HANDBOOKS

# SAN JUAN ISLANDS

DON PITCHER

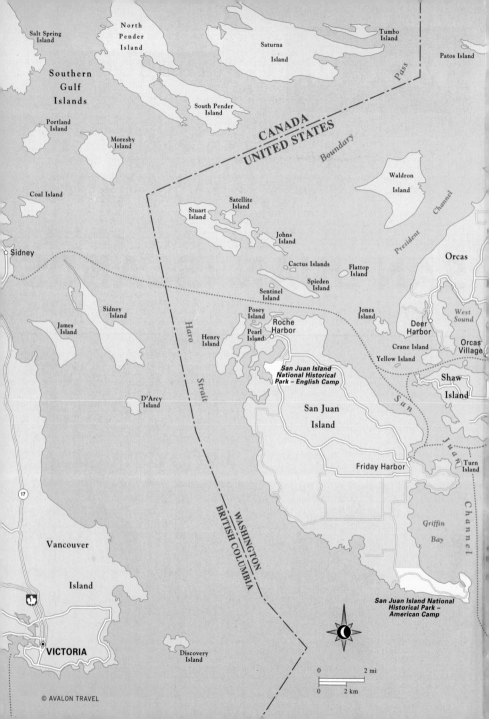

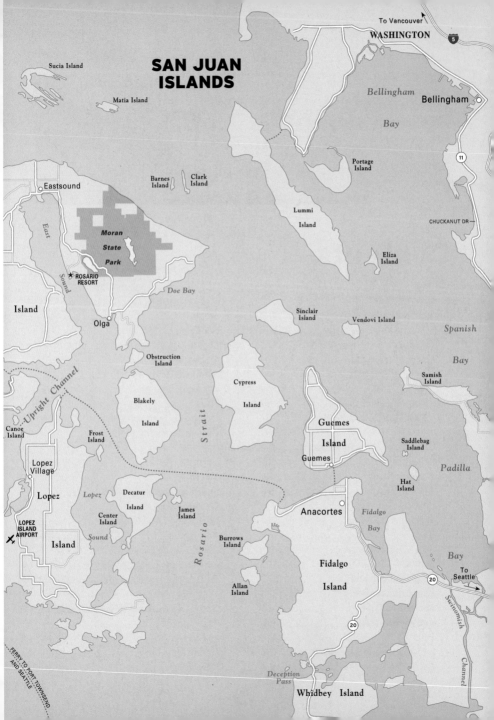

# Contents

# Discover the San Juan Islands

Nestled between the Washington mainland and Vancouver Island, the San Juan Islands offer a perfect weekend or one- to two-week getaway. The islands are equidistant from two major Northwest cities, Seattle to the south and Vancouver to the north. Despite this proximity, they remain largely rural, with no fast-food restaurants or big-box discount stores anywhere. Instead, you'll find a host of small bed-and-breakfasts, distinctive art galleries, specialty farms selling everything from alpaca garments to oysters, family-run whale-watching and sea-kayaking companies, and fine restaurants where the owner might also be your waiter.

From the air, it's easy to imagine the San Juan archipelago as broken pieces from a shattered plate. They encompass 176 named islands, and a total of 743 islands, islets, and reefs at low tide (or 428 at high tide). Thirty of these are inhabited. Some 16,000 people live on the islands year-round, half of them on San Juan Island, home to Friday Harbor, the islands' only incorporated town. The three largest islands – Orcas, San Juan, and Lopez – form a cluster of oddly shaped puzzle pieces around Shaw Island, with many of the smaller islands strewn outward to the north and east from this hub.

The San Juans tend to attract an upscale clientele who appreciate

luxurious inns and acclaimed restaurants, but travelers on a budget can also enjoy the islands. Families can opt to rent a vacation home for a week or more, taking the time to explore the San Juans at their own pace. Backpacking visitors and cyclists will find hostels on San Juan and Orcas Islands, and several summer camps provide fun options for kids.

With their dark evergreen forests and rocky shorelines, the islands have become one of Washington's favorite places to get away, and when summer rolls around, they are flooded with tourists, temporarily doubling the population. Visiting the San Juans means escaping to a place where the natural world dominates and where folks raise a hand to wave as you pass. When the ferry leaves the dock at Anacortes, a sense of timelessness seems to descend upon all onboard. Children wave excitedly to passing sailboats, clusters of cyclists huddle around maps, locals read books and sip coffee at window tables, and birders gather outside to watch for eagles or murres. The pace of life here is slow; the San Juan Islands are best enjoyed in a leisurely way.

# Planning Your Trip

## ▶ WHERE TO GO

### Gateways to the Islands

Most visitors to the San Juan Islands arrive onboard Washington State Ferries that depart from the town of Anacortes. Nearby is popular Deception Pass State Park, and farther south is bucolic Whidbey Island, with the artsy towns of Coupeville and Langley. The island provides a scenic access route for people driving up from Seattle. Another entry point is Bellingham, with its museums, historic Fairhaven neighborhood, and shore-hugging Chuckanut Drive. Victoria, the elegant capital of British Columbia, Canada, lies on the southern tip of Vancouver Island.

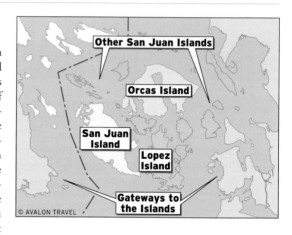

### San Juan Island

San Juan Island is a favorite island destination. The main town, Friday Harbor, is a picturesque spot, with The Whale Museum, fine dining and lodging, and abundant

Roche Harbor on San Juan Island

opportunities for whale-watching and sea kayaking. Roche Harbor has a busy marina, gorgeous grounds, historic buildings, and a sculpture garden. San Juan Island National Historical Park reveals the island's vivid history with protected English Camp on the western shore and great beaches at American Camp. Other island attractions include a much-photographed lighthouse, the only whale-watching park in the nation at Lime Kiln Point State Park, wineries, a lavender farm, and an alpaca farm.

## Orcas Island

The "Gem of the San Juans," Orcas Island is both the largest and most diverse island in the archipelago. The main settlement is Eastsound, with its picture-perfect inns, cozy cafés, earthy farmers market, and even a skateboard park. Elsewhere on Orcas are marinas, resorts, and pottery studios. The east side of the island is dominated by woodsy Moran State Park, with mountaintop vistas, miles of trails, camping, and lakes for swimming. Nearby is the century-old mansion at Rosario Resort.

## IF YOU HAVE . . .

- **A WEEKEND:** Visit San Juan Island.

- **A WEEK:** Add Orcas Island.

- **10 DAYS:** Add Lopez Island.

- **TWO WEEKS:** Add outer island state parks.

- **THREE WEEKS:** Add Whidbey Island and Victoria.

kayakers at Obstruction Pass off Orcas Island

horse and colt grazing on Orcas Island

## Lopez Island

Quiet and slow-paced, Lopez is a destination for bicyclists who pedal a 30-mile paved loop that traverses gently rolling farm country. "The Wave" isn't a surfer's term here, but one applied to the ubiquitous hands that lift off the steering wheel to acknowledge every passing car or bike. B&Bs and vacation rentals are scattered around the island, and Lopez Village has shops, restaurants, a little museum, and a nearby organic vineyard. Spencer Spit State Park is popular for camping, a long beach, and kayaking.

## Other San Juan Islands

Once you get beyond the three largest islands, the number of visitors decreases markedly. State ferries visit Shaw Island, but not the other islands, where access is by water taxi, boat, kayak, or plane. Shaw Island offers hiking and camping options. Lummi Island provides snug lodging and four-star dining. Many of the smaller islands in the San

Cedar Rock Biological Preserve on Shaw Island

Juans are maintained as marine state parks, most notably Sucia Island, Jones Island, and Stuart Island, all with protected coves and hiking trails.

## ▶ WHEN TO GO

The San Juans are primarily a summertime destination, and anyone heading to the islands between mid-June and early September will find throngs of fellow travelers. Many of the best accommodations fill up far in advance, especially on weekends, when some resorts are booked a year or more ahead. Summers are primarily warm and dry, with lush floral displays and plenty of chances to view killer whales just offshore. If you don't mind the wait for a table at the restaurants and lengthy ferry lines—and if you can get lodging reservations—this is a great time to visit. On weekends, leave your vehicle in Anacortes to avoid lengthy waits at the ferry terminal. Both Orcas and San Juan Islands have car rentals, and a shuttle bus service is available on San Juan Island.

Spring and fall provide ideal times to visit. By May, many plants are already flowering—don't miss the wildflower displays on Yellow Island—but school is still in session, so most folks haven't yet headed out on vacation. Lodging prices aren't at peak summer rates, and businesses welcome travelers. Fall brings a bit of color to the trees, cooler temperatures, and the chance to soak up the beauty in relative peace and quiet. By mid-November, long ferry lines are gone, prices drop, B&Bs have rooms on short notice, and it's easy to take a romantic walk down an unpopulated beach. Holiday weekends get busy again, but for much of the winter, you'll pretty much have the place to yourself. This is also the chilliest and rainiest part of the year, with an occasional dusting of snow.

# ▶ BEFORE YOU GO

The San Juan Islands cover a relatively small area—it's less than 30 miles across the archipelago—and there are no bridges to or between the islands, so everyone and everything (from oranges to cement) must get to the islands onboard boats, ferries, or planes. Fortunately, the islands have good transportation, along with excellent lodging, food, and recreational opportunities, making them easy for travelers.

Orcas, the largest of the islands, covers 57 square miles and stretches a dozen miles across by eight miles north to south. San Juan Island is 55 square miles, while Lopez Island covers 30 square miles. These are followed by several mid-size islands—Cypress, Shaw, Blakely, Waldron, and Decatur—and a multitude of smaller ones.

Whether you're aboard a state ferry threading its way through the islands or in a small floatplane dipping down to a watery landing, getting to the islands is half the fun. Access is primarily by Washington State Ferries from the town of Anacortes (an 80-mile drive north from Seattle along I-5); but quite a few visitors fly in, while others ride private passenger ferries, motorboats, or sailboats to the islands. The state ferry system links the four main islands—San Juan, Orcas, Lopez, and Shaw—with Anacortes, with some ferries continuing westward to the Canadian port of Sidney (20 miles north of Victoria) on Vancouver Island. Bikes and kayaks are welcome onboard these ferries, making the islands an ideal destination for adventurous travelers. Private ferries and tour boats run from Seattle, Bellingham, and Port Townsend, and scheduled flights are available out of Seattle, Anacortes, and Bellingham. Many island visitors bring their own vehicles onboard the state ferries, but you can also rent a car or take a local taxi once you arrive. San Juan Island has a reasonably priced shuttle bus.

Summers on the San Juans are mild and often sunny, so you won't need down jackets or heavy raingear. July and August each average only an inch of rain per month, and May, June, and September are also reasonably dry. Short pants and T-shirts are ubiquitous throughout the summer, though you will want long-sleeve shirts and pants for cooler evenings and cloudy or rainy days. Carry a light jacket for rainy days or on-the-water trips. As a general rule, keep it casual when it comes to clothing. Even the most upscale island restaurants don't require a sports jacket or tie.

For winter travel, plan your packing around dressing in layers, and be sure to have a sweater or two and Gore-Tex or another breathable rain jacket.

A few other items you shouldn't forget include binoculars, camera, cell phone, laptop or tablet computer, sunscreen, sunglasses, and insect repellent, along with passports if you plan any cross-border travel into Canada.

Cattle Point, San Juan Island

whale-watching off San Juan Island

# Explore the San Juan Islands

## ▶ QUICK GETAWAYS

The San Juan Islands are an easy half-day drive and ferry ride from Seattle and Vancouver. Because of this, the islands are exceptionally popular destinations, particularly on summer weekends. Avoid the crowds by visiting in the off-season or in the middle of the week if possible. But even at their most crowded, the San Juans are still much more peaceful than city living.

For a weekend trip, it is probably best to leave your vehicle in Anacortes to avoid the lengthy ferry lines. Both Orcas and San Juan Islands have taxis and car rentals; an excellent shuttle service is available on San Juan Island. Some lodgings also provide limited transportation.

### San Juan Island

Always a favorite of visitors, San Juan Island is great for an extra-long weekend escape, with plenty to do and a range of lodging and food choices. The ferry docks right at Friday Harbor, making this a good base for your trip.

**DAY 1**

Drive to Anacortes, stopping to see Washington Park and other sights, before boarding the Washington State Ferries for the town of Friday Harbor on San Juan Island. There are many lodging choices in Friday Harbor, including well-maintained budget rooms at Orca Inn, swanky rooms at

camel waiting for a handout on San Juan Island

Lime Kiln Point Lighthouse on San Juan Island

formal gardens at English Camp in San Juan Island National Historical Park

Island Inn at 123 West, or cheery country digs at Juniper Lane Guest House.

### DAY 2

In Friday Harbor visit The Whale Museum, and then take a half-day whale-watching trip or head to Lime Kiln Point State Park to watch from the shore (recommended to reduce impact). Drive south along the coast, stopping at tiny Westside Scenic Preserve to soak up the view before visiting fragrant Pelindaba Lavender Farm, the cuddly alpacas at Krystal Acres Ranch, and the tasting rooms at San Juan Vineyards and Westcott Bay Cider.

### DAY 3

Time for a history lesson. This is a full day, so get an early start or choose a couple of sights instead of trying to see them all. Drive over to English Camp for a hike up Mount Young in this portion of San Juan Island National Historical Park, then on to beautiful Roche Harbor for lunch and a saunter through the IMA Sculpture Park. Continue south to American Camp for a hike through the flower-filled meadows or a stroll along

South Beach—one of the finest beaches in the islands. End the day with dinner in Friday Harbor (reservations advised) at Coho Restaurant or Backdoor Kitchen.

### DAY 4

Max out your time in Friday Harbor before ferrying back to Anacortes. Do a little browsing at Griffin Bay Bookstore, buy an ice cream cone from The Sweet Retreat & Espresso, browse the galleries, or rent a bike and pedal the loop road around Pear Point, stopping for a picnic lunch at Jacksons Beach.

## Orcas Island

Orcas Island is too big to really take in over a long weekend, but this short trip provides a sampler that will make you wish for more time there.

### DAY 1

Catch an early ferry for a timely start on this diverse island. With a central base in the Eastsound area, you can easily get to most of the sights on the island. Outlook Inn features a great in-town setting and a variety of room choices, including inexpensive ones in

dining in the sun at Orcas Hotel on Orcas Island

the historic main building. Families will enjoy the condos at Landmark Inn or the staterooms at Inn at Ship Bay.

On this day you may want to spend time exploring the sights around Eastsound, such as the Orcas Island Historical Museum, or rent a sit-on-top kayak from Crescent Beach Kayaks to paddle the protected bay.

### DAY 2

Explore Moran State Park, including the paved road to the stone tower atop Mount Constitution. Hike the trails, try some mountain biking, or play in the waters of Cascade Lake. Be sure to take the detour to Rosario Resort for a visit to this historic getaway.

### DAY 3

Take it easy on your last day on Orcas Island. Grab brunch at Roses Bakery Café and tour the local galleries and gift shops in Eastsound before heading back to the ferry.

## Lopez Island

Lopez is all about relaxing, so this weekend adventure is short on activities and long on letting go.

### DAY 1

Arrive at the Anacortes ferry terminal and get onboard for a truly relaxing weekend. In Lopez Village wander through the handful of shops, the museum, and over to Weeks Wetland Preserve to watch migrating birds.

Once you've settled into your lodging place (MacKaye Harbor Inn and Lopez Farm Cottages are especially nice), enjoy a waterside dinner at Galley Restaurant and Lounge and then take a sunset walk along the beach at Otis Perkins County Park.

Lopez Island is an idyllic place for a weekend stroll.

### DAY 2

Get a gourmet picnic lunch from Vita's Wildly Delicious, and if you're in town on a summer Saturday, walk across the road to check out the Lopez Island Farmers Market. Rent a bike from Lopez Bicycle Works or Village Cycles to see the island at an appropriately slow pace, stopping for a leisurely break at one of the beaches; Watmough Bay and Agate Beach are great choices. If you'd rather explore Lopez from a "see" level, join Cascadia Kayak Tours for a half-day sea-kayak paddle.

### DAY 3

Drop by Caffé la Boheme in Lopez Village for a cappuccino and head next door to Holly B's Bakery for a giant cinnamon roll before catching the ferry back to Anacortes. If you have the time, drive the scenic route south to Seattle via Deception Pass State Park and Whidbey Island.

# ROMANCING THE ISLANDS

The San Juan Islands are a perfect destination for romance, with beautiful scenery, cozy cottages, candlelit restaurants, upscale day spas, and lots of fun adventures. They're a favorite spot for both weddings and honeymoons, but also draw couples looking to relax in a luxurious bed-and-breakfast. Here are a few romantic inns and restaurants, and wild places to start your romantic getaway.

## SAN JUAN ISLAND

### Romantic Lodging

- Roche Harbor Resort, page 139

- Trumpeter Inn B&B, page 144

- Wildwood Manor, page 145

### Fine Dining

- Backdoor Kitchen, page 148

- Coho Restaurant, page 148

- Duck Soup Inn, page 149

### Outdoor Escapes

- South Beach, page 112

- Lime Kiln Point Lighthouse, page 115

- San Juan Vineyards, page 121

- Pelindaba Lavender Farm, page 122

## ORCAS ISLAND

### Romantic Lodging

- Beach Haven Resort, page 188

- Cabins-on-the-Point, page 194

- The Inn on Orcas Island, page 197

### Fine Dining

- Inn at Ship Bay, page 204

- New Leaf Café, page 204

- West Sound Café, page 207

### Outdoor Escapes:

- Mount Constitution , page 164

- Howe Art Gallery, page 172

- Doe Bay Resort and Retreat, page 182

## LOPEZ ISLAND

### Romantic Lodging

- Bay House and Garden Cottages, page 225

- Lopez Farm Cottages, page 227

- MacKaye Harbor Inn, page 228

### Casual Dining

- Holly B's Bakery, page 230

- Caffé la Boheme, page 230

- Vita's Wildly Delicious, page 230

### Outdoor Escapes

- Spencer Spit State Park, page 217

- Iceberg Point, page 219

- Watmough Head, page 220

Wildwood Manor on San Juan Island

# ► CAMPING WITH THE KIDS

Family trips don't have to resemble the 1983 comedy, *National Lampoon's Vacation*. On the San Juan Islands, it's easy to bring the family, rent a cottage or house (around $900–1,300/week), and launch out on day trips from this base. The itinerary below is a low-rent version to Lopez and Orcas Islands; similar weeklong trips are also very popular on San Juan Island.

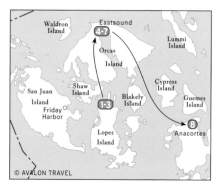

© AVALON TRAVEL

## Day 1

Load up the minivan and drive to Anacortes, where you have time to stock up on snacks and diapers at The Market. After an interminable wait, roll onboard a ferry heading toward Lopez Island and set up camp at Spencer Spit State Park.

## Day 2

If you brought bikes along, everyone can hop on for a ride around the island; if not, they're available for rent from Lopez Bicycle Works or Village Cycles. Afterwards, return to

Spencer Spit, where the kids can roast marshmallows over a campfire.

## Day 3

Enjoy another day of biking around the island; break up the ride with a hike through the forest at Shark Reef Park and the chance to look for colorful stones at Agate Beach County Park. Get burgers and grilled cheese sandwiches at Lopez Island Soda Fountain,

Shark Reef Park on Lopez Island

waterfall in Moran State Park on Orcas Island

Orcas Island Pottery

and wander the handful of shops and galleries in nearby Lopez Village.

## Day 4

Pack everyone up and take the ferry to Orcas Island. Drive up to Eastsound for lunch at Mia's Café, then continue out the eastern end to Moran State Park with its abundant campsites among the trees (best ones are at South End Campground).

## Day 5

Drive the twisting road up Mount Constitution to take in the island vistas and head back down to Cascade Lake for swimming with other families and a balanced lunch of hot dogs, lemonade, and popcorn. Everyone knows sugar works wonders in helping kids relax, so throw in an ice cream cone or three.

## Day 6

Lots of options today. Join a guided morning hike through Gnat's Nature Hikes, or hop on a whale-watching trip through Deer Harbor Charters. Browse pottery galleries on the east side of Orcas before a side trip to watch the daredevils at Orcas Island Skateboard Park, or spend an afternoon at The Funhouse for something more intellectually stimulating.

## Day 7

Put the kids in day care at Orcas Island Children's House or Kaleidoscope and take the time to explore the shops of Eastsound, brunching at Roses Bakery Café. If you're feeling ambitious, join a day trip to Sucia Island from Shearwater Kayaks, or rent a mountain bike from Wildlife Cycles. On your way to get the kids, stop by Homegrown Market to pick up fresh seafood to cook back at the campsite.

## Day 8

It's time to exit the islands, but if you take an afternoon ferry, you'll have time for a short hike in Obstruction Pass State Park before heading out. Waiting in your car as the ferry approaches the terminal, with the kids sleeping peacefully in the backseat, you may think that family trips aren't so bad after all.

# FARM FRESH

Orcas Island farm

A revitalized back-to-the-land movement is leading to a focus on regionally produced foods, and the San Juans are home to a growing number of small farms, farmers markets, and organic products. Many local restaurants make a point of buying fresh island products. Find summertime farmers markets on Saturdays in Friday Harbor, Eastsound, and Lopez Village, plus Anacortes, Bellingham, and Whidbey Island. Here are a few additional farm fresh options:

## SAN JUAN ISLAND

- Heritage Farm, page 120
- Krystal Acres Ranch, page 120
- San Juan Vineyards, page 121
- Westcott Bay Cider, page 121
- Pelindaba Lavender Farm, page 122

## ORCAS ISLAND

- Orcas Moon Alpacas, page 182
- Once in a Blue Moon Farm, page 195

## LOPEZ ISLAND

- Lopez Island Vineyards & Winery, page 216
- Horse Drawn Farm, page 217
- Lopez Island Farm, page 217

## OTHER ISLANDS

- Whidbey Island Greenbank Farm, Whidbey Island, page 49
- Meerkerk Rhododendron Gardens, Whidbey Island, page 50
- Butchart Gardens, Vancouver Island, page 83
- Victoria Butterfly Gardens, Vancouver Island, page 86
- Our Lady of the Rock Monastery, Shaw Island, page 241
- Nettles Farm, Lummi Island, page 247

# ▶ EXPLORING THE OUTER ISLANDS

The vast majority of visitors to the San Juans focus all their attention on the most accessible islands—San Juan, Orcas, and Lopez—but with a little effort (and some cash), you can discover an entirely different world. The following tour mixes time on the main islands with trips to lesser-known islands and state marine parks. All sorts of other options exist, and if you want to create your own itinerary, you should consider hiking and camping on Cypress Island (access by water taxi from Anacortes), Stuart Island (water taxi from San Juan Island), or Matia Island (water taxi from Anacortes). The trip below begins in Bellingham and assumes that you have a car.

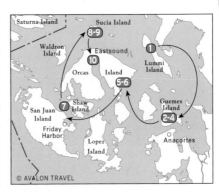

## Day 1

Drive northwest from Bellingham on I-5 and take Exit 260 to the ferry for Lummi Island. Stop at Beach Store Café for lunch, check out the art at Sisters Bountiful Mercantile, then tour the island roads before settling in for a gourmet dinner and plush accommodations at The Willows Inn.

## Days 2-4

Return to the mainland in the morning, stopping in Bellingham's Fairhaven district for a foamy espresso at Tony's Coffee & Teas. Then you're off down winding Chuckanut Drive with its arching trees, bay vistas, and seafood restaurants, but be sure to turn off on the narrow side road to Taylor Shellfish Farms for some fresh Manila clams. Chuckanut Drive eventually connects to U.S. Highway 20 and Anacortes—an interesting

kayaks on a Jones Island beach

sunset off Sucia island

along the way to check out the shops and galleries, and have dinner at Chimayo Restaurant. Orcas is a fine base to explore surrounding islands and has its own array of attractions.

## Day 6

This easy day begins with a short kayak tour from Spring Bay Inn and a big breakfast (both included in your stay). Do a bit of hiking within nearby Obstruction Pass State Park, or drive the roads of Orcas Island to see local sights. Dinner is a vegetarian affair at frumpy and earthy Doe Bay Resort.

## Day 7

If you're traveling in May or June—when flowers are at their peak—a day trip to Yellow Island is a vividly verdant option. Shearwater Adventures has kayak day trips to the island, and Gnat's Nature Hikes combines a boat ride with a guided hike; both depart from Deer Harbor on Orcas Island. As an alternative, rent a skiff from Deer Harbor Charters and head over to nearby Jones Island for an easy forest hike with deer, raccoons, and other creatures for company.

## Days 8-9

You've sampled kayaking, and now it's time for something more substantial. San Juan Island-based Discovery Sea Kayaks leads multi-night tours that include time on Patos Island with its picturesque lighthouse and Sucia Island with its maze of trails leading to hidden coves. This is a good introduction to kayaking; several other companies on Orcas, San Juan, and Lopez islands offer extended sea kayak trips.

## Day 10

Return to Orcas Island and catch the ferry back to Anacortes.

town with several fine restaurants—but we're stopping here, for a lunch or early dinner at friendly Adrift Restaurant. Then catch the little ferry from Anacortes to Guemes Island. You've booked three tranquil nights at Guemes Island Resort, with a choice of attractive cabins on the water or rustic yurts beneath tall trees. The low-key resort is a delightful place to chill out, so bring a book or two, set up a massage, relax in the sauna, play ping pong with the kids, or borrow a rowboat to drop a crab pot for dinner. Groceries and excellent meals are available on Guemes from Anderson's General Store.

## Day 5

Leave the Guemes Island world behind and drive onto the ferry to Anacortes again. Get a hearty breakfast at Calico Cupboard Café & Bakery before catching a state ferry to Orcas Island, where you've booked two nights at The Cabin on Spring Bay. Stop at Eastsound

# GATEWAYS TO THE ISLANDS

Located 80 miles north of Seattle, the town of Anacortes is Washington's primary gateway to the San Juan Islands, with state ferries departing several times a day year-round. Immediately south of Anacortes is Whidbey Island, a scenic access route for people driving up from Seattle. The city of Bellingham is on the mainland northeast of the San Juans, with tours to the islands. Beautiful Victoria, capital of British Columbia, is just a ferry ride from the San Juans. Seattle is another gateway, with a private passenger ferry and air taxis connecting to the San Juans. All these places are described in this chapter, with complete coverage for Anacortes and Victoria, and more limited details on Whidbey Island, Bellingham, and Seattle.

## PLANNING YOUR TIME

Most visitors en route to the San Juans start from Anacortes on Fidalgo Island. It offers a good mix of restaurants, reasonably priced lodging, and sights to see, including **Washington Park** and the historic sternwheeler **W.T. Preston.** A few miles south of town is **Deception Pass State Park,** famous for the high arched bridge that links Fidalgo Island with Whidbey Island to the south.

One of the longest islands in America, Whidbey has one large town (Oak Harbor) and two smaller—and far more interesting—ones: Langley and Coupeville. Colorful **Whidbey Island Greenbank Farm** is a fun stop, with loganberry wines and other treats for sale, and just up the road is **Meerkerk Rhododendron**

# HIGHLIGHTS

◖ **W.T. Preston:** Now landlocked along the Anacortes waterfront, this historic stern-wheeler operated around Puget Sound from 1940 through the 1970s. Today, it's open for self-guided tours (page 28).

◖ **Washington Park:** Covering 200 prime waterfront acres, this Anacortes park has camping, hiking trails, and a very scenic two-mile loop road (page 29).

◖ **Deception Pass State Park:** Best known for the arching bridge that links Whidbey and Fidalgo Islands, this very popular park has hundreds of campsites, miles of hiking trails, freshwater lakes for swimming, and sandy beaches (page 30).

◖ **Whidbey Island Greenbank Farm:** Famous for its big red-and-white barn and loganberry wines, this historic farm is a top attraction on Whidbey Island (page 49).

◖ **Ebey's Landing National Historical Reserve:** Managed by the National Park Service, this reserve is a mix of preserved agricultural lands bordered by an impressive shoreline of cliffs and beaches (page 51).

◖ **Fairhaven:** Bellingham's famous historic district is a great place to search for that perfect gift or enjoy a fine meal while waiting for your train, bus, boat, or ferry (page 59).

◖ **Whatcom Museum:** Newly transformed with the addition of the striking Lightcatcher building, this museum houses changing exhibits of art. Old City Hall atop a nearby hill contains historical collections (page 62).

◖ **Chuckanut Drive:** This exceptionally scenic road stretches south from Fairhaven, with tall trees, the waters of Samish Bay, and several notable restaurants, before emerging onto the farmland of Skagit Valley (page 63).

◖ **Craigdarroch Castle:** To get a feeling for the wealth of Victorian-era Victoria, take a tour of this extravagant castle (page 80).

◖ **Butchart Gardens:** Even if you have only one day in Victoria, make time to visit one of the world's most delightful gardens (page 83).

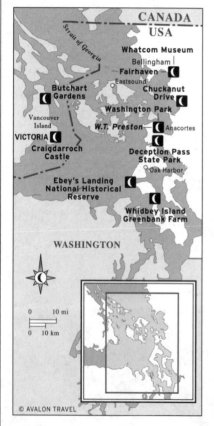

LOOK FOR ◖ TO FIND RECOMMENDED SIGHTS, ACTIVITIES, DINING, AND LODGING.

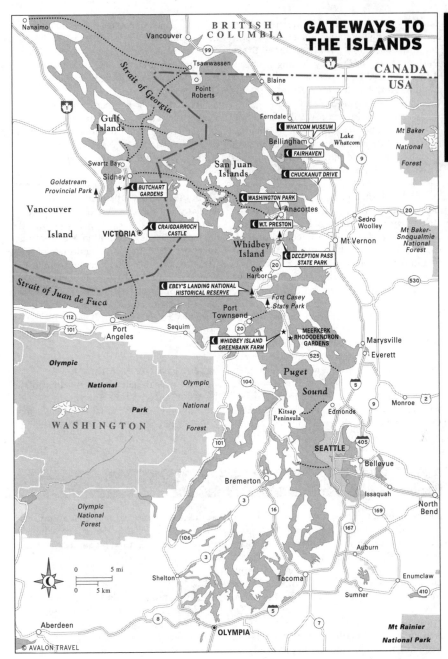

# GATEWAYS TO THE ISLANDS

**BRITISH COLUMBIA**

Nanaimo

Vancouver

Tsawwassen

**99**

Blaine

**CANADA**
**USA**

**5**

Point Roberts

Strait of Georgia

Ferndale

Lake Whatcom

Mt Baker

*National*

*Forest*

**WHATCOM MUSEUM**

Bellingham

**9**

Gulf Islands

**FAIRHAVEN**

Swartz Bay

San Juan Islands

**CHUCKANUT DRIVE**

Sidney

Goldstream Provincial Park

**BUTCHART GARDENS**

**WASHINGTON PARK**

Anacortes

Sedro Woolley

**20**

**Vancouver**

**W.T. PRESTON**

Mt Vernon

Mt Baker-Snoqualmie National Forest

**Island**

**VICTORIA**

**CRAIGDARROCH CASTLE**

Whidbey Island

**DECEPTION PASS STATE PARK**

**530**

Oak Harbor

**20**

Strait of Juan de Fuca

**EBEY'S LANDING NATIONAL HISTORICAL RESERVE**

Fort Casey State Park

**112**

**101**

Port Angeles

Sequim

Port Townsend

**20**

**MEERKERK RHODODENDRON GARDENS**

Marysville

**Olympic**

Olympic

**104**

**WHIDBEY ISLAND GREENBANK FARM**

**525**

Everett

*National*

*National*

**Puget**

**9**

**Park**

*Forest*

**5**

Monroe

**2**

**WASHINGTON**

**101**

**Sound**

Kitsap Peninsula

Edmonds

**SEATTLE**

**405**

Bellevue

Bremerton

Issaquah

**169**

North Bend

Olympic National Forest

**3**

**16**

**167**

**106**

**3**

Auburn

Enumclaw

0   5 mi

0   5 km

Shelton

Tacoma

**410**

Sumner

**8**

**5**

Aberdeen

**OLYMPIA**

**7**

Mt Rainier

National Park

© AVALON TRAVEL

Gardens, which shows 1,500 varieties in late spring, including Washington's state flower, the coast rhododendron. Visit **Fort Casey State Park** to check out the disappearing guns and Admiralty Head Lighthouse, or nearby **Ebey's Landing National Historical Reserve** for verdant fields and a gorgeous coastline.

The city of Bellingham is a destination in its own right, but also provides a jumping-off point for whale-watching tours to the San Juan Islands. The historic **Fairhaven** district boasts a collection of nicely restored buildings from the 1880s, many fine shops, and the multimodal transportation center for trains, buses, boats, and the Alaska State Ferry. Downtown Bellingham is home to the **Whatcom Museum** and a couple of more offbeat collections, including the American Radio Museum and Mindport—filled with amusing and educational junk. South of Bellingham, **Chuckanut Drive** is one of the most scenic roads in the region, hugging the coast through lush forests before opening into the farm country northeast of Anacortes.

Seattle is the primary access point for people flying into the area and has enough attractions to keep visitors busy for a week (or a decade). Take the time to explore **Pike Place Market,** with its bustling arts and crafts market, delectable eats, and chaotic fun. Take in **Seattle Center,** where you'll find the city's landmark **Space Needle,** the fun and educational Pacific Science Center, and the mesmerizing Experience Music Project/Science Fiction Museum. If you have time, visit Pioneer Square, the Museum of Flight, the Burke Museum on the University of Washington campus, or one of the city's funky neighborhoods.

Situated on the southern tip of Canada's Vancouver Island, the picture-perfect city of Victoria is a major destination in its own right. This is as close as you'll come to London on this side of the Atlantic, with traditional high tea, double-decker bus tours, and formal gardens. Surrounding its famed **Inner Harbour** are the parliament buildings and the Fairmont Empress, Victoria's most memorable landmark. Other must-sees include the **Royal British Columbia Museum** and **Butchart Gardens,** plus a multitude of wild attractions farther afield, including the ancient forests of Goldstream Provincial Park. Washington State ferries depart for the San Juan Islands from the town of Sidney, 20 miles north of Victoria, and British Columbia ferries head out to Tsawwassen (Vancouver) and the Gulf Islands.

## Getting to the Islands

Access to the San Juan Islands is primarily via the **Washington State Ferries** (206/464-6400 or 888/808-7977, www.wsdot.wa.gov/ferries), with connections from Anacortes and Sidney, British Columbia.

# Anacortes

Many visitors know Anacortes (anna-KOR-tez) only as the launching point for the San Juan Islands, but this city of 15,000 is far more than a ferry dock. With a casual end-of-the-road atmosphere, it's also one of the more pleasant cities of its size in Puget Sound. The city is 80 miles north of Seattle and 90 miles south of Vancouver.

Although it looks like part of the mainland, Anacortes is officially on **Fidalgo Island;** Swinomish Slough cuts a sluggish, narrow swath from the La Conner area around the hills known as Fidalgo Head. The slough is kept open for boaters and is spanned by a beautiful curving arc of a bridge.

## History

Anglos first resided on the island in the 1850s, but William Munks, who called himself "The King of Fidalgo Island," claimed to be the first permanent settler and opened a store in 1869. A geologist named Amos Bowman

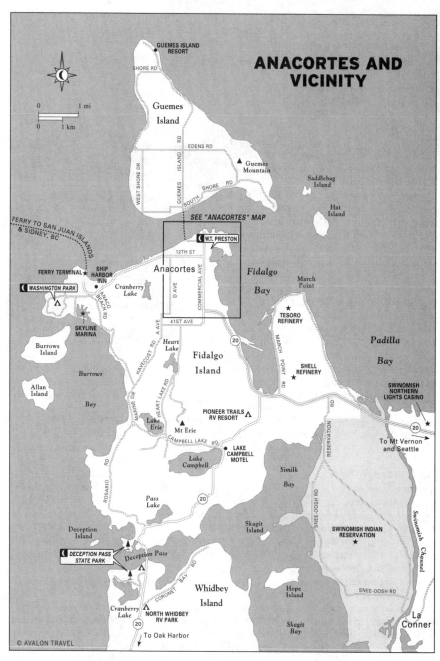

# ANACORTES AND VICINITY

0   1 mi
0   1 km

Guemes Island Resort

SHORE RD

Guemes Island

GUEMES ISLAND RD

EDENS RD

WEST SHORE DR

GUEMES ISLAND RD

SOUTH SHORE RD

Guemes Mountain

Saddlebag Island

Hat Island

SEE "ANACORTES" MAP

FERRY TO SAN JUAN ISLANDS & SIDNEY, BC

W.T. PRESTON

12TH ST

FERRY TERMINAL ★   SHIP HARBOR INN

Anacortes

Fidalgo Bay

March Point

WASHINGTON PARK

Cranberry Lake

ANACO BEACH RD

COMMERCIAL AVE

D AVE

41ST AVE

TESORO REFINERY ★

Burrows Island

SKYLINE MARINA

HAVECOST RD

A AVE

Heart Lake

20

MARCH POINT RD

SHELL REFINERY ★

Padilla Bay

Allan Island

Burrows Bay

MARINE DR

HEART LAKE RD

Fidalgo Island

SWINOMISH NORTHERN LIGHTS CASINO

Lake Erie

PIONEER TRAILS RV RESORT

20

To Mt Vernon and Seattle

Mt Erie

CAMPBELL LAKE RD

LAKE CAMPBELL MOTEL

RESERVATION RD

ROSARIO RD

Lake Campbell

Similk Bay

Swinomish Channel

Pass Lake

20

SNEE-OOSH RD

SWINOMISH INDIAN RESERVATION ★

Deception Island

Deception Pass

Skagit Island

DECEPTION PASS STATE PARK

CORONET BAY RD

Whidbey Island

Hope Island

SNEE-OOSH RD

La Conner

Cranberry Lake

NORTH WHIDBEY RV PARK

20

Skagit Bay

To Oak Harbor

© AVALON TRAVEL

tried to persuade the company he worked for, the Canadian Pacific Railroad, to establish its western terminus at Fidalgo—despite the fact that Bowman had never seen the island. When the railroad refused, Bowman came down to check out the land himself, bought 168 acres of it, and opened a store, a wharf, and the Anna Curtis Post Office, named after his wife, in 1879. Bowman was so determined to get a railroad—any railroad—into Anacortes that he published a newspaper, *The Northwest Enterprise,* to draw people and businesses to his town.

He was so convincing that the population boomed to more than 3,000 people, even though, by 1890, the town's five railroad depots had yet to see a train pull up. The Burlington Northern Railroad eventually came, and residents found financial success in salmon canneries, shingle factories, and lumber mills. Anacortes grew to prominence as a shipping and fishing port; by its heyday in 1911, it was home to seven canneries and proclaimed itself "salmon canning capital of the world." Workers were needed for all these plants, and Anacortes became a major entry point of illegal laborers from China and Japan; several outlaws made a prosperous living smuggling in both workers and opium. Anacortes's title for salmon canning has long since been lost as salmon stocks dwindled in Puget Sound due to overfishing, but the city still maintains a strong seaward orientation.

### Anacortes Today
Anacortes relies on the Tesoro and Shell oil refineries, the Dakota Creek shipyard, two seafood processing plants (including the Trident Seafoods plant, which turns Alaskan pollock into fish burgers for Burger King and Long John Silver's), and tourists en route to the San Juan Islands. A fleet of gillnetters and seiners supplies salmon for local markets, and many of the boats here head north to Alaska each summer. In recent years, the city has grown with the increase in tourism as well as retirees who enjoy the mild, relatively dry weather. A gateway arch at the corner of Commercial

© DON PITCHER

**Washington State Ferries serve Anacortes.**

Avenue and 11th Street welcomes visitors to downtown Anacortes—now a National Historic District—and a number of the historic Victorian buildings have been restored.

## SIGHTS
### Museums and Historic Sites
The **Anacortes Museum** (1305 8th St., 360/293-1915, http://museum.cityofanacortes. org, 10 A.M.–4 P.M. Mon.–Tues., Thurs.–Sat., 1–4 P.M. Sun., year-round, donation) has changing exhibits on local history. Drop by the visitors center for a *Walking Tour of Historic Downtown Anacortes* brochure detailing 30 historic buildings. Dozens of small **historical murals** adorn local buildings, including the mural of Anna Curtis across the street from the visitors center.

Don't miss **Causland Park,** which covers a city block at 8th Street and N Avenue (right across from the museum). The park's playfully ornate mosaic walls, gazebo, and amphitheater were built in 1920 with colorful stones from area islands. Nearby are a number of 1890s

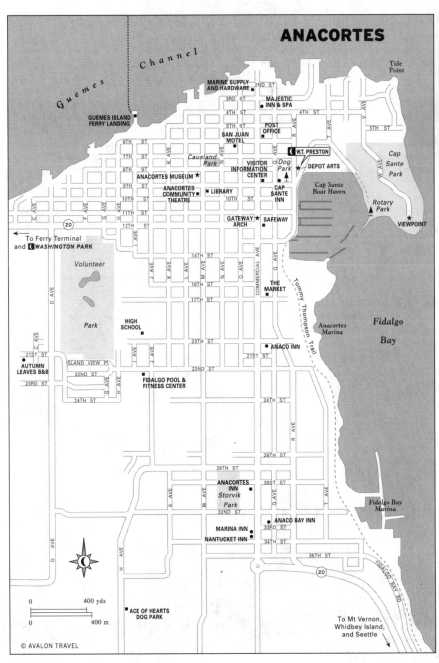

# ANACORTES

Channel

Guemes

Tide Point

MARINE SUPPLY AND HARDWARE ■

2ND ST

3RD ST

MAJESTIC INN & SPA ■

4TH ST

4TH AVE

V AVE

4TH ST

GUEMES ISLAND FERRY LANDING ■

5TH ST

POST OFFICE ■

5TH ST

SAN JUAN MOTEL ■

6TH ST

7TH ST

K AVE

Causland Park

N AVE

W.T. PRESTON ■

Cap Sante Park

8TH ST

VISITOR INFORMATION CENTER ■

Dog Park

DEPOT ARTS ■

ANACORTES MUSEUM ★

9TH ST

Cap Sante Boat Haven

10TH ST

ANACORTES COMMUNITY THEATRE ■

■ LIBRARY

10TH ST

CAP SANTE INN

Rotary Park

11TH ST

12TH ST

GATEWAY ARCH ★

SAFEWAY ■

VIEWPOINT ★

20

To Ferry Terminal and ◖WASHINGTON PARK

D AVE

C AVE

Volunteer

14TH ST

COMMERCIAL AVE

Q AVE

Park

16TH ST

THE MARKET ■

17TH ST

Anacortes Marina

Fidalgo

HIGH SCHOOL ■

20TH ST

Bay

21ST ST

ANACO INN ●

21ST ST

AUTUMN LEAVES B&B ■

C AVE

ISLAND VIEW PL

22ND ST

22ND ST

FIDALGO POOL & FITNESS CENTER ■

23RD ST

G AVE

H AVE

24TH ST

24TH ST

R AVE

28TH ST

29TH ST

ANACORTES INN ●

30ST ST

Storvik Park

K AVE

Q AVE

Fidalgo Bay Marina

32ND ST

MARINA INN ●

ANACO BAY INN ●

33RD ST

NANTUCKET INN ●

34TH ST

D AVE

H AVE

35TH ST

20

FIDALGO BAY RD

0      400 yds

0      400 m

■ ACE OF HEARTS DOG PARK

To Mt Vernon, Whidbey Island, and Seattle

© AVALON TRAVEL

GATEWAYS TO THE ISLANDS

homes and buildings, many restored to their original splendor. The home owned and built by Amos and Anna Curtis Bowman in 1891 stands at 1815 8th Street. At 807 4th Street, an architect's office is now housed in what was probably the finest bordello in the county in the 1890s. The little church at 5th and R was built by its Presbyterian congregation in 1889; still in use is the Episcopal Church at 7th and M, built in 1896.

Founded in 1913, **Marine Supply & Hardware Co.** (2nd and Commercial Ave., 360/293-3014, www.marinesupplyandhardware.com) is the oldest continuously operating marine supply store west of the Mississippi. The original oiled wood floors and oak cabinets are still here, along with a potpourri of supplies. It's a fascinating place to visit, with three generations of the Demopoulos family running things.

## ◖ *W.T. Preston*

Remnants of Anacortes's earlier days are scattered throughout town, including the fascinating historic sternwheeler *W.T. Preston,* next to the marina at 7th Street and R Avenue (360/293-1916, http://museum.cityofanacortes.org, 10 A.M.–4 P.M. Thurs.–Tues. June–Aug., 10 A.M.–4 P.M. Sat., 11 A.M.–4 P.M. Sun. Apr.–May and Sept.–Oct., closed Nov.–Mar., $3 adults, $2 seniors, $1 kids, free for children under eight). Now a National Historic Landmark, the *Preston* operated as a snagboat for the U.S. Army Corps of Engineers from 1940 till 1981, when she was given to the city of Anacortes. The last sternwheeler operating on Puget Sound, it kept waterways clear of debris by towing off snags, logs, and stumps that piled up against bridge supports. Step into the **Maritime Heritage Center** (360/299-1984) for an introduction to the importance of fishing and boat building, and then walk up the ramp for a self-guided tour of the vessel.

Adjacent to the *Preston* is the 1911 Burlington Northern Railroad Depot at 7th and R, now home to the Depot Arts Center, plus the Anacortes Farmers Market on summer Saturdays.

historic snagboat *W.T. Preston*

© DON PITCHER

## Viewpoints

Five miles south of downtown Anacortes, 1,270-foot **Mount Erie** is the tallest hill on Fidalgo Island. A steep and winding road rises 1.5 miles to a partially wooded summit, where four short trails lead to dizzying views of the Olympics, Mount Baker, Mount Rainier, and Puget Sound. Don't miss the two lower overlooks, located 0.25 mile downhill from the summit. Get to Mount Erie by following Heart Lake Road south from town past Heart Lake to the signed turnoff at Mount Erie Road. Trails lead from various points along Mount Erie Road into other parts of Anacortes Community Forest Lands.

For a low-elevation viewpoint of Anacortes, the Cascades, and Skagit Valley, visit **Cap Sante Park** on the city's east side, following 4th Street to West Avenue. Scramble up the boulders for a better look at Mount Baker, the San Juans, and the Anacortes refineries that turn Alaskan oil into gasoline. Not far away, a short paved trail leads to **Rotary Park** next to Cap Sante Boat Haven, where you'll find picnic tables overlooking the busy harbor.

## 【 Washington Park

Three miles west of downtown Anacortes, Washington Park is a strikingly beautiful preserve with 220 waterfront acres on Rosario Strait affording views of the San Juans and Olympics. Walk, bike, or drive the skinny two-mile paved scenic loop, and stop off at one of many waterfront picnic areas. Other facilities include a busy boat launch, several miles of hiking trails offering views of the San Juans and the Olympics, a playground, and crowded campsites with showers and laundry facilities. Pick up a detailed map and description of the park at the downtown visitors center. The original park acreage was donated by one of Fidalgo Island's earliest pioneers, Tonjes Havekost, who said, "Make my cemetery a park for everybody." His grave stands on the southern edge of the park, overlooking Burrows Channel. The Anacortes Women's Club bought additional acreage in 1922 from

© DON PITCHER

enjoying the view from Cap Sante Park in Anacortes

the sale of lemon pies—they paid just $2,500 for 75 beachfront acres.

## Guemes Island

Skagit County operates a **ferry** (www.skagit-county.net, $10 round-trip for a car and driver) to residential Guemes (GWEE-mes) Island from 6th Street and I Avenue. Take your bicycle along for a scenic tour of this rural, almost level island that is home to 500 year-round residents, and twice that many in the summer. You'll find a mile-long public shoreline on the southwest end, with a pleasant agate-strewn beach; the best access is by turning left off the ferry and following South Shore Drive to its junction with West Shore Drive. Kids will enjoy the playground near the center of Guemes. **Guemes Island Resort** on the north end of the island provides lodging. If you aren't staying here, stop at the adjacent **Young's Park** for a delightful beach picnic. Learn more about the island at www.linetime.org.

A 1.2-mile hiking trail climbs to the 700-foot summit of **Guemes Mountain**—highest point on the island—providing vistas in all directions. Access the trailhead by driving straight from the ferry landing for 1.5 miles and turning right on Edens Road. Continue another 1.5 miles, where you'll see a small parking area and the trailhead on the left side. Find details at www.skagitlandtrust.org.

Next to the ferry landing on Guemes, the welcoming **Anderson's General Store** (7885 Guemes Island Rd., 360/293-4548, www.guemesislandstore.com, 8 A.M.–7 P.M. daily) has groceries and supplies. Its motto: "If we don't have it, we'll explain how you can get along without it." Stop by for delicious breakfasts (try the lingonberry crepes), giant cinnamon rolls, lunchtime burgers and salads, and light dinners, with beer on draft at the small bar and a covered deck to take in the ferry action. Live music is offered most Friday nights, and Wi-Fi is free.

The **Friends of Guemes Island** (www.friendsofguemesisland.org) works to preserve the rural character of the island.

## Padilla Bay

This shallow bay east of Anacortes is home to the **Breazeale Interpretive Center** (10441 Bayview-Edison Rd., 360-428-1558, www.padillabay.gov, 10 A.M.–5 P.M. Wed.–Sun., free). Stop by to learn more about this important estuary; there's even a hands-on room for kids. Nearby is tiny **Bay View State Park** (360/757-0227, www.parks.wa.gov), with access to the bay, a two-mile shoreline trail, and campsites for $21–28; reservations for $10 extra at 888/226-7688 or through the park website.

## ◖ Deception Pass State Park

Washington's most popular state park, Deception Pass (360/675-2417, www.parks.wa.gov) has facilities that rival those of national parks: swimming at two lakes, four miles of shoreline, 28 miles of hiking trails, freshwater and saltwater fishing, boating, picnicking, rowboat rentals, boat launches, viewpoints, an environmental learning center, and several hundred campsites. The park, nine miles south of Anacortes on Highway 20, covers almost 3,600 forested acres on both sides of spectacular **Deception Pass Bridge.** (The north side is on Fidalgo Island, while the south end is on Whidbey Island.)

When Captain George Vancouver first sighted this waterway in 1792, he called it Port Gardner. But when he realized the inlet was actually a tidal passage between two islands, he renamed it "Deception Pass." Because of the strong tidal currents that can reach nine knots twice a day, the passage was avoided by sailing ships until 1852, when Captain Thomas Coupe (for whom nearby Coupeville is named) sailed a fully rigged three-masted vessel through the narrow entrance.

For a unique perspective, take a speedy catamaran tour through the passage from **Deception Pass Tours** (360/914-0096 or 888/909-8687, www.deceptionpasstours.com). These hour-long trips start in Oak Harbor and cost $25 adults or $21 for seniors and kids.

## THE MAIDEN OF DECEPTION PASS

The Samish Indians told the story of the beautiful maiden of Deception Pass, Ko-Kwal-Alwoot. She was gathering shellfish along the beach when the sea spirit saw her and was at once enamored; when he took her hand, Ko-Kwal-Alwoot became terrified, but the sea spirit reassured her, saying he only wished to gaze upon her loveliness. She returned often, listening to the sea spirit's declarations of love.

One day a young man came from the sea to ask Ko-Kwal-Alwoot's father for permission to marry her. Her father, suspecting that living underwater would be hazardous to his daughter's health, refused, despite the sea spirit's claim that Ko-Kwal-Alwoot would have eternal life. Miffed, the sea spirit brought drought and famine to the old man's people until he agreed to give his daughter away. There was one condition: that she return once every year so the old man could be sure she was properly cared for. The agreement was made, and the people watched as Ko-Kwal-Alwoot walked into the water until only her hair, floating in the current, was visible. The famine and drought ended at once.

Ko-Kwal-Alwoot kept her promise for the next four years, returning to visit her people, but every time she came she was covered with more and more barnacles and seemed anxious to return to the sea. On her last visit, her people told her she need not return unless she wanted to; ever since that time, she has provided abundant shellfish and clean spring water to that area. Legend has it that her hair can be seen floating to and fro with the tide in Deception Pass.

Today, this Samish legend is inscribed on a story pole on Fidalgo Island within Deception Pass State Park. To get there, follow Highway 20 to Fidalgo Island; go west at Pass Lake, following the signs for Bowman Bay and Rosario Beach, and hike the trail toward Rosario Head.

## DECEPTION PASS BRIDGE

Completed in 1935, Deception Pass Bridge, a steel cantilever-truss structure, links Fidalgo, Pass, and Whidbey Islands. Much of the work was done by the Civilian Conservation Corps (CCC), which also built many other park structures. The bridge towers 182 feet above the water. It's estimated that each year more than three million people stop at the bridge to peer over the edge at the turbulent water and whirlpools far below, or to enjoy the sunset vistas. A delightful and very scenic trail leads down from the southwest side of the bridge to a beautiful beach. The beach is also accessible by taking the road to the North Beach picnic area.

## OTHER SIGHTS

**Bowman Bay** is just north of the bridge on the west side of the highway and has campsites, a boat launch, and a fishing pier, plus a **CCC Interpretive Center** (Thurs.–Mon. hours

© DON PITCHER

Deception Pass Bridge at Deception Pass State Park

vary, summers only) inside one of the attractive structures the corps built. Three rooms contain displays on the CCC and the men who worked for it in the 1930s. You may find one of the original CCC workers on duty, ready to talk about the old times. **Anacortes Kayak Tours** (360/588-1117 or 800/992-1801, www.anacorteskayaktours.com) guides 1.5-hour paddles ($35) from its kiosk here.

**Rosario Beach,** just north of Bowman Bay, features a delightful picnic ground with CCC-built stone shelters. A 0.5-mile hiking trail circles Rosario Head, the wooded point of land that juts into Rosario Bay (technically this is part of the 75-acre Sharpe County Park). The shoreline is a fine place to explore tidepools. The **Maiden of Deception Pass** totem pole commemorates the tale of a Samish girl who became the bride of the water spirit. Walla Walla College Marine Station (www.wwc.edu) is adjacent to Rosario Beach, and an underwater park offshore is popular with scuba divers.

A mile south of the Deception Pass Bridge is the turnoff to Coronet Bay Road. This road ends three miles out at **Hoypus Point,** a good place to fish for salmon or to ride bikes, with striking views of Mount Baker.

### LAKES AND HIKES

Only electric motors, canoes, and rowboats are allowed on the park's lakes. You can observe beaver dams, muskrats, and mink in the marshes on the south side of shallow **Cranberry Lake,** which also hosts a seasonal concession stand. Trout fishing is good here, and the warm water makes it a favorite swimming hole. North of the bridge is **Pass Lake,** another place to fish or paddle.

A 15-minute hike to the highest point on the island, 400-foot **Goose Rock,** provides views of the San Juan Islands, Mount Baker, Victoria, and Fidalgo Island. You may possibly see a bald eagle soaring overhead. The trail starts at the south end of the bridge, heading east from either side of the highway; take the wide trail as it follows the pass, and then take one of the unmarked spur trails uphill to the top. Other hiking trails lead throughout the park, ranging from short nature paths to unimproved trails for experienced hikers only.

## ENTERTAINMENT AND EVENTS

The **Anacortes Community Theatre** (918 M St., 360/293-6829, www.acttheatre.com) stages plays, musicals, and annual Christmas performances. The **Vela Luka Croatian Dancers** (www.velaluka.org) is a local group that performs all over the world. This is the most obvious example of Anacortes's strong Croatian community; an estimated 25 percent of the local population is of Croatian descent.

The small **Anacortes Cinemas** (4th and O Sts., 360/293-7000, www.farawayentertainment.com/anacortes.html) shows first-run films. Find live music on weekends at three downtown bars, all of which sometimes share a cover charge: **Rockfish Grill & Anacortes Brewery** (320 Commercial Ave., 360/293-3666, www.rockfishgrill.com), **Brown Lantern Ale House** (412 Commercial Ave., 360/293-2544, www.brownlantern.com), and **Watertown Pub** (314 Commercial Ave., 360/293-3587).

Drop some cash at **Swinomish Northern Lights Casino & Bingo** (just across the Highway 20 bridge on Fidalgo Island, 360/293-2691 or 888/288-8883, www.swinomishcasino.com), which offers gambling—including bingo, slots, craps, roulette, blackjack, poker, keno, and off-track betting. The gift shop sells native arts, and the lounge has live music (no cover) on Saturday nights and comedy every Friday. A free shuttle is available from town, and a 100-room hotel and a convention center are in the works.

### Festivals and Events

Throughout the month of April, the ever-popular **Skagit Valley Tulip Festival** (360/428-5959, www.tulipfestival.org) brings activities to Anacortes, La Conner, and Mount Vernon, including everything from garden tours to a quilt show. Another popular April event is the **Spring Wine Festival,** with tastings from 30 regional wineries and food sampling from six local restaurants.

**The Heart of Anacortes** (www.theheartof-anacortes.com) is an outdoor venue for music and performance on 4th Street behind Rockfish Grill, with lots of action all summer and fall.

The **Anacortes Waterfront Festival,** held at Cap Sante Boat Haven on Q Avenue the third weekend of May, celebrates the city's maritime heritage with a food court and beer garden, live music, free boat rides, craft booths, marine swap meet, and kids' activities.

Anacortes, like every other town in America, has a parade and fireworks on the **Fourth of July.** During **Shipwreck Days Flea Market** on the third Saturday in July, more than 300 vendors turn downtown Anacortes into a giant garage sale.

The **Anacortes Arts Festival** (360/293-6211, www.anacortesartsfestival.com), the first weekend of August, attracts more than 70,000 people with a juried fine art show, 250 arts and crafts booths, kids' events, ethnic foods, classic cars, and plenty of live music and entertainment. Don't miss this one! Especially fun is the quick-and-dirty boat building contest, which gives participants five hours to construct a wooden boat.

The **Anacortes Eagles' Barbecue,** the third weekend of August, has been going on for nearly six decades, with a block-long array of salmon, chicken, and ribs (but no eagles, alas). **Oyster Run** (360/757-1515, www.oysterrun.org), the last weekend of September, brings thousands of bikers to Anacortes; it's a great place for leather lovers. You'll also find stunt motorcyclists, a beer garden, vendors, and oysters on the half shell. More drinking takes place at the annual **Oktoberfest Bier on the Pier,** where 30 breweries roll out the tasting barrels. The **Deception Pass Dash** (www.outdooradventurecenter.com) in December attracts some 200 kayakers for a paddle through the pass.

## SHOPPING

Anacortes is becoming a popular destination for antiquing, with a number of downtown shops specializing in historical Northwest items. Meet regional authors during book and poetry readings at **Watermark Book Co.** (612 Commercial Ave., 360/293-4277).

Local galleries present changing exhibits during monthly **First Friday Art Walks** (www.anacortesart.com). Several downtown galleries line Commercial Avenue, the best of which are **Anne Martin McCool Gallery** (711 Commercial Ave., 360/293-3577, www.mccoolart.com), which displays her vivid watercolors; **Scott Milo Gallery** (420 Commercial Ave., 360/293-6938, www.scottmilo.com), with a variety of artists and changing exhibits; and **Insights Gallery** (516 Commercial Ave., 360/588-8044, www.insightsgallery.com), featuring contemporary artists. **Depot Arts Center** (611 R Ave., 360/293-3663, www.depotartscenter.com, 1–4 P.M. Tues.–Sun.) houses a gallery showcasing local talent. It's adjacent to the historic *W.T. Preston.*

## SPORTS AND RECREATION
### Hiking and Biking

The **Tommy Thompson Parkway** is a paved 3.5-mile bike/running path that starts at the downtown marina, extends south to Fidalgo Bay RV Park, and then crosses to March Point atop an old railway trestle over Fidalgo Bay. Rent bikes at **Skagit Cycle Center** (1620 Commercial Ave., 360/588-8776, www.skagitcyclecenter.com).

Some of the finest local hiking is at Deception Pass State Park. Stop by the Anacortes visitors center for a guide to trails within the 2,800-acre **Anacortes Community Forest Lands** (360/293-1918, www.cityofanacortes.org) around Mount Erie and Cranberry, Whistle, and Heart Lakes. More than 50 miles of trails are here, and many of them can be linked into loop hikes; get a map for $10.

The 3.5-mile **Whistle Lake Shore Loop** circles small Whistle Lake, offering water views, lots of bird life, and old-growth stands of Douglas fir and western red cedar. An easy and almost level path, the **Erie View Trail** departs from Heart Lake Road and follows a seasonal creek to a fine view of Mount Erie a mile out. Return the same way.

From the trailhead at the intersection of Mount Erie and Heart Lake Roads, hike the 0.5-mile **Pine Ridge Loop Trail** for more views of Mount Erie and Sugarloaf. This moderately difficult hike takes from one to two hours. Another short hike is the 1.6-mile **Sugarloaf Trail,** starting on Ray Auld Drive, six miles from its intersection with Heart Lake Road. Follow the trail from the marshy trailhead straight up, ignoring side trails. To the west, enjoy views of Port Townsend, the San Juan Islands, and the Strait of Juan de Fuca; to the north, Bellingham.

The Cranberry Lake area also has a number of hiking paths, including the mile-long **John M. Morrison Loop Trail,** which starts at the end of 29th Street. This easy loop hike provides bluff-top views of Cranberry Lake and old-growth Douglas fir forests, where some trees are seven feet in diameter.

## Sea Kayaking

**The Sea Kayak Shop** (2515 Commercial Ave., 360/299-2300, www.seakayakshop.com) is a full-service shop with classes for all levels of ability, kayak rentals to experienced paddlers, and occasional guided tours.

**Anacortes Kayak Tours** (1801 Commercial Ave., 360/588-1117 or 800/992-1801, www.anacorteskayaktours.com) operates from the Island Adventures Center, which also leads whale-watching trips. Nearby Burrows Island is a popular destination for three-hour ($74) or five-hour paddles ($99) departing from Skyline Marina. The company's most popular trips are inexpensive 1.5-hour paddles ($35) from Bowman Bay at Deception Pass State Park.

## Boating and Fishing

Anacortes is home to the second largest bareboat charter fleet in the world. You'll find dozens of power yachts and sailboats heading out from two impressive marinas: **Anacortes Marina** (2415 T Ave., 360/293-4543, www.anaortesmarina.com) and **Cap Sante Boat Haven** (1019 Q Ave., 360/293-0694, www.

portofanacortes.com). Cap Sante has guest moorage. The largest charter companies are **ABC Yacht Charters** (360/293-9533 or 800/426-2313, www.abcyachtcharters.com), **Anacortes Yacht Charters** (360/293-4555 or 800/233-3004, www.ayc.com), and **Ship Harbor Yacht Charters** (360/299-9193 or 877/772-6582, www.shipharboryachts.com).

For fishing trips, contact **Highliner Charters** (360/770-0341, www.highlinercharters.com), **Jolly Mon Charters** (360/202-2664, www.jollymonanacortes.com), **R&R Charters** (360/293-2992, www.randrfishingcharters.com), or **Catchmore Charters** (360/293-7093, www.catchmorecharters.com).

## Whale-Watching

Two local companies offer five- to six-hour whale-watching trips from Anacortes, both using large 100-foot vessels. **Island Adventures** (1801 Commercial Ave., 360/293-2428 or 800/465-4604, www.island-adventures.com, $109 adults, $89 seniors, and $49 kids) boasts a fast 150-passenger boat that can find orcas even when they've moved into Canadian waters around the Southern Gulf Islands. The company operates most of the year, shifting to humpback and gray whales in the winter and spring months.

**Mystic Sea Charters** (819 Commercial Ave., 360/588-8000 or 800/308-9387, www.mysticseacharters.com, $89 adults, $79 seniors, or $49 kids under 18) offers five-hour whale-watching trips on a comfortable boat with room for 75 folks.

## Other Recreation

**Similk Beach Golf Course** (12518 Christianson Rd., 360/293-3444, greens fees $32) is an 18-hole course with Puget Sound vistas. Swim at the public **Fidalgo Pool and Fitness Center** (1603 22nd St., 360/293-0673, www.fidalgopool.com, $5); a complete exercise center is also available here. **Bayside Fitness** (8212 S. March's Point Rd., 360/293-0123, www.baysidefitness.com) has day passes for $10; child care and massage are available.

**Anacortes Diving & Supply** (2502 Commercial Ave., 360/293-2070, www.anacortesdiving.com) is a full-service shop that runs dive trips to the San Juans and surrounding areas. **Diver's Dream Charters** (360/202-0076, www.lujacsquest.com) provides dive transportation onboard the 42-foot *Lu-Jac's Quest*.

## ACCOMMODATIONS

Anacortes is blessed with an abundance of comfortable hotels, motels, and B&Bs. Make reservations far ahead for the summer months since some places fill up by March for the peak season in July and August. The Anacortes Chamber of Commerce website (www.anacortes.org) has links to many local lodging options, including guesthouses and cottages.

### Hotels and Inns

Centrally located **San Juan Motel** (1103 6th St., 360/293-5105 or 800/533-8009, www.sanjuanmotelwa.com, $80 d) is a clean, quiet place where the rooms include two queen-size beds, kitchenettes, and Wi-Fi.

Downtown across from the marina, **Cap Sante Inn** (906 9th St., 360/293-0602 or 800/852-0846, www.capsanteinn.com, $95–99 d) is an excellent mid-priced motel offering attractive rooms, comfy beds, fine linens, Wi-Fi, plus microwaves and fridges. A two-bedroom suite sleeps six for $160. Pets ($10 extra) are allowed. Guests are likely to be greeted by the owner's dogs, and there's a dog park less than a block away.

Similar rates are offered at **Anacortes Inn** (3006 Commercial Ave., 360/293-3153 or 800/327-7976, www.anacortesinn.com, $90–105 d), where rooms include fridges and microwaves (some full kitchens with dishes) and guests enjoy a seasonal outdoor pool, Wi-Fi, and continental breakfast. Special rates are often available, so call ahead.

**Lake Campbell Lodging** (1377 Hwy. 20, 360/293-5314 or 888/399-1077, www.lakecampbelllodging.com, ($59–76 d), four miles south of Anacortes, is a good family spot with clean rooms that include fridges, microwaves, and Wi-Fi. Larger units with two bedrooms and

kitchenettes ($86–96 d) can sleep up to seven. Pretty Lake Campbell is right across Highway 20 from the motel, but traffic can be heavy. Closed the last two weeks of December.

**Islands Inn** (3401 Commercial Ave., 360/293-4644 or 866/331-3328, www.islandsinn.com, $89–99 d) offers comfortable motel rooms—most with fireplaces and some with separate bedrooms—plus a large suite ($149 d) containing a fireplace and jetted tub. An outdoor pool and hot tub are on the premises, and guests are treated to a complimentary breakfast buffet in the lobby. Petite Wine Bar serves tapas and other light fare for dinner.

In the heart of town, **◖ Majestic Inn** (419 Commercial Ave., 360/299-1400 or 877/370-0100, www.majesticinnandspa.com, $169–259 d) exudes historic elegance. It was built in 1889, but the building has been completely updated with such amenities as a fine-dining restaurant and lounge, full-service spa, and Wi-Fi. Twenty guest rooms and a luxury suite ($249 d) all include a continental breakfast.

On the south end of town, **Anaco Bay Inn** (916 33rd St., 360/299-3320 or 877/299-3320, www.anacobayinn.com, $99–124 d) is Anacortes's newest lodging place. The immaculate rooms have gas fireplaces, and larger ones include kitchenettes and jetted tubs; suites ($129 d) and two-bedroom apartments with full kitchens ($139 d) are also available. A continental breakfast, Wi-Fi, and large indoor hot tub are included.

Just up the street is **Marina Inn** (3300 Commercial Ave., 360/293-1100 or 800/231-5198, www.marinainnwa.com, $99–119 d), with big and immaculate rooms, in-room fridges and microwaves, a light breakfast, and Wi-Fi.

**Anaco Inn** (905 20th St., 360/293-8833 or 888/293-8833, www.anacoinn.com) is another well-kept, newer place. Basic rooms are $89–109 d, suites with jetted tubs and kitchens cost $119–129 d, and apartment units run $149 d. Guests appreciate the continental breakfast and Wi-Fi. There's a two-night minimum on weekends (when the rate goes up $10).

Anyone heading out to the San Juans should consider homey ◖ **Anacortes Ship Harbor Inn** (5316 Ferry Terminal Rd., 360/293-5177 or 800/852-8568, www.shipharborinn.com), located close to the ferry west of town. It's quiet and peaceful, with water vistas, Wi-Fi, a BBQ area, clean rooms ($99 d), cottages with kitchenettes and fireplaces ($149 d), and suites ($179 d) with jetted tubs and plasma TVs. A hot breakfast is included, and you're likely to encounter deer and rabbits on the lawn.

Built in 1925, **Nantucket Inn** (3402 Commercial Ave., 360/333-5282, www.nantucketinnanacortes.com) is a classic three-story Colonial-style home with eight guest rooms, all with private baths, light breakfasts, and Wi-Fi. The two queen-bed rooms are $99 d, while king rooms run $129–159 d. The grounds are popular for weddings and family reunions.

## Bed-and-Breakfasts

**Autumn Leaves B&B** (2301 21st St., 360/293-4920 or 866/293-4929, www.autumn-leaves.com, $160 d) is a large contemporary home with three romantic guest rooms furnished with French antiques, gas fireplaces, and jetted tubs. Rates include a gourmet breakfast. No kids under 14.

Sail over to **The Ship House Inn B&B** (12876 Marine Dr., 360/293-1093, www.shiphouseinn.com, $125–159 d), where the nautical theme carries through three cute cottages, one of which has a boat-shaped space to watch the sunset. The smallest units have twin bunk beds. A filling breakfast is served in the galley room facing the water. Older kids only due to the clifftop location.

## Cottages and Suites

Several private cottages and suites are available around Anacortes. **Lowman House Suites/Smugglers Cottage** (701 K Ave., 360/293-0590, www.lowmanhouse.com) rents two very comfortable suites in a 1907 home for $700 per week, plus a 1920 three-bedroom cottage for $770 per week. All units include full kitchens and private baths.

**Town Cottages** (360/293-1252 or 877/293-1252, www.towncottages.com) rents two cottages and a dozen condos for $450–730 per week (one-week minimum stay). All are fully furnished with kitchens, laundry, off-street parking, and Wi-Fi.

**Troll House Guest Cottage** (3895 Sea Breeze Ln., 360/293-5750, www.thetrollhouse.com, $125–150/night) is a delightful two-person place with a kitchenette, hot tub, and private deck.

**Serenity by the Sea** (360/588-0472, www.serenityanacortes.com, $125 weekdays, $150 weekends) has a single apartment in a contemporary home with nice views from the windows, a full kitchen, and Wi-Fi. No children under age 16.

## Resorts

Located on the north end of Guemes Island and accessible via a five-minute ferry ride ($10 round-trip) from Anacortes, **Guemes Island Resort** (325 Guemes Island Rd., 360/293-6643 or 800/965-6643, www.guemesislandresort.com, $165–220 nightly, $1,072–1,188/week) is a delightful family escape. Eight waterfront cabins—each with a kitchen and woodstove—face a grassy lawn with views of Mount Baker. The larger units sleep up to six. Other options include three private houses ($240–465/night) or five comfortable yurts ($75–115 d) for upscale camping in the trees. No TVs, radios, or room phones in any of these, but guests are welcome to use the rowboats, sea kayaks, wood-fired sauna, Ping-Pong table, yard games, hiking trail, boat launch, Wi-Fi, and crab pots. Massage and a Dutchtub (wood-fired hot tub filled with saltwater) are available. The resort books far ahead for the peak Dungeness crabbing season from mid-July through September. There's a minimum stay of three nights (four nights for the houses) during the summer and holidays.

## Camping

Three miles west of Anacortes and close to the ferry terminal, city-run **Washington Park** (360/293-1918, www.cityofanacortes.org,

© DON PITCHER

Guemes Island Resort

$15–17 tents or $19–23 RV hookups) has 75 crowded campsites in a peaceful wooded setting, as well as showers, picnic tables, boat launches, and a delightful beach and playground. No reservations, but the campground is open all year.

Nine miles south of Anacortes, **Deception Pass State Park** (360/675-2417, www.parks.wa.gov, $22–25 tents, $31–36 RVs, $12 bikes) has some of the finest camping in this part of Washington, with tall Douglas firs and a gorgeous lakeside location. Unfortunately, the park's popularity means that you'll be accompanied by a multitude of fellow visitors. There are 310 tent and RV sites at Deception Pass, with hot showers and dump stations. The primary campground along Cranberry Lake has year-round sites, and a second seasonal campground is just north of the bridge at Bowman Bay, with additional sites at the former Sunrise Resort. If possible, make reservations ($9 extra) well in advance of a midsummer visit at 888/226-7688, www.parks.wa.gov. Head to the park's

outdoor amphitheater on weekend evenings in the summer for natural history lectures and presentations.

Exceptionally popular with RVers—and with good reason—**Pioneer Trails RV Resort** (527 Miller Rd., 360/293-5355 or 888/777-5355, www.pioneertrails.com) sits on 28 acres of forested land south of town off Highway 20. Immaculate sites cost $32 ($50 for those with a private cabana), and cabins are $48–59. No tent camping.

A sprawling RV park just south of town, **Fidalgo Bay Resort** (4701 Fidalgo Bay Rd., 360/293-5353 or 800/727-5478, www.fidalgobay.com, $32–58) has beach access, seafood cookouts, a fitness center, and Wi-Fi. Other RV options include **Swinomish Northern Lights Casino** (12885 Casino Dr., 360/293-2691 or 800/877-7529, www.swinomishcasino.com, $22–25) or **Lighthouse RV Park** (6060 Sands Way, 360/770-4334, $23). The last of these isn't much more than a gravel lot with crammed-together sites near Skyline Marina. You can also park RVs at Cap Sante Marina in

Anacortes; check in at the harbormasters office (360/293-0694).

**North Whidbey RV Park** (565 W. Cornet Bay Rd., 360/675-9597 or 888/462-2674, www.northwhidbeyrvpark.com, $30) is nine miles south of Anacortes and across the road from Deception Pass State Park.

# FOOD
## Breakfast and Lunch
Start your day at **Calico Cupboard Café & Bakery** (901 Commercial Ave., 360/293-7315, www.calicocupboardcafe.com, 7 A.M.–3 P.M. daily, $9–12) for homemade country breakfasts—served all day—and healthy lunches. Save room for dessert; the fudge pecan pie and apple dumplings are legendary. Get there early on weekends to avoid a wait.

**Penguin Coffee** (2110 Commercial Ave., 360/588-8321, www.penguincoffee.com) and **Johnny Picasso's** (501 Commercial Ave., 360/299-2755, 8 A.M.–6 P.M. Mon.–Fri., 9 A.M.–6 P.M. Sat., 10 A.M.–4 P.M. Sun.) both offer start-me-up espresso and free Wi-Fi. They're fun spots to relax, and the latter houses a studio where you can paint ceramic pottery or craft fused-glass pieces.

Just looking to maximize your calorie, fat, and sugar consumption? Get a dozen to go at **Donut House** (2719 Commercial Ave., 360/293-4053, 24 hours daily); the drive-up window obviates the need to expend needless energy walking inside. Free Wi-Fi too.

## Seafood
**Anthony's** (1207 Q Ave., 360/588-0333, www.anthonys.com, 11:30 A.M.–9:30 P.M. Mon.–Thurs., 11:30 A.M.–10:30 P.M. Fri.–Sat., 10 A.M.–9:30 P.M. Sun., $19–32 entrées) is the local incarnation of this Northwest chain of upmarket restaurants. Enormous windows provide a Cap Sante Marina view, while two large decks and a covered patio with an outdoor fireplace add to the lively appeal. The menu encompasses regional seafood and steaks, along with a $20 early bird four-course dinner on weeknights before 6 P.M.

**Bob's Chowder Bar** (3320 Commercial Ave., 360/299-8000, www.bobschowderbar. com, 11 A.M.–8 P.M. Mon.–Sat.) is the spot for quick seafood meals such as oyster burgers, clam chowder, fish tacos, chicken strip baskets, and grilled wild salmon. The priciest item is $11, making Bob's popular with families.

## Fine Dining
If you eat just one meal in Anacortes, make sure it's at the nautically themed **C** **Adrift Restaurant** (510 Commercial Ave., 360/588-0653, www.adriftrestaurant.com, 8 A.M.–9 P.M. Mon.–Thurs., 8 A.M.–10 P.M. Fri.–Sat., $10–30 dinner entrées). Unpretentious and quirky, Adrift is open three meals a day with a raucous atmosphere and from-scratch meals from the open kitchen. Owners Nichole and Maggi Holbert crank out unusual breakfasts (served till 4 P.M.) and creative lunches. Try the fried egg sandwich with bacon and cheese, cottage cheese pancakes, or the Skagit burger ($12 for a quarter-pounder) topped with garlic aioli. Many items are locally grown and organic. Dinner entrées start around $14 for a pulled-pork, black bean, and sweet potato taco. The menu changes often, but always has several staples, including an amazing cioppino ($28) with a rich tomato wine sauce and big chunks of clams, mussels, halibut, salmon, and crab, all seasoned with saffron and fennel. Nightly seafood and steak specials are worth considering, along with the Dungeness crabcake appetizers. This is slow food worth the wait. If you get bored, peruse the eclectic collection of old books (including some first editions); I found *The Muzzleloading Hunter* and *Offset Lithographic Printmaking* next to each other. If you find one you like, buy it for $5. There are no reservations here.

**5th St. Bistro at Majestic Inn** (419 Commercial Ave., 360/299-1400 or 877/370-0100, www.majesticinnandspa.com, 4–9 P.M. Sun.–Mon., 4–10 P.M. Tues.–Thurs., 4 P.M.–midnight Fri.–Sat., $13–29) is an upscale destination spot where a big garden is a favorite summertime wedding spot. Dinners include filet mignon, Caesar salads, grilled salmon, and a spicy mac-n-cheese. The casual-dining lounge is popular for oysters on the half shell, steamed mussels, and Kobe beef burgers.

Located in the heart of town, **Cameron's Living Room Dining** (904 Commercial Ave., 360/299-4567, www.cameronslivingroomdining.com, 5–9 P.M. Mon.–Thurs., 5–10 P.M. Fri.–Sat., closed Sun., $24–28 entrées) features an exquisite setting to match the food. Chef David Burdette is best known for such specialties as Dutch oven braise lamb shank, panko-crusted black cod, and grilled ribeye steak Delmonico. A tad pricey, but a fine place for a romantic evening. Diners are treated to piano music on Friday and Saturday evenings.

### International

Find fine Italian dining at **Il Posto** (21210 Commercial Ave., 360/293-7600, www.ilpostoristorante.com, 4:30–9:30 P.M. Wed.–Mon., $18–25 entrées). House specialties include cioppino, penne alla vodka, and calamari peperonati.

Often crowded with locals, **Greek Islands Restaurant** (2001 Commercial Ave., 360/293-6911, www.greekislana.com, 11 A.M.–2 P.M., 4 P.M.–closing Tues.–Sun.) serves lamb souvlaki, moussaka, chicken a la Greka, spanakopita, and other Mediterranean specialties. Everything is made from scratch at this authentic slice of the Old World, where chef Emmanuel Chondroyannos cooks the food and his friendly wife Anna greets diners. This is the real deal.

For Japanese food, try **Teriyaki Time** (910 11th St., 360/588-8025, 11 A.M.–9 P.M. Mon.–Fri., 11 A.M.–8 P.M. Sat.) or **Tokyo Restaurant** (818 Commercial Ave., 360/293-9898, 11 A.M.–9 P.M. Mon.–Fri., 3:30–9 P.M. Sat.) The latter has a sushi bar and $8 bento box lunches.

Find traditional Mexican plates, seafood, burritos, and vegetarian dishes at **Agave Taqueria** (2520 Commercial Ave., 360/588-1288, 11 A.M.–10 P.M. daily). It's the hometown spot for south-of-the-border meals, filling with locals for fast and tasty meals. Pull up to the drive-through if you're in a hurry. Big burritos are $8–9, while traditional Mexican plates cost $11–14.

For delicious Thai food, including vegetarian specialties, visit **Thai Season Restaurant** (710 Commercial Ave., 360/293-4004, www.thaiseasonanacortes.com, 11 A.M.–9 P.M. Mon.–Thurs., 11 A.M.–10 P.M. Fri., noon–10 P.M. Sat., noon–9 P.M. Sun., $13–20 entrées).

### Pubs and Pizza

You certainly won't go wrong with a lunch or dinner at **C Rockfish Grill & Anacortes Brewery** (320 Commercial Ave., 360/588-1720, www.rockfishgrill.com, 11 A.M.–11 P.M. Sun.–Thurs., 11 A.M.–midnight Fri.–Sat.), where the menu includes local seafood, small wood-fired pizzas, and burgers, along with nachos, wings, and fresh ales from the on-the-premises brewery. Dinner entrées are $18–24, but you can get a pizza or great fish and chips for $10. It's a bar, but families are welcome.

Just down the street is **Brown Lantern Ale House** (412 Commercial Ave., 360/293-2544, www.brownlantern.com), where the burgers and the halibut and chips are noteworthy and the pool table and shuffleboard see plenty of action.

**Village Pizza** (807 Commercial Ave., 360/293-7847, 11 A.M.–10 P.M. daily ) has pizzas and mini-pizzas, subs, grinders, and more; a medium cheese pizza is $13.

### Markets and Wines

Stock up on groceries for the San Juans at two big stores along Commercial Avenue: **Safeway** (911 11th St., 360/293-5393, www.safeway.com, daily 24 hours) and **The Market** (1519 Commercial Ave., 360/588-8181, www.themarketsllc.com, 6 A.M.–11 P.M. daily).

**Seabear Smokehouse** (605 30th St., 360/260-1082 or 800/645-3474, www.seabear.com) sells smoked Alaska salmon, Washington-made items, and other treats. Drop by to sample the fish or watch a video on the processing operation; salmon chowder is available Wednesdays in the summer.

The **Anacortes Farmers Market** (7th St.

and R Ave., 360/293-7922, www.anacortes-farmersmarket.org, 9 A.M.–2 P.M. Sat. mid-May–mid-Oct.) takes place at the Depot Arts Center. It's a good place to buy fresh produce, baked goods, flowers, artisan cheeses, hand-made crafts, clothing, and jams.

For an impressive selection of wines—including the most extensive selection of Washington wines anywhere—stop by **Compass Wines** (1405 Commercial Ave., 360/293-6500, www.compasswines.com). Free delivery is offered to local marinas.

## INFORMATION

For maps, brochures, and up-to-date information, drop by the **Anacortes Visitor Information Center** (819 Commercial Ave., 360/293-3832, www.anacortes.org, 9 A.M.–5 P.M. Mon.–Fri., 10 A.M.–3 P.M. Sat.–Sun. year-round). Across the street is a mural of Anna Curtis, for whom the town was named. Also check out the *Anacortes American* newspaper's website (www.goanacortes.com) for local information and news.

## SERVICES

**Island Hospital** (1211 24th St., 360/299-1300, www.islandhospital.org) has a 24-hour emergency room and 43 beds. The only hospital on the San Juan Islands is a limited facility in Friday Harbor, so this is the primary regional facility for the islands. Both **Anacortes Family Medicine** (2511 M Ave., 360/299-4211, www.islandhospital.org) and **Fidalgo Island Walk-In Clinic** (1500 Commercial Ave., 360/299-2650, www.fidalgowalk-in.com) provide same-day appointments.

If your pet gets sick or hurt, head to **Anacortes Animal Hospital** (2504 Commercial Ave., 360/293-3431) or **Fidalgo Animal Medical Center** (3303 Commercial Ave., 360/293-2186, www.fidalgovets.com). Leave your dogs or cats at **Sunnyhill Kennels & Catterey** (8033 Summit Rd., 360/293-3434, www.sunnyhillkennels.com) if you don't want to have them on the San Juans. Dog lovers will appreciate the big fenced-in **Ace of**

**Hearts Dog Park** (H Ave. at 38th Ave., www.anacortesdogpark.com).

Spacious **Anacortes Library** (1220 10th St., 360/293-1910, http://library.cityofanacortes.org, 1–5 P.M. Mon., 11 A.M.–8 P.M. Tues.–Wed., 9 A.M.–8 P.M. Thurs.–Fri., noon–5 P.M. Sat.) has a kids' room and a dozen computers with free Internet access and Wi-Fi.

## GETTING THERE AND AROUND
### Washington State Ferries

To reach the San Juan Islands or Sidney, British Columbia, via state ferry, you have no choice but to leave from Anacortes—and ferry traffic keeps a good portion of local businesses in business. The **Washington State Ferries** website (www.wsdot.wa.gov/ferries) has details on the ferry system, including current wait times in Anacortes. Call 206/464-6400 or 888/808-7977 for information and reservations. Ferries between Anacortes and the San Juans have onboard Wi-Fi for a daily or monthly charge.

### ANACORTES TERMINAL

Located on 12th Street, the Anacortes ferry terminal has a small gift shop, and the **Cheesecake Café** (360/588-0234), which serves sandwiches, sweets, and espresso. Warning: Anacortes police often stop folks speeding in an attempt to catch the ferry. Keep your speed down or you might get delayed considerably longer, with a fine to boot!

If you're bringing your car, be prepared for a lengthy wait in peak season. Get there at least two hours in advance for midsummer weekend travel, and bring a book to read. A small beach nearby is fun for a stroll or to keep the kids from bugging you too much, but keep an eye on the ferry traffic so you don't find yourself at the other end of the beach when cars start loading. Avoid delays by leaving your car in the parking lot next to the terminal (800/828-4197, $25 for three days or $40 for a week); there's always space for walk-on passengers.

© DON PITCHER

The Anacortes ferry terminal is especially busy on summer weekends.

## TO THE SAN JUANS

For travel to the San Juan Islands, the state ferries charge higher rates in summer (May–Sept.) than in the off-season. Peak-season summertime fares from Anacortes to Friday Harbor—the last American stop—are $11.50 for adult passengers and walk-ons, or $53.80 for a car and driver. Bikes are $4 extra, and kayaks cost $17.50 more. Car-and-driver fares to the other islands from Anacortes are a few dollars less, and child rates are discounted.

**Westbound interisland travel** (such as from Lopez to Orcas) is free for passengers or $23.50 for a car and driver. Ferry travelers are only charged in the westbound direction; eastbound travel within the San Juans or from the islands to Anacortes is free. If you're planning to visit all the islands, save money by heading straight to Friday Harbor, and then work your way back through the others at no additional charge. Credit cards are accepted at all ferry terminals, but checks are not.

Want to save time at the tollbooth? You can purchase **Wave2Go** tickets online in advance

of your trip, but doing so does not mean you will be on a given ferry since boarding is on a first-come, first-served basis. Advance ticket purchases through the Wave2Go system can also be made at special kiosks in the terminals. All tickets are good for 90 days from the date of purchase.

## TO VANCOUVER ISLAND

Twice a day (once daily in winter; no service Jan.–Mar.), a ferry heads from Anacortes to **Sidney, British Columbia,** 20 miles north of Victoria on Vancouver Island. One-way peak-season fares to Sidney are $16.85 for passengers and walk-ons or $56.45 for a car and driver. Vehicle reservations are highly recommended for this route and should be made at least 24 hours in advance. Make reservations online (www.wsdot.wa.gov/ferries) or by calling 206/464-6400 or 888/808-7977. Vehicles heading eastbound from Sidney to Anacortes can stop off in the San Juans at no additional charge. You will be crossing an international border, so passports are required (for kids a passport or birth certificate will do).

## Other Transportation
### GUEMES FERRY

Skagit County operates the small **Guemes Island Ferry** (6th St. and I Ave., 360/293-6356, www.skagitcounty.net) to this nearby residential island. The five-minute crossing costs $10 round-trip for a car and driver, and $3.50 adults, $2 kids round-trip for passengers or walk-ons. The ferry departs hourly (more often during commute hours) from 6:30 A.M. till at least 8 P.M. daily (till 11 P.M. on weekends). It doesn't run between 11:30 A.M. and 1 P.M.

### WATER TAXIS

Based at Skyline Marina in Anacortes, **Island Express Charters** (360/299-2875 or 877/473-9777, www.islandexpresscharters.com) has two high-speed landing crafts with plenty of space for kayaks, bikes, and gear. They'll head most anywhere in the San Juans for set prices, starting around $75 per person round-trip to the closer islands. Add $12 round-trip for bikes or $30 for kayaks. Free parking while you're on the islands.

In business since 1992, **Paraclete Charters** (Skyline Marina, 360/293-5920 or 800/808-2999, www.paracletecharters.com) runs three boats (the largest can carry 64 folks) from Anacortes. Prices depend on your destination and number of people, but you don't need to charter an entire boat, and there's space for kayaks, bikes, and pets.

### BY AIR

Departing from **Anacortes Airport** (www.portofanacortes.com/airport.shtml), **San Juan Airlines** (360/293-4691 or 800/874-4434, www.sanjuanairlines.com) offers commuter flights year-round to Lopez, San Juan, Orcas, Decatur, and Blakely Islands in the San Juans, plus flightseeing and air charters.

### BY BUS AND SHUTTLE VAN

**Skagit Transit** (360/299-2424, www.skagittransit.org, $1) has daily bus connections from Anacortes (including the ferry terminal, Guemes Island ferry terminal, and Washington Park) to Mount Vernon, La Conner, and other parts of Skagit County. All buses have bike racks. **Airporter Shuttle** (360/380-8800 or 800/235-5247, www.airporter.com) runs vans between Anacortes and Sea-Tac Airport at least 10 times daily year-round; the fare is $33 one-way ($20 kids) to the Anacortes ferry terminal.

### BY TAXI AND CAR

Call **Mert's Taxi** (360/708-6358) for rides around town or out to the ferry terminal. Car rentals are available from **U-Save Auto Rental** (360/293-8686 or 877/451-6985, www.usave.net) and **Enterprise Rent a Car** (360/293-4325 or 800/261-7331, www.enterprise.com).

# Whidbey Island

One of the longest islands in the lower 48 states, Whidbey Island encompasses 208 square miles in its 45-mile length. No spot on it is more than 5 miles from the water.

Whidbey is a favorite place for a Sunday-afternoon drive, with Deception Pass State Park the primary "stop and gawk" spot along the way. Also popular are the quaint towns of Coupeville and Langley, the quiet shoreline and picturesque agricultural land of Ebey's Landing National Historical Reserve, and wild places such as South Whidbey State Park and Fort Casey State Park. The largest metropolitan center, Oak Harbor, is home to Whidbey Naval Air Station.

## Exploring the Island

Whidbey is a perfect destination for a day trip or a weekend outing, with lots to explore and a wide variety of places to stay. The island is also great for cyclists, with many miles of quiet back roads and well-maintained bike paths.

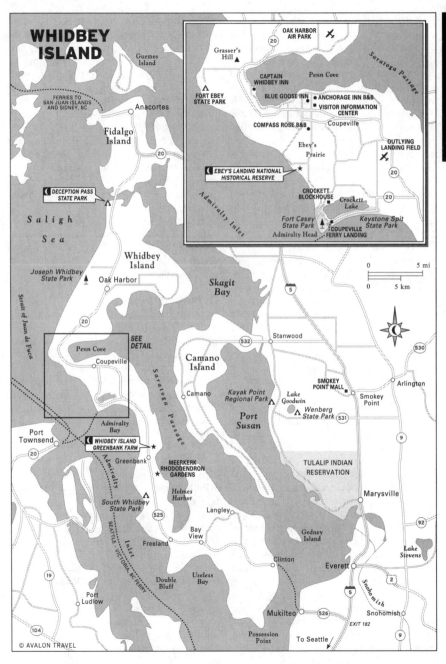

# WHIDBEY ISLAND

Guemes Island

FERRIES TO SAN JUAN ISLANDS AND SIDNEY, BC

Anacortes

Fidalgo Island

20

**DECEPTION PASS STATE PARK**

S a l i g h

S e a

Joseph Whidbey State Park

Oak Harbor

Whidbey Island

Skagit Bay

5

SEE DETAIL

Penn Cove

Coupeville

Camano Island

Stanwood

532

530

Saratoga Passage

Camano

Kayak Point Regional Park

Lake Goodwin

SMOKEY POINT MALL

Smokey Point

Arlington

Strait of Juan de Fuca

20

Admiralty Bay

Port Townsend

20

**WHIDBEY ISLAND GREENBANK FARM**

Greenbank

MEERKERK RHODODENDRON GARDENS

Holmes Harbor

Port Susan

Wenberg State Park

531

9

TULALIP INDIAN RESERVATION

Marysville

South Whidbey State Park

525

Langley

Bay View

Freeland

Gedney Island

92

Lake Stevens

19

Double Bluff

Useless Bay

Clinton

Everett

2

Port Ludlow

104

Snohomish

5

Mukilteo

526

EXIT 182

Snohomish

9

Possession Point

To Seattle

© AVALON TRAVEL

0 ___ 5 mi

0 ___ 5 km

### Detail inset

Grasser's Hill

OAK HARBOR AIR PARK

20

Saratoga Passage

CAPTAIN WHIDBEY INN

Penn Cove

**FORT EBEY STATE PARK**

BLUE GOOSE INN

ANCHORAGE INN B&B

VISITOR INFORMATION CENTER

COMPASS ROSE B&B

Coupeville

OUTLYING LANDING FIELD

Ebey's Prairie

20

**EBEY'S LANDING NATIONAL HISTORICAL RESERVE**

20

CROCKETT BLOCKHOUSE

Crockett Lake

Admiralty Inlet

Fort Casey State Park

Admiralty Head

COUPEVILLE FERRY LANDING

Keystone Spit State Park

The charm of the picturesque towns of Langley and Coupeville is natural—a result of their history, not a theme created to attract tourism.

For a fast day tour, ride the Mukilteo-Clinton ferry to the south end of the island and take a leisurely drive up-island, with stops in each town and park. To really see Whidbey right, you'll need more than a day. Take the time to explore the many natural areas and historic sites, camping out in one of the excellent state parks or staying in a local bed-and-breakfast. Reservations are highly recommended for summer weekends.

Contact **Whidbey-Camano Tourism** (888/747-7777, www.whidbeycamanoislands. com) for information on Whidbey.

## Getting There

To drive onto Whidbey Island, you've got only one option: the Deception Pass Bridge at the island's north end. To get there, go west on Highway 20 from I-5. Access to the south end of Whidbey is a relaxing **Washington State Ferries** (206/464-6400 for general info or 888/808-7977 in Washington and British Columbia only) ride from Mukilteo or Port Townsend. Find all the details—including current ferry wait times—at www.wsdot. wa.gov/ferries.

The **Mukilteo-Clinton** ferry departs every half hour or so 5 A.M.–2 A.M., and the 20-minute crossing costs $4.20 round-trip for passengers or walk-ons, $1 extra for bikes, and $9 one-way for a car and driver. (No charge for eastbound passengers and bikes.) Busiest times are during the weekday commute (westbound in the morning and eastbound in the evening), on Saturday mornings (after 9 A.M. en route to the island), and late in the afternoon on Sundays. Sunday evenings after 7 P.M. are quieter, so just enjoy the island and let folks in a hurry wait in the traffic jams while you sit on a beach or in a café.

From the Olympic Peninsula, board the ferry in **Port Townsend** to arrive at the **Coupeville** landing next to Fort Casey State Park a half hour later. These perpetually full ferries operate every 90 minutes between 6:30 A.M. and 8:30 P.M. in the summer, and one-way fares are $2.75 for passengers ($0.50 extra one-way for bikes), or $9.35 for a car and driver. Unlike most other Washington State Ferries, reservations are highly recommended for this one. Be sure to make a **ferry reservation** within 24 hours of your departure at www.wsdot.wa.gov/ferries, or by calling 206/464-6400 or 888/808-7977. You can also make a reservation at the tollbooth a few hours prior to your sailing, or take your chances without one (not advised). Twenty spaces are kept for vehicles without reservations, but you may be waiting for hours if you miss the boat.

Heading to Whidbey from Sea-Tac Airport? Take the **Whidbey-Sea-Tac Shuttle** (360/679-4003 or 877/679-4003, www. seatacshuttle.com), with frequent daily runs up the island.

## Getting Around

Whidbey Island seems like it was designed for biking. The rolling hills, clean air, and beautiful weather are inspiring enough; occasional whale and eagle sightings add to the pleasure. **Island Transit** (360/678-7771 or 800/240-8747, www.islandtransit.org) is a *free* bus system that operates Monday–Saturday all across Whidbey Island, from Clinton on the south to Deception Pass on the north. All buses have bike racks.

# LANGLEY

This tiny waterfront artists' community (pop. 1,100) is a great browsing stop, and several of its lodging establishments have views across Saratoga Passage to Camano Island and beyond. You'll find a number of gourmet restaurants, boutiques, bed-and-breakfasts, bookstores, and art galleries.

Langley may be the only Washington town founded by a teenager. In 1880, an ambitious 15-year-old German immigrant, Jacob Anthes, settled here. Because he was too young to file for a homestead, Anthes spent $100 to buy 120 acres of land, adding to his holdings with a 160-acre homestead claim when he reached

© DON PITCHER

Lilacs drape an archway in Langley.

21. He later built a store and post office and teamed up with Judge J. W. Langley to plat the new town.

## Sights

Langley's main attraction is simply the town itself, situated right along Puget Sound. A favorite downtown spot for photos is the life-size bronze **Boy and Dog,** by local sculptor Georgia Gerber. The 160-foot fishing pier offers water views and a chance to pull out your fishing pole, and the beach is popular for picnicking and swimming. Tiny **South Whidbey Historical Museum** (312 2nd St., 360/730-3367, www.southwhidbeyhistory. org, 1–4 P.M. Fri.–Sun. June–Aug., 1–4 P.M. Sat.–Sun. Sept.–May) has local memorabilia in a century-old building. Across the street at the corner is a small park with a colorful shelter and tables.

**Seawall Park** off 1st Street is the spot for a beach fix. Watch for eagles, herons, and gray whales—especially in spring. Ring the whale bell if you see one.

## Entertainment and Events

**Clyde Theatre** (217 1st St., 360/221-5525, www.theclyde.net) is the only place to watch first-run movies on the south end of Whidbey.

In late February, the **Langley Mystery Weekend** attracts sleuths in search of a make-believe murderer. Clues are planted all over town, and actors serve up information to help (or confuse) hundreds of amateur detectives. The main summertime event—it's been around for almost 40 years—is **Choochokam Festival of the Arts** (www.choochokamarts. org) on the second weekend in July. The festival attracts thousands of visitors to First Street with live music, art exhibits, a street dance, beer garden, and half-marathon race. A free shuttle bus runs from the Clinton ferry terminal, so you won't need to bring a car.

**Island County Fair** (360/221-4677, www. islandweb.org/fair) is a four-day event the third week of August that includes a carnival, parade, music, and 4-H exhibits. For something a bit less countrified, return to Langley for

**DjangoFest Northwest** (www.djangofest.com) in mid-September, with Gypsy jazz celebrating the life and music of Django Reinhardt.

## Shopping

Tiny Langley is home to several fine art galleries, most notably **Museo Gallery** (215 1st St., 360/221-7737, www.museo.cc) and **Brackenwood Gallery** (302 1st St., 360/221-2978, www.brackenwoodgallery.com), both of which feature unusual and highly creative pieces. Brackenwood has works by internationally known sculptor Georgia Gerber, whose ever-popular metal pig is a Pike Place Market landmark. Cooperatively run **Whidbey Art Gallery** (220 2nd St., 360/221-7675) features interesting pieces by Whidbey artists.

The **Whidbey Island Center for the Arts** (565 Camano Ave., 360/221-8268 or 800/638-7631, www.wicaonline.com) has concerts and plays throughout the year. Housed within the old fire station, **Callahan's FireHouse Studio & Gallery** (179 2nd St., 360/221-1242, www.callahansfirehouse.com) is a fun place to watch glassblowers at work or to produce your own pieces. In a half-hour session ($55), you get to create a colorful sea float, tumbler, or paperweight.

For wearable art, don't miss **Eddy's** (306 1st St., 360/321-3339, www.eddysonwhidbey-island.com), with fun and colorful organic cotton T-shirts ($38), many featuring designs by Whidbey artists.

**Lowry-James Rare Prints & Books** (101 Anthes Ave., 360/221-0477, www.lowryjames.com) is one of the Northwest's premier shops for natural history engravings and lithographs. Just a block away is **Gregor Rare Books** (197 2nd St., 360/221-8331, www.gregorbooks.com), specializing in 20th-century masterpieces. The shops are owned by a husband and wife team, David Gregor and Priscilla Lowry-Gregor, both of whom are experts in their respective fields. **Moonraker Books** (209 1st St., 360/221-6962) carries a fine selection of regional titles.

**Whidbey Island Winery** (5237 S. Langley Rd., 360/221-2040, www.whidbeyislandwinery.

com, tastings 11 A.M.–5 P.M. Wed.–Mon.) is a family operation that produces white wines from estate-grown Madeleine Angevine and Madeleine Sylvaner grapes, along with surprisingly good rhubarb wines and a number of reds crafted from eastern Washington grapes. Stop for a picnic overlooking the adjacent vineyard and apple orchard. Situated near the center of the island, **Greenbank Cellars** (3112 Day Rd. near Greenbank, 360/678-3964, www.greenbankcellars.com, tasting 11 A.M.–5 P.M. Sat.–Mon.) crafts wines from their Siegerrebe and Madeline Angevine vineyard. The small family winery is housed in a century-old barn.

## Recreation

Adjacent to the Star Store at Bayview Corner, **Half Link Bicycle Shop** (360/331-7980, www.halflinkbikes.com) rents mountain and hybrid bikes and has free Whidbey Island road and trail maps. **Whidbey Island Kayaking Company** (360/661-5183 or 800/233-4319, www.whidbeyislandkayaking.com) leads two-hour kayak trips ($49) from the south end of the island.

## Accommodations

The Langley Visitors Center has details on a multitude of local bed-and-breakfasts and inns and keeps track of vacancies. Stop by the visitors center to see photos of each place. Add a 10.4 percent lodging tax to all rates.

### HOTELS AND INNS

The 16-room **Saratoga Inn** (201 Cascade Ave., 360/221-5801 or 800/698-2910, www.saratogainnwhidbeyisland.com, $175–235 d) combines the privacy of a hotel with other amenities, including a buffet breakfast and afternoon wine and hors d'oeuvres. Spacious rooms are attractively appointed, and all include gas fireplaces, guest robes, Wi-Fi, and bikes to roll around town. Honeymooners will love the carriage house suite ($315 d) with its privacy, two-person tub, and full kitchen.

Designed by the architect-owner, **Langley Motel** (526 B Camano Ave., 360/221-6070 or 866/276-8292, www.langleymotel.com,

$105–135 d) has four units with 1950s retro-style rooms and full kitchens. Two-night minimum on weekends.

The luxurious 26-unit ◖ **Inn at Langley** (400 1st St., 360/221-3033, www.innatlangley.com) has rooms ($325–345 d), suites ($395–595 d), and cottages ($495 d), each with its own private patio overlooking Saratoga Passage, a jetted tub, wood-burning fireplace, continental breakfast, and Wi-Fi. A two-night minimum is in place on weekends, and no kids under age 12 are permitted, but pets are accepted for an extra fee. Also on the premises is a renowned restaurant, along with Spa Essencia, providing massage, aromatherapy, body masks, and more.

Located right along the beach and just up from the marina, **Boatyard Inn** (200 Wharf St., 360/221-5120, www.boatyardinn.com, $200–295 d) has spacious and modern studio units, loft suites, and a townhouse. Most of these feature waterfront decks, and all include mini-kitchens and Wi-Fi.

◖ **Eagles Nest Inn** (4680 Saratoga Rd., 360/221-5331 or 800/243-5536, www.eaglesnestinn.com, $150–195 d) is a delightful bed-and-breakfast getaway in a lush forested setting. The octagonal house is capped with an "eagle's nest" room ($180 d) with windows on all sides and a view to match. Three other guest rooms are a bit larger, and the Saratoga room ($195 d) has a private balcony, fireplace, and soaking tub. Amenities include a full breakfast, outdoor hot tub, private baths, Wi-Fi, and hiking trails within adjacent Saratoga Woods Preserve. The feeders outside attract birds and chipmunks, and deer are frequent visitors to the grounds.

### BED-AND-BREAKFASTS

Find links to local bed-and-breakfasts at www.langleylodging.com or www.whidbeyislandbandb.com. Most of these require a two-night minimum stay on summer weekends.

**Country Cottage of Langley B&B** (215 6th St., 360/221-8709 or 800/713-3860, www.acountrycottage.com, $139–189 d) is a 1920s Craftsman-style farmhouse with six cottages, all with water views, private entrances, and decks. A gourmet breakfast is served in the main house or brought to your cottage. Three cottages also feature in-room Jacuzzis and fireplaces. Kids are welcome, and pets are accepted (fee).

Situated on a secluded high bluff on the west side of Whidbey, **Cliff House** (360/331-1566 or 800/297-4118, www.cliffhouse.net) is a gorgeous two-bedroom home with a large kitchen, sunset views, and access to miles of beaches. The house rents for $495 d or $595 for four people, including a self-serve continental breakfast each morning. Also available is an adorable cottage with private bath, kitchenette, and a stairway to the beach for $195 d. A two-night minimum is required, and no kids are allowed due to the cliff-top location.

### CAMPING

Camp at nearby **South Whidbey State Park** (360/331-4559, www.parks.wa.gov, $22–25 tents, $29–34 RVs). **Island County Fairgrounds** (819 Camano Ave., 360/221-4677, www.islandweb.org/fair) has year-round tent sites and RV hookups with showers. Coin-operated showers are located at the marina at the foot of Wharf Street.

## Food

Langley is blessed with fine and surprisingly reasonable restaurants. Start your morning at the ever-busy ◖ **Useless Bay Coffee** (121 2nd St., 360/221-4515, www.uselessbaycoffee.com, 7:30 A.M.–4:30 P.M. Mon.–Tues., 7:30 A.M.–9 P.M. Wed.–Sun.), where owner Des Rock is a coffee connoisseur, roasting his own beans in a small on-the-premises roaster. Get a morning latte, a grilled panini on homemade bread, a breakfast taco, or a granola parfait. Take your coffee outside to enjoy it amid the flowers. Dinners ($9–18) at Useless Bay are equally notable; the menu stars smokehouse comfort food with a Latin twist such as blackened salmon tostadas, Yucatan pulled pork, black bean chile, and chicken tinga, plus beer and wine. Check the blackboard for the day's specials. There's occasional live music in an adjacent band shell.

A bit hard to find—but worth the search—is **Mukilteo Coffee Roasters/Cabuni Café** (3228 Lake Leo Way, 360/321-5270, www.cabuni.com, 8 A.M.–4 P.M. Mon.–Sat., closed Sun., $8–11). The café has a peaceful in-the-woods setting, with a menu of lunchtime salads, wraps, and burgers. There's evening music, along with beer, wine, and free Wi-Fi. It's located south of Bayview Corner between Langley and the main highway.

For comfort food, **Braeburn Restaurant** (197 2nd St., 360/221-3211, www.braeburnlangley.com, 8 A.M.–3 P.M. Mon.–Fri., 7 A.M.–4 P.M. Sat.–Sun., $8–12) serves stuffed apple bread French toast or corned beef mash for breakfast along with curry chicken salad or meatloaf sandwich (and lots more) for lunch. Enjoy patio dining in the summer.

**Mo's Pub & Eatery** (317 2nd St., 360/221-1131, 4–10 P.M. Tues.–Wed., 4–11 P.M. Thurs., 4 P.M.–midnight Fri., noon–midnight Sat., noon–10 P.M. Sun., $9–11) serves British pastries, chicken pot pie, sausage rolls, shepherd's pie, burgers, and more. Stick around for a game of darts or live music some nights.

A French-inspired Northwest bistro, **Prima Bistro** (upstairs at 201 1st St., 360/221-4060, www.primabistro.com, 11:30 A.M.–9 P.M. daily, $13–19), serves steak frites, seafood specials, burgers, and salads. Get beer on tap and mixed drinks at the cozy bar, or step out on the deck for alfresco dining with a water view. Live music every Thursday. Call ahead for reservations on busy summer weekends. Downstairs, the **Star Store** (360/221-5222, www.starstorewhidbey.com) is a fun place to explore, with gourmet groceries, clothing, housewares, and imported items. A second Star Store is at Bayview Corner at the intersection of Bayview Road and Highway 525.

Up the street a bit, the Garibyan brothers have gained an enormous local following for their artfully presented Greek and Middle Eastern dishes at ◖ **Café Langley** (113 1st St., 360/221-3090, www.cafelangley.com, 11:30 A.M.–2:30 P.M., 5–9 P.M. daily, $15–21). Try the chicken marsala gnocchi or pappardelle seafood pasta.

Across the street is tiny **Village Pizzeria** (106 1st St., 360/221-3363, 11:30 A.M.–9 P.M. daily), where the New York–style thin-crust pizza packs folks in on weekends. Get a $3 slice or pie to go if you're in a hurry. Credit cards aren't accepted, but there's an ATM if you're short on cash.

**Mosquito Fleet Chili** (12 Front St., 360/678-2900, 7 A.M.–4 P.M. Mon.–Sat.) serves traditional American breakfasts in a waterside setting. Great homemade chili and cornbread, or try the salmon quiche, tomato basil soup, mussel chowder, or just a big slice of pecan pie.

The **South Whidbey Tilth Farmers Market** (Hwy. 525 at Thompson Rd., 360/579-2892, www.southwhidbeytilth.org, 11:30 A.M.–3:30 P.M. Sun., May–early Oct.) has all-organic fruits and vegetables, plus flowers, baked goods, and seafood. The **Bayview Farmers Market** (360/321-4302, www.bayviewfarmersmarket.com, 10 A.M.–2 P.M. Sat. May–Oct.) is located behind the Star Store at the intersection of Bayview Road and Highway 525.

At the top of the hill on 2nd Street, **Living Green Natural Food & Apothecary** (630 2nd St., 360/221-8242, 9 A.M.–6 P.M. Mon.–Sat., $7–8) is a vegetarian café with wraps, rice bowls, salads, smoothies, raw foods, vegan gluten-free baked goods, organic espresso, and natural foods.

Focused exclusively on wines from Washington state, **2nd St. Wine Shop** (221 2nd St., 360/221-3121, 10 A.M.–7 P.M. Wed.–Mon.) has wine tasting: $4 to sample eight wines.

The ◖ **Inn at Langley** (400 1st St., 360/221-3033, www.innatlangley.com, Thurs.–Sun. summer, Fri.–Sun. rest of the year) is Whidbey's four-star restaurant, serving memorable six-course Northwest cuisine dinners that emphasize local ingredients. Celebrity chef Matt Costello puts on quite a performance in the open kitchen, explaining each step of the meal as he prepares it. Highly recommended, but you'll need to reserve a week or two ahead, or a month in advance for Saturday nights. The cost for these memorable culinary extravaganzas is $105 per person; add $85 per person if you want paired wines with your dinner.

## Information

Drop by the **Langley Visitors Center** (208 Anthes Ave., 360/221-6765 or 888/232-2080, www.visitlangley.com, 11 A.M.–4 P.M. daily year-round) for the full scoop on Langley. You can also get brochures from a visitors kiosk at Langley Road and Highway 525; it's staffed on summer weekends.

## SOUTH WHIDBEY STATE PARK

Easily the island's most underrated park, South Whidbey State Park (360/331-4559, www.parks.wa.gov) has outstanding hiking and picnicking, plus clamming and crabbing on a narrow sandy beach, campsites, and striking Olympic Mountains views. The 85 acres of old-growth Douglas fir and western red cedar protect resident black-tailed deer, foxes, raccoons, rabbits, bald eagles, ospreys, and pileated woodpeckers. Be sure to hike **Wilbert Trail,** a mile-long path that circles through these ancient forests; it starts directly across from the park entrance. State park campsites are $22–25 for tents, or $29–34 for RVs with hookups. Make reservations ($9 extra) at 888/226-7688 or through the park website. Get to the park by heading east from Freeland on Bush Point Road; it becomes Smugglers Cove Road and continues past the park, a distance of seven miles.

## ◖ WHIDBEY ISLAND GREENBANK FARM

The large red barn at Whidbey Island Greenbank Farm (14 miles north of the ferry dock at Clinton, 360/678-7700, www.greenbankfarm.com) is a well-known sight to anyone driving across Whidbey Island. Once the largest loganberry farm in the world, it is now owned by the county. The farm's wine shop sells loganberry wine (produced elsewhere), along with grape and fruit wines from local wineries. Besides wines, the shop has preserves,

© DON PITCHER

Whidbey Island Greenbank Farm

jellies, and loganberry wine–filled chocolates. The buildings also houses **Whidbey Pies Café** (360/678-1288, www.whidbeypies.com), serving eight kinds of pies daily at $4 per slice. Three fine art galleries are also worth a look at Greenbank Farm.

Greenbank Farm is open daily 10 A.M.–5 P.M. in the summer, Monday–Friday 11 A.M.–5 P.M., Saturday–Sunday 10 A.M.–5 P.M. the rest of the year. A **farmers market** (360/678-7710, www.greenbankfarm.com) takes place Sunday 11 A.M.–3 P.M. May–September.

## MEERKERK RHODODENDRON GARDENS

This delightful garden (360/678-1912, www.meerkerkgardens.org, 9 A.M.–4 P.M. daily, $8, free for children) boasts more than 1,500 varieties of rhododendron species and hybrids on a 53-acre site just south of Greenbank off Resort Road. Begun by Max and Anne Meerkerk in the 1960s, the gardens are now maintained by the not-for-profit Seattle Rhododendron Society. Peak season for "rhodies" is in late April and early May. By the way, the coast rhododendron is Washington's state flower.

## FORT CASEY STATE PARK

Fort Casey State Park (360/678-4519, www.parks.wa.gov) is a historic U.S. Army post three miles south of Coupeville next to the Keystone ferry dock. It has two miles of beach, an underwater park, a boat ramp, hiking trails, picnic areas, spectacular Olympics views, and campsites, plus good fishing in remarkably clear water.

Fort Casey was one of the "Iron Triangle" of forts that guarded the entrance to Puget Sound and the Bremerton Naval Shipyard at the turn of the 20th century. This deadly crossfire consisted of Fort Casey, Fort Worden at Port Townsend, and Fort Flagler on Marrowstone Island; fortunately, the guns were never fired at an enemy vessel. Fort Casey's big weapons were the ingenious 10-inch disappearing carriage guns; the recoil sent them swinging back down out of sight for reloading, giving the sighter a terrific ride. By 1920, advances in naval warfare made them obsolete, so they

disappearing carriage gun, Fort Casey State Park

were melted down. During World War II, Fort Casey was primarily a training site, although anti-aircraft guns were mounted on the fortifications. The fort was closed after the war and purchased by the State of Washington in 1956 for a state park.

## Sights

If you're arriving on Whidbey Island by ferry from Port Townsend, get to Fort Casey by taking an immediate left onto Engle Road as soon as you exit the ferry terminal. Much of the fort is open for public viewing, including ammunition bunkers, observation towers, underground storage facilities (bring your flashlight), gun catwalks, and the main attraction: two disappearing guns. Because the originals are long gone, these were brought here in 1968 from an old American fort in the Philippines.

Be sure to visit the **Admiralty Head Lighthouse Interpretive Center** (360/240-5584, www.admiraltyhead.wsu.edu, 11 A.M.–5 P.M. daily June–Aug., reduced hours Sept.–May, free) where you can learn about coast artillery and the 1890 defense post. The lighthouse itself has not been used since 1927, but you can climb to the top for a wonderful view of Puget Sound and the Olympic Mountains. The hilltop location is a great place to watch ferries crossing from Port Townsend, and kids will have fun on the beach.

The fort's historic buildings are now used as a conference center and the Fort Casey Inn, both run by Seattle Pacific University (www.fortcaseyinn.com). Also nearby is shallow **Crockett Lake,** a good place to look for migratory and resident birds. The **Crockett Blockhouse,** one of four remaining fortifications built in the 1850s to defend against Indian attacks, stands on the north shore of the lake. An offshore underwater park is popular with divers. Northeast of Crockett Lake is Outlying Landing Field, used by Navy pilots to simulate aircraft-carrier landings.

## Camping

The small and crowded campground ($22–25 for tents, $29–34 for RVs hookups) at Fort Casey is open year-round and has showers. These exposed sites are right on the water next to the busy ferry terminal. Pleasant hiking trails lead through the wooded grounds and uphill to the fort's cannons. No reservations are taken, so get here early on summer weekends.

## ◖ EBEY'S LANDING NATIONAL HISTORICAL RESERVE

Ebey's Landing (360/678-6084, www.nps.gov/ebla), two miles southwest of Coupeville center, has easily the most striking coastal view on the island; no wonder portions of the 1999 movie *Snow Falling on Cedars* were filmed here. As the roads wind through acres of rich farmland, the glimpses of water and cliff might remind you of the northern California or Oregon coastline; the majestic Olympics add to the drama.

The native Skagit people were generally friendly toward the white settlers, but their northern neighbors were considerably less forgiving of the invaders. Alaska's Kake tribe of the Tlingit people had a fierce reputation, as exemplified by the following incident recorded by Richard Meade (1871):

*In 1855 a party of Kakes, on a visit south to Puget Sound, became involved in some trouble there, which caused a United States vessel to open fire on them, and during the affair one of the Kake chiefs was killed. This took place over 800 miles from the Kake settlements on Kupreanof Island. The very next year the tribe sent a canoe-load of fighting men all the way from Clarence Straits in Russian America to Whidby's Island in Washington Territory, and attacked and beheaded an ex-collector – not of internal revenue, for that might have been pardonable – but of customs, and returned safely with his skull and scalp to their villages. Such people are, therefore, not to be despised, and are quite capable of giving much trouble in the future unless wisely and firmly governed.*

© DON PITCHER

Jacob Ebey House at Ebey's Landing National Historical Reserve

The beheaded man was Colonel Isaac Ebey, the first settler on Whidbey Island; his head was eventually recovered and reunited with his body before being buried at Sunnyside Cemetery. To fend off further attacks (which never came), the pioneers built seven block-houses in the 1850s, four of which still stand.

The Anglo settlers were attracted to this part of Whidbey Island by the expansive prairies and fertile black soil. These prairies occupy the sites of shallow Ice Age lakes; when the water dried up, the rich, deep soil remained. The in-digenous practice of burning helped keep them open over the centuries that followed, and the white settlers simply took up residence on this prime land.

Managed by the National Park Service and covering 17,400 acres, Ebey's Landing National Historical Reserve helps keep this land rural and agricultural through scenic easements, land donations, tax incentives, and zoning. Approximately 90 percent of the land remains in private hands. Created in 1978, this was America's first national historical reserve.

## Sights

The main attraction at Ebey's Landing National Historical Reserve is simply the country itself: bucolic farmland, densely wooded ridges, and steep coastal bluffs. At the Coupeville mu-seum, pick up an informative driving and bi-cycling brochure that provides a detailed tour of Ebey's Landing.

For a scenic bike ride or drive, turn onto Hill Road (two miles south of Coupeville) and follow it through the second-growth stand of Douglas fir trees. It emerges on a high bluff overlooking Admiralty Inlet before dropping to the shoreline at tiny **Ebey's Landing State Park.** From the small parking area at the wa-ter's edge, hike the 1.5-mile trail along the bluff above **Parego Lagoon** for a view of the coastline, Olympics, and the Strait of Juan de Fuca that shouldn't be missed. The lagoon is a fine place to look for migratory birds. Return along the beach, or continue northward to Fort Ebey State Park (three miles from Ebey's Landing). Along the way, keep your eyes open for gem-quality stones, such as agate, jasper, and black and green jade, plus quartz and petrified wood.

Several historical sights are out Cemetery Road, accessible from Cook Road. Colonel Isaac Ebey is buried at **Sunnyside Cemetery.** The **Davis Blockhouse,** another of the blockhouses used to defend against Tlingit and Haida attacks, stands at the edge of the cemetery; it was moved here in 1915. Park your car at the aptly named **Prairie Overlook.** Farms spread out below, and the horizon is marked by snowcapped Mount Baker to the north and Mount Rainier to the south. Walk up the dirt road past the little park headquarters building (9 A.M.–5 P.M. Mon.–Fri.) to the restored **Jacob Ebey House** (staffed 10 A.M.–4 P.M. Thurs.–Sun. June–Sept.), containing historical exhibits in the two front rooms. A blockhouse is right out front. The home was built in 1855 by the father of Isaac Ebey.

## COUPEVILLE

The second oldest town in Washington, the "Port of Sea Captains" was founded and laid out in 1852 by Captain Thomas Coupe, the first man to sail through Deception Pass. The protected harbor at Penn Cove was a perfect site for the village that became Coupeville (pop. 1,700). Timber from Whidbey was shipped to San Francisco to feed the building boom created by the gold rush. Today, modern businesses operate from Victorian-era buildings amid the nation's largest historical preservation district. Coupeville is the county seat for Island County and has the only public hospital on Whidbey. Downtown has an immaculate cluster of false-fronted shops and restaurants right on the harbor and a long wharf once used to ship local produce and logs to the mainland. This is a cat-friendly town; perhaps half the downtown businesses have one inside. Summer weekends are busy times, but in the winter months, life in Coupeville slows to a crawl and downtown is a very quiet place.

### Sights

The town's most obvious attraction is picturesque **Coupeville Wharf,** which extends into

Penn Cove. Find several marine exhibits (including a gray whale skeleton suspended from the ceiling) in the building at the end of the wharf. Also here are a café and **Harbor Gift & Kayak Rental** (360/678-3625), with double kayaks for $30 per hour.

**Island County Museum** (908 NW Alexander St., 360/678-3310, www.islandhistory.org, 10 A.M.–4 P.M. Mon.–Sat., 11 A.M.–4 P.M. Sun., $3 adults, $2.50 seniors and kids, $6 families, free for kids under five) has pioneer relics, including a shadow box with flowers made from human hair, interesting newsreels from the 1930s on the Indian Water Festival, a 1902 Holsman car (first car on Whidbey), woolly mammoth bones, and changing exhibits. Out front is a lovely garden with drought-tolerant native plants and herbs.

Another of the original Whidbey Island fortifications, the **Alexander Blockhouse,** built in 1855, stands outside the museum, along with a shelter housing two turn-of-the-20th-century Native American racing canoes.

One of the more unique local attractions is **Earth Sanctuary** (360/331-6667, www.earthsanctuary.org, $7), a 72-acre preserve where art and ecology mix in a druid-friendly, sacred-aura, in-touch-with-the-earth locale that includes two miles of trails, a stone circle (tallest in the world), prayer wheel, labyrinth, and more. It's open daily during daylight hours.

Also on the spiritual path to enlightenment is **Whidbey Institute at Chinook** (360/341-1884, www.whidbeyinstitute.org), a "place of deep inquiry and inspiration" near the town of Clinton, with a variety of educational and environmental events. The 70-acre site has lovely wooded trails and a spacious retreat center.

Get a taste of Coupeville's sailing past onboard the **Cutty Sark** (360/678-5567, www.svcuttysark.com), a classic 52-foot ketch, built from teak in 1960. Join Captain John Colby Stone for a day sail from Coupeville: $185 for up to six people on a two-hour sail. Overnight and multi-night trips to the San Juan Islands are also available.

© DON PITCHER

The Coupeville Wharf extends into Penn Cove.

## Penn Cove

For a scenic drive, head northwest from Coupeville along Madrona Way, named for the Pacific madrone (also called madrona) trees whose distinctive red bark and leathery green leaves line the roadway. Quite a few summer cottages and cozy homes can be found here, along with the one-of-a-kind Captain Whidbey Inn. Offshore are dozens of floating pens where mussels grow on lines hanging in Penn Cove. On the northwest corner of Penn Cove, Highway 20 passes scenic **Grasser's Hill,** where hedgerows alternate with open farmland. Development restrictions prevent this open country from becoming a mass of condos. Just north of here are the historic **San de Fuca schoolhouse** (now a vacation rental) and Whidbey Inn.

## Fort Ebey State Park

Located southwest of Coupeville on Admiralty Inlet, Fort Ebey State Park (360/678-4636, www.parks.wa.gov) has campsites, a large picnic area, three miles of beach, and several miles of hiking trails within its 644 acres. The fort was constructed during World War II, though its gun batteries were never needed. The concrete platforms remain, along with cavernous bunkers, but the big guns have long since been removed. Thanks to its location in the Olympics' rain shadow, the park is one of the few places in western Washington where cactus grows, but it also has stands of second-growth forest and great views across the Strait of Juan de Fuca.

Although not as well known as other parks on Whidbey, Fort Ebey is still a favorite summertime spot. Much of its popularity stems from tiny **Lake Pondilla,** a glacial sinkhole—and a bass fisher's and swimmer's delight. Follow the signs from the north parking lot for a two-block hike to the lake; half a dozen picnic tables and a camping area are reserved for hikers and bicyclists. Other trails lead along the bluffs south from here and down to the beach. Adventurous folks (after consulting a tide chart and with a bit of care) can walk all the way to Fort Casey State Park, eight miles away.

## Entertainment and Events

**Pacific Northwest Art School** (15 NW Birch St., 360/678-3396 or 866/678-3396, www.coupevillearts.org) teaches dozens of workshops throughout the year, from photography and watercolor painting to lost wax jewelry and Japanese stencil making.

The **Penn Cove Water Festival** (www.penncovewaterfestival.com) in mid-May brings tribal canoe races, dance performances, Native American arts and crafts, traditional foods, and games for kids. The event attracts tribes and visitors from all over Puget Sound. In existence for nearly 50 years, the mid-August **Coupeville Arts and Crafts Festival** (www.coupevilleartsandcraftsfestival.org) is another big event, with musical entertainment, arts and crafts, gallery openings, kids' activities, and food.

**Concerts on the Cove** (360/678-6821, www.concertsonthecove.org) includes all sorts of productions, from Peking acrobats to Maria

Muldaur. Their Sundays in the Park series provides a fine way to spend a lazy afternoon during July and August.

## Shopping

Two adjacent art galleries are at 9 NW Front Street: **Hunter Art Studio** (360/678-3653 or 888/877-5841) and the cooperatively run **Penn Cove Gallery** (360/678-1176, www.penncovegallery.com).

## Accommodations

Coupeville is blessed with many historic buildings, several of which have been turned into bed-and-breakfasts and inns, but be sure to make advance reservations for summer weekends. Useful websites with links to local lodgings are www.coupevillelodging.com and www.cometocoupeville.com.

### HOTELS AND INNS

Right in town, **Coupeville Inn** (200 NW Coveland St., 360/678-6668 or 800/247-6162, www.thecoupevilleinn.com, $105–140 d) is a French mansard-style inn. The 24 hotel rooms provide waterside views of Penn Cove. Other options include a two-bedroom apartment unit ($195 d), a beach suite ($175 d), and a lovely two-bedroom house ($225 for up to four people). All rooms have fridges, private baths, Wi-Fi, and a continental breakfast. A variety of stay-and-sail packages are offered to combine lodging with sailing trips.

At **Captain Whidbey Inn** (2072 W. Captain Whidbey Inn Rd., 360/678-4097 or 800/366-4097, www.captainwhidbey.com)—a classic two-story inn built in 1907 from madrone logs—rooms in the main lodge are $94–105 d, or $171 d for log-walled suites. All of these have "European-style" shared baths down the hall. Newer guest rooms with private baths are $165–190 d, and four modern cabins containing wood-burning fireplaces, decks, private baths, and hot tub access cost $193 d. Add $15 for each additional person. Continental breakfast is available in the dining room each morning. The expansive grounds, studded with Pacific madrone trees, face Penn Cove. Even if

you aren't staying here, be sure to stop and take in the scenery, or order a martini in the bar or enjoy a meal in the restaurant.

Adjacent to Fort Casey State Park, **Fort Casey Inn** (1124 S. Engle Rd., 360/678-5050 or 866/661-6604, www.fortcaseyinn.com) consists of 10 restored Georgian Revival homes that served as officers' quarters during World War I. Most of these large two-story homes are divided into two units each, with complete kitchens, private baths, and access to a heated outdoor pool, but no phones, TVs, or Wi-Fi. These are authentically historic places, not luxury condos—so ignore those negative TripAdvisor reviews! Basements were built to be used as bomb shelters in case of attack, and some still have the original steel-shuttered windows. The duplexes sleep four or five guests for $175 per night. The old doctor's house ($185) is separate from the others, providing more privacy, and a single motel-style unit is also available for $85 d. You're likely to encounter deer on the lawn most evenings. Fort Casey Inn is owned by Seattle Pacific University.

### BED-AND-BREAKFASTS

**Anchorage Inn B&B** (807 N. Main St., 360/678-5581 or 877/230-1313, www.anchorage-inn.com, $95–155 d) has seven guest rooms with private baths in a large and luxurious Victorian-style home. The largest room fills the third floor, providing views of Penn Cove and Mount Baker. A big sit-down breakfast is included, plus Wi-Fi. The historic two-bedroom Calista cottage next door is perfect for families; $180 for up to six (no breakfast and there's a two-night minimum).

One of the most striking local places is **Compass Rose B&B** (508 S. Main St., 360/678-5318 or 800/237-3881, www.compassrosebandb.com, $115 d), a Queen Anne Victorian built in 1890 and packed with antiques and Persian rugs. It's almost like stepping into a museum. The two guest rooms have queen-size or king-size beds, and an elegant candlelight breakfast is served on fine china and crystal. "Extremely well-behaved" kids (antiques, after all) are welcome. Gregarious owners Jan and Marshall Bronson—he's a retired naval captain—also own a vintage 1933 Packard.

Occupying two adjacent Victorian-era homes—both on the National Register of Historic Places—**[( The Blue Goose Inn** (702 N. Main St., 360/678-4284 or 877/678-4284, www.bluegoosecoupeville.com, $99–159 d) provides tasteful B&B accommodations. The inn consists of Kineth House and Coupe House—built in 1887 and 1891, respectively—with a total of eight guest rooms, private baths, full breakfasts, and Wi-Fi. The location is perfect, right in the heart of Coupeville. No children under 12 are permitted.

Just a five-minute walk from downtown, **Lovejoy Inn B&B** (5 NW 8th St., 360/678-1204, www.thelovejoyinn.com) is a relaxing place where three guest rooms ($79–130 d with a light breakfast) have private baths and Wi-Fi. The carriage house studio ($135 d with continental breakfast) has a private entrance, kitchenette, king-size bed, and deck. Children are welcome.

**Garden Isle Guest Cottages** (207 NW Coveland, 360/678-5641, www.gardenisle-cottages.com) consists of two immaculate cottages ($130–140 d) with mini-kitchens, a hot tub, private baths, continental breakfast, and Wi-Fi. A separate vacation house ($200 d, add $15 each for extra guests) has three bedrooms, three baths, a full kitchen, and more; two-night minimum required.

### CAMPING

Find year-round camping ($22–25 tents or $29–34 RVs) at **Fort Casey State Park** (three miles south of Coupeville, 360/678-4519) or **Fort Ebey State Park** (five miles west of Coupeville, 360/678-4636, www.parks.wa.gov). No advance reservations for Fort Casey, but campsites at Fort Ebey can be reserved ($10 extra) at 888/226-7688 or through the park website.

**Rhododendron Park,** a Washington Department of Natural Resources park, is two miles east of Coupeville on Highway 20. It's easy to miss; look for the small blue camping sign on the highway. Here you'll find eight free in-the-woods campsites (with water) in a second-growth stand of Douglas firs. The understory blooms with rhododendrons in April and May.

### Food

Pastry aficionados shouldn't miss **Knead & Feed** (4 Front St., 360/678-5431, www.kneadandfeed.com, 9 A.M.–3 P.M. Mon.–Fri., 8 A.M.–4 P.M. Sat.–Sun., $4–10), where tempting marionberry bear claws, slices of rhubarb pie, and enormous walnut caramel rolls await. Breakfast scrambles and lunchtime sandwiches and homemade soups provide more substantial fare.

For an upscale dining experience with a superb waterside view, it's hard to beat **Front Street Grill** (20 Front St., 360/682-2551, www.fsgcoupeville.com, 11 A.M.–9 P.M. Sun.–Thurs., 11 A.M.–10 P.M. Fri.–Sat.). Start with Penn Cove mussels steamed in coconut green curry, and then order a Kobe beef burger ($17) or Dan's spicy seafood fettuccine ($25), topping the evening off with a raspberry pomegranate margarita and orange crème brûlée. The restaurant has live music every Wednesday evening.

Find dependably good pub grub—including fish and chips, Reuben sandwiches, and steamed mussels—inside **Toby's Tavern** (8 NW Front St., 360/678-4222, www.tobysuds.com, $10–19). The 1884 red building contains a pool table and is open to all ages, with food service till 9 or 10 P.M.

Owner/chef Andreas Wurzrainer has transformed **[( Christopher's** (103 NW Coveland St., 360/678-5480, www.christophersonwhidbey.com, 11:30 A.M.–2 P.M., 5 P.M.–closing Mon.–Fri., noon–2:30 P.M., 5 P.M.–closing Sat.–Sun., $16–23 entrées) into one of the finest dining choices on Whidbey. The restaurant has an upscale setting and such specialties as bacon-wrapped pork tenderloin and raspberry barbecued salmon, along with classic clam chowder from the soup pot. Save space for the decadent chocolate mousse served in a dark chocolate tulip shell. Reservations are advised. There's live piano music on Friday and Saturday nights.

🄲 **The Oystercatcher** (901 Grace St., 360/678-0683, www.oystercatcherwhidbey. com, 5–8 P.M. Thurs.–Sun., $23–29 entrées) is a wonderful place where the limited menu changes nightly. Owner/chefs Joe and Jamie Scott serve fresh seafood, including Penn Cove mussel hors d'oeuvres, with a nice selection of wines as accompaniment. It's casually elegant, but kids are welcome. Call ahead for reservations since only eight tables are available. Dine on the small deck if the weather cooperates.

The **Coupeville Farmers Market** (360/678-4288, 10 A.M.–2 P.M. Sat. Apr.–Oct.) takes place behind the library at 8th and Alexander Streets.

## Information and Services

For local information and brochures, stop by the **Central Whidbey Visitor & Information Center** (905 NW Alexander St., 360/678-5434, www.centralwhidbeychamber.com, 10 A.M.–2 P.M. Mon.–Fri.), housed within the old firehouse. Another helpful website is www.cometocoupeville.com.

**Whidbey General Hospital** (101 N. Main St., 360/678-5151, www.whidbeygen.org) is the only public hospital on the island.

## OAK HARBOR

Settled first by sea captains, then the Irish, and at the turn of the 20th century by immigrants from Holland, Oak Harbor (pop. 22,000) takes its name from the many ancient Garry oak trees that grew here; those remaining are protected by law. The city was founded by three men in the early 1850s: a Swiss named Ulrich Freund, a Norwegian named Martin Tafton, and a New Englander named C. W. Sumner. The military arrived during World War II and remain the primary economic force.

Oak Harbor's historic waterside downtown retains a bit of character, but the main drag—Highway 20—is yet another sad example of the malling of America, complete with Kmart, Wal-Mart, and other middlebrow attractions. This is the only place on the island where you'll find burger joints, shopping malls, traffic jams, and noise. It's on a far smaller scale than many Puget Sound cities, but comes as a shock if you've just driven in from genteel Coupeville and Langley.

## Whidbey Island Naval Air Station

Oak Harbor's main employer is the largest naval air base in the Northwest, Whidbey Island Naval Air Station (360/257-2211, www. cnic.navy.mil/whidbey). It is home to electronic warfare squadrons, including reconnaissance aircraft (EA-6B Prowlers and EA-18G Growlers), along with surveillance planes (P-3 Orion and EP-3 Aries). The base employs more than 10,000 military and civilian personnel and is a favorite of Navy personnel. The area is filled with military retirees who appreciate the scenic setting and mild weather.

The **PBY Memorial Foundation** maintains a small military museum (315 W. Pioneer Way, 360/240-9500, www.pbyma. org, 11 A.M.–5 P.M. Wed.–Sat.) at the Navy's Seaplane Base in Oak Harbor. Out front is the main attraction, a lovingly restored PBY Catalina, an amphibious plane used to patrol the Pacific during World War II. The museum is open to the public, but you'll need ID to enter the gate.

## Entertainment and Events

**Whidbey Playhouse** (730 SE Midway Blvd., 360/679-2237, www.whidbeyplayhouse.com) puts on plays throughout the year. Here since 1959, **Blue Fox Drive-In Theatre** (two miles south of town at 1403 Monroe Landing Rd., 360/675-5667, www.bluefoxdrivein.com) is one of only five surviving outdoor movie theaters in Washington. Locals say they serve the best pizzas in Oak Harbor.

**Whidbey Island Marathon** (www.whidbeyislandmarathon.com) in mid-April attracts 2,000 or so runners. A bit less grueling, **Holland Happening** (www.hollandhappening.org) on the last weekend of April includes a street fair, parade, and international dance festival. The **4th of July** festivities include a parade and fireworks, followed in mid-July by

**Whidbey Island Race Week** (www.whidbeyislandraceweek.com), one of the world's top 20 yachting regattas.

## Recreation

**Windjammer Park** (360/279-4500, www.oakharbor.org), on Beeksma Drive, has a sandy beach with piles of driftwood, sheltered picnic tables, saltwater swimming and wading pools, a gazebo, tennis courts, baseball diamonds, tent and RV campsites, and a monumental **Dutch-style windmill.** There's a nice view of the peaceful and protected harbor from here, and a great kiddie playground. Look for ducks along the shore. **Smith Park** at Midway Boulevard has old Garry oak trees and a large boulder left behind by the last Ice Age.

**Joseph Whidbey State Park** (360/902-8844, www.parks.wa.gov), just south of Whidbey Island Naval Air Station on Swantown Road, is largely undeveloped, with picnic tables and a few trails. The real attraction here is a long and scenic beach, one of the finest on the island. No camping is permitted.

The hip-roofed **Neil Barn** (100 E. Whidbey Ave., 360/240-9273, hours vary) was once the largest barn on the West Coast. Today it houses a roller-skating rink operated by the local Boys and Girls Club. The distinctive **water tower** out front houses a small historical museum that's open occasionally. **Hummingbird Farm Nursery** (2319 Zylstra Rd., 360/679-5044, www.hummingbirdfarmnursery.com, 10 A.M.–6 P.M. Wed.–Sun.) has extensive display gardens and a garden shop.

Swim outdoors at the seasonal **Windjammer Park** (360/579-5551, free) or indoors year-round at **John Vanderzicht Memorial Pool** (85 SE Jerome St., 360/675-7665, www.oakharborpool.com, $3.25), which also includes a sauna, two hot tubs, a ball swing, inflatable octopus, and wading pool.

For golf enthusiasts, the 18-hole **Gallery Golf Course** (360/257-2178, www.gallerygolfcourse.com, $24 for 9 holes, $33 for 18 holes) is out on Crosby Road.

At **Lavender Wind Farm** (2530 Darst Rd., 360/678-0919 or 877/242-7716, www.lavenderwind.com), owner Sarah Richards grows nine varieties of organic lavender for bouquets and various products, including her homemade lavender ice cream. The farm is north of Fort Ebey State Park off West Beach Road.

## Accommodations

Oak Harbor has the least-expensive lodging on Whidbey, but as always, location matters, and you won't find the charm of Coupeville or Langley here. **Queen Ann Motel** (450 SE Pioneer Way, 360/675-2209, $59 d) is an affordable option, with attractive rooms and an outdoor pool.

At **Best Western Plus Harbor Plaza** (33175 State Rt. 20, 360/679-4567 or 800/927-5478, www.bestwestern.com/harborplaza, $141–160 d) amenities include an outdoor heated pool, hot tub, fitness center, microwaves, fridges, Wi-Fi, and continental breakfast.

Rooms at **Coachman Inn** (35959 State Rt. 20, 360/675-0727 or 800/635-0043, www.thecoachmaninn.com) range from standard units ($105–130 d) and Jacuzzi suites $139–179 d) to a two-bedroom townhouse apartment ($159 for up to six) and a penthouse suite ($209). The hotel includes an outdoor pool, exercise room, fridges, Wi-Fi, and a hot breakfast.

### CAMPING

City-run **Staysail RV Park** (at the end of Beeksma Dr., 360/279-4500, www.oakharbor.org, $12 tents, $20 RVs with full hookups) has camping along the lagoon within Windjammer Park. There are no reservations available, but the park does have hot showers.

Beautiful **Deception Pass State Park** (360/675-2417, www.parks.wa.gov, $22–25 tents, $31–36 RVs, $12 bikes) is nine miles north; it's described in the *Anacortes* section. In addition, the local Wal-Mart parking lot (1250 SW Erie St., 360/279-0665) becomes an unofficial RV park each summer.

## Food

As might be expected given the strong military presence in Oak Harbor, most restaurants serve up the traditional American food groups: McDonald's, pizza, and steak, but one place serves as the notable exception: **Frasers Gourmet Hideaway** (1191 SE Dock St., 360/279-1231, www.frasersgh.com, 4:30–10:30 P.M. Tues.–Sat., closed Sun. and Mon., $24–39). The town's fine dining establishment, Frasers serves beef tenderloin, rack of lamb, lobster pappardelle, and more in a classy downtown setting. Be sure to try the spicy Singapore prawn appetizer, Frasers's signature dish. The restaurant has several tables on the wraparound porch.

Get authentic Mexican fare at **Mi Pueblo** (916 SE Bayshore Dr., 360/240-0813, www.mipueblobythebay.com, 11 A.M.–10 P.M. Sun.–Thurs., 11 A.M.–11 P.M. Fri.–Sat., $11–15) downtown. There's karaoke and dancing till 2 A.M. most weekends, salsa dance lessons on Thursday nights, water views any evening, and the best margaritas on Whidbey.

**Seabolt's Smokehouse & Deli** (31640 State Rte. 20, 360/675-6485 or 800/574-1120, www.seabolts.com, 9 A.M.–8 P.M. Mon.–Sat., 8 A.M.–3 P.M. Sun., $8–14) attracts locals with halibut and chips, seafood gumbo, fish tacos, and more.

**Sweet Rice Thai Cuisine** (885 SE Pioneer Way, 360/679-8268, 11 A.M.–9 P.M. Mon. and Wed.–Fri., noon–9 P.M. Sat.–Sun.) has an all-you-can-eat lunch buffet most weekdays. Equally popular (and reasonable) is **1-2-3 Thai** (31595 State Rte. 20, 360/679-7600, www.123thaifood.webs.com, 11 A.M.–9 P.M. daily).

**Zorba's Restaurant** (32955 State Rte. 20, 360/279-8322, www.zorbasoakharbor.com, 11 A.M.–9 P.M. daily) has a diverse menu (from teriyaki chicken burgers to three-meat ravioli), but is best known for Greek specialties such as spanakopita, moussaka, and lamb gyros. Reasonable prices too; most entrées are under $13.

The **Oak Harbor Public Market** (360/675-0472, 4–7 P.M. Thurs., mid-May–late Sept.) takes place in Tree Park next to the visitors center along Highway 20.

## Information
The **Oak Harbor Visitor Center** (32630 Hwy. 20, 360/675-3735, www.oakharborchamber.com, 9 A.M.–5 P.M. Mon.–Fri. year-round, 10 A.M.–2 P.M. Sat. May–Sept.) is located next to the appropriately named Tree Park.

# Bellingham

With a population topping 82,000, Bellingham is no longer a town, though it still maintains a friendly small-town feel. The city is an almost perfect blend of the old and the new, with stately homes, extraordinary museums, and an abundance of cultural events, plus many fine shops and restaurants. Bellingham's big paper mill closed in 2007, but the town continues to flourish with Western Washington University—third largest university in the state—and increasing numbers of tourists. The town pegs the "livability" meter, consistently getting stellar reviews in those "best places to live" magazine rankings.

Bellingham is a jumping-off point for private ferries and whale-watching trips to the San Juan Islands; it is also where northbound travelers catch Alaska Marine Highway ferries. The terminal for all these boats is in Bellingham's historic Fairhaven district. In addition, it is only 43 miles to the ferry terminal at Anacortes, and the route takes you along beautiful Chuckanut Drive. Because of this, Bellingham is a popular stopping point for people driving down from Vancouver en route to the San Juans, and a regional shopping destination.

## SIGHTS
### ◖ Fairhaven
This historic section of Bellingham has quite a few buildings constructed in the late 1880s. At the time, rumors were circulating that

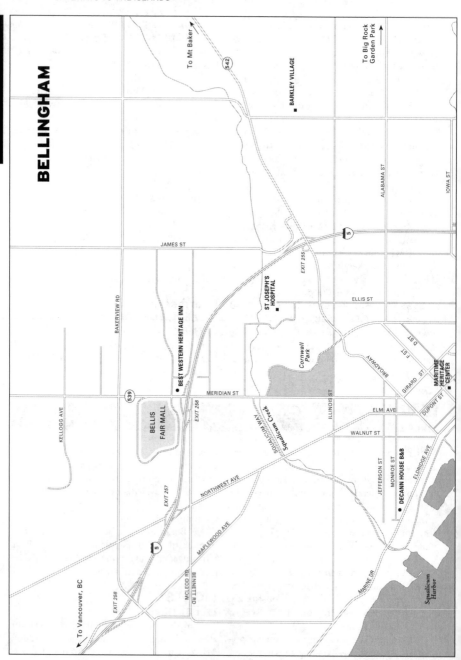

# BELLINGHAM

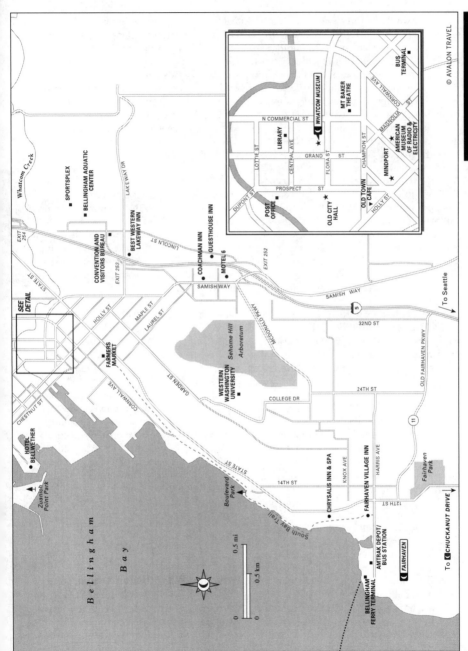

© AVALON TRAVEL

Fairhaven would be the western terminus for the Great Northern Railroad. The railroad chose Tacoma instead, and the buildings are now part of the Fairhaven Historic District; pick up a walking-tour map from the visitors center. A wonderful two-mile walkway connects Fairhaven with downtown Bellingham, including a portion that extends over the bay.

Several interesting shops and galleries can be found in the district. **Good Earth Pottery** (1000 Harris Ave., 360/671-3998, www.goodearthpots.com) has fine ceramics. In the same building, the cooperatively owned **Artwood** (360/647-1628, www.artwoodgallery.com) sells handcrafted woodworking. **Chuckanut Bay Gallery** (700 Chuckanut Dr., 360/734-4885, www.chuckanutbaygallery.com) is a lovely stop a mile or so south of Fairhaven at the start of Chuckanut Drive, with quality pieces by regional artisans.

One of the most popular places in Fairhaven—or in all of Bellingham for that matter—**Village Books** (1200 11th St., 360/671-2626 or 800/392-2665, www.villagebooks.com)—has frequent book readings, workshops, and signings. Look for used titles just up the street at **Eclipse Bookstore** (1104 11th Ave., 360/647-8165).

## Whatcom Museum

In the last few years, Bellingham's stodgy old downtown museum has been transformed into a modern cultural center—the Art District—surrounded by burgeoning cafés, galleries, and other businesses. Whatcom Museum (360/778-8933, www.whatcommuseum.org) consists of Old City Hill and the new Lightcatcher building. Commanding a high bluff at 121 Prospect Street, **Old City Hall** (noon–5 P.M. Thurs.–Sun.) is an ornate redbrick building capped by a four-corner cupola and a central clock tower. Constructed in 1892, it remained in use until 1939. The building now houses historical displays from Bellingham's early days.

**The Lightcatcher** (250 Flora St., noon–5 P.M. Tues.–Sun.) provides a vastly different experience. Designed by architect Jim Olson, this 42,000-square-foot museum debuted in 2009. A curving translucent wall of glass—37 feet high and 180 feet long—dominates the building, separating the exterior courtyard from interior galleries. The building integrates natural materials and even has a green roof covered with plants and solar arrays. Exhibition spaces contain changing exhibits of art, and a family gallery has activities for kids. Admission to both The Lightcatcher and Old City Hall is $10 adults, $8 seniors and students, and $4.50 for children under age five.

## Other Museums

Make it a point to visit **Mindport** (210 W. Holly St., 360/647-5614, www.mindport.org, noon–6 P.M. Wed.–Fri., 10 A.M.–5 P.M. Sat., noon–4 P.M. Sun., $2), a creative science center that will amuse, fascinate, and educate both kids and adults. The exhibits are mostly made from reused old junk, with a touch of whimsy thrown in. Great fun.

Don't miss the fascinating **American Museum of Radio & Electricity** (1312 Bay St., 360/738-3886, www.americanradiomuseum.org, noon–6 P.M. Wed.–Fri., 10 A.M.–5 P.M. Sat., noon–4 P.M. Sun., $5 adults, $2 kids under age 12), with more than a thousand radios, some dating from the early 1900s. But this place isn't just about radios, it's also about the dawn of the electrical age and all the bizarre creations of that era, including a Theremin you can play. In this age of computers, this throwback to the past still entertains kids of all ages. Don't miss the summertime coil demonstrations; they're literally shocking.

The **Bellingham Railway Museum** (1320 Commercial St., 360/393-7540, www.bellinghamrailwaymuseum.org, noon–5 P.M. Tues. and Thurs.–Sat., $4 adults, $2 kids) features model-railroad displays and exhibits on historic railroads.

## Western Washington University

The 215-acre campus of Western Washington University (I-5 Exit 252, 360/650-3861, www.wwu.edu) is home to 12,000 students. Visitors appreciate the **Outdoor Sculpture Garden,** with two-dozen works scattered across the campus. Overlooking Bellingham Bay and accessible via a footpath from the university, **Sehome Hill Arboretum** provides 3.5 miles of trails and splendid views of the San Juans and Mount Baker, plus 180 acres of tall Douglas firs, wildflowers, and big-leaf maples.

## ◖ CHUCKANUT DRIVE

One of the most scenic stretches of highway in the state, Chuckanut Drive (Hwy. 11) stretches south from Fairhaven and then across Skagit Valley. The Bellingham visitors center has a helpful brochure detailing attractions along the way, or visit www.chuckanutdrive.com. The road doesn't have a straight stretch for seven miles as it swoops and swerves along the face of a cliff. Grand views span across to Anacortes, Guemes Island, and, farther north, the San Juan Islands. With no shoulder, a narrow strip of pavement, and tight corners, it's a bit dicey for bikes (especially on weekends when traffic is heaviest), but the views are stunning. Several excellent restaurants dot Chuckanut Drive. You will also pass the road to **Taylor**

© DON PITCHER

**wooded creek along Chuckanut Drive**

**Shellfish Farms** (360/766-6002, www.taylorshellfishfarms.com), which has fresh oysters, clams (including geoduck), and mussels; it's the largest producer of Manila clams in the United States.

### Larrabee State Park

Established in 1923, this was the first state park in Washington. Larrabee (360/676-2093, www.parks.wa.gov) occupies one of the most beautiful stretches of mountainous country along Chuckanut Drive and has a popular campground. Covering more than 2,500 acres, the park borders Samish Bay and boasts a boat launch, a sandy beach for sunning, and tidepools for marine explorations. Nine miles of hiking trails include the southern end of the **Interurban Trail,** connecting the park with Bellingham. Other trails lead to scenic Fragrance and Lost Lakes for trout fishing and to dramatic vistas from the 1,941-foot summit of **Chuckanut Mountain** (also accessible via a gravel road).

## CITY AND COUNTY PARKS

**Whatcom County** (360/676-6985, www.co.whatcom.wa.us/parks) has one of the best collections of city- and county-owned parks in the state. In Bellingham alone, there are more than 35 places that qualify as parks, including greenbelts, fitness areas, and trails. These parks range from less than half an acre to more than a thousand acres.

Beautiful **Samish Park** (at I-5 Exit 246 south of Bellingham, 360/733-2362) is a 39-acre county park along Lake Samish with swimming, fishing, boating, picnicking, hiking, boat rentals, and a playground.

**Whatcom Falls Park** (near Lake Whatcom at 1401 Electric Ave.) has hiking trails, tennis courts, a playground, a picnic area, and a state fish hatchery on 241 acres. With 12 acres on the lake itself, **Bloedel Donovan Park** (2214 Electric Ave.) includes a swimming beach, boat launch, playground, and picnic area.

Covering more than 1,000 acres, **Lake Padden Park** (4882 Samish Way; I-5 Exit 252) has hiking and horse trails, a golf course, picnic areas, and a playground, plus swimming, fishing, and nonmotorized boating.

**Stimpson Family Nature Reserve** has four miles of hiking trails through lush old-growth forests, with two ponds and wetland areas. It's near Lake Whatcom about five miles east of downtown.

Overlooking Squalicum Harbor, **Zuanich Point Park** is an outstanding place for picnics, kite flying, and play. A children's play area, paved bike path, and dock add to the appeal.

## ENTERTAINMENT AND EVENTS

Opened in 1927 as a vaudeville and movie palace, historic **Mt. Baker Theatre** (106 N. Commercial St., 360/733-5793, www.mtbakertheatre.com) hosts the **Whatcom Symphony Orchestra** (360/756-6752, www.whatcomsymphony.com), as well as many other musical and theatrical performances. A **Brown Bag Music Series** (360/647-2060) features concerts on the public library lawn each Friday mid-June–August.

**Pickford Film Center** (1318 Bay St., 360/647-1300, www.pickfordcinema.org) opened its new, state of the art downtown cinema in 2011, showing independent, art house, and foreign films.

Founded by comedian—and Bellingham resident—Ryan Stiles, **The Upfront Theatre** (1208 Bay St., 360/733-8855, www.theupfront.com) is a 100-seat cabaret-style venue with live improv comedy Thursday–Saturday nights.

For the latest on the local music scene, pick up a copy of *Cascadia Weekly* (www.cascadiaweekly.com) or *Bellingham Herald's Take Five* (www.bellinghamherald.com). **Wild Buffalo** (208 W. Holly St., 360/752-0848) and **Boundary Bay Brewery & Bistro** (1107 Railroad Ave., 360/647-5593, www.bbaybrewery.com) are good first stops for live bands. **Green Frog Café** (902 N. State St., 360/756-1213, www.acoustictavern.com) attracts singer-songwriter artists with a tiny stage and more than 20 microbrews on tap. **Temple Bar** (306 W. Champion St., 360/676-8660, www.templebarbellingham.com) is a great little wine bar with live music every Saturday and surprisingly good food. It's especially popular during happy hour, when a featured bottle of wine and a small plate of cheese, bread, olives, and fruit is just $15.

**Downtown Art Walks** bring out gallery enthusiasts the first Friday of each month. Bellingham's **Ski to Sea Race** (360/746-8861, www.skitosea.com), held Memorial Day weekend, tests the physical endurance and athletic skills of its participants over an 85-mile course that includes cross-country and downhill skiing, running, bicycling, canoeing, mountain biking, and finally kayaking across Bellingham Bay to the finish in the Fairhaven district. An annual event since 1973, the race is the highlight of a weeklong festival that includes parades, a street fair with crafts, live music and dancing, food, and a beer garden on Sunday after the race.

There's a big **Fourth of July** fireworks show over Bellingham Harbor each summer, and each July, the city hosts the two-week **Bellingham Festival of Music** (360/676-5997, www.bellinghamfestival.org), with outstanding classical and jazz performances. Around the same time, the **Chalk Artfest** (360/676-8548, www.alliedarts.org) attracts a wide range of talent, from kids to serious artists. Great fun as everyone gets to draw on the city's sidewalks and not get arrested.

## SHOPPING

Bellingham has a diverse arts community, with a number of fine galleries. **Allied Arts of Whatcom County** (1418 Cornwall Ave., 360/676-8548, www.alliedarts.org) has a large downtown gallery. **Blue Horse Gallery** (301 W. Holly St., 360/671-2305, www.bluehorsegallery.com) shows works from two-dozen regional artists. Each October, the **Whatcom Artist Studio Tour** (www.studiotour.net) provides an open house for more than 50 local artisans.

## RECREATION
### Hiking

Stop by the visitors center for descriptions and maps of more than 20 hiking trails in and around Bellingham, including trails in Whatcom Falls Park, Sehome Hill Arboretum, and the nearby Mt. Baker-Snoqualmie National Forest.

The **Interurban Trail** is a nine-mile path that follows a former railroad bed from Old Fairhaven Parkway south to Larrabee State Park. Continue north from Fairhaven to Bellingham via the paved two-mile **South Bay Trail,** a portion of which is on pilings over Bellingham Bay. It's a great place for a jog or bike ride.

## Swimming and Skating

Bellingham's **Arne Hanna Aquatic Center** (1114 Potter St., 360/657-7665, www.ci.bellingham.wa.us/parks/aqua) has an indoor pool, wading pool, diving tank, and water slide. A second pool is available at **Whatcom Family YMCA** (1256 N. State St., 360/763-8630, www.whatcomymca.org). In the summer, you can also swim at **Lake Padden Park** (4882 Samish Way, 360/676-6985), **Lake Samish** (673 N. Lake Samish Dr., 360/733-2362), and **Bloedel Donovan Park** (2214 Electric Ave., 360/676-6985).

For year-round indoor ice skating, head to **Sportsplex** (1225 Civic Field Way, 360/733-9999, www.bellinghamsportsplex.com).

## Boating

The visitors bureau has a complete listing of sailing and fishing charter operators and cruises. For day sailings, contact **Gato Verde Adventure Sailing** (360/220-3215, www.gatoverde.com), **Shawmanee Charters** (360/734-9849, www.bellinghamsailing.com), or **Schooner Zodiac** (206/719-7622, www.schoonerzodiac.com).

Bellingham is a major center for boaters heading to the San Juans, with the following companies offering powerboat or sailing charters: **Bellhaven Charters** (360/733-6636 or 877/310-9471, www.bellhaven.net), **Bellingham Yachts Sales and Charters** (360/671-0990 or 877/310-9446, www.bellinghamyachts.com), **Northwest Explorations** (360/676-1248 or 800/826-1430, www.

nwexplorations.com), **Par Yacht Charters** (360/200-6800, www.parcharters.com), **San Juan Sailing** (360/671-4300 or 800/677-7245, www.sanjuansailing.com), and **San Juan Yachting** (360/671-4300 or 800/670-8089, www.sanjuanyachting.com).

## Kayaking

**Moondance Sea Kayaking Adventures** (360/738-7664, www.moondancekayak.com) leads sea kayak tours in the area, from half-day paddles ($65) to five-day San Juan trips ($625).

**Elakah Expeditions** (360/734-7270 or 800/434-7270, www.elakah.com) guides sea kayaking trips of varying lengths. All-day trips (4–5 hours on the water) to Lummi Island cost $90 including a gourmet lunch. Elakah also leads multi-day kayaking-and-camping tours to the outlying islands: $380 for three days or $625 for five days. Kayaking lessons are also available.

## Whale-Watching

**Island Mariner Cruises** (2621 S. Harbor Loop Dr., 360/734-8867 or 877/734-8866, www.orcawatch.com) operates the largest whale-watching boat in the area, the 110-foot *Island Caper,* with space for 100 passengers. Seven-hour trips are $69 adults, $59 youths, and $39 kids. Also popular are 2.5-hour narrated historical harbor cruises for $35 per person. These are offered Thursday evenings late June to mid-August.

**San Juan Cruises** (360/738-8099 or 800/443-4552, www.whales.com, Fri.–Sat. May–Sept.) departs Bellingham for all-day cruises to the San Juan Islands on the 149-passenger *Victoria Star 2*. These trips combine a two-hour stop in Friday Harbor with a three-hour whale-watching voyage and lunch; $99 adults, $50 ages 6–17, free for younger kids. San Juan Cruises also operates a three-day cruise to the San Juan Islands, along with a day tour of Chuckanut Bay.

## Outfitters

Located in Fairhaven, **Brenthaven** (909 Harris Ave., 360/671-0495 or 800/803-7225, www.brenthaven.com) sells high-quality daypacks, laptop and tablet computer bags, and soft luggage. Rent bikes from **Fairhaven Bike and Ski** (1108 11th St., 360/733-4433, www.fairhavenbike.com) or **Jack's Bicycle Center** (1907 Iowa St., 360/733-1955, www.jacksbicyclecenter.net).

## ACCOMMODATIONS

**Bellingham Whatcom Tourism** (904 Potter St., 360/671-3990 or 800/487-2032, www.bellingham.org) keeps track of local lodging availability on summer weekends. Stop by the office for brochures, discount coupons, or to check out photographs of local bed-and-breakfasts. An abundance of weekend soccer tournaments creates unbelievably crowded conditions in summer, so lodging can be a challenge. Call months ahead for the peak of summer to ensure a space. The tourism center also operates **Bellingham Best Buys** (888/261-7795, www.bellingham.org), a program with substantial discounts—up to 50 percent in the off-season—for selected hotels.

Surprisingly, there are no hostels in Bellingham. The closest one is the seasonal **Birch Bay Hostel** (360/371-2180, www.birchbayhostel.org, $28/person), 20 miles north of Bellingham.

### Under $100

**Coachman Inn** (120 N. Samish Way, 360/671-9000 or 800/962-6641, www.coachmaninnmotel.com, $89–99 d) has simple but well-maintained rooms, fridges, Wi-Fi, a sauna, continental breakfast, and a small seasonal pool.

**Motel 6** (3701 Byron St., I-5 Exit 252, 360/671-4494 or 800/466-8356, www.motel6.com, $65 d) has an outdoor pool and Wi-Fi, but avoid rooms on the noisy freeway side if you're a light sleeper.

**GuestHouse Inn** (805 Lakeway Dr., 360/671-9600 or 800/214-8378, www.guesthouseintl.com, $90–100 d) is a fine moderately priced option, with newly remodeled rooms, a filling hot breakfast, indoor hot tub, and Wi-Fi. It's right off I-5 at Exit 253.

### Over $100

Popular with business travelers and convenient to the airport, **Hampton Inn Bellingham Airport** (3985 Bennett Dr., 360/676-7700 or 800/426-7866, www.hamptoninn.com, $159 d) includes a heated seasonal outdoor pool, buffet breakfast, and airport and ferry shuttle. Some rooms have jetted tubs.

**Best Western Plus Heritage Inn** (151 E. McLeod Rd., 360/647-1912 or 800/528-1234, www.bestwestern.com/heritageinnbellingham) has the look of a New England Colonial building and features attractive grounds, 91 fashionable rooms, a seasonal outdoor pool, indoor hot tub, fitness center, airport shuttle, Wi-Fi, and a filling hot breakfast. Reserve a room facing away from I-5. Most rooms are $160 weekends and $130 weekdays, while the three suites are $190 weekends and $160 weekdays.

Another of Bellingham's finer hotels, the **Best Western Plus Lakeway Inn** (714 Lakeway Dr., I-5 Exit 256, 360/671-1011 or 888/671-1011, www.bellingham-hotel.com, $200–240 d) has an indoor pool, exercise room, hot tub, flat-screen TVs, sauna, Wi-Fi, and an airport shuttle. Business travelers appreciate the comfortable beds and conference center.

A 22-room boutique hotel, **☾ Fairhaven Village Inn** (1200 10th St., 360/733-1311 or 877/733-1100, www.fairhavenvillageinn.com, $189–219 d) blends well with its historic Fairhaven neighbors. Rooms are spacious and include gas fireplaces, plush king-size beds, small decks, a continental breakfast, Wi-Fi, and other amenities. A luxurious two-room suite with jetted tub costs $249 d. The Interurban Trail starts nearby, providing a good spot for a morning run.

One of Bellingham's most indulgent lodging choices, **Hotel Bellwether** (1 Bellwether Way, 360/392-3100 or 877/411-1200, www.hotelbellwether.com) offers a waterfront location, large rooms (many with king-size beds), balconies, Italian furnishings, gas fireplaces, large TVs, marble baths with jetted tubs, a lavish breakfast buffet, and Wi-Fi. Peak season weekend rates start at $277 d for the smaller rooms facing the plaza, $349–519 d for more spacious ones, all the way up to $989 d for the lavish three-level lighthouse suite. Downstairs is the classy Harborside Restaurant and Lounge, and golfers will appreciate the small putting green.

The acclaimed **Chrysalis Inn & Spa** (804 10th St, 360/756-0005 or 888/808-0005, www.thechrysalisinn.com, $199–324 d) is another gorgeous waterside option with ultra-luxurious rooms (two-person baths, gas fireplaces, and window seats), a breakfast buffet, an impressive lobby, wine bar, and decadent spa. Unfortunately, the hotel's trackside location means train noise throughout the night.

## Bed-and-Breakfasts

**⟨ Tree Frog Night Inn** (1727 Mt. Baker Hwy., 360/676-2300, www.treefrognight.com, $185 d, add $30 each for extra guests) consists of a gorgeous, environmentally friendly cottage with two guest suites, each of which can sleep four. Nearby are gardens, a forest, and a pond. Suites have small porches, luxurious furnishings, private baths, and flat-screen TVs, Wi-Fi, robes, organic breakfasts, and a bottle of local wine. Private massage and spa packages are available.

**DeCann House B&B** (2610 Eldridge Ave., 360/734-9172, www.decannhouse.com, $115–135 d for one night or $99–115 d for multiple nights) is a 1902 Victorian home accentuated with stained glass, an antique pool table, and fine views of the San Juan Islands. The two guest rooms include private baths and a full breakfast.

Located along scenic Chuckanut Drive south of Bellingham, **Chuckanut B&B** (3056 Chuckanut Dr., 360/766-6191, www.chuckanutmanor.com, $160 d or $230 for four) is a two-bedroom suite with a large deck facing Samish Bay, including a full kitchen and private bath with jetted tub. A continental breakfast is provided, and Chuckanut Manor Seafood & Grill is downstairs. Railroad tracks are just down the hill, so trains may sing to you in the night.

On the woodsy shore of Whatcom Lake just east of Bellingham, **⟨ MoonDance Inn** (4737 Cable St., 360/647-2997, www.bellingham-bandb.com, $135–180 d) provides a beautiful setting, luxury accommodations, full breakfasts, a private dock, firepit, lakeside beach, canoes, kayaks, volleyball, and Wi-Fi. Five guest rooms all have private baths, and kids are accepted.

## Camping

The closest public campsites are seven miles south of Bellingham at **Larrabee State Park** (360/676-2093, www.parks.wa.gov, $22–25 tents, $29–34 RVs). Year-round sites are available, along with showers. Make reservations ($10 extra) at 888/226-7688 or via the park website.

At **Bellingham RV Park** (3939 Bennett Dr., 360/752-1224 or 888/372-1224, www.bellinghamrvpark.com), RV hookups cost $30.

## FOOD

Bellingham has an amazing variety of creative eating establishments. Head to Fairhaven and just walk around to see what looks interesting, or visit the downtown Arts District surrounding the Whatcom Museum.

### Breakfast and Lunch

Enjoy great breakfasts and lunches at **⟨ Old Town Café** (316 W. Holly St., 360/671-4431, 6:30 A.M.–3 P.M. Mon.–Sat., 8 A.M.–2 P.M. Sun., $7–9 breakfasts), an earthy downtown brunch place where the line of customers stretches out the door most mornings. Try the Number Nine: two poached eggs on a biscuit with cheese sauce, tomatoes, and homefries. The atmosphere is laid-back and noisy.

A different dining experience can be found a few blocks away at **The Little Cheerful Café** (113 E. Holly St., 360/738-8824, www.littlecheerful.com, 7 A.M.–2 P.M. daily, $6–14), where the staff is, of course, very cheerful. The setting is casual, and the breakfasts are always great—especially the house favorites, eggs Benedict and California hash browns—with ample portions. Everything on the menu is available all day, so you can start your morning with an egg McStupid (scrambled egg, cheese, and bacon on a bun, with hash browns), and end it with the aptly named myocardia infarction burger (2,500 calories). Outside sidewalk seating is available, but be prepared to wait if you show up after 10 A.M. on weekends.

A Victorian building in Fairhaven houses spacious **Skylark's Hidden Café** (1308 11th St., 360/715-3642, www.skylarkshiddencafe. com, 8 A.M.–midnight daily, $14–30 dinner entrées), serving filling breakfasts, deli sandwiches, soups, fresh seafood, and more. Everything is made in-house. No longer hidden, the café has expanded from its backstreet location to a beautiful two-level building with a hardwood bar (14 single malt scotches) and live jazz most weekends.

## Coffee

Many Bellingham places make espresso, but one stands out: **Tony's Coffee & Teas** (1101 Harris Ave. in Fairhaven, 360/733-6319, www. tonyscoffee.com), where the smell of roasting coffee wafts through the air. There's another location downtown, but the Fairhaven one is the real deal. Read the newspaper, sample the carrot cake, play a game of chess, or just lean back and take in the scene (sans Wi-Fi, alas). This is as close to Berkeley as you'll get this far north. The owners also run **Harris Ave. Café** (360/738-0802, www.harrisavecafe.com, 8 A.M.–2 P.M. daily, $6–11) next door, with delicious brunches and a shady patio.

A popular regional chain, **Wood's Coffee** (www.thewoodscoffee.com) has several local stores—all with Wi-Fi—including a striking one in the historic Flatiron Building at Meridian and Stuart (360/733-9570). For killer views with your cappuccino, stop by their shop in Boulevard Park (470 Bay View Rd., 360/738-4771); it's right on the water, with a deck and windows fronting Bellingham Bay. All Wood's Coffee shops are open daily, generally from 6 or 7 A.M. to 8 or 9 P.M. In addition to all the standard coffee drinks, they have sandwiches, salads, and baked goods.

## Quick Bites

**Swan Café** inside the Community Food Co-Op (1059 N. State St., 360/734-8158, www.communityfood.coop, $5–6) serves hearty soups, salads, and sandwiches. This is a fine place for an inexpensive downtown lunch.

If you're in Fairhaven and want great sandwiches, bagels, quiche, a slice of famous peanut butter pie, or just a scoop of ice cream, drop by **Colophon Café** inside Village Books (1210 11th St., 360/671-2626, www.colophoncafe.com, 9 A.M.–8 P.M. Mon.–Thurs., 9 A.M.–10 P.M. Fri.–Sat., 10 A.M.–8 P.M. Sun.).

**D'Anna's Italian Café** (1317 N. State St., 360/714-0188, www.dannascafeitaliano.com, $13–22 entrées) is a bright bistro serving homemade pasta, lasagna, sandwiches, salads, and lattes, with a couple of outside tables.

## International

Newly relocated to the Bellingham Marina near the Bellwether Hotel, **Giuseppe's Al Porto Ristorante Italiano** (21 Bellwether Way, 360/714-8412, www.giuseppesitalian.com, 11:30 A.M.–9 P.M. Sun.–Thurs., 11:30 A.M.–10 P.M. Fri.–Sat.) has delicious pastas and a large outside terrazza for waterside dining. You can choose a simple spaghetti dish for $16, all the way up to a $33 rack of lamb.

Fairhaven's **Dos Padres Restaurante** (1111 Harris Ave., 360/733-9900, www.dospadres.com, 11:30 A.M.–9 P.M. Sun.–Thurs., 11:30 A.M.–9:30 P.M. Fri.–Sat., $9–15) has an extensive selection of Mexican dishes with a Southwest twist, along with locally famous margaritas and house-special chile rellenos. It's been here since 1973.

**India Grill** (1215 Cornwall Ave., 360/714-0314, www.indiagrill.us) is *the* place for Indian lunches and dinners, including tandoori and vegetarian specials. The lunch buffet is just $8. Several local places have flavorful Thai food; two of the best are **Busara Thai Cuisine** (404 36th St., 360/734-8088) and **Thai House Restaurant** (187 Telegraph Rd., 360/734-5111).

**Little Tokyo** (2915 Newmarket Place in

Barkley Village, 360/752-2222, www.littleto-kyowa.com) is a casual sushi bar and Japanese restaurant open for lunch and dinner.

## American and Eclectic

Fairhaven's **Dirty Dan Harris' Restaurant** (1211 11th St., 360/676-1011, www.dirtydan-harris.com, 5–10 P.M. daily, $20–30 entrées) serves prime rib, steaks, and fresh seafood dinners in a classy 1800s-style saloon. It's named for Daniel Jefferson Harris, a feisty eccentric best known for his bathing habits—or lack thereof—who platted the town's streets, built a dock, and sold lots to the thousands of folks who rolled into Fairhaven in 1883. He made a small fortune in the process.

If you aren't looking for the gourmet-variety burger, **Boomer's Drive-In** (310 N. Samish Way, 360/647-2666, www.boomersdrivein.com) has the finest anywhere around.

It isn't in Bellingham, but **Rhododendron Café** (360/766-6667, www.rhodycafe.com, 11:30 A.M.–9 P.M. Wed.–Fri., 9 A.M.–9 P.M. Sat.–Sun., $10–30) is certainly worth the drive. This little country café is a centerpiece for the town of Bow near the south end of Chuckanut Drive. Weekend brunch is always a draw. Check the blackboard for lunch and dinner treats, including various ethnic specialties and Northwest cuisine.

## Seafood

Perpetually crowded, **Big Fat Fish Co.** (1304 12th St., 360/733-2284, www.bigfatfishco.com, 11:30 A.M.–9:30 P.M. Sun.–Thurs., 11:30 A.M.–10 P.M. Fri.–Sat., $14–28 entrées) is a Fairhaven hit, with stylish sushi and "seafood with attitude." Dinner entrées include everything from halibut puttanesca and sesame calamari to big fat Kobe burgers. Three-course dinner specials—salad, fresh seafood, and dessert—are just $19. Lunchtime burgers, seafood tacos, sandwiches, and chowder cost around $12.

A trio of seafood places hug **Chuckanut Drive** south of Bellingham; all are open for lunch and dinner. At the southernmost end of the drive, **Chuckanut Manor Seafood &** Grill (360/766-6191, www.chuckanutmanor.com, lunch and dinner daily) specializes in fresh seafood and continental dishes, a Friday night seafood and prime rib smorgasbord ($33), and Sunday champagne brunches ($23). Reservations are recommended. It's been here since 1963.

Clinging to the side of a hill, **The Oyster Bar** (240 Chuckanut Dr., 360/766-6185, www.theoysterbar.net, 11:30 A.M.–10 P.M. daily, $26–35 entrées) has two levels of windows facing the San Juan Islands. It serves oysters (of course), but fresh fish and other seafood are featured attractions on the always-changing menu, and the wine list is equally notable. Reservations are essential, especially on weekends.

Specializing in Northwest food and wine in a romantic setting, **Oyster Creek Inn** (2190 Chuckanut Dr., 360/766-6179, www.oystercreekinn.net, 11:30 A.M.–9 P.M. daily, $30–50) serves seafood (including fresh oysters from Taylor Shellfish Farms, just down the hill), roast duckling, lamb, and other dishes. This "treehouse" of a place is perched along a cascading creek; outside diners are surrounded by ferns and tall trees. Reservations are advised.

## Pubs and Pizza

Find award-winning brews at **Boundary Bay Brewery & Bistro** (1107 Railroad Ave., 360/647-5593, www.bbaybrewery.com, $15–22 entrées), with seven beers on tap and a pub menu of steak, fish, pizza, salads, sandwiches, and more. The big doors open onto a flower-filled deck and beer garden.

**Chuckanut Brewery & Kitchen** (601 W. Holly St., 360/752-3377, www.chuckanut-breweryandkitchen.com, 11:30 A.M.–9 P.M. Sun.–Thurs., 11:30 A.M.–10 P.M. Fri.–Sat.) specializes in German lagers—including the award-winning Chuckanut Helles Lager—but crafts nearly 20 variations on the beer theme. The diverse menu encompasses wood stone pizzas ($12–14), Chuckanut chowder ($8), roasted yam fries ($7), brewmaster's meatloaf ($14), or brat and beer ($9 with a pint). You know they must be doing something right, since the brew-pub won as "small brewing company & brewer of the year" at the 2011 Great American Beer Festival. Brewery tours are only offered once a month, so call ahead for the next one.

For pizzas, **La Fiamma** (200 E. Chestnut, 360/647-0060, www.lafiamma.com, 11 A.M.–9 P.M. Mon.–Thurs., 11 A.M.–10 P.M. Fri.–Sat., noon–9 P.M.) is a stylish but family-friendly spot with crunchy wood-fired pizzas (even a moo shu pork version), panini sandwiches, and salads. A large cheese pizza costs $14; locals call it the best in town. Another great pizza option is **New York Pizza and Bar** (902 N. State St., 360/733-3171, www.newyorkpizzaandbar.com, 11 A.M.–midnight Sun.–Wed., 11 A.M.–2 A.M. Thurs.–Sat.), with a pizza/pasta restaurant on one side and a bar on the other.

### Markets and Bakeries

Bellingham's **Community Food Co-Op** (1220 N. Forest St., 360/734-8158, www.communityfood.coop, 7 A.M.–10 P.M. daily) is a spacious natural foods market and home to the Swan Café & Deli.

Find European-style breads, plus sandwiches and soups, at **Avenue Bread Co.** (1313 Railroad Ave., 360/715-3354, www.avenuebread.com, 7 A.M.–4 P.M. Mon.–Sat., 9 A.M.–4 P.M. Sun., $7–8). A few doors away is **The Bagelry** (1319 Railroad Ave., 360/676-5288, www.bagelrybellingham.com, 7 A.M.–4 P.M. Mon.–Fri., 7:30 A.M.–4 P.M. Sat., 8 A.M.–3 P.M., most items under $7), a popular place with New York–style bagels, bagel sandwiches, and omelets.

The exceptionally popular **Mount Bakery Café** (308 W. Champion St., 360/715-2195, www.mountbakery.com, 8 A.M.–3:30 P.M. daily, $6–11) serves savory and sweet crepes, waffles, BLTs, quiche of the day, and amazing tarts, croissants, chocolate truffle cakes, and other sweet treats. The crème brûlée is to die for. Mount Bakery Café is in the heart of the Art District, with a second shop in Fairhaven at 1217 Harris Avenue.

The **Bellingham Farmers Market** (1200 Railroad Ave., 360/647-2060, www.bellinghamfarmers.org, 10 A.M.–3 P.M. Sat. Apr.–Dec.) is housed within Depot Market Square. A second farmers market takes place behind Village Books in Fairhaven Wednesday noon–5 P.M. June–September.

## INFORMATION

For maps, a slew of brochures, historic walking tours, and general information, visit the **Bellingham Whatcom Tourism Visitors Center** (904 Potter St., I-5 Exit 253, 360/671-3990 or 800/487-2032, www.bellingham.org, 9 A.M.–5 P.M. daily). An information kiosk is inside the Bellingham Cruise Terminal, where the Alaska ferry docks.

## GETTING THERE AND AROUND

The **Bellingham Cruise Terminal** (www.portofbellingham.com), three blocks downhill from Fairhaven, is where you can catch whale-watching boats to the San Juans, and the **Alaska Marine Highway** (360/676-8445 or 800/642-0066, www.ferryalaska.com) ferries to Alaska.

### By Car

**Avis** (360/676-8840 or 800/331-1212, www.avis.com) has rentals at the airport, with a second location inside the ferry terminal if you're arriving on the Alaska ferry or by train. Enterprise, Hertz, and Budget also have airport car rentals.

### By Train

**Amtrak** (360/734-8851 or 800/872-7245, www.amtrakcascades.com) provides twice-daily train connections on its *Cascades* train north to Vancouver, British Columbia, and south to Mount Vernon, Everett, Edmonds, and Seattle. It stops at the Fairhaven depot, just a short walk from the Bellingham Cruise Terminal.

### By Air

Located just north of the city, **Bellingham International Airport** (360/671-5674, www.

portofbellingham.com) is a popular departure point for many Canadians because they can get more convenient flights to some U.S. destinations and cheaper tickets; the parking—$6 per day—is a big savings too. Because of this, air traffic has grown rapidly in the last decade.

**Alaska Airlines** (800/252-7522, www.alaskaair.com) and its subsidiary **Horizon Air** (800/547-9308, www.horizonair.com) connect Bellingham with Sea-Tac, Las Vegas, and Honolulu. **Allegiant Air** (702/505-8888, www.allegiantair.com) connects Bellingham with Los Angeles, Las Vegas, Long Beach, Oakland, Palm Springs, San Diego, and Phoenix.

**San Juan Airlines** (360/293-4691 or 800/874-4434, www.sanjuanairlines.com) has daily service to San Juan, Orcas, Lopez, Blakely, and Decatur in the San Juan Islands, along with charter flights and flightseeing.

**Northwest Sky Ferry** (360/696-9999, www.nwskyferry.com) has twice-daily flights from Bellingham to San Juan, Orcas, and Lopez Islands, with flightpooling charters to other destinations throughout the San Juan Islands.

If you're flying into Sea-Tac Airport, catch the **Airporter Shuttle** (360/380-8800 or 866/235-5247, www.airporter.com) van to Bellingham for $30 one-way ($18 kids). **Quick Shuttle Service** (604/940-4428 or 800/665-2122, www.quickcoach.com) has service to Vancouver for $28 one-way ($16 kids).

## By Bus

Locally, **Whatcom Transit Authority** (360/676-7433, www.ridewta.com, $1)—better known as WTA—provides daily bus service throughout Bellingham and the rest of the county, including Ferndale, Lynden, Blaine, and the Lummi Indian Reservation. **Greyhound** (401 Harris Ave., 360/733-5252 or 800/231-2222, www.greyhound.com) has nationwide bus connections from the Amtrak depot in Fairhaven.

# Seattle

Seattle is not only the largest city in the Pacific Northwest, but also a delightful place to spend several days—or years—of adventurous sightseeing. Below is a skim-the-surface version of the city.

## SIGHTS

If you only have a day in the city, be sure to take in **Pike Place Market** (85 Pike St., 206/682-7453, www.pikeplacemarket.org) for a wonderful introduction to Seattle at its best. Located downtown at the waterfront end of Stewart Street, it's open daily. The true heart and soul of Seattle, Pike Place is where visitors and locals buy the freshest fish, most colorful flowers, and most squeezable produce in town. Listen to the street musicians, enjoy the parade of humanity, pose with the pig (sculpted by a Whidbey Island artist), and explore a myriad of shops and eateries, but watch out for flying fish.

Other not-to-be-missed downtown sights include the **Seattle Art Museum** (1300 1st St., 206/625-8900, www.seattleartmuseum.org); **Pioneer Square,** with its juxtaposition of fine art galleries, hip nightclubs, and down-in-the-dumps alcoholics; and the **Seattle Aquarium** (Pier 59, 206/386-4300, www.seattleaquarium.org). A short distance north of downtown is **Seattle Center,** where you'll find the city's landmark **Space Needle** (206/443-2111 or 800/937-9582, www.spaceneedle.com), kid-friendly **Pacific Science Center** (206/443-2001 or 866/414-1912, www.pacsci.org), and mesmerizing **Experience Music Project/ Science Fiction Museum** (206/770-2700 or 877/367-7361, www.empmuseum.org)—where everyone gets to be 17 again. The building's curvy metal exterior is certain to elicit "wows" from the kids. Just south of downtown are modern baseball and football stadiums, and farther to the south is the **Museum of Flight** (9404 E. Marginal Way, 206/764-5720, www. museumofflight.org), with a world-class collection of aircraft. For discounts on these and other attractions, buy a **Seattle CityPass** (www.citypass.com/seattle); you can visit up to six attractions for $59 adults, $39 kids. The pass is good for nine days from the first use, and includes all the places described above.

Check out **Lake Union** with its quaint houseboats, sailboats, kayaks, and maritime exhibits. If you're flying to the San Juans on Kenmore Air, you'll probably depart from here. **Recreation Equipment Inc.** (222 Yale Ave. N., 206/223-1944, www.rei.com), known to most folks as REI, is a must-stop for anyone interested in the outdoors, and a great place to get ready for a trip to the San Juans. Its enormous flagship store is located up the hill from Lake Union.

The **University District** (U-District) is home to—you guessed it—the University of Washington and has all the usual student-oriented shops, including a plethora of great ethnic eateries. While here, be sure to visit the **Burke Museum** (206/543-5590, www.washington.edu/burkemuseum) and **Henry Art Gallery** (206/543-2280, www.henryart.org).

Other neighborhoods well worth exploring include **Capitol Hill,** with its fun shops, great food, and strong gay presence; **Fremont,** where funky is always in vogue; and the **International District,** with a wide diversity of Asian shops and restaurants.

## ACCOMMODATIONS

Seattle's lodging choices cover the spectrum from basic hostels all the way up to five-star hotels. The Seattle Convention and Visitors Bureau's **Seattle SuperSaver** (206/461-5882 or 800/535-7071, www.seattlesupersaver.com) is a one-stop place to find a room in your price range. The online lodging guide is categorized by location and price, with direct links to hundreds of local options. For the best deals on a hotel, you may want to try bidding via Priceline.com or a similar website.

Backpacking travelers willing to sleep in a

bunk bed should check out the **Green Tortoise Hostel** (105 Pike St., 206/340-1222, www. greentortoise.net, $28–32/person).

If you have a car, decent and inexpensive options include two U-District places: **The College Inn** (4000 University Way NE, 206/633-4441, www.collegeinnseattle.com, $65–95 d) and **University Inn** (4140 Roosevelt Way NE, 206/632-5055 or 800/733-3855, www.universityinnseattle.com, $149–209 d), along with **Mediterranean Inn** (425 Queen Anne Ave., 206/428-4700, www.mediterranean-inn.com, $169–199 d), close to the Space Needle. For airport lodging that won't break the bank, try **Red Roof Inn Seattle Airport** 16838 International Blvd., 206/248-0901 or 800/733-7663, www.redroof.com, $93–98 d).

Looking for something more upscale? Try a pair of downtown places: **Inn at Queen Anne** (505 First Ave. N, 206/282-7357 or 800/952-5043, www.innatqueenanne.com, $130–140 d) or **Pensione Nichols B&B** (1923 1st Ave., 206/441-7125, www.pensionenichols.com, $130–150 d with breakfast).

At the $300-and-up end of the price spectrum, you won't go wrong at **The Edgewater** (2411 Alaskan Way, 206/728-7000 or 800/624-0670, www.edgewaterhotel.com) or the elegant **Inn at the Market** (86 Pine St., 206/443-3600 or 877/711-8646, www.innatthemarket.com). Find homier lodging choices through the **Seattle B&B Association** (206/547-1020 or 800/348-5630, www.lodginginseattle.com).

## INFORMATION

The **Seattle Convention and Visitors Bureau** (7th Ave. at Pike St., 206/461-5840 or 866/732-2695, www.visitseattle.org) stocks the *Seattle Visitors Guide,* a fat compendium of local entertainment, shopping, and sights. Also check out the CVB's useful lodging and restaurant guides. Sea-Tac Airport has a small information center with the usual blizzard of brochures and freebie papers. It's near the baggage claim area.

Located inside the REI store, the **Outdoor Recreation Information Center** (206/470-4060, www.nps.gov/ccso/oric.htm) has complete details on natural areas around the state, including National Park Service, Washington State Parks, and Department of Natural Resources lands.

Useful websites for Seattle information include the **City of Seattle's** official website (www.seattle.gov), Microsoft's **Citysearch** site (www.seattle.citysearch.com), and those of local newspapers: *Seattle Times* (www.seattletimes.nwsource.com) and *Seattle Weekly* (www.seattleweekly.com).

## GETTING THERE AND AROUND

The San Juan Islands are 65 air miles northeast of Seattle, with a variety of transportation options to get you there.

### Ferries

You will see a constant parade of Washington State Ferries departing from downtown Seattle, but none of these go to the San Juans. Instead, you'll need to get to Anacortes, where state ferries head to the islands. There is, however, a private ferry with daily service to the islands from Seattle, the passenger-only **Victoria Clipper** (206/448-5000 or 800/888-2535, www.clippervacations.com), a family of three large high-speed catamarans with day trips between Seattle and San Juan Island. The round-trip cost is $80 adults, $40 kids if you wait till the last minute, but you can save substantially by booking at least a day ahead: $70 round-trip for adults and free for kids under 12. Combine transportation from Seattle with a 2.5-hour whale-watching trip for $30–40 extra. Cruises operate daily mid-May–early September, and on weekends only the rest of September. The company has a multitude of other travel options in the Northwest, including packages that add a night's lodging on San Juan Island, or a three-day/two-night visit to San Juan Island and Victoria. You can also use this as transportation to the islands from Seattle, going up on one day and returning at a later date. In addition, *Victoria Clipper* has year-round service between Seattle and Victoria for $107–147 round-trip.

© EVA BROWNING/123RF

Seattle city skyline

## Shuttles

Getting to the islands from Seattle is easy. **Airporter Shuttle** (360/380-8800 or 866/235-5247, www.airporter.com, $33 one-way adults, $20 kids) makes connections between Sea-Tac and the ferry terminal at Anacortes, along with Bellingham and points north all the way to Vancouver.

**Island Airporter** (360/378-7438, www.islandairporter.com) provides direct van service daily from Sea-Tac to San Juan Island. The bus departs the airport and heads straight to the Anacortes ferry, where it drives on for San Juan Island, and then continues to Friday Harbor ($50) and Roche Harbor ($60). You'll need to add the ferry fare, but it's approximately half the standard rate since you're on a bus. Vans operate once a day in each direction Monday–Saturday in summer and Monday–Friday in winter.

## By Train and Bus

**Amtrak** trains serve Seattle from the King Street Station (3rd Ave. S. and S. King St., 206/464-1930 or 800/872-7245, www.amtrakcascades.com). The Amtrak *Cascades* train connects Seattle with Vancouver, stopping at Mount Vernon twice daily in each direction. Trains do not stop in Anacortes (where Washington State Ferries depart for the San Juan Islands), and the Mount Vernon station is 18 miles away.

**Greyhound** (206/628-5526 or 800/231-2222, www.greyhound.com) has daily bus service throughout the lower 48 and to Vancouver, British Columbia, from its bus terminal at 9th and Stewart. It's the same story here as for Amtrak; Greyhound's closest stop is the town of Mount Vernon.

## By Car

If you're driving from Seattle, it's 80 miles (92 miles from Sea-Tac) to Anacortes, where you catch the Washington State Ferries to the San Juans. The ride is very straightforward: follow I-5 north to Mount Vernon at Exit 230 and turn west onto Highway 20, which goes straight into Anacortes. The ferry terminal is three miles west of downtown Anacortes via 12th Street. Sea-Tac has all the national **car rental** companies downstairs next to the baggage claim; visit www.travelocity.com to find the lowest rates.

Be sure to fill your tank in Anacortes before driving on the ferry. Because of the extra cost of shipping fuel (and because they can get away with it), gas stations on the islands charge at least 30 percent more than on the mainland.

## By Air

Seattle's airport is 12 miles south of the city and midway between Seattle and Tacoma, hence the name, **Sea-Tac International Airport** (www.portseattle.org/seatac). It's the primary entry point for flights into Washington state, but there are no direct flights from Sea-Tac to the San Juan Islands; you'll need to go to either Lake Union or Boeing Field in Seattle.

The islands are served by **Kenmore Air** (425/486-1257 or 866/435-9524, www.kenmoreair.com)—the world's largest seaplane operation—with flights to San Juan, Orcas, and Lopez Islands from Seattle's Lake Union. Pack light for your trip since a 24-pound baggage weight limit is in effect, and excess baggage costs $1 per pound. A free shuttle provides transport to Lake Union from Sea-Tac. Wheeled-plane flights to San Juan and Orcas Islands depart from Boeing Field (www.kingcounty.gov) on the south end of Seattle; the baggage weight limit on these is 70 pounds. Kenmore also offers flightseeing trips and charters to other destinations in the San Juans—including Cypress, Sucia, Stuart, and Jones Islands.

Charter flights to the San Juans can be cheaper than scheduled flights if you have four or more passengers. Both **San Juan Airlines** (360/293-4691 or 800/874-4434, www.sanjuanairlines.com) and **Island Air** (360/378-2376 or 888/378-2376, www.sanjuan-islandair.com) provide charter flights from Boeing Field.

# Victoria

Many people view the city of Victoria (pop. 335,000), at the southern tip of Vancouver Island, for the first time from the Inner Harbour, coming in by boat the way people have for almost 150 years. Ferries, fishing boats, and seaplanes bob in the Harbour, with a backdrop of manicured lawns and flower gardens, quiet residential suburbs, and striking inner-city architecture. High tea, double-decker bus tours, and exploring formal gardens are some of the true joys in Victoria.

## DOWNTOWN SIGHTS

The epicenter of downtown Victoria is the foreshore of the Inner Harbour, which is flanked by the parliament buildings, the city's main museum, and the landmark Fairmont Empress hotel. Government Street leads uphill from the waterfront through a concentration of touristy shops and restaurants while, parallel to the west, Douglas Street is the core street of a smallish central business district.

### Inner Harbour

Initially, the Harbour extended farther inland; before the construction of the massive stone causeway that now forms the marina, the area on which the impressive Empress now stands was a deep, oozing mudflat. Walk along the lower level and then up the steps in the middle to come face-to-face with an unamused Captain James Cook; the bronze statue commemorates the first recorded British landing, in 1778, on the territory that would later become British Columbia. Above the northeast corner of the Harbour is the **Victoria Visitor Centre** (812 Wharf St., 250/953-2033, www.tourismvictoria.com, 9 A.M.–5 P.M. daily), the perfect place to start your city exploration. Be sure to return to the Inner Harbour after dark, when the parliament buildings are outlined in lights and the Empress Hotel is floodlit.

### Fairmont Empress

Overlooking the Inner Harbour, the

© DON PITCHER

Victoria's famous Inner Harbour

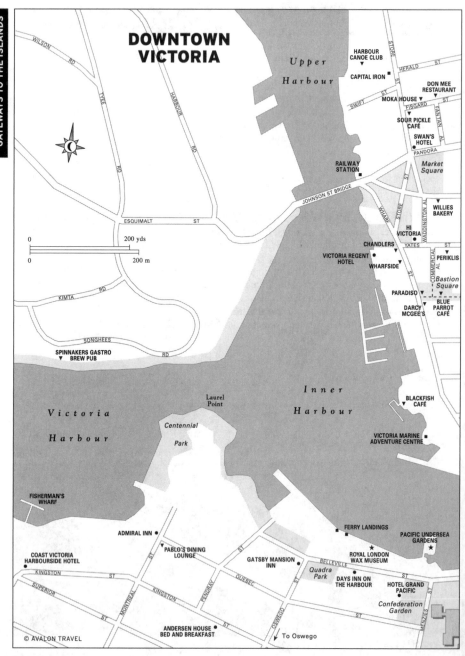

# DOWNTOWN VICTORIA

WILSON RD

TYEE RD

HARBOUR RD

*Upper Harbour*

HARBOUR CANOE CLUB
CAPITAL IRON
STORE ST
HERALD ST
DON MEE RESTAURANT
SWIFT ST
MOKA HOUSE
FISGARD ST
FANTAN AL
SOUR PICKLE CAFÉ
SWAN'S HOTEL
PANDORA ST

*Market Square*

ESQUIMALT ST

RAILWAY STATION

JOHNSON ST BRIDGE

WHARF ST

STORE ST
WADDINGTON AL
WILLIES BAKERY

HI VICTORIA
YATES ST
COMMERCIAL AL
PERIKLIS

0        200 yds
0        200 m

CHANDLERS
VICTORIA REGENT HOTEL
WHARFSIDE
*Bastion Square*
PARADISO
DARCY MCGEE'S
BLUE PARROT CAFÉ

KIMTA RD

SONGHEES RD

SPINNAKERS GASTRO BREW PUB

*Inner Harbour*

BLACKFISH CAFÉ

Laurel Point

*Victoria Harbour*

*Centennial Park*

VICTORIA MARINE ADVENTURE CENTRE

FISHERMAN'S WHARF

ADMIRAL INN
PABLO'S DINING LOUNGE
COAST VICTORIA HARBOURSIDE HOTEL
KINGSTON ST
SUPERIOR ST
MONTREAL ST
KINGSTON ST
PENDRAY ST
GATSBY MANSION INN
QUEBEC ST
*Quadra Park*
BELLEVILLE ST
FERRY LANDINGS
PACIFIC UNDERSEA GARDENS
ROYAL LONDON WAX MUSEUM
DAYS INN ON THE HARBOUR
HOTEL GRAND PACIFIC
*Confederation Garden*
MENZIES ST

ANDERSEN HOUSE BED AND BREAKFAST
OSWEGO ST
↓ To Oswego

© AVALON TRAVEL

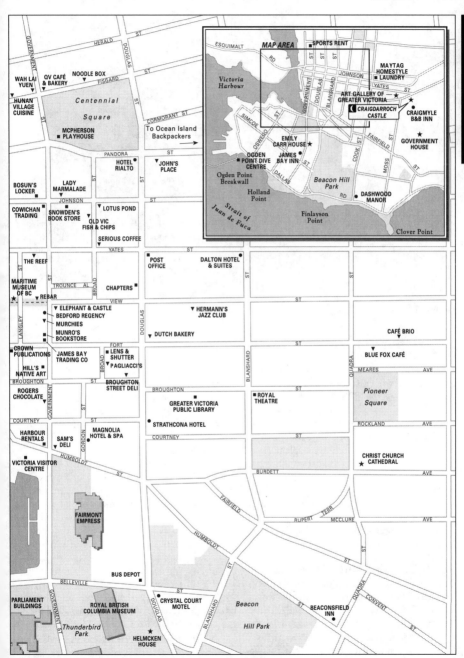

Fairmont Empress hotel

© DON PITCHER

pompous, ivy-covered 1908 Fairmont Empress is Victoria's most recognizable landmark. Its architect was the well-known Francis Rattenbury, who also designed the parliament buildings, the CPR steamship terminal, and Crystal Garden. It's worthwhile walking through the hotel lobby to gaze—head back, mouth agape—at the interior razzle-dazzle, and to watch people-watching people partake in traditional afternoon tea Browse through the conservatory and gift shops, drool over the menus of the various restaurants, see what tours are available, and exchange currency if you're desperate (banks give a better exchange rate). Get a feeling for the hotel's history by joining a tour.

## Royal British Columbia Museum

Canada's most-visited museum and easily one of North America's best, the Royal British Columbia Museum (675 Belleville St., 250/356-7226, 10 A.M.–5 P.M. daily, adult CAN$15, senior and youth CAN$9.50) is a must-see attraction for even the most jaded museum-goer. Its fine Natural History Gallery displays are extraordinarily true to life, complete with appropriate sounds and smells. Come face-to-face with an Ice Age woolly mammoth, stroll through a coastal forest full of deer and tweeting birds, meander along a seashore or tidal marsh, and then descend into the Open Ocean Exhibit via submarine—a very real trip that's not recommended for claustrophobics. The First Peoples Gallery holds a fine collection of artifacts from the island's first human inhabitants, the Nuu-chah-nulth (Nootka). Many of the pieces were collected by Charles Newcombe, who paid the Nuu-chah-nulth for them on collection sorties in the early 1900s. More modern human history is also explored here in creative ways. Take a tour through time via the time capsules; walk along an early-1900s street; and experience hands-on exhibits on industrialization, the gold rush, and the exploration of British Columbia by land and sea in the Modern History and 20th Century Galleries.

## Parliament Buildings

Satisfy your lust for governmental, historical, and architectural knowledge all in one by taking a free tour of the Harbourside Provincial Legislative Buildings, aka the parliament buildings. These prominent buildings were designed by Francis Rattenbury and completed in 1897. The exterior is British Columbia Haddington Island stone, and if you walk around the buildings you'll no doubt spot many a stern or gruesome face staring down from the stonework.

On either side of the main entrance stand statues of Sir James Douglas, who chose the location of Victoria, and Sir Matthew Baillie Begbie, who was in charge of law and order during the gold rush period. Atop the copper-covered dome stands a gilded statue of Captain George Vancouver, the first mariner to circumnavigate Vancouver Island. Walk through the main entrance and into the memorial rotunda, look skyward for a dramatic view of the central dome, and then continue upstairs to peer into the legislative chamber, the home of the democratic government of British Columbia. Free guided tours are offered every 20 minutes, 9 A.M.–noon and 1–5 P.M. in summer, less frequently (Mon.–Fri. only) in winter. Tour times differ according to the goings-on inside; for current times, call the tour office at 250/387-3046.

## Laurel Point

For an enjoyable short walk from downtown, continue along Belleville Street from the parliament buildings, passing a conglomeration of modern hotels, ferry terminals, and some intriguing architecture dating back to the late 19th century. A path leads down through a shady park to Laurel Point, hugging the waterfront and providing good views of the Inner Harbour en route. If you're feeling really energetic, continue to **Fisherman's Wharf,** where an eclectic array of floating homes are tied up to floating wharves.

## OLD TOWN

The oldest section of Victoria lies immediately north of the Inner Harbour between Wharf and Government Streets. Start by walking north from the Inner Harbour along historic Wharf Street, where Hudson's Bay Company furs were loaded onto ships bound for England, gold seekers arrived in search of fortune, and shopkeepers first established businesses. Cross the road to cobblestoned **Bastion Square,** lined with old gas lamps and decorative architecture dating from the 1860s to 1890s. This was the original site chosen by James Douglas in 1843 for Fort Victoria, the Hudson's Bay Company trading post. At one time the square held a courthouse, jail, and gallows. Today, restored buildings house trendy restaurants, cafés, nightclubs, and fashionable offices.

## Maritime Museum of British Columbia

At the top (east) end of Bastion Square, the Maritime Museum of British Columbia (28 Bastion Square, 250/385-4222, 9:30 A.M.–4:30 P.M. daily, until 5 P.M. in summer, adult CAN$12, senior CAN$10, child CAN$5) is housed in the old provincial courthouse building. It traces the history of seafaring exploration, adventure, commercial ventures, and passenger travel through displays of dugout canoes, model ships, Royal Navy charts, figureheads, photographs, naval uniforms, and bells. One room is devoted to exhibits chronicling the circumnavigation of the world, and another holds a theater. The museum also has a nautically oriented gift shop.

## SOUTH OF THE INNER HARBOUR

### Emily Carr House

In 1871 artist Emily Carr was born in this typical upper-class 1864 Victorian-era home (207 Government St., 250/383-5843, 11 A.M.–4 P.M. Tues.–Sat. mid-May–Sept., adult CAN$5.50, senior and student CAN$4.50, child CAN$3.25). Carr moved to the mainland at an early age, escaping the confines of the capital to draw and write about the British Columbian native people and the wilderness in which she lived. She is best remembered today for her painting, a medium she took up in later years.

## Beacon Hill Park

This large, hilly city park—a lush, sea-edged oasis of grass and flowers—extends from the back of the museum along Douglas Street out to cliffs that offer spectacular views of Juan de Fuca Strait and, on a clear day, the distant Olympic Mountains. Add a handful of rocky points to scramble on and many protected pebble-and-sand beaches, and you've found yourself a perfect spot to indulge your senses. Catch a sea breeze and gaze at all the strolling, cycling, dog-walking, and pram-pushing Victorians passing by. On a bright sunny day, you'll swear that most of Victoria is here too. The park is within easy walking distance from downtown and can also be reached by bus 5. For a tidbit of history, walk through the park to rocky Finlayson Point, once the site of an ancient fortified native village. Between 1878 and 1892, two enormous guns protected the point against an expected but unrealized Russian invasion.

## ROCKLAND

This historic part of downtown lies behind the Inner Harbour, east of Douglas Street, and is easily accessible on foot.

### Christ Church Cathedral

On the corner of Quadra and Courtney Streets, Christ Church Cathedral (250/383-2714) is the seat of the Bishop of the Diocese of British Columbia. Built in 1896, in 13th-century Gothic style, it's one of Canada's largest churches. Self-guided tours are possible (8:30 A.M.–5 P.M. Mon.–Fri., 7:30 A.M.–8:30 P.M. Sun., free). In summer, the cathedral sponsors free choral recitals each Saturday at 4 P.M. The park next to the cathedral is a shady haven to rest weary feet, and the gravestones make fascinating reading.

### Art Gallery of Greater Victoria

From Christ Church Cathedral, walk up Rockland Avenue for four blocks through the historic Rockland district, passing stately mansions and colorful gardens on tree-lined streets. Turn left on Moss Street and you'll come to the 1889 Spencer Mansion and its modern wing, which together make up the Art Gallery of Greater Victoria (1040 Moss St., 250/384-4101, 10 A.M.–5 P.M. daily, Thurs. until 9 P.M., adult CAN$13, senior CAN$11, child CAN$2.50). The gallery contains Canada's finest collection of Japanese art, a range of contemporary art, an Emily Carr gallery, and traveling exhibits, as well as a Japanese garden with a Shinto shrine. The Gallery Shop sells art books, reproductions, and handcrafted jewelry, pottery, and glass.

## Government House

Continue up Rockland Avenue from the art gallery to reach Government House (1401 Rockland Ave., 250/387-2080, www.ltgov.bc.ca/default.htm, grounds open dawn–dusk daily, free), the official residence of the lieutenant governor, the queen's representative in British Columbia. The surrounding gardens, including an English-style garden, rose garden, and rhododendron garden, along with green velvet lawns and picture-perfect flower beds, are open to the public throughout the year. On the front side of the property, vegetation has been left in a more natural state, with gravel paths leading to benches that invite pausing to take in the city panorama.

## ◖ Craigdarroch Castle

A short walk up (east) from the art gallery along Rockland Avenue and left on Joan Crescent brings you to the baronial four-story mansion known as Craigdarroch Castle (1050 Joan Crescent, 250/592-5323, 9 A.M.–7 P.M. daily in summer and 10 A.M.–4:30 P.M. the rest of the year, adult CAN$13.75, senior CAN$12.75, child CAN$5). From downtown, take bus 11 (Uplands) or 14 (University) to Joan Crescent, then walk 100 meters (110 yards) up the hill. The architectural masterpiece was built in 1890 for Robert Dunsmuir, a wealthy industrialist and politician who died just before the building was completed.

For all the nitty-gritties, tour the mansion with volunteer guides who really know their Dunsmuir, and then admire at your leisure all the polished wood, stained-glass windows, Victorian-era furnishings, and the great city views from upstairs.

## SCENIC ROUTE TO OAK BAY

This route starts south of the Inner Harbour and follows the coastline all the way to the University of Victoria. If you have your own transportation, this is a "must-do" in Victoria; if you don't, most city tours take in the sights along the route. You can take Douglas Street south alongside Beacon Hill Park to access the coast, but it's possible to continue east along the Inner Harbour to the mouth of Victoria Harbour proper, passing the Canadian Coast Guard Base and the **Ogden Point Breakwall,** the official start of the Scenic Marine Drive (marked by blue signs). The breakwall is only three meters (10 feet) wide, but it extends for 800 meters (0.5 mile) into the bay. It's a super-popular stroll, especially in the early morning.

For the first few kilometers beyond the breakwall, the Olympic Mountains in Washington state are clearly visible across the Strait of Georgia, and many lookouts allow you to stop and take in the panorama, including **Clover Point.** A few hundred meters beyond Clover Point, **Ross Bay Cemetery** is the final resting place of many of early Victoria's most prominent residents. Volunteer hosts are on hand throughout the summer to point out the graves of Emily Carr; British Columbia's first governor, Sir James Douglas; members of the coal-baron Dunsmuir family; and Billy Barker, of gold rush fame. The gates are open weekdays during daylight hours.

Continuing east, Dallas Road takes you through quiet residential areas, past small pebble beaches covered in driftwood, and into the ritzy mansion district east of downtown, where the residents have grand houses, manicured gardens, and stunning water views.

Continue through the well-manicured fairways of Victoria Golf Club on Gonzales Point to Cadboro Bay, home to the **Royal Victoria Yacht Club.** The **University of Victoria** lies

© DON PITCHER

a beach along the scenic route to Oak Bay

on a ridge above Cadboro Bay; from here head southwest along Cadboro Bay Road and then Yates Street to get back downtown, or to go north take Sinclair Road and then Mackenzie Avenue to reach Highway 17, the main route north up the Saanich Peninsula toward famous Butchart Gardens.

## WEST OF DOWNTOWN
### Goldstream Provincial Park

Lying 20 kilometers (12.4 miles) from the heart of Victoria, this 390-hectare (960-acre) park straddles Highway 1 northwest of downtown. The park's main natural feature is the Goldstream River, which flows north into the Finlayson Arm of Saanich Inlet. Forests of ancient Douglas fir and western red cedar flank the river; orchids flourish in forested glades; and at higher elevations forests of lodgepole pine, western hemlock, and maple thrive.

The park's highlight event occurs late October–December, when chum, coho, and chinook salmon fight their way upriver to spawn themselves out on the same shallow gravel bars where they were born four years previously. Bald eagles begin arriving in December, feeding off the spawned-out salmon until February. From the picnic area parking lot, two kilometers (1.2 miles) north of the campground turnoff, a trail leads 400 meters (440 yards) along the Goldstream River to **Freeman King Visitor Centre** (250/478-9414, 9 A.M.–5 P.M. daily), where the life cycle of salmon is described.

Even if the salmon aren't spawning, Goldstream is a great place to visit at any time of year, with hikes suitable to all fitness levels. Starting from the visitors center, the 200-meter (220-yard) **Marsh Trail** will reward you with panoramic water views from the mouth of the Goldstream River. Another popular destination is **Goldstream Falls**, at the south end of the park. This trail leaves from the back of the park campground and descends to the picturesque falls in around 300 meters (330 yards). Non-campers should park at the campground entrance, from where it's 1.2 kilometers (0.7 mile) to the falls. One of the park's longer hikes

Goldstream Falls is a natural highlight in Goldstream Provincial Park.

© DON PITCHER

is the **Goldmine Trail,** which begins from a parking lot on the west side of Highway 1 halfway between the campground and picnic area. This trail winds two kilometers (1.2 miles) each way through a mixed forest of lodgepole pine, maple, and western hemlock, passing the site of a short-lived gold rush and coming to **Niagara Falls,** a poor relation of its eastern namesake but still a picturesque flow of water. Of a similar length, but more strenuous, is the trail to the summit of 419-meter (1,374-foot) **Mount Finlayson,** which takes around one hour each way and rewards successful summiteers with views back across the city and north along Saanich Inlet. The trail is accessed from Finlayson Arm Road.

Park admission is CAN$1 per vehicle per hour to a maximum of CAN$3 for a day pass.

## SAANICH PENINSULA

The Saanich Peninsula is the finger of land that extends north from downtown. It holds Victoria's most famous attraction, Butchart Gardens, as well as Victoria International

Airport and the main arrival point for ferries from Tsawwassen. If you've caught the ferry over to Vancouver Island from Tsawwassen, you'll have arrived at **Swartz Bay,** on the northern tip of the Saanich Peninsula; from here it's a clear run down Highway 17 to downtown Victoria. If you've been in Goldstream Provincial Park or are traveling down the island from Nanaimo on Highway 1, head north and south, respectively, to **Mill Bay,** where a ferry departs regularly for **Brentwood Bay** on the Saanich Peninsula. (Brentwood Bay is home to Butchart Gardens.) Ferries run in both directions nine times daily 7:30 A.M.–6 P.M. Peak one-way fares for the 25-minute crossing are adult CAN$6.35, child CAN$3.20, vehicle CAN$14.80. For exact times, contact **BC Ferries** (250/386-3431, www.bcferries.com).

## ❰ Butchart Gardens

Carved from an abandoned quarry, these delightful gardens are Victoria's best-known attraction. They're approximately 20 kilometers (12.4 miles) north of downtown (800 Benvenuto Dr., Brentwood Bay, 250/652-4422, www.butchartgardens.com). The gardens are open every day of the year from 9 A.M., closing in summer at 10 P.M. and in winter at 4 P.M., with varying closing hours in other seasons. Admission in summer is adult CAN$28, youth 13–17 CAN$14, children 5–12 CAN$3; admission in winter is around 60 percent of those rates.

A Canadian cement pioneer, R. P. Butchart, built a mansion near his quarries. He and his wife, Jennie, traveled extensively, collecting rare and exotic shrubs, trees, and plants from around the world. By 1904, the quarries had been abandoned, and the couple began to beautify them by transplanting their collection into formal gardens interspersed with concrete footpaths, small bridges, waterfalls, ponds, and fountains. The gardens now contain more than 5,000 varieties of flowers, and the extensive nurseries test-grow some 35,000 new bulbs and more than 100 new roses every year. Go there in spring, summer, or early autumn to treat your eyes and nose to a marvelous sensual experience (many a gardener would give both

© DON PITCHER

Butchart Gardens

hands to be able to work in these gardens). Highlights include the Sunken Garden (the original quarry site) with its water features and annuals; the formal Rose Garden, set around a central lawn; and the Japanese Garden, from where views extend to Saanich Inlet. In winter, when little is blooming and the entire landscape is green, the basic design of the gardens can best be appreciated. Summer visitors are in for a special treat on Saturday nights (July and August only), when a spectacular fireworks display lights up the garden.

As you may imagine, the attraction is super busy throughout spring and summer. For this reason, try and arrive as early as possible, before the tour buses arrive. Once through the tollgate and in the sprawling parking lot, make a note of where you park your vehicle. Once on the grounds, pick up a flower guide and follow the suggested route. After you've done the rounds (allow at least two hours), you can choose from a variety of eateries. You'll also find a gift shop specializing in—you guessed it—floral items, as well as a store selling seeds.

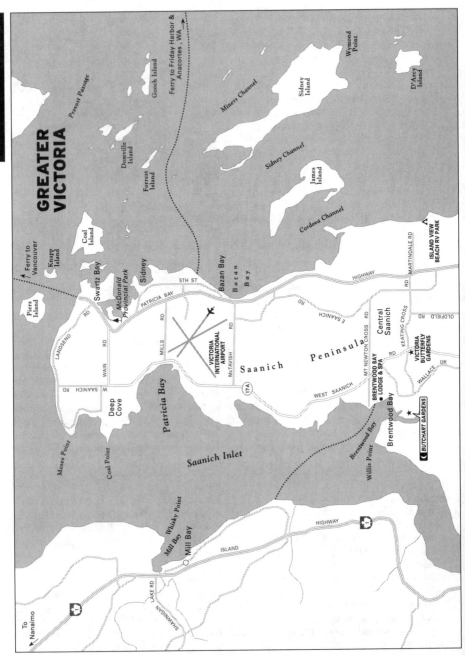

GREATER VICTORIA

Ferry to Friday Harbor & Anacortes, WA

Wymond Point

D'Arcy Island

Gooch Island

Miners Channel

Sidney Island

Prevost Passage

Donville Island

Sidney Channel

Forrest Island

James Island

Cordova Channel

Ferry to Vancouver

Coal Island

Knapp Island

Swartz Bay

McDonald Provincial Park

Sidney

5TH ST

Bazan Bay

Bazan Bay

HIGHWAY

MARTINDALE RD

ISLAND VIEW BEACH RV PARK

Piers Island

PATRICIA BAY

RD

VICTORIA INTERNATIONAL AIRPORT

17A

Saanich

Peninsula

E SAANICH RD

Central Saanich

KEATING CROSS RD

OLDFIELD RD

LANDS END RD

WAIN RD

MILLS RD

McTAVISH

WEST SAANICH RD

MT NEWTON CROSS RD

BRENTWOOD BAY LODGE & SPA

VICTORIA BUTTERFLY GARDENS

WALLACE DR

W SAANICH RD

Moses Point

Deep Cove

Patricia Bay

Brentwood Bay

Brentwood Bay

BUTCHART GARDENS

Coal Point

Saanich Inlet

Willis Point

Whisky Point

Mill Bay

Mill Bay

ISLAND

HIGHWAY

LAKE RD

SHAWNIGAN

To Nanaimo

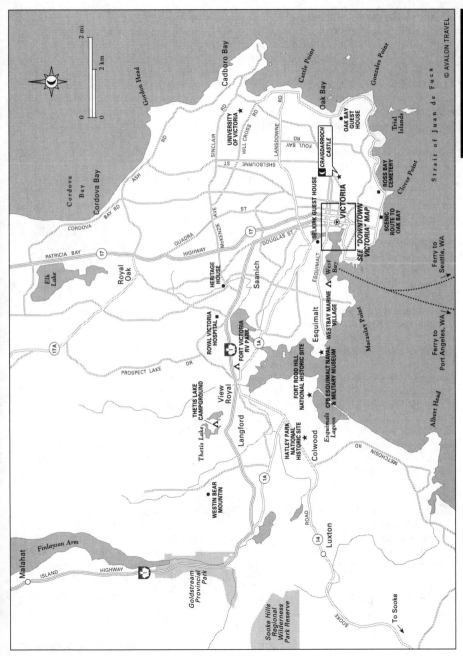

© AVALON TRAVEL

### Victoria Butterfly Gardens

In the same vicinity as Butchart Gardens, Victoria Butterfly Gardens (1461 Benvenuto Dr., 250/652-3822, 9 A.M.–5:30 P.M. daily mid-May–Sept., 9:30 A.M.–4:30 P.M. daily Mar.–mid-May and Oct., adult CAN$12.50, senior CAN$11.50, child CAN$6.50) offers you the opportunity to view and photograph some of the world's most spectacular butterflies at close range. Thousands of these beautiful creatures—species from around the world—live here, flying freely around the enclosed gardens and feeding on the nectar provided by colorful tropical plants. You'll also be able to get up close and personal with exotic birds such as parrots and cockatoos.

### Sidney

The bustling seaside town of Sidney lies on the east side of the Saanich Peninsula, overlooking the Strait of Georgia. As well as being the departure point for ferries to the San Juan Islands, Sidney has a charming waterfront precinct anchored by the impressive Sidney Pier Hotel & Spa. It's a pleasant spot to explore on foot—enjoying the many outdoor cafés, walking out onto the pier, and soaking up the nautical ambience. Beside the hotel, at the **Shaw Ocean Discovery Centre** (9811 Seaport Place, 250/665-7511, 10 A.M.–5 P.M. daily, adult CAN$12, child CAN$6), the underwater world of the Strait of Georgia unravels itself through aquariums, interpretive panels, and a marine education center. From the nearby marina, **Eco Cruising** (250/655-5211, June–Sept.) runs two different tours daily—one around the Harbour and the other to Piers Island (both adult CAN$43, senior CAN$33, child CAN$23). Back along the main street, **Sidney Museum** (2423 Beacon Ave., 250/655-6355, 10 A.M.–4 P.M. daily, donation) provides an interesting insight into the peninsula's earliest settlers.

## ENTERTAINMENT AND EVENTS

Victoria has a vibrant performing arts community, with unique events designed especially for the summer crowds. The city lacks the wild nightlife scene of neighboring Vancouver, but a large influx of summer workers keeps the bars crowded and a few nightclubs jumping during the busy season. The city does have more than its fair share of British-style pubs, and you can usually get a good meal along with a pint of lager. The magazine *Monday* (www.mondaymag.com) offers a comprehensive arts and entertainment section.

### Bars

The **Strathcona Hotel** (919 Douglas St., 250/383-7137) is Victoria's largest entertainment venue, featuring four bars, including one with a magnificent rooftop patio (with a volleyball court) and the Sticky Wicket, an English bar complete with mahogany paneling.

Closer to the Inner Harbour and converted from an old grain warehouse is **Swans Hotel** (506 Pandora St., 250/361-3310, daily from 11 A.M.), which brews its own beer. Unlike many other smaller brewing operations, this one uses traditional ingredients and methods, such as allowing the brew to settle naturally rather than be filtered. The beer is available at the hotel's bar, in its restaurants, and in the attached liquor store.

A few blocks farther north and right on the water is the **Harbour Canoe Club** (450 Swift St., 250/361-1940), housed in an 1894 redbrick building that was at one time home to generators that powered Victoria's streetlights. This place is popular with the downtown crowd and has a great deck.

Also offering magnificent water views is **Spinnakers Gastro Brewpub,** across the Inner Harbour from downtown (308 Catherine St., 250/386-2739, 11 A.M.–2 A.M. daily). Having opened in 1984 as Canada's first brewpub, Spinnakers continues to produce its own European-style ales, including the popular Spinnakers Ale. The original downstairs brewpub is now a restaurant, while upstairs is now the bar. Most important, both levels have outdoor tables with water views.

Victoria's many English-style pubs usually feature a wide variety of beers, congenial atmosphere, and inexpensive meals. The closest of these to downtown is the **James Bay Inn** (270 Government St., 250/384-7151). Farther out, **Six Mile Pub** (494 Island Hwy., 250/478-3121) is a classic Tudor-style English pub that was established in 1885, making it the province's oldest pub.

## Nightclubs

Most of Victoria's nightclubs double as live music venues attracting a great variety of acts. **Legends,** in the Strathcona Hotel (919 Douglas St., 250/383-7137), has been a city hot spot for more than 30 years. It comes alive with live rock-and-roll some nights and a DJ spinning the latest dance tunes on other nights. In the same hotel, **Big Bad John's** is the city's main country music venue. At the bottom of Bastion Square, **Darcy's Pub** (1127 Wharf St., 250/380-1322) is a great place for lunch or an afternoon drink, while after dark, it dishes up live rock to a working-class crowd. A popular nightclub is **Plan B** (1318 Broad St., 250/384-3557), a small dance club venue with attitude.

Victoria boasts several good jazz venues. The best of these is **Hermann's Jazz Club** (753 View St., 250/388-9166, Wed.–Sat.). **Steamers** (570 Yates St., 250/381-4340) draws diverse acts but generally features jazz and blues on Tuesday and Wednesday nights. Check the Victoria Jazz Society website (www.jazzvictoria.ca) for a schedule of local jazz performances.

## Festivals and Events

The birthday of Queen Victoria has been celebrated in Canada since 1834 and is especially relevant to those who call her namesake city home. The Inner Harbour is alive with weekend festivities that culminate in the **Victoria Day Parade.** (Although Queen Victoria's actual birthday was May 24, the event is celebrated with a public holiday on the Monday preceding May 25.)

Hosted by the Royal Victoria Yacht Club and with more than 60 years of history behind it, **Swiftsure International Yacht Race**

(250/592-9098, www.swiftsure.org, last weekend of May) attracts thousands of spectators to the shoreline of the Inner Harbour to watch a wide variety of vessels cross the finish line in six different classes, including the popular pre-1970 Classics division.

At **Symphony Splash** (250/385-9771, www.victoriasymphony.ca, first Sun. in Aug.), the local symphony orchestra performs from a barge moored in the Inner Harbour to masses crowded around the shore. This unique musical event attracts upwards of 40,000 spectators who line the shore or watch and listen from kayaks.

The water comes alive during the **Victoria Dragon Boat Festival** (250/704-2500, www.victoriadragonboat.com, middle weekend of Aug.), with 90 dragon boat teams competing along a short course stretching across the Inner Harbour. Onshore entertainment includes the Forbidden City Food Court, classic music performances, First Nations dancing, and lots of children's events.

The **Victoria Fringe Theatre Festival** (250/383-2663, www.victoriafringe.com, last week of Aug.) is a celebration of alternative theater, with more than 350 acts performing at six venues throughout the city, including outside along the Harbour foreshore and inside at the Conservatory of Music on Pandora Street. All tickets are around CAN$10–15.

## SHOPPING

Victoria is a shopper's delight. Most shops and all major department stores are generally open Mon.–Sat. 9:30 A.M.–5:30 P.M. and stay open for late-night shopping Thursday and Friday nights until 9 P.M. The touristy shops around the Inner Harbour and along Government Street are all open on Sundays. Government Street is the main strip of tourist and gift shops. The bottom end, behind the Empress Hotel, is where you'll pick up all those tacky T-shirts and such. Farther up the street are more stylish shops, such as **James Bay Trading Co.** (1102 Government St., 250/388-5477), which specializes in native arts from coastal communities; **Hill's Native Art** (1008 Government St.,

250/385-3911), selling a wide range of authentic native souvenirs; and **Cowichan Trading** (1328 Government St., 250/383-0321), featuring Cowichan sweaters. Traditions continue at **Rogers Chocolates** (913 Government St., 250/881-8771), which is set up like a candy store of the early 1900s, when Charles Rogers first began selling his homemade chocolates to the local kids.

## Old Town
In Old Town, the colorful, two-story **Market Square** courtyard complex was once the haunt of sailors, sealers, and whalers, who came ashore looking for booze and brothels. It's been jazzed up, and today shops here specialize in everything from kayaks to condoms. Walk out of Market Square on Johnson Street to find camping supply stores and the interesting **Bosun's Locker** (580 Johnson St., 250/386-1308), filled to the brim with nautical knickknacks. Follow Store Street north from Market Square to find a concentration of arts-and-crafts shops along Herald Street. In the vicinity, **Capital Iron** is the real thing. Housed in a building that dates to 1863, this business began in the 1930s by offering the public goods salvaged from ships. In the 80-odd years since, it's evolved into a department store stocking an eclectic variety of hardware and homeware products.

## Bookstores
Don't be put off by the touristy location of **Munro's Books** (1108 Government St., 250/382-2464 or 888/243-2464), in a magnificent neoclassical building that originally opened as the Royal Bank in 1909. It holds a comprehensive collection of fiction and nonfiction titles related to Victoria, the island, and Canada in general.

Munro's may be the grandest bookstore in town, but it's not the largest. That distinction goes to **Chapters** (1212 Douglas St., 250/380-9009, 8 A.M.–11 P.M. Mon.–Sat., 9 A.M.–11 P.M. Sun.). **Crown Publications** (106 Ontario St., 250/386-4636, www.crownpub.bc.ca) is a specialty bookstore with a great selection of western Canadiana and maps. In seaside Oak Bay, **Ivy's Bookshop** (2188 Oak Bay Ave., 250/598-2713) is a friendly little spot with a wide-ranging selection from local literature to current best sellers.

## SPORTS AND RECREATION
### Walking and Biking
All of Vancouver Island is a recreational paradise, but Victorians find plenty to do around their own city. Walking and biking are especially popular, and from the Inner Harbour, it's possible to travel on foot or by pedal power all the way along the waterfront to Oak Bay.

If you're feeling energetic—or even if you're not—plan on walking or biking at least a small section of the Scenic Marine Drive, which follows the shoreline of Juan de Fuca Strait from Ogden Point all the way to Oak Bay. The section immediately south of downtown, between Holland Point Park and Ross Bay Cemetery, is extremely popular with early-rising locals, who start streaming onto the pedestrian pathway before the sun rises. Out of town, **Goldstream Provincial Park,** beside Highway 1, and **East Sooke Regional Park,** off Highway 14 west of downtown, offer the best hiking opportunities.

The **Galloping Goose Regional Trail** follows a rail line that once linked Victoria and Sooke. For 55 kilometers (34 miles) it parallels residential back streets, follows waterways, and passes through forested parkland. The rail bed has been graded the entire way, making it suitable for both walkers and cyclists. The official starting point is the defunct railway station at the top end of downtown where Wharf and Johnson Streets merge, and from the end of the trail in Sooke, bus 1 will bring you back to the city. Obviously you can't walk the entire trail in a day, but even traversing a couple of short sections during your stay is worthwhile for the variety of landscapes en route.

For those keen on getting around by bike, it doesn't get much better than the bike path following the coastline of the peninsula on which Victoria lies. From downtown, ride down Government Street to Dallas Road, where you'll pick up the separate bike path running east along the coast to the charming seaside suburb of Oak Bay. From there, Oak Bay Road will take you back into the heart of the city for a round-trip of 20 kilometers (12.4 miles). You can rent bikes at **Sports Rent,** just north of downtown (1950 Government St., 250/385-7368), starting at CAN$16–24 for two hours, CAN$29–39 per day.

## Whale-Watching

Heading out from Victoria in search of whales is something that can be enjoyed by everyone. Both resident and transient whales are sighted during the local whale-watching season (mid-April–October), along with sea lions, porpoises, and seals. Trips last 2–3 hours, are generally made in sturdy inflatable boats with an onboard naturalist, and cost CAN$75–100 per person. Recommended operators departing from the Inner Harbour include **Cuda Marine Adventures** (250/383-8411 or 888/672-6722), **Great Pacific Adventures** (250/386-2277 or 877/733-6722), **Orca Spirit Adventures** (250/383-8411 or 888/672-6722), and **Prince of Whales** (250/383-4884 or 888/383-4884). **Sea Quest Adventures** (250/656-7599 or 888/656-7599) is based in Sidney, on the Saanich Peninsula, and offers three-hour whale-watching cruises on the Strait of Georgia for CAN$95 per person. The waters here are calmer than those experienced on trips departing the Inner Harbour. This company also has kayak tours and rentals.

## Kayaking

Daily through summer, **Ocean River Sports** (1824 Store St., 250/381-4233 or 800/909-4233, www.oceanriver.com) organizes guided three-hour paddles in the Inner Harbour (CAN$60 pp). They also offer kayaking courses, sell and rent kayaks and other equipment, and offer overnight tours as far away as the Queen Charlotte Islands.

## Swimming and Sunbathing

The best beaches are east of downtown. At **Willows Beach,** in Oak Bay, most of the summer crowds spend the day sunbathing, although a few hardy individuals brave a swim; the water temperature here tops out at around 17°C (63°F). Closer to downtown, at the foot of Douglas Street, the foreshore is mostly rocky, but you can find a couple of short, sandy stretches here and there. **Elk Lake,** toward the Saanich Peninsula, and **Thetis Lake,** west of downtown along Highway 1, are also popular swimming and sunbathing spots. Within walking distance of downtown, **Crystal Pool** (2275 Quadra St., 250/361-0732) has an Olympic-size pool as well as diving facilities, a kids' pool, sauna, and whirlpool.

## ACCOMMODATIONS

Victoria accommodations come in all shapes and sizes. A couple of downtown hostels cater to travelers on a budget, and there are also a surprising number of convenient roadside motels with rooms for under CAN$100, including one right off the Inner Harbour. Bed-and-breakfasts, however, are where Victoria really shines, with more than 300 at last count. You'll be able to find bed-and-breakfast rooms for under CAN$100, but to fully immerse yourself in the historical charm of the city, expect to pay more. In the same price range are boutique hotels such as the Bedford Regency—older hotels that have been restored and come with top-notch amenities and full service. Most of the upscale hotel chains are not represented downtown—the city has no Four Seasons, Hilton, Hotel Inter-Continental, Hyatt, Marriott, Radisson, or Regent.

In the off-season (Oct.–May), the nightly rates quoted here are discounted up to 50 percent, but occupancy rates are high as Canadians flock to the country's winter hot spot. No matter what time of year you plan to visit, arriving in Victoria without a reservation is unwise, but it's especially so in the summer months, when gaggles of tourists compete for a relative paucity of rooms. As a last resort, staff at the **Victoria Visitor Centre** (Wharf St., 250/953-2022 or 800/663-3883, www.victoriatourism.com, 9 A.M.–5 P.M. daily) can offer help finding a room.

## Downtown

All but a couple of the accommodations within this section are within easy walking distance of the Inner Harbour. If you're traveling to Victoria outside of summer, don't be put off by the quoted rates because the downtown hotels offer the biggest off-season discounts.

If you're simply looking for a motel room and don't want to pay for the location, check the British Columbia *Accommodations* guide for options along the routes leading into downtown from the north. Locally owned **Traveller's Inn** (www.travellersinn.com) has several motels offering rooms for under CAN$100, while along Gorge Road (Hwy. 1A), you'll find a Days Inn and a Howard Johnson.

### UNDER CAN$100

Budget travelers are well catered to in Victoria, and while the accommodation choices in the capital are more varied than in Vancouver, there is no one backpacker lodge that stands out above the rest.

In the heart of downtown Victoria's oldest section is **HI-Victoria** (516 Yates St., 250/385-4511 or 888/883-0099, www.hihostels.ca). The totally renovated 108-bed hostel enjoys a great location only a stone's throw from the Harbour. Separate dorms and bathroom facilities for men and women are complemented by two fully equipped kitchens, a large meeting room, lounge, library, game room, travel services, public Internet terminals, and an informative bulletin board. Members of Hostelling International pay CAN$35 per night, nonmembers CAN$38.50; a limited number of private rooms range CAN$88–105 s or d.

Housed in the upper stories of an old commercial building, **Ocean Island Backpackers Inn** (791 Pandora Ave., 250/385-1788 or 888/888-4180, www.oceanisland.com) lies just a couple of blocks from downtown. This a party place—exactly what some young travelers are looking for. On the plus side, the lodging is clean, modern, and welcoming throughout. Guests have use of kitchen facilities, a laundry room, and a computer for Internet access. There's also plenty of space to relax, such as a reading room, music room (guitars supplied), television room, and street-level bar open until midnight. Dorm beds are CAN$28 per person while private rooms range from CAN$34 for a super-small single to CAN$117 for an ensuite that sleeps a family of four.

### CAN$100-200

Dating to 1911 and once home to artist Emily Carr, **James Bay Inn** (270 Government St., 250/384-7151 or 800/836-2649, www.james-bayinn.com, CAN$139–189 s or d) is five blocks from the Harbour and within easy walking distance of all city sights and Beacon Hill Park. From the outside, the hotel has a clunky, uninspiring look, but a bright and breezy decor and new beds in the simply furnished rooms make it a pleasant place to rest your head.

East of downtown in the suburb of Oak Bay, the Tudor-style **Oak Bay Guest House,** one block from the waterfront (1052 Newport Ave., 250/598-3812 or 800/575-3812, www.oakbayguesthouse.com, CAN$107–189 s or d), has been taking in guests since 1922. It offers 11 smallish antiques-filled rooms, each with a private balcony and a bathroom. The Sun Lounge holds a small library and tea- and coffee-making facilities, while the Foyer Lounge features plush chairs set around an open fireplace. Rates include a delicious four-course breakfast.

**Traveller's Inn** (www.travellersinn.com) is a local chain of 11 properties strung out along the main highways into downtown. The company advertises *everywhere* with an eye-catching CAN$40 room rate. That's what you'll pay for a single room in the middle of winter, midweek, and with a CAN$10 discount coupon (from the Traveller's Inn website or brochure). Rates at other times of year are competitive and a good value, but still a little less enticing than at first impression. The two best choices are **Traveller's Inn Downtown** (1850 Douglas St., 250/381-1000 or 888/254-6476) and **Traveller's Inn-City Center** (1961 Douglas St., 250/953-1000 or 888/877-9444). Rates at both are CAN$109.95 s, CAN$120 d in July and August, discounted at other times of the year and throughout the week outside of summer. These rates include a light breakfast.

If you're looking for a modern feel, centrally located [C] **Swans Suite Hotel** (506 Pandora Ave., 250/361-3310 or 800/668-7926, www.swanshotel.com, CAN$199–359 s or d) is an excellent choice. Located above a restaurant/pub complex that was built in the 1880s as a grain storehouse, each of the 30 split-level suites holds a loft, full kitchen, dining area, and bedroom. The furnishings are casual yet elegantly rustic, with West Coast artwork adorning the walls and fresh flowers in every room.

Around the southern end of the Inner Harbour, the **Admiral Inn** (257 Belleville St., 250/388-6267 or 888/823-6472, www.admiral.bc.ca, CAN$159–229 s or d) is an excellent place to stay away from the downtown crowd but still within walking distance of the main attractions and best restaurants. Spacious rooms come with a balcony or patio, while extras include free parking, a light breakfast, kitchens in many rooms, and discount coupons for local attractions. Throw in friendly owner-operators, and you have a good value.

Separated from downtown by Beacon Hill Park, **Dashwood Manor** (1 Cook St., 250/385-5517 or 800/667-5517, www.dashwoodmanor.com, CAN$189–289 s or d), a 1912 Tudor-style heritage house on a bluff overlooking Juan de Fuca Strait, enjoys a panoramic view of the entire Olympic mountain range. The 11 guest rooms are elegantly furnished, and hosts Dave and Sharon Layzell will happily recount the historical details of each room. The Oxford Grand room (CAN$269) holds a chandelier, stone fireplace, and antiques.

Just four blocks from the Inner Harbour, the 1905 [C] **Beaconsfield Inn** (988 Humboldt St., 250/384-4044 or 888/884-4044, www.beaconsfieldinn.com, CAN$169–299 s or d) is exactly what you may imagine a Victorian bed-and-breakfast should be. Original mahogany floors, high ceilings, classical moldings, imported antiques, and fresh flowers from the garden create an upscale historical charm throughout. Each of the nine guest rooms is individually decorated in a style matching the Edwardian era. The Emily Carr Suite, named for the renowned artist who spent her early years in the city, has a rich burgundy and green color scheme, Emily Carr prints on the walls, a regal mahogany bed topped by a goose-down comforter, an oversized bathroom and double-jetted tub, and a separate sitting area with a fireplace. After checking in, you'll be invited to join other guests for high tea in the library and then encouraged to return for a glass of sherry before heading out for dinner. As you might expect, breakfast—served in a formal dining room or more casual conservatory—is a grand affair, with multiple courses of hearty fare delivered to your table by your impeccably presented host.

### OVER CAN$200

Very different from Victoria's traditional accommodations is the contemporary **Parkside Victoria** (810 Humboldt St., 250/716-2651 or 866/941-4175, www.parksidevictoria.com, CAN$249–399 s or d). Within walking distance of the Inner Harbour, the guest rooms have a contemporary ambience, and each has one or two bedrooms, a full kitchen with stainless steel appliances, and large wall-mounted TVs. Rooms on the upper floors have city views. Other highlights include a fitness room, indoor pool, theater, and underground parking.

Sitting on a point of land jutting into the Inner Harbour, the **Laurel Point Inn** (680 Montreal St., 250/386-8721 or 800/663-7667, www.laurelpoint.com, from CAN$249 s or d) offers a distinct resort atmosphere within walking distance of downtown. Two wings hold around 200 rooms; each has a water view and private balcony, but well worth the extra money are the Terrace Suites. Amenities include an indoor pool, beautifully landscaped Japanese-style gardens, a sauna, a small fitness facility, two restaurants, a lounge, and a gift shop.

The [C] **Magnolia Hotel & Spa** (623 Courtney St., 250/381-0999 or 877/624-6654, www.magnoliahotel.com, from CAN$269 s or d) is a European-style boutique hotel just up the hill from the Harbour. It features an elegant interior with mahogany-paneled walls, Persian rugs, chandeliers, a gold-leafed ceiling, and fresh flowers throughout the public areas. The rooms are elegantly furnished and feature floor-to-ceiling windows, heritage-style furniture in a contemporary room layout, richly colored fabrics, down duvets, and coffee-making facilities. Many also feature a gas fireplace. The bathrooms are huge, with marble trim, a soaker tub, and separate shower stall. The hotel is also home to the Magnolia Spa and a stylish steakhouse. Rates include a light breakfast, daily newspaper, passes to a nearby fitness facility, and, unlike at most other downtown hotels, free parking.

The grand old **Fairmont Empress** (721 Government St., 250/384-8111 or 800/257-7544, www.fairmont.com, from CAN$359 s or d) is Victoria's best-loved accommodation. Covered in ivy and with only magnificent gardens separating it from the Inner Harbour, it's also in the city's best location. Designed by Francis Rattenbury in 1908, the Empress is one of the original Canadian Pacific Railway hotels. Rooms are offered in 90 different configurations, but as in other hotels of the era, most are small. Each is filled with Victorian period furnishings and antiques. The least expensive Fairmont Rooms start at CAN$359, but if you really want to stay in this Canadian landmark, consider upgrading to a Fairmont Gold room. Although not necessarily larger, these rooms have views, a private check-in, nightly turndown service, and a private lounge where hors d'oeuvres are served in the evening; CAN$469–529 includes a light breakfast. If you can't afford to stay at the Empress, plan on at least visiting one of the restaurants or the regal Bengal Lounge.

## Saanich Peninsula

With the exception of the sparkling new Brentwood Bay Lodge & Spa, these accommodations are along Highway 17, the main route between downtown Victoria and the BC Ferries terminal at Swartz Bay. These properties are best suited to travelers arriving at or departing from the airport or ferry terminal, but are also handy to Butchart Gardens.

Right beside the highway, **Western 66 Motel** (2401 Mt. Newton Cross Rd., 250/652-4464 or 800/463-4464, www.western66motel.com, CAN$92–99 s or d) has a large variety of affordable rooms, English-style gardens, complimentary coffee in the lobby each morning, and an inexpensive restaurant on the premises. Traveling families will want to upgrade to the super-spacious family rooms, which sleep up to six people for around CAN$115.

Just off the main highway between the ferry terminal and downtown, on the road into downtown Sidney, is **€ The Cedarwood** (9522 Lochside Dr., 250/656-5551 or 877/656-5551, www.thecedarwood.ca, rooms CAN$125–139 s or d, suites and cottages from CAN$135), highlighted by a colorful garden with outdoor seating overlooking the Strait of Georgia. Regular motel rooms are clean and comfortable, but a better deal are the individually furnished log cottages, some with full kitchens.

At the same intersection as the Western 66 is **Quality Inn Waddling Dog** (2476 Mt. Newton Cross Rd., 250/652-1146 or 800/567-8466, www.qualityinnvictoria.com, CAN$129–139 s or d), styled as an old English guesthouse complete with an English pub. The Waddling Dog offers several well-priced packages that include admission to Butchart Gardens.

You'll feel like you're a million miles from the city at **Brentwood Bay Resort** (849 Verdier Ave., Brentwood Bay, 250/544-2079 or 888/544-2079, www.brentwoodbayresort.com, CAN$329–549 s or d), an upscale retreat overlooking Saanich Inlet. It's one of only three Canadian properties with a Small Luxury Hotels of the World designation, and you will want for nothing. You can learn to scuba dive, take a water taxi to Butchart Gardens, enjoy the latest spa treatments, or join a kayak tour. The guest rooms take understated elegance to new heights. Filled with natural light, they feature contemporary West Coast styling (lots of polished wood and natural colors), the finest Italian sheets on king-size beds, and private balconies. Modern conveniences like DVD entertainment systems, wireless Internet, and free calls within North America are a given. Dining options include a beautiful restaurant specializing in Vancouver Island produce and local seafood and an upscale pub with a waterfront patio.

If you're the camping sort, consider staying at **McDonald Provincial Park,** near the tip of the Saanich Peninsula 31 kilometers (19 miles) north of the city center. Facilities are limited (no showers or hookups); campsites are CAN$21 per night. Also on the peninsula, halfway between downtown Victoria and Sidney, is **Island View Beach Regional Park** (Homathko Dr., 250/652-0548, mid-May–early Sept., CAN$15–20), right on the beach three kilometers (1.9 miles) east of Highway 17.

## Camping

The closest camping to downtown is at **Westbay Marine Village** (453 Head St., Esquimalt, 250/385-1831 or 866/937-8229, www.westbay.bc.ca, CAN$35–47.50), across Victoria Harbour from downtown. Facilities at this RV-only campground include full hookups and laundry facilities. It is part of a marina complex comprising floating residences and commercial businesses, such as fishing charter operators and restaurants. Water taxis connect the "village" to downtown. Rates range depending on the view (the most expensive sites have unobstructed views across to the Inner Harbour).

**Fort Victoria RV Park** (340 Island Hwy., 250/479-8112, www.fortvictoria.ca, CAN$38) is six kilometers (3.7 miles) northwest of the city center on Highway 1A. This campground provides full hookups (including cable TV), free showers, laundry facilities, wireless Internet (CAN$2/night), and opportunities to join charter salmon-fishing trips.

## FOOD

While Victoria doesn't have a reputation as a culinary hot spot, over the past decade things have improved greatly with the opening of numerous restaurants serving top-notch cuisine with influences from around the world. Local chefs are big on produce organically grown and sourced from island farms. Seafood—halibut, shrimp, mussels, crab, and salmon—also features prominently on many menus.

Because of the thriving tourist trade centered on the Inner Harbour, chances are you will find something to suit your tastes and budget close at hand—Italian, Mexican, Californian, or even vegan cuisine. Mixed in with a few tourist traps are several excellent Harbourfront choices that are as popular with the locals as with visitors. Unlike in many cities and aside from a small Chinatown, ethnic restaurants are not confined to particular streets. On the other hand, Fort Street east of Douglas has a proliferation of restaurants that are as trendy as it gets on the island.

You will still find great interest in traditional English fare, including afternoon tea, which is served everywhere from motherly corner cafés to the grand Fairmont Empress. English cooking in general is much maligned but worth trying. For the full experience, choose kippers and poached eggs for breakfast, a ploughman's lunch (crusty bread, a chunk of cheese, pickled onions), and then roast beef with Yorkshire pudding (a crispy pastry made with drippings and doused with gravy) in the evening.

## Coffee

While Victoria is generally associated with high tea, there are some serious coffee lovers in the capital. A good percentage of these consider **Moka House** (various locations, including 345 Cook St., 250/388-7377, 6:30 A.M.–9 P.M. Mon.–Sat., 7 A.M.–7 P.M. Sun.) as pouring the best coffee. As a bonus, the bagels are excellent and wireless Internet is free. The focus at minimalist **Habit Coffee** (552 Pandora St., 250/294-1127, 7 A.M.–6 P.M. Mon.–Sat., 8 A.M.–6 P.M. Sun.) is most definitely the coffee, although there's an eclectic collection of magazines to browse through.

## Bakeries

In Old Town, **Willies Bakery** (537 Johnson St., 250/381-8414, 7 A.M.–4 P.M. Mon.–Fri., 8:30 A.M.–4 P.M. Sat., 8 A.M.–4 P.M. Sun., lunches CAN$5.50–9.50) is an old-style café offering cakes, pastries, and sodas, with a quiet cobbled courtyard in which to enjoy them.

On the same side of downtown, **Cascadia Bakery** (1812 Government St., 250/380-6606, 7:30 A.M.–5:30 P.M. Mon.–Fri., 8:30 A.M.–5:30 P.M. Sat., 9 A.M.–3 P.M. Sun., lunches CAN$6.50–9) is best known for its hand-shaped, preservative-free breads, but also offers freshly made granola and tasty lunches.

## Cafés

In the heart of downtown, **Broughton Street Deli** (648 Broughton St., 250/380-9988, 7:30 A.M.–4 P.M. Mon.–Fri.) occupies a tiny space at street level of a historic redbrick building. Soups made from scratch daily are CAN$4 and sandwiches just CAN$5.

**Lady Marmalade** (608 Johnson St., 250/381-2872, 8:30 A.M.–10 P.M. Tues.–Sat., 8:30 A.M.–4 P.M. Sun.–Mon., lunches CAN$7.50–12) is a funky café with a delightful array of breakfast choices (think brie and avocado eggs benedict) and healthy lunches, including an avocado, brie, and bacon baguette.

With walls decorated with original art and an eclectic array of table arrangements, **Mo:Le** (554 Pandora St., 250/385-6653, 8 A.M.–3 P.M. Mon.–Fri., 8 A.M.–4 P.M. Sat.–Sun., lunches CAN$10–16) impresses with creative yet well-priced cooking—think shrimp eggs benedict, yam omelet, maple-balsam grilled vegetable sandwich, and more.

Well worth searching out, there's nearly always a lineup for tables at **Blue Fox** (919 Fort St., 250/380-1683, 7:30 A.M.–4 P.M. Mon.–Fri., 8 A.M.–3 P.M. Sat.–Sun., lunches CAN$7–12). Breakfast includes Eggs Benedict Pacifico (with smoked salmon and avocado) and Apple Charlotte (French toast with apples and maple syrup). At lunch, try an oversized Waldorf salad or a curried chicken burger with sweet date chutney.

## Casual Dining

At the foot of Bastion Square, a cobbled pedestrian mall, **Local Kitchen** (1205 Wharf St., 250/385-1999, 11:30 A.M.–10 P.M. Mon.–Sat., 11 A.M.–5 P.M. Sun., CAN$14–25) offers a menu of simple, globally inspired cooking, although the outdoor tables are reason enough to stop by. The West Coast seafood kebab, the vegetable curry—it's all excellent.

Touristy **Wharfside Eatery** (1208 Wharf St., 250/360-1808, daily for lunch and dinner, CAN$15–31) is a bustling waterfront complex with a maritime theme and family atmosphere. Behind a small café section and a bar is the main dining room and a two-story deck, where almost every table has a stunning water view. Seafood starters to share include a tasting plate of salmon and mussels steamed in a creamy tomato broth. The lunchtime appetizers run through to the evening menu, which also includes wood-fired pizza, standard seafood dishes under CAN$30, and a delicious smoked chicken and wild mushroom penne. The cheesecake is heavenly.

## Seafood

Victoria's many seafood restaurants come in all forms. Fish and chips is a British tradition and is sold as such at **Old Vic Fish & Chips** (1316 Broad St., 250/383-4536, 11 A.M.–8 P.M. Mon.–Sat., CAN$11–17), which has been in business since 1930. Pay the extra for halibut.

Occupying a prime location on a floating dock amid whale-watching boats, seaplanes, and shiny white leisure craft, the **🄲 Flying Otter Grill** (950 Wharf St., 250/414-4220, 8 A.M.–10 P.M. daily, CAN$16–31) is just steps from the main tourist trail, but it's far enough removed to make it a popular haunt with locals wanting a quiet, casual waterfront meal. The setting alone makes the Flying Otter a winner, but the menu is a knockout. Choose pan-fried oysters or grilled chili-lime-marinated prawns to share, and then move on to mains like seafood risotto. To get there, walk north along the Harbour from the information center.

Away from the tourist-clogged streets of the Inner Harbour is **🄲 Barb's Place** (Fisherman's Wharf, at the foot of St. Lawrence St., 250/384-6515, daily from 8 A.M., CAN$8–18), a sea-level eatery on a floating dock. It's not a restaurant as such, but a shack surrounded by outdoor table settings, some protected from the elements by a canvas tent. The food is as fresh as it gets. Choose cod and chips, halibut and chips, or clam chowder, or splash out on a steamed crab. Adding to the charm are the surrounding floating houses, and seals that hang out waiting for handouts. An enjoyable way to reach Barb's is by ferry from the Inner Harbour.

## Pub Meals

Right in the heart of downtown is the **Elephant and Castle** (corner of Government St. and View St., 250/383-5858, lunch and dinner daily, CAN$10–18.50). This English-style pub features exposed beams, oak paneling, and traditional pub decor. A few umbrella-shaded tables line the sidewalk out front. You'll find all the traditional favorites, such as steak and kidney pie and fish and chips.

**Swan's Hotel** (506 Pandora St., 250/361-3310, 7 A.M.–1 A.M. daily, CAN$11–18) is home to a stylish brewpub with matching food, such as a portobello burger and a smoked salmon wrap. As well as the typical pub pews, the hotel has covered a section of the sidewalk with a glass-enclosed atrium.

While all the above pubs exude the English traditions for which Victoria is famous, **Spinnakers Gastro Brewpub** (308 Catherine St., Esquimalt, 250/386-2739, daily from 11 A.M., CAN$12–26) is in a class by itself. It was Canada's first in-house brewpub, and it's as popular today as when it opened in 1985. The crowds come for the beer, but also for great food served up in a casual, modern atmosphere. British-style pub fare, such as a ploughman's lunch, is served in the bar, while West Coast and seafood dishes such as sea bass basted in an ale sauce are offered in the downstairs restaurant.

## Italian

The energetic atmosphere at **⟨ Café Brio** (944 Fort St., 250/383-0009, daily from 5:30 P.M., CAN$17–32) is contagious, and the food is as good as anywhere in Victoria.

The Mediterranean-inspired dining room is adorned with lively artwork and built around a U-shaped bar, while out front are a handful of tables on an alfresco terrace. A creative menu combines local, seasonal produce with Italian expertise and flair. The charcuterie, prepared in-house, is always a good choice to begin with, followed by wild salmon prepared however your server suggests. Order the chocolate cake smothered in chocolate espresso sauce, even if you're full.

One of the most popular restaurants in town is **Pagliacci's** (1011 Broad St., 250/386-1662, 11:30 A.M.–3 P.M., 5:30–10 P.M. daily, CAN$12–27), known for hearty Italian food, homemade bread, great desserts, and loads of atmosphere. Small and always busy, the restaurant attracts a lively local crowd, many with children; you'll inevitably have to wait for a table during the busiest times (no reservations taken). Pastas include a prawn fettuccine topped with tomato mint sauce.

## Caribbean

**The Reef** (533 Yates St., 250/388-5375, lunch and dinner daily, CAN$12–17.50) is as un-Victoria-like as one could imagine, but it's incredibly popular for its upbeat atmosphere, tasty food, and island-friendly service. The kitchen concentrates on the Caribbean classics, with jerk seasoning and tropical fruit juices featured in most dishes. Highlights include any of the West Indian curries, *ackee* (fruit) with salted cod fish, plantain chips with jerk mayo, and chicken marinated in coconut milk and then roasted. Of course, you'll need to order a fruity drink for the full effect—a traditional favorite like a piña colada or something a little more hip, like a rum-infused banana smoothie.

## Vegetarian

**⟨ Rebar** (50 Bastion Square, 250/361-9223, 8:30 A.M.–9 P.M. Mon.–Sat., 8:30 A.M.–3:30 P.M. Sun., CAN$7.50–16) is a cheerful, always-busy, 1970s-style vegetarian restaurant with a loyal local following. Dishes such as the almond burger at lunch and Thai tiger prawn curry at dinner are full of flavor and made with only the freshest ingredients. Still hungry? Try the nutty carrot cake. Children are catered to with fun choices such as banana and peanut butter on sunflower seed bread. It's worth stopping by just for juice: Vegetable and fruit juices, power tonics, and wheatgrass infusions are made to order for CAN$6.

## Chinese

Victoria's small Chinatown surrounds a short, colorful strip of Fisgard Street between Store and Government Streets. The restaurants welcome everyone, and generally the menus are filled with all the familiar Westernized Chinese choices. Near the top (east) end of Fisgard is **QV Café and Bakery** (1701 Government St., 250/384-8831), offering inexpensive Western-style breakfasts in the morning and Chinese delicacies the rest of the day.

One of the least expensive places in the area is **Wah Lai Yuen** (560 Fisgard St., 250/381-5355, 10 A.M.–8 P.M. daily, CAN$7–16), a simply decorated, well-lit restaurant with fast and efficient service. The wonton soups are particularly good; try the Szechwan prawns, or get adventurous and order salted squid. Out front is a bakery with offerings such as peanut almond soft cake.

## Southeast Asian

**Noodle Box** (626 Fisgard St., 250/360-1312, daily from 11 A.M., CAN$7.50–15) started out as a street stall and now has multiple locations, including along Fisgard Street near the entrance to Chinatown. The concept is simple—an inexpensive noodle bar serving up fare similar to what you'd find on the streets of Southeast Asia.

Step into the world of British colonialism at the ◖ **Bengal Lounge,** in the Fairmont Empress (721 Government St., 250/389-2727). The curry lunch buffet (11:30 A.M.–2 P.M. daily, CAN$28) and curry dinner buffet (6–9 P.M. daily, CAN$30) come with the three condiments I love to have with curry: shaved coconut, mango chutney, and mixed nuts.

If you've never tried Thai cuisine, you're in for a treat at **Sookjai Thai** (893 Fort St.,

Victoria's Chinatown is a good place to search out an inexpensive meal.

© DON PITCHER

250/383-9945, 11:30 A.M.–2:30 P.M. Mon.–Fri., 5–8:30 P.M. Mon.–Sat., CAN$10–18). The tranquil setting is the perfect place to sample traditional delights such as *tom yum goong* (a prawn and mushroom soup with a hint of tangy citrus) and baked red snapper sprinkled with spices sourced from Thailand. The snapper is the most expensive main, with several inspiring vegetarian choices around CAN$10.

Seating just 20 diners, **Planet Thai Bistro** (615 Johnson St., 250/380-7878, 11:30 A.M.–2:30 P.M. Mon.–Sat., 5 P.M.–closing daily, CAN$9–15) offers up inexpensive fare, including sweet corn cakes (CAN$6.50) to start and prawns roasted in sweet chili sauce (CAN$14) as a main.

## INFORMATION

Tourism Victoria runs the bright, modern **Victoria Visitor Centre** (812 Wharf St., 250/953-2033 or 800/663-3883, www.tourismvictoria.com, 9 A.M.–5 P.M. daily), which overlooks the Inner Harbour. The friendly staff can answer most of your questions. They also book accommodations, tours and charters, restaurants, entertainment, and transportation, all at no extra cost; sell local bus passes and map books with detailed area-by-area maps; and stock an enormous selection of tourist brochures. Also collect the free *Accommodations* publication and the free local news and entertainment papers—the best way to find out what's happening in Victoria while you're in town.

The best place to get information on a wide variety of recreation opportunities is the **Victoria Marine Adventure Centre,** based on a floating dock just around the corner from the information center (950 Wharf St., 250/995-2211 or 800/575-6700, www.marine-adventures.com).

The central branch of the **Greater Victoria Public Library** (735 Broughton St., at the corner of Courtney St., 250/382-7241, www.gvpl.ca, 9 A.M.–6 P.M. Mon., Fri.–Sat., 9 A.M.–9 P.M. Tues.–Thurs., 1–5 P.M. Sun., closed Sun. in summer) has a special collection focusing on the history and people of Vancouver Island.

## Tours

The classic way to see Victoria is from the comfort of a horse-drawn carriage. Throughout the day and into the evening, **Victoria Carriage Tours** (250/383-2207 or 877/663-2207) has horse carriages lined up along Menzies Street at Belleville Street awaiting passengers. A 30-minute tour costs CAN$90 per carriage (seating up to six people), a 45-minute tour costs CAN$130, and a 60-minute Royal Tour costs CAN$170. Tours run 9 A.M.–midnight, and bookings aren't necessary, although there's often a line.

Big red double-decker buses are as much a part of the Victoria tour scene as horse-drawn carriages. These are operated by **Gray Line** (250/744-3566 or 800/663-8390, www.grayline.ca) from beside the Inner Harbour. There are many tours to choose from, but to get yourself oriented while also learning some city history, take the 90-minute Grand City Drive Tour. It departs from the Harbourfront every half hour 9:30 A.M.–4 P.M., adult CAN$32, child CAN$16. The most popular of Gray Line's other tours is the one to Butchart Gardens (CAN$56, including admission price).

**Victoria Harbour Ferry** (250/708-0201) offers boat tours of the Harbour and Gorge Waterway. The company's funny-looking boats each seat around 20 passengers and depart regularly 9 A.M.–8:15 P.M. from below the Empress Hotel. The 45-minute loop tour allows passengers the chance to get on and off at will; adult CAN$22, senior CAN$20, child CAN$10, or travel just pieces of the entire loop for adult CAN$5–8.

## SERVICES

In a medical emergency, call 911 or contact **Victoria General Hospital** (1 Hospital Way, 250/727-4212). For non-urgent cases, a handy facility is **James Bay Medical Treatment Centre** (230 Menzies St., 250/388-9934).

The main **post office** is on the corner of Yates and Douglas Streets.

All of Victoria's downtown accommodations have in-room Internet access. A good option for travelers on the run is the small café on the lower level of the Hotel Grand Pacific (463 Belleville St., 7 A.M.–7 P.M. daily), where public Internet access is free with a purchase.

# GETTING THERE
## Arriving by Air
**Air Canada** (604/688-5515 or 888/247-2262, www.aircanada.ca), **Pacific Coastal** (604/273-8666 or 800/663-2872, www.pacificcoastal.com), and **WestJet** (604/606-5525 or 800/538-5696, www.westjet.com) have scheduled flights between Vancouver and Victoria, but the flight is so short that the attendants don't even have time to throw a bag of peanuts in your lap. These flights are really only practical if you have an onward destination—flying out of Victoria, for example, with Los Angeles as a final destination.

Several companies operate seaplanes between downtown Vancouver and downtown Victoria. From Coal Harbour, on Burrard Inlet, **Harbour Air** (604/274-1277 or 800/665-0212, www.harbour-air.com) and **West Coast Air** (604/606-6888 or 800/347-2222, www.westcoastair.com) have scheduled floatplane flights to Victoria's Inner Harbour. Expect to pay around CAN$120 per person each way for any of these flights.

Victoria International Airport (www.victoriaairport.com), the island's main airport, is on the Saanich Peninsula, 20 kilometers (12.4 miles) north of Victoria's city center. Once you've collected your baggage from the carousels, it's impossible to miss the rental car outlets (Avis, Budget, Hertz, and National) across the room, where you'll also find a currency exchange and information booth. Outside is a taxi stand and ticket booth for the airporter shuttle. The modern terminal also houses a lounge, various eateries, and a profusion of greenery.

The **AKAL Airport Shuttle Bus** (250/386-2525 or 877/386-2525, www.victoriaairporter.com) operates buses between the airport and major downtown hotels every 30 minutes (adult CAN$19, child CAN$12 each way). The first

departure from downtown to the airport is at 5 A.M. A taxi costs approximately CAN$65 to downtown.

## Ferry from Vancouver
**BC Ferries** (250/386-3431 or 888/223-3779, www.bcferries.com) links Vancouver and Victoria with a fleet of ferries that operate year-round. Ferries depart Vancouver from **Tsawwassen,** south of Vancouver International Airport (allow one hour by road from downtown Vancouver) and **Horseshoe Bay,** on Vancouver's North Shore. They terminate on Vancouver Island at **Swartz Bay,** 32 kilometers (20 miles) north of Victoria. On weekends and holidays, the one-way fare on either route is adult CAN$14, child 5–11 CAN$7, vehicle CAN$46.75; rates for motor vehicles are slightly lower on weekdays, and all fares are reduced mid-September–late June. Limited vehicle reservations (CAN$15/booking) are accepted at 604/444-2890 or 888/724-5223, or online at www.bcferries.com. Seniors travel free Monday–Thursday but must pay for their vehicles.

In high season (late June–mid-Sept.), the ferries run about once an hour 7 A.M.–10 P.M. The rest of the year they run a little less frequently. Both crossings take around 90 minutes. Expect a wait in summer, particularly if you have an oversized vehicle (each ferry can accommodate far fewer large vehicles than standard-size cars and trucks).

Try to plan your travel outside peak times, which include summer weekends, especially Friday afternoon sailings from Tsawwassen and Sunday afternoon sailings from Swartz Bay. Most travelers don't make reservations but simply arrive and prepare themselves to wait for the next ferry if the first one fills. Both terminals have shops with food and magazines as well as summertime booths selling everything from crafts to mini donuts.

## Ferry from Washington State
From downtown Seattle (Pier 69), **Clipper Navigation** (800/888-2535, www.clippervacations.com, adult US$93 one-way, US$155

round-trip) runs passenger-only ferries to Victoria's Inner Harbour. In summer, sailings are made five times daily, with the service running the rest of the year on a reduced schedule. Travel is discounted off-season and year-round for seniors and children.

North of Seattle, Anacortes is the departure point for **Washington State Ferries** (206/464-6400, 250/381-1551, or 888/808-7977, www.wsdof.wa.gov/ferries, US$16.85, vehicle and driver US$56.45) to Sidney (on Vancouver Island, 32 kilometers/20 miles north of Victoria), with a stop made en route in the San Juan Islands. Make reservations at least 24 hours in advance in either direction.

The final option is to travel from Port Angeles to Victoria. Two companies offer service on this route. The **MV Coho** (250/386-2202 or 360/457-4491, www.cohoferry.com, adult US$15.50, child US$7.75, vehicle and driver US$55) runs year-round, with up to four crossings daily in summer. The passenger-only **Victoria Express** (250/361-9144 or 360/452-8088, www.victoriaexpress.com, US$12.50 pp each way) makes the crossing with 2–4 sailings daily June–September.

### By Bus

The main **bus depot** (710 Douglas St.) is behind the Fairmont Empress. **Pacific Coach Lines** (604/662-7575 or 800/661-1725, www.pacificcoach.com) operates bus service between Vancouver's Pacific Central Station and downtown Victoria, via the Tsawwassen–Swartz Bay ferry. In summer the coaches run hourly 6 A.M.–9 P.M.; rates are CAN$42 one-way and CAN$82 round-trip, which includes the ferry fare. The trip takes 3.5 hours. This same company also runs buses to the Victoria depot from downtown Vancouver hotels (CAN$48 one-way, CAN$90 round-trip) and from Vancouver

International Airport (CAN$52 one-way, CAN$94 round-trip).

## GETTING AROUND
### By Bus

Most of the inner-city attractions can be reached on foot. However, the **Victoria Regional Transit System** (250/385-2551, www.transitbc.com) is excellent, and it's easy to jump on and off and get everywhere you want to go. Pick up an *Explore Victoria* brochure at the information center for details of all the major sights, parks, beaches, and shopping areas and the buses needed to reach them. Bus fare for travel within the entire city is adult CAN$2.50, senior or student CAN$1.60. Transfers are good for travel in one direction within 90 minutes of purchase. A DayPass, valid for one day's unlimited bus travel, costs adult CAN$7.70, senior or student CAN$5.50.

### By Bike

Victoria doesn't have the great network of bicycle paths that Vancouver boasts, but bike-rental shops are nevertheless plentiful. Try **Sports Rent** (1950 Government St., 250/385-7368) or **Oak Bay Bicycles** (1990 Oak Bay Ave., 250/598-4111). Expect to pay from around CAN$10 per hour, CAN$40 per day. As well as renting bikes, **Great Pacific Adventures** (around the Harbour from the visitors center in the West Coast Air terminal at 1000 Wharf St., 250/386-2277) rents strollers, scooters, and watercraft.

### By Taxi

Taxis operate on a meter system, charging CAN$2.75 at the initial flag drop plus around CAN$2 per kilometer. Call **Blue Bird Cabs** (250/382-8294 or 800/665-7055), **Empress Taxi** (250/381-2222), or **Victoria Taxi** (250/383-7111).

# SAN JUAN ISLAND

Second largest island in the archipelago (Orcas is slightly bigger), San Juan Island is 20 miles long and 7 miles wide, covering a total of 55 square miles. Picturesque and tidy **Friday Harbor** sits along the west side, its marina protected by Brown Island. It has all the charm of a coastal Maine town, with white clapboard buildings, busy shops, art galleries, and fine restaurants tucked into hills surrounding the harbor. Friday Harbor is the only incorporated town in the chain, and it is also the county seat, the commercial center of the San Juans, and home to around a third of San Juan Island's 7,400 residents. It is a U.S. Customs port of entry, as is **Roche Harbor** on the other side of the island. Roche Harbor is regionally famous for its superb deep-water marina and historic buildings that are now part of a popular resort.

Once you leave Friday Harbor, the country quickly opens into expansive farms and fields, forests, hills, and rocky shorelines. It is a delightfully diverse island with something to please almost any traveler. On the south end of San Juan, the land is grassy and open, with a couple of long beaches. The western shore is relatively undeveloped and rugged, with the only whale-watching park in the nation at **Lime Kiln Point State Park.** Two historic and especially scenic areas—English Camp on the west side and American Camp on the southeast end of the island—lie within **San Juan Island National Historical Park.**

A handful of celebrity types have homes on San Juan, including 1970s rocker Steve Miller and Richard Nixon's one-time head of the Environmental Protection Agency, William

© DON PITCHER

# HIGHLIGHTS

◖ **The Whale Museum:** Learn about orca whales and other marine mammals at this very informative museum in Friday Harbor. Kids love to try on the whale costumes (page 105).

◖ **San Juan Island National Historical Park:** This park commemorates the conflict

Roche Harbor
◖

San Juan Island
◖ National
Historical Park

Orcas
Island

San Juan Channel

Shaw
Island

San Juan ◖
Vineyards

Sea
Kayaking
◖

The Whale
Museum

Friday
Harbor

Lime Kiln Point
State Park

◖ — Whale-Watching

◖

Friday
Harbor

◖

Pelindaba
Lavender Farm

Jackle's
Lagoon

◖

San Juan Island
National Historical Park

0          2 mi

0          2 km

© AVALON TRAVEL

between the United States and Britain for control of the San Juan Islands. English Camp has historic buildings and a formal garden along a protected cove, while American Camp is a windswept, open spot with grand scenery and the best beaches anywhere on the San Juans (page 108).

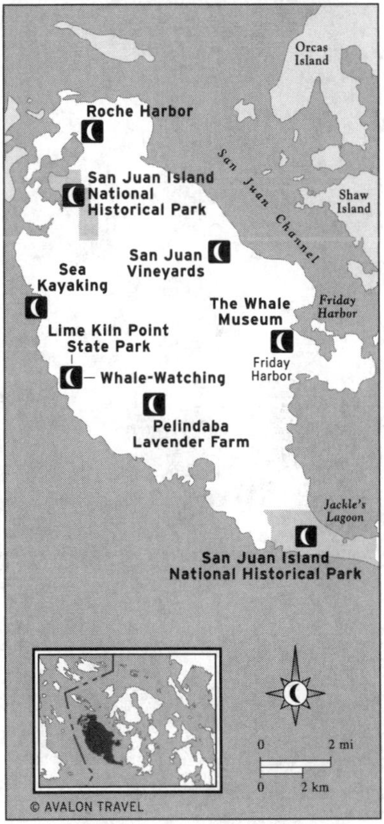

◖ **Roche Harbor:** Beautifully maintained, this marina and resort has a historic hotel, flower-packed gardens, and abundant recreation options (page 113).

◖ **Lime Kiln Point State Park:** Often called Whale Watch Park, this west-side natural area has a photogenic lighthouse and underwater hydrophones to listen for the orca (killer) whales that often pass just offshore (page 115).

◖ **San Juan Vineyards:** A boutique winery here produces wines from 10 acres of Madeleine Angevine and Siegerrebe grapes (page 121).

◖ **Pelindaba Lavender Farm:** The fragrance often reaches you before you ever see the 20 acres of organic lavender used for a wide range of culinary and other products. The owners also have a shop featuring their wares in the heart of Friday Harbor (page 122).

◖ **Sea Kayaking:** A favorite of adventurous visitors, kayaking is the perfect way to explore the waters around San Juan Island. A number of companies lead short day trips or multi-night paddles to surrounding marine state parks (page 127).

◖ **Whale-Watching:** Each year, more than a half-million people board whale-watching boats in the San Juans, many of which depart from Friday Harbor, Roche Harbor, or Snug Harbor (page 129).

LOOK FOR ◖ TO FIND RECOMMENDED SIGHTS, ACTIVITIES, DINING, AND LODGING.

SAN JUAN ISLAND

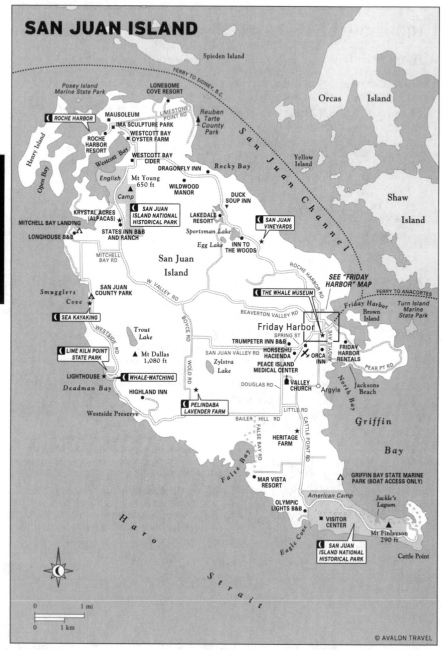

# SAN JUAN ISLAND

Spieden Island

Orcas    Island

FERRY TO SIDNEY, B.C.

Posey Island
Marine State Park

LONESOME
COVE RESORT

MAUSOLEUM

ROCHE HARBOR

IMA SCULPTURE PARK

WESTCOTT BAY
OYSTER FARM

ROCHE
HARBOR
RESORT

LIMESTONE
POINT RD

Reuben
Tarte
County
Park

Yellow
Island

Shaw

Island

Henry Island

Westcott Bay

WESTCOTT BAY
CIDER

DRAGONFLY INN

Rocky Bay

San Juan Channel

Open Bay

English

Camp

Mt Young
650 ft

WILDWOOD
MANOR

DUCK
SOUP INN

LAKEDALE
RESORT

SAN JUAN
VINEYARDS

KRYSTAL ACRES
(ALPACAS)

SAN JUAN
ISLAND NATIONAL
HISTORICAL PARK

Sportsman Lake

MITCHELL BAY LANDING

STATES INN B&B
AND RANCH

Egg Lake

INN TO
THE WOODS

LONGHOUSE B&B

MITCHELL
BAY RD

San Juan
Island

Roche Harbor Rd

SEE "FRIDAY
HARBOR" MAP

FERRY TO ANACORTES

Smugglers
Cove

SAN JUAN
COUNTY PARK

W VALLEY RD

THE WHALE MUSEUM

Friday Harbor
Brown
Island

Turn Island
Marine
State Park

SEA KAYAKING

Trout
Lake

BOYCE RD

BEAVERTON VALLEY RD

Friday Harbor

SPRING ST

ARGYLE AVE

FRIDAY
HARBOR
RENTALS

LIME KILN POINT
STATE PARK

Mt Dallas
1,080 ft

TRUMPETER INN B&B

HORSESHU
HACIENDA

PEACE ISLAND
MEDICAL CENTER

ORCA
INN

PEAR PT RD

LIGHTHOUSE

WHALE-WATCHING

WOLD RD

SAN JUAN VALLEY RD

Zylstra
Lake

North Bay

Jacksons
Beach

Deadman Bay

HIGHLAND INN

DOUGLAS RD

VALLEY
CHURCH

Argyle

Westside Preserve

PELINDABA
LAVENDER FARM

LITTLE RD

Griffin

BAILER HILL RD

CATTLE POINT RD

Bay

FALSE BAY RD

HERITAGE
FARM

False Bay

MAR VISTA
RESORT

GRIFFIN BAY STATE MARINE
PARK (BOAT ACCESS ONLY)

Haro

American Camp

Jackle's
Lagoon

OLYMPIC
LIGHTS B&B

VISITOR
CENTER

Eagle Cove

SAN JUAN ISLAND NATIONAL
HISTORICAL PARK

Mt Finlayson
290 ft

Cattle Point

Strait

WESTSIDE RD

0    1 mi

0    1 km

© AVALON TRAVEL

Ruckelshaus. Heading farther back in time, the late John Wayne often stayed on the island, particularly at Roche Harbor. (Wayne owned nearby Spieden Island for a number of years.) And U.S. presidents Theodore Roosevelt and Howard Taft overnighted at Roche Harbor while in office.

## HISTORY

The Pig War, a turf battle between the United States and Britain, threatened to escalate into violent conflict in 1859. Once tensions eased, both sides stationed troops on San Juan Island to protect their interests until a settlement could be reached. That settlement did not come until 1872, when the United States was awarded the islands by an arbitrator, Kaiser Wilhelm I of Germany.

### San Juan Town and Friday Harbor

Shortly after American soldiers landed on the southern end of San Juan Island in 1859, a settlement sprang up along nearby Griffin Bay. Originally called San Juan Town, it would later be known as Old Town. The turmoil over ownership of the islands made them ripe for all sorts of illicit activities, the primary one being the uncontrolled selling of alcohol. Within a year, the entire area was verging on anarchy, with robberies, attacks on women at any time of the day or night, rampant drunkenness by both Native Americans and whites, saloon brawls, prostitution, and even murder. The American military stepped in to restore order, but San Juan Town's reputation was already ruined.

The name Friday Harbor comes from an early settler called **Joe Friday.** Born in Hawaii, Friday was brought to the San Juans by the Hudson's Bay Company to tend sheep. His original name is unknown, but it's possible the British sailors who recruited him wanted something they could pronounce, naming him after Friday, the fictional character in *Robinson Crusoe.* Joe Friday settled along the protected cove others came to call Friday's Harbor, and the town grew up on land where his sheep had grazed. Friday was one of many Hawaiians

English Camp, once the English base of the Pig War conflict

who were brought to the San Juan Islands and Gulf Islands by the British. The Hawaiians were called Kanakas by others, and Kanaka Bay on the southwest side of San Juan Island is named for them. There was a mass exodus of Kanakans from the San Juans after the islands were awarded to the Americans in 1872. Many moved to Victoria, while others followed their flocks of sheep to Salt Spring Island in the Gulf Islands. Of course, it didn't help that Kanakans were given citizenship by the British, while Americans viewed them with suspicion, denying them basic rights. (As a total aside—courtesy of author Mark Billington—the word *Friday* had its origins in the word *Frigg,* the goddess of love in Norse mythology.)

One of the few reputable civilians on San Juan in the early years was **Edward Warbass,** who came to the island to run the U.S. Army's post store and stayed around to become justice of the peace, a state legislator, and the crafter of a bill that created San Juan County. Warbass is best known today as the father of Friday Harbor. Fed up with the boozing reputation of San Juan Town, he resolved to create a grand metropolis at a protected harbor on the west side of the island. He claimed that it would rival Seattle.

In 1873, Warbass staked 160 acres for the new San Juan County seat on the shores of Friday's harbor, erected a shack for the courthouse, and waited in vain for the hordes to arrive. It was three years before the first settler, other than Warbass, finally moved in to open a store, and almost a decade before the town contained more than a handful of homes and residents. In 1882, a second store opened at Friday Harbor, creating competition that led the owners to add a backroom bar. This was what folks really needed: cheap beer. Within a few months, the island's economic focus shifted to Friday Harbor, and over the next few years, San Juan Town became a ghost town. A fire in 1890 destroyed all that remained of Old Town, but nobody shed any tears. Friday Harbor was now clearly the chief—and only— town on the islands, and it remains so today, with some 2,200 permanent residents.

## The Lime King

Today, Roche Harbor is famous for its beautiful protected harbor, large marina, and immaculately maintained historic buildings, which operate as the largest resort on San Juan Island. The harbor was discovered early, and by 1850 the Hudson's Bay Company had built a log trading post along the shore. In 1881, the brothers Robert and Richard Scurr bought the harbor and began mining an incredibly rich deposit of lime.

In 1884, **John S. McMillin,** a Tacoma lawyer, learned of the limestone and bought the land for $40,000. By 1886, McMillin's Tacoma and Roche Harbor Lime Company had begun operation. The old Hudson's Bay cabin became the basis for his Hotel de Haro, a still-standing structure that has hosted presidents and paupers over the decades. Business boomed, and by the 1890s, Roche Harbor had become not only the primary employer in the San Juans, but also the largest producer of lime west of the Mississippi. The lime was mined from 13 hillside quarries.

Workers drilled holes for dynamite and then used sledgehammers to crush the rock once it had been blasted loose. The rock was hauled to kilns by horse-drawn wagon. In later years, a steam locomotive carried the ore, and this in turn was replaced by trucks.

The limestone was processed in brick-lined kilns along the shore of Roche Harbor. The rock was dumped into steel receptacles lined with firebrick and then heated with wood fires. The intense heat eventually changed the rock into lime. It took 4,000 acres of forest just to keep the kilns running; each kiln burned 10 cords of wood every six hours! The company had its own small fleet of ships to transport the lime to markets as far away as San Francisco and Hawaii.

The company continued to grow, adding a modern lime factory and a barrel works, along with docks and warehouses that extended hundreds of feet into the bay. McMillin built a company town that included segregated housing for nearly 800 Asian and white employees. Single men were barracked in large bunkhouses, and families were housed in rows of trim and well-kept cottages. Payment was in scrip, useable only at the company store on the wharf, alcohol was banned, and the company even owned a school and church.

McMillin prospered immensely from all this development, buying out his partners and running his various businesses in ways that would lead to fraud charges (they were later dismissed). For half a century, John McMillin was the undisputed king of San Juan Island. When union organizers demanded a wage increase at the quarries, he summarily fired 50 men associated with the union. McMillin also used his money, power, and influence to dictate local politics for years, handpicking candidates for office who toed the pro-business Republican line. On the plus side, McMillin did continue to provide jobs when hard times came in the Depression of the 1930s. He died in 1936 and is buried in the Masonic symbol–covered family mausoleum just above Roche Harbor—built, of course, with cement from the local limeworks.

The quarries at Roche Harbor finally closed in 1956, and a Seattle businessman and physician, Dr. Reuben J. Tarte, purchased all 4,000 acres and 12 miles of coastline. Over the next three decades, he and his family restored the aging hotel and other buildings. The complex has been sold twice since and is currently owned by Rich Komen and SaltChuk Resources (the billion-dollar parent of Totem Ocean Trailer Express, Foss Maritime, and other companies; www.marineresourcesgroup. com), who have continued the process of transforming this old lime operation into the finest resort in the San Juans.

## PLANNING YOUR TIME

San Juan Island is popular both for weekend vacationers and those with more time on their hands. It's possible to fly directly to the island, but most folks arrive by state ferry. A ferry trip requires getting to Anacortes (or Sidney if you're visiting from Vancouver Island), waiting in line for an hour or more, and then sailing to Friday Harbor. Unless you get a very early start and leave late the evening of your return, you can lose big chunks of your weekend to travel. Take as much time as you can afford, but even a short trip can be fun.

Friday Harbor is the center of action on San Juan Island, and a good base from which to explore surrounding areas. It's also home to the fun and educational **Whale Museum,** several fine restaurants, and a multitude of gift shops and galleries. After visiting the museum, many visitors climb onboard one of the many **whale-watching** boats that converge on killer whales feeding in nearby waters. There is controversy over the impacts of whale-watching boats, with the museum recommending onshore whale-watching. The best place for that is **Lime Kiln Point State Park** on the undeveloped west side of the island. Just north of here is a small county park that serves as a popular put-in point for guided and private groups of **sea kayakers.**

**San Juan Island National Historical Park** and **Roche Harbor** mix history with grand scenery. The park commemorates the Pig War, with historic bases once occupied by American and British soldiers, while Roche Harbor features gracious gardens, an old clapboard hotel, a busy harbor, and an intriguing mix of nature and art at **IMA Sculpture Park.**

On the south end of the island, **Pelindaba Lavender Farm** grows fragrant lavender flowers for a variety of uses and has a big shop in the heart of Friday Harbor. These attractions are just a starting point, and inveterate travelers will discover all sorts of other delights on San Juan Island.

# Sights

It's easy to see Friday Harbor sights on foot, but for many of the most interesting spots around San Juan, you'll need transport. **San Juan Transit** (360/378-8887 or 800/887-8387, www.sanjuantransit.com, daily mid-May–early Sept., $5 one-way, $10 round-trip, $15 all-day pass, discounts for children) provides an inexpensive way to see the sights in the summer, with stops at many destinations, including Roche Harbor, IMA Sculpture Park, San Juan Vineyards, Pelindaba Lavender Farm, Lakedale Resort, Krystal Acres Alpaca Ranch, English Camp,

and Lime Kiln Point State Park (whale-watching).

## ( THE WHALE MUSEUM

One of the must-see places on San Juan Island, The Whale Museum (62 1st St. N. in Friday Harbor, 360/378-4710 or 800/946-7227, www.whalemuseum.org, 9 A.M.–6 P.M. daily late May–Sept., 10 A.M.–5 P.M. daily the rest of the year; closed Thanksgiving, Christmas, and in early January, $6 adults, $5 seniors, $3 ages 5–18 and college students, free for kids under 5) opened its doors in 1979 as the first

SAN JUAN ISLAND

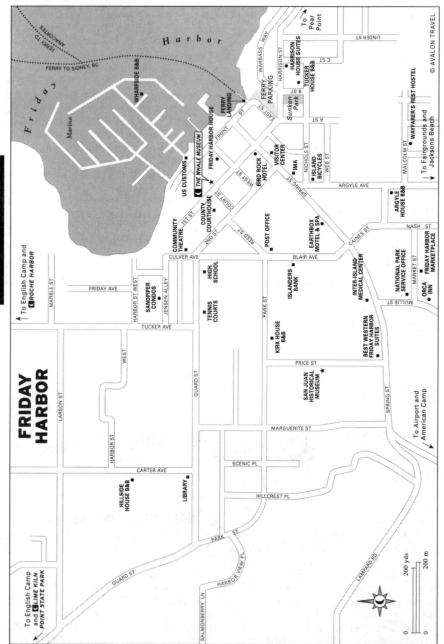

# FRIDAY HARBOR

© AVALON TRAVEL

Harbor

Friday

FERRY TO ANACORTES

FERRY TO SIDNEY, BC

To Pear Point

WARBASS WAY

HARRISON ST

HARRISON HOUSE SUITES

TUCKER HOUSE B&B

LINDER ST

C ST

B ST

Marina

WHARFSIDE B&B

FERRY LANDING

FERRY PARKING

Sunken Park

WAYFARER'S REST HOSTEL

MALCOM ST

To Fairgrounds and Jacksons Beach

A ST

FRIDAY HARBOR HOUSE

THE WHALE MUSEUM

US CUSTOMS

FRONT ST

EAST ST

VISITOR CENTER

BIRD ROCK HOTEL

NICHOLS ST

IMA

ISLAND BICYCLES

WEB ST

SPRING ST

ARGYLE AVE

WEST ST

COURT ST

COMMUNITY THEATRE

COUNTY COURTHOUSE

1ST ST

2ND ST

REED ST

POST OFFICE

EARTHBOX MOTEL & SPA

CAINES ST

ARGYLE HOUSE B&B

NASH ST

FRIDAY HARBOR MARKETPLACE

NATIONAL PARK SERVICE OFFICE

MARKET ST

CULVER AVE

BLAIR AVE

INTER-ISLAND MEDICAL CENTER

MULLIS ST

ORCA INN

To English Camp and ROCHE HARBOR

MARBLE ST

FRIDAY AVE

HARBOR ST WEST

SANDPIPER CONDOS

JENSEN ALLEY

HIGH SCHOOL

PARK ST

ISLANDERS BANK

TUCKER AVE

TENNIS COURTS

KIRK HOUSE B&B

BEST WESTERN FRIDAY HARBOR SUITES

PRICE ST

WEST ST

GUARD ST

SAN JUAN HISTORICAL MUSEUM

SPRING ST

LARSON ST

MARGUERITE ST

To Airport and American Camp

HARBOR ST

CARTER AVE

SCENIC PL

HILLSIDE HOUSE B&B

LIBRARY

HILLCREST PL

To English Camp and LIME KILN POINT STATE PARK

PARK ST

GUARD ST

HARBOR VIEW PL

SALMONBERRY LN

LAMPARD RD

0    200 yds
0    200 m

© DON PITCHER

The Whale Museum

museum in America dedicated to the interpretation of living whales in the wild. Exhibits focus on whale biology and human-whale interactions, with a particular spotlight on the famous resident killer whale (orca) populations of the Salish Sea.

Downstairs are several free exhibits that introduce you to these incredible animals, including details on recent sightings. The main collection is up a narrow staircase bordered by a colorful whale mural. You are introduced to these creatures through the legends of the Salish people who first lived here. One room in the museum shows a video about orca whales in the Salish Sea; sit in for an excellent overview. Another small room has exhibits especially for children, and they'll love the chance to dress up with orca fins and tails for photos to send to the grandparents. The large exhibit hall upstairs contains life-size models and the full skeletons of a baby gray whale, plus adult killer and minke whales. A big wall chart shows the genealogy of local pods. Step into a phone booth to hear the songs of various whales and other

marine mammals; learn about hydrophones and how the noises from vessels can be a problem for whales; examine whale fetuses; and compare the pickled brains of a spotted dolphin, a fin whale, and a human. The museum operates a network of hydrophones to monitor whale locations, vocalizations, and noise from vessel traffic.

There's also an art gallery, plus a gift shop with books on whales, educational toys, games, videos and CDs, clothing, T-shirts, and jewelry. Group tours and educational programs are available year-round. You can "adopt" one of the local orcas (population of 88 in 2011) for $35. If you come upon a stranded seal, sea lion, or other marine mammal, do not handle it, but instead immediately call the museum's **Stranded Marine Mammal Hotline** at 800/562-8832.

## SAN JUAN HISTORICAL MUSEUM

In 1894, James King built a two-story farmhouse that now houses the San Juan Historical Museum (405 Price St., 360/378-3949, www.sjmuseum.org, 10 A.M.–4 P.M. Wed.–Sat.

1–4 P.M. Sun., May–Sept., 1–4 P.M. Sat. Apr. and Oct., by appointment only in winter, $5 adults, $4 seniors, $3 ages 6–18, free for kids under 5). Inside are fascinating antiques, old photos, and historical artifacts, while outside you'll find a variety of old farm equipment, the first county jail, a log cabin, barn, milk house, and carriage house. Those interested in a more in-depth look at local history will want to check out the resource center here, with its extensive collection of historic photos, oral histories, and genealogical information. The little gift shop sells books, cards, and toys. A variety of museum activities take place throughout the year, including outdoor concerts Wednesday evenings mid-July–mid-August and the Fourth of July Pig War picnic.

You may want to also check out the **American Legion Veterans Museum** (360/298-1940, www.wateringholegallery.com/museum, 10 A.M.–2 P.M. Fri.–Sun. summers, free) next to The Whale Museum on 1st Street. Housed within are weapons and memorabilia from past wars, most notably a unique Union flag from the Battle of Shiloh during the Civil War.

A number of other historic structures dot the island. One of the nicest is **Valley Church,** on Madden Lane two miles south of Friday Harbor. The church was built in 1892, and two cemeteries are nearby.

## OTHER FRIDAY HARBOR SIGHTS

Head up Front Street from the ferry landing for a couple of hidden attractions. Next to the ferry is **Spring Street Landing** (www.portoffridayharbor.org), a collection of shops with an interesting 400-gallon **saltwater aquarium** containing surf perch, sea stars, anemones, sea cucumbers, tube worms, scallops, sea urchins, and other creatures from nearby waters.

A short distance farther at Waterfront Park is *Interaction,* a large and striking wood sculpture by First Nations Canadian artist Susan Point. The piece is inspired by traditional Coast Salish house posts but uses contemporary techniques to represent the interface between people and their environment on San Juan Island.

## SAN JUAN ISLAND NATIONAL HISTORICAL PARK

In one of the stranger pieces of Northwest history, the killing of a pig by an American settler nearly set off a war between the United States and Britain. Conflict was averted when saner heads prevailed, and the San Juan Islands were eventually declared American territory. The sites where the American and British forces were based during the standoff are now part of San Juan Island National Historical Park, with administrative offices in Friday Harbor (650 Mullis St., 360/378-2240, www.nps.gov/sajh). The park itself is in two sections on different sides of the island: American Camp on the south end and English Camp on the western shore. Both sites have small visitors centers, along with picnic areas and beach access for day use only. The grounds of both are open year-round, but they do not have campgrounds.

Summertime activities include guided historical and nature walks on weekends at American Camp, living history exhibitions Saturday 12:30–3:30 P.M. at English Camp, and various talks and demonstrations on summer weekends. Check the park website for details on these and other program offerings.

### American Camp

On the southeast corner of San Juan Island, 1,200-acre American Camp sits on a windswept grassy peninsula six miles from Friday Harbor. This is a magnificent place on a sunny summer afternoon, with both the Cascades and Olympics in view. It's also a deliciously lonely place to explore on a rainy winter day.

The **American Camp Visitor Center** (360/378-2240, 8:30 A.M.–5 P.M. daily late May–early Sept., 8:30 A.M.–4:30 P.M. Wed.–Sun. the rest of the year) houses a few historical exhibits, along with bottles, pipes, marbles, a comb, a chamber pot, and other small items found in archaeological excavations of the military encampments. Be sure to pick up the park brochure at trailheads for a self-guided mile-long walking tour.

Three original buildings remain at American Camp from the occupation in the 1860s—two officers' quarters and a laundress's quarters—along with an earthen gun fortification (redoubt) that was constructed by an army engineer named **Henry M. Robert.** You probably know him from a still-in-print book he wrote in 1876: *Robert's Rules of Order,* the internationally used manual of parliamentary procedure. A long white picket fence circles the grounds, and a trail leads downhill past the site of **Belle Vue Farm** near Grandma's Cove. Belle Vue was the old Hudson's Bay Company Farm and the home of the British-owned pig that American Lyman Cutlar shot.

American Camp is a fun place for a hike at any time of the year, with all-encompassing vistas, a long sandy beach, three bird-filled lagoons, and a protected cove with tall trees. Bright orange poppies line the slopes in early summer, and **killer whales** are often visible offshore; just look for the cluster of small boats trailing them. If the weather is sunny and the wind isn't too strong, you certainly won't go wrong with a trek up the towering summit of **Mount Finlayson.** OK, it's hardly a mountain at just 290 feet, so leave your climbing ropes and carabiners at home, but you're bound to be pleased at the summit panorama. On a clear day, you can pick out Mount Baker, Mount Rainier, the Olympic Mountains, and Vancouver Island. There are several routes up the hill; a good one starts at the Jakle's Lagoon Trailhead, where parking is available. The path climbs grassy and flower-filled slopes (with scattered boulders for variety), and for the next mile you can take deep breaths of fresh air, practice a little tai chi, pull out the binoculars to check for whales, eat a peanut butter sandwich, or kiss your sweetie. Once you reach the end near Third Lagoon, you can return on a separate path above Griffin Bay. Follow an old roadbed through a canopy of Douglas fir, western red cedar, and Western hemlock along **Jakle's Lagoon** to reach your original starting point. The total loop is around 3.5 miles, but you can come up with shorter versions if you just want a quick view from the hill or a one-mile round-trip saunter to the lagoon.

© DON PITCHER

American Camp

# THE PIG WAR

Because of vague wording in the Oregon Treaty of 1846 – the document that established the boundary between the United States and Canada – the San Juan Islands were not only the subject of a territorial dispute, but also the stage for an international incident commonly referred to as the Pig War. The treaty noted that the boundary would extend "to the middle of the channel which separates the continent from Vancouver's Island and thence southerly through the middle of the said channel, and of Fuca's Straits, to the Pacific Ocean." Unfortunately, there are actually two main channels. Britain said the boundary was Rosario Strait, the channel between the mainland and the San Juans, while the United States claimed Haro Strait – which separated the San Juans from Vancouver Island – as the border. In between were the San Juan Islands, claimed by both England and America.

## COLLISION COURSE

Britain lacked a strong presence in the Pacific Northwest, so the powerful Hudson's Bay Company was given free rein on Vancouver Island, with the head of the company also serving as governor of British Columbia. In the 1850s and 1860s, western Canada was under the control of a man with fierce loyalties to both the company and England, James Douglas. In 1851 he set up a fishing operation on the island. Two years later, he sent John Charles Griffin – for whom Griffin Bay is named – to establish Belle Vue Farm on the southern end of the island. Hawaiian (Kanaka) shepherds tended 1,400 sheep, crops were planted, and a few pigs rounded out the farm.

The United States also showed a keen interest in the San Juans by 1859, around 18 American settlers had moved onto San Juan Island. The relationship between the two sides grew strained. Several tit-for-tat incidents raised the level of tension, but a dead pig brought everything to a boil.

## HOG WILD

Lyman A. Cutlar arrived on San Juan Island in April 1859, took a Native American wife, and soon began clearing land for a home and a potato patch. Unfortunately, the place he had chosen was smack in the midst of land grazed by Hudson's Bay Company sheep. A boar from Belle Vue Farm kept wandering into Cutlar's potatoes, and each time he'd have to chase it out. Complaints to Charles Griffin got him nowhere; he suggested the problem was Cutlar's weak fence. On June 15, 1859, Cutlar awoke to see Griffin's Hawaiian herdsman laughing as the pig rooted in the potatoes once again. With a shot from his rifle, the offending pig was dead.

Cutlar decided honesty was now the best course, and he walked over to Belle Vue to pay Griffin for the pig. Griffin's response: "You Americans are nothing but a nuisance on the island and you have no business here." He then claimed the boar was worth $100, and Cutlar stormed out. Later that day, a Hudson's Bay ship arrived, and another heated discussion ensued, with the British threatening to haul Cutlar off to Victoria for trial and Cutlar threatening to shoot anyone who attempted to do so. By the time July 4 arrived two weeks later, American settlers on San Juan were agitating for U.S. sovereignty.

Into this fracas stepped William Harney, a brash U.S. Army brigadier general. Within days, an American steamer arrived, carrying a company of soldiers under Captain George E. Pickett.

The troops landed and quickly set up a camp near the Hudson's Bay Company wharf. It was an odd choice. Instead of putting his men out of range of British naval guns, Pickett chose a totally exposed beach. When the number of warships grew, he moved to the opposite beach. This really puzzled the British officers. Of course, they didn't know he had graduated last in his class at West Point: 59th out of 59.

## AN ESCALATING CRISIS

Governor James Douglas didn't take kindly to the sudden American military presence. He ordered three British warships under Captain Geoffrey Hornby to occupy the island but to avoid a military collision. That confrontation nearly came on August 3, when Hornby told Pickett that his British troops would be landing that day. Pickett's forces were vastly outnumbered, but he said they would fight to the last man. Fortunately, Captain Hornby had the presence of mind to avoid bloodshed, though his warships did stay threateningly close to shore.

Instead of landing his men, Hornby decided to wait for word from Douglas's superior, Rear Admiral Robert L. Baynes, who was expected back soon from Chile. When he arrived two days later, Baynes was appalled. He told Douglas that he would not "involve two great nations in a war over a squabble about a pig," and ordered his men to "not on any account whatever take the initiative in commencing hostilities." Still, five of Her Majesty's ships stood ready to land Royal Marines and to open fire on the Americans.

In the meantime, General Harney continued to build up his forces on San Juan, and by the end of August, 461 American soldiers – protected by an earthen redoubt, 14 field pieces, and eight naval guns – faced off against the British ships. All this military buildup and bluster had taken place without any instructions from Washington DC, and when President James Buchanan heard the news, he sent Lieutenant General Winfred Scott, commanding general of the U.S. Army, to seek a peaceful settlement. After much bickering, both sides agreed to leave a token force of men until a final settlement could be brokered.

## SHARING THE ISLAND

The Americans stayed on the south end of the island at **"Fort Pickett,"** as American Camp came to be called, building a small cluster of structures on this lonely and windswept spot. Crushing boredom, bad food, and dreadful quarters made this a hardship post. On March 21, 1860, a contingent of British Royal Marines landed on the west side of the island at beautiful **Garrison Bay,** an important winter village site for Coast Salish peoples for a thousand tyears. The British built a comfortable camp with prim white buildings and a formal garden, but the men here were no less unhappy and bored than those at American Camp. Desertions and even suicides took place. In the years that followed, the two camps gradually developed a camaraderie that led to joint celebrations of the Fourth of July and Queen Victoria's birthday.

The sudden flare-up on San Juan died down almost as quickly, perhaps in large part because attentions turned elsewhere. A much bigger event was steaming over the horizon: the Civil War. By 1861, nearly everyone had forgotten about the silly argument over an island in Puget Sound.

## AMERICA TAKES OVER

The Civil War and other matters kept the issue of boundary claims on a back burner for a dozen years, and settlers from both sides occupied the islands. Finally, in 1871, a deal was struck to let an arbitrator make the final boundary decision. The man they chose was Kaiser Wilhelm I of Germany, and on October 21, 1872, he pronounced Haro Strait the dividing channel, awarding the San Juan Islands to the United States. On November 25, 1872, the Royal Marines withdrew from English Camp. Within days, nearly all the British settlers on the islands had rushed to change their citizenship, allowing them to keep their land as American homesteaders.

The Pig War is barely a footnote to history today, but it marked a turning point in relations between Britain and America. No more would the two countries view each other as enemies. Their last conflict had just one casualty, the pig. The National Park Service took over the sites of American Camp and English Camp in 1966 and now maintains them as San Juan Island National Historical Park.

A maze of short trails covers the open country around the American Camp Visitor Center, taking you to the historic locations (marked by signs) of the Hudson's Bay Company Farm, the officers' quarters, laundress's quarters, and redoubt, and then downhill to the shore along pretty **Grandma's Cove.** This cove is less than a mile roundtrip from the visitors center. The prairie at American Camp is home to the **island marble butterfly,** a species long thought extinct. Prior to its discovery in 1998, the butterfly hadn't been seen for 90 years!

If beaches are your thing, don't miss driftwood-jammed **South Beach,** a truly wonderful place for a sunset walk (or run). A parking lot is right next to South Beach, and you can hike a mile or so in either direction on this, San Juan Island's longest public beach. It's also one of the best beaches anywhere in the archipelago. It can become a log-walk at the highest tides, so check a tide chart before heading out. This is also a good place to watch for birds, including terns, gulls, plovers, ruddy turnstones, greater and lesser yellowlegs, and bald eagles. Tidepools on the western end of the beach have a multitude of marine life. Restrooms and picnic tables are available.

On the north side of the peninsula along Griffin Bay, **Fourth of July Beach** is another easy walk. It's a short hike from the parking area to the beach, and from here you can walk to Old Town Lagoon, site of the rougharound-the-edges town when American Camp was occupied.

Near the tip of the peninsula is tiny **Cattle Point Interpretive Area,** where you'll find a picnic shelter housed in an old powerhouse. You can walk to **Cattle Point Lighthouse** via a trail that starts 150 yards down the road to the south. Two pretty pocket-size beaches are just down from the powerhouse parking area. A number of private residences are located on the eastern end of the peninsula, as this area lies outside the boundaries of San Juan Island National Historical Park.

## English Camp

Nine miles from Friday Harbor on the northwest side of the island, English Camp (360/378-4409, 9 A.M.–5 P.M. daily June–early Sept., closed the rest of the year) covers 841 acres and includes four buildings from the 1860s that have been restored: a small white barracks, hospital, commissary, and a picturesque **blockhouse.** The latter sits right at the water's edge and has a peculiar design. The second story is rotated 45 degrees from the bottom level, allowing troops to repel attacks from any side. Fortunately, the attack never came. Befitting the civilized British modus operandi, the camp had a small **formal garden,** an impressive replica of which has been reestablished.

Park volunteers staff the buildings during the summer and show a video that explains the Pig War. Be sure to pick up the park brochure for a self-guided walking tour of the historic sites. As with American Camp, it's day use only here, with no camping allowed. A spotting scope is often set up outside the barracks, providing a good view of an active osprey nest on a nearby snag.

English Camp is a quiet and peaceful spot with protected waters on both sides of Bell Point. It contrasts sharply with American Camp's exposed and windswept location. The grounds include several old pear trees from a homestead family who lived here after the British military departed in 1872. Enormous bigleaf maples are also on the grounds, one of which was once officially the world's largest. The loss of two major limbs reduced its spread, so the tree is now simply a very big and beautiful maple. It is estimated to be over 340 years old.

A 650-foot hill, **Mount Young,** rises directly behind Garrison Bay, with meadow openings atop its forested slopes. The 0.75-mile Mount Young Trail starts at the far end of the English Camp parking lot, crosses the road, and climbs to the little **British cemetery** where six Royal Marines are buried—though none of them died in a battle over the islands. One especially poignant gravestone reads:

*William Taylor*
*Aged 34 years*
*Who was accidentally shot*
*By his Brother*
*Jan. 26th 1868.*
*This Tablet is erected by his*
*Sorrowing Brother.*

Beyond this, the trail continues up through second-growth forests to the open summit of Mount Young, where you are treated to outstanding vistas across the archipelago. Old Garry oak trees grow up here as well.

An easy alternative walk departs from the blockhouse and leads along an almost-level path to the tip of **Bell Point** and then back along Westcott Bay; it's about a mile roundtrip. This little wooded peninsula is a great place for a picnic lunch. Keep your eyes open for Canada geese and wild turkeys below, and bald eagles and turkey vultures overhead.

## ◖ ROCHE HARBOR

On the north end of San Juan Island, 10 miles from Friday Harbor, Roche Harbor (360/378-2155 or 800/451-8910, www.rocheharbor.com) is a delightful step into the past. (By the way, locals pronounce Roche as ro-SHAY, not roach.)

John McMillin's **Hotel de Haro** began as a log cabin built by the Hudson's Bay Company, but later grew into the distinctive three-story mansion of today. President Theodore Roosevelt visited it twice, in 1906 and 1907, and it later hosted President William Howard Taft. The quarries operated till 1956, when they were essentially mined out. Pick up the fascinating walking tour brochure at the hotel and start your exploration of this picturesque harbor.

Roche Harbor is named for Richard Roche, a British surveyor and midshipman during two 19th-century expeditions of the area. Hotel de Haro is named for nearby Haro Strait, which in turn got its name from Lopez Gonzales de Haro, a Spanish sailor and the first European to discover the San Juan Islands.

### Resort and Marina

The white-clapboard Hotel de Haro, now on the National Register of Historic Places, has been lovingly restored. If it isn't occupied, you can peek in the presidential suite (room 2A) upstairs where Roosevelt stayed, or see his 1907 signature in the guest book below his portrait. The hotel's sloping floors, creaking steps, and crooked windows add charm and provide a gracious setting for the antique furnishings.

Take some time to explore the area around the hotel. Out front is a wonderful **formal garden** with rose trellises and brilliant swaths of various flowers throughout the summer. The yellow brick road between the garden and the hotel was built from firebricks that once lined the limekilns. McMillin's home is now a waterside restaurant, facing the protected and busy harbor filled with sailboats, motorboats, and kayaks. Roche Harbor is still the primary U.S. Customs port of entry for boaters heading to the San Juans from Canadian waters. The old general store is still in use and well worth a visit. Behind it, warehouses once stretched hundreds of feet into the bay, holding up to 20,000 barrels of lime. Across the parking lot are the two original **stone kilns** built by the Scurr brothers in 1881. The 13 old lime quarries are uphill behind the resort, but you need to exercise caution since the slopes are unstable.

Join a free game of bocce ball on the courts nearby, or saunter down the row of **Artist Kiosks** showcasing photography, jewelry, hand-knit pieces, and watercolors—not to mention scoops of ice cream. The booths are next to the parking lot and are open daily late June–early September and on weekends in the spring and fall. Midsummer moped and bike rentals are available across from the IMA Sculpture Park, uphill from Roche Harbor.

Just up from the hotel is the quaint little New England–style **Our Lady of Good Voyage Chapel,** built in 1892. John McMillin was a devout Methodist, but when Reuben Tarte bought Roche Harbor in 1956, he turned it into the only privately owned Catholic church

Afterglow Vista Mausoleum at Roche Harbor

© DON PITCHER

in America. Mass is held on Easter Sunday and periodically throughout the summer. Other denominations also use the chapel, and it's a favorite spot for a wedding-with-a-view. A carillon was added in 1972, followed a few years later by a stained-glass window that depicts two of the late Dr. Tarte's devotions: medicine and tennis.

A short walk north of the church are nine simple cottages once used by McMillin's employees; they're now rented out to guests. Ten larger cottages were torn down, along with the old Japanese settlement on the south side of the harbor. The Japanese buildings were replaced by ugly condos in the 1970s, a glaring affront to this historic site. More recent developments have been more appropriate to the site, including tasteful additions in the last few years of upscale lodging, a spa, and other facilities behind and adjacent to Hotel de Haro.

A moving—and simultaneously comical—**Colors Ceremony** takes place each evening at sunset mid-May–late September, as the U.S., Canadian, and British flags are lowered as the national anthems play, followed by taps and a shot from the cannon. This event always attracts a big crowd. Surprise your friends by having a message read to them during the ceremony; just leave the message at the front desk of Hotel de Haro in advance.

## Afterglow Vista Mausoleum

The exuberant McMillin family mausoleum, Afterglow Vista, is about a mile from Hotel de Haro. Located north of the cottages and a 0.25-mile hike up a dirt trail (signed), the mausoleum's centerpiece is a stone temple packed with Masonic symbols and containing the family's ashes in chair-shaped crypts around a limestone (of course) table. There's even a broken column symbolizing the "unfinished state" of life, but the planned bronze dome with a Maltese cross was never added to this once-grandiose mausoleum. Some folks claim that on full moon nights, a ghostly McMillen family can be seen talking and laughing around the mausoleum table. Could this be the true meaning of that creepy Afterglow Vista name?

Hotel de Haro at Roche Harbor Resort

## IMA Sculpture Park

Covering 19 acres near the entrance to Roche Harbor, IMA Sculpture Park (360/370-5050, www.sjima.org, daily dawn–dusk, $5 donation, kids under 12 free) is home to more than 100 large stone, wood, bronze, glass, and metal sculptures created by noted Northwest artists. Trails wend through a diverse habitat of forest, meadow, pond, wetland, and shoreline. The sculptures change every few months, so there's always something new to see (and touch). All of these are also for sale if you have a few thousand dollars lying around; just peruse the binder inside the gatehouse for prices and artist info. Birders should pick up the brochure on the 120 or so species that have been seen in this diverse habitat. Bring your kids to the free **Family Art Days** on Saturdays in July and August, with lots of hands-on activities. The IMA Sculpture Park is part of the San Juan Islands Museum of Art & Sculpture Park, with a separate gallery in Friday Harbor. Nearby is a **fly-in aviation community,** where planes taxi down Cessna Avenue and park in hangars next to the houses.

## ◖ LIME KILN POINT STATE PARK

Locally known as **Whale Watch Park** (360/378-2044, www.parks.wa.gov), this is a premier spot to look for killer whales as they pass along Haro Strait on the island's west side. It's the only park in the nation dedicated primarily to whale-watching. Sit here long enough on a summer day (it may be quite a while), and you're likely to see killer whales and possibly minke whales, Dall's porpoises, or harbor porpoises. Day use of the park costs $10 per vehicle.

Picturesque **Lime Kiln Point Lighthouse** was completed in 1919. Researchers from The Whale Museum use the lighthouse as a base to observe whale and vessel behavior, as well as to study whale vocalizations and underwater noise via offshore hydrophones. If there aren't any whales, you can take in the vistas that stretch from Vancouver Island to the Olympic

© DON PITCHER

"Resting Dancer" by Tuck Langdon in the IMA Sculpture Park

Peninsula. If it's foggy, you'll get a fine view of the fog.

The park has plenty of parking and a wheelchair-accessible trail to the whale-viewing area. A small **interpretive center** next to the parking lot is staffed daily 10 A.M.–6 P.M. in the summer, but it closes when whales are passing by the lighthouse. No camping, but there are picnic tables, drinking water, and privies. Tune your radio to 88.1 FM when you approach the park to hear a broadcast of underwater sounds—including whales if they happen to be in the area.

In the summer, park staff, volunteers, and researchers lead lighthouse tours (7 P.M.–sunset Thurs. and Sat. late May–early Sept.) and interpretive **orca whale talks** (3 P.M. Fri. and Sat. June–mid-Aug.). At other times, you can watch a video on whales at the interpretive center, listen to underwater sounds from the hydrophone, take in the view at the lighthouse, or pull out binoculars to scan for orcas and marine birds.

A loop hike leads past one of the restored limekilns and several in disrepair and then heads south to the old quarry and Deadman Bay. The trail continues out of the park and onto adjacent land within the **Limekiln Preserve,** owned by the San Juan County Land Bank. South of Limekiln, West Side Road hugs the steep shoreline of San Juan Island. This stretch of road is part of the Land Bank's **Westside Scenic Preserve,** where three pullouts provide additional chances to watch for whales and to take in panoramic views of Vancouver Island and the Olympic Mountains.

## SAN JUAN COUNTY PARK

On the west side of the island at Smallpox Bay, San Juan County Park (360/378-8420, www.co.san-juan.wa.us/parks) is the only public camping spot on San Juan Island. In addition to camping, the 12-acre park has a grassy day-use area overlooking the water, a pebble beach, pretty forests, picnic tables, restrooms,

© DON PITCHER

Lime Kiln Point Lighthouse

drinking water, and a boat launch. The waters here are popular with kayakers and divers, and this is a good place to watch for wild turkeys on land and killer whales offshore. Portions of the 1998 film *Practical Magic* were filmed in the park.

**Smallpox Bay** got its name in the 1860s when two sick sailors from an unknown boat were put ashore to prevent them from contaminating the rest of the crew with smallpox. Local Coast Salish people, who had no immunity to the disease, helped the men, and smallpox quickly spread across San Juan Island. The feverish victims jumped into the bay to cool off and died of pneumonia. The few survivors burned their possessions and fled the island.

## REUBEN TARTE COUNTY PARK

This tiny day-use-only area (360/378-8420, www.co.san-juan.wa.us/parks) is a secluded and delightful place to escape the Friday Harbor crowds. Located on the north end of the island near Limestone Point, it consists of a rocky point with two minor coves facing Haro Strait. The ferry connecting the islands with Sidney, British Columbia, goes right past the park. This is one of the few pieces of public land on the north end of San Juan Island; everything else around here is posted No Trespassing.

Get to Reuben Tarte by following Roche Harbor Road eight miles from Friday Harbor and turning right onto Rouleau Road. Follow it a mile, then turn right onto Limestone Point Road. After another mile, turn right again onto San Juan Drive and continue 0.25 mile to the park, located on the left. You should probably park at the top and hike down the steep paved road to Reuben Tarte, as only a couple of parking spaces are available at the bottom. There are no facilities (other than an outhouse) here, but bring your picnic lunch for a delightful afternoon along the shore.

## FALSE BAY BIOLOGICAL RESERVE

Owned by the University of Washington, False Bay is a half-mile-wide undeveloped bay on the south end of San Juan Island. This large and shallow bay becomes a mudflat when the tide is out, though there are some sandy stretches along the shore. It's an easy stroll, and a good place to look for shorebirds. Access is from a pullout off False Bay Road; Mar Vista Resort is a short distance southeast of here.

## BEACHES AND OTHER NATURE AREAS

A number of other day-use-only spots are scattered around San Juan Island. **Jacksons Beach** is a small public beach a mile south of Friday Harbor off Argyle Avenue. It has a sandy shore littered with driftwood, a boat ramp, picnic tables, sand volleyball courts, and restrooms.

**Eagle Cove** sits on the south end of the island just west of American Camp and is a favorite of sports fishers who enjoy the delightful

# KILLER WHALES

Killer whales (also called orcas) are a major attraction for visitors to the San Juan Islands. Each year more than 500,000 people board commercial whale-watching trips in the waters off Washington and British Columbia, pumping $10 million into the economy. In addition, several thousand other boaters head out to watch whales on private vessels each year.

Why all this attention? Perhaps it is just a simple human interest in the natural world – and large mammals in particular. But anyone who has seen these magnificent creatures in the wild will tell you that it is something more significant, for here are intelligent and beautifully patterned animals who share close family bonds, communicate long distances underwater, enjoy play, and share our taste for salmon (though theirs is in the raw, sashimi form).

## NATURAL HISTORY

With a range from tropical seas south to the edge of Antarctica and north into the Bering Sea, killer whales are the second most widely distributed mammals on the planet; only humans range farther. And like humans, some females may live a century or longer (males have a shorter lifespan), with sexual maturity around age 15. At birth, the calves are 8 feet long and weigh more than 400 pounds. By adulthood, females are around 23 feet long, while males can reach 30 feet. A member of the order of cetaceans – whales, dolphins, and porpoises – the killer whale might best be viewed as a large dolphin that happens to have *whale* in its name.

Killer whales, *Orcinus orca,* have long had a reputation befitting their murderous name. Historically, they were regarded as bloodthirsty predators and a threat to humans on or in the water. More recently, the "Save the Whales" crowd has promoted them as lovable creatures that should instead be called by

the more lyrical name, orcas. (Ironically, the word "orca" comes from a Latin word meaning "kingdom of the dead.") The orca frenzy was fueled in part by the three sappy *Free Willy* movies that played fast and loose with the facts. (Portions of *Free Willy I* and *Free Willy II* were shot on the San Juans.) The truth is actually much more complex; some killer whales known as residents hunt only fish. Others, called transient killer whales, kill marine mammals, including sea lions, porpoises, other whales, and even sea otters.

Orcas travel in matrilineal groups called pods. These consist of extended families that follow the eldest female. Even the males may remain for life within these extended families. Surprisingly, not all mating takes place with other pods, and there is some evidence of inbreeding within the pods. Intensive research has revealed that orcas have a highly complex social structure and diverse patterns of behavior, including a vocal dialect for each pod that is distinctive from one population to the next.

Killer whales can be surprisingly kind to members of their own pod. In 1973, a British Columbia ferry collided with a young killer whale, seriously injuring it with the propeller. Other members of the pod rushed to the calf's aid, physically supporting it for two weeks to help it breathe. Unfortunately, the animal later died of its wounds.

## RESIDENT KILLER WHALES

The whales most commonly seen around the San Juans are considered residents, though some of the pods migrate out of the area seasonally. Ninety percent of their diet is salmon, particularly the fatty chinook (king) salmon.

Nearly 300 resident killer whales swim in the waters along Washington and British Columbia. They are divided into two groups: a large northern community of approximately

215 whales in 16 pods found mainly in British Columbia's Johnstone Strait area, and a smaller southern community of whales that spend much of their time in the Salish Sea around the San Juan Islands. These southern residents are subdivided into family groups known as J, K, and L pods. Each pod contains closely related whales around an older female; she is often the mother or grandmother of others in the pod. The matriarch of J pod was born in 1911, with four generations of descendents for this centurnarian.

With a few more than 40 members, L pod is the largest, followed by J pod with more than 25 members and K pod with around 20 indivuduals. The J pod is the one most often seen by whale-watchers because it spends time in local waters year-round. During the winter J pod are often offshore, returning to the Salish Sea for brief visits. Both K and L pods head to the outer coast of Washington and Vancouver Island, and even as far south as Monterey Bay, California, during the winter and spring.

## SAVING THE WHALES

When intensive research on the orcas began in 1976, the southern community (J, K, and L pods) consisted of 71 individuals. It gradually increased to a peak of 98 in 1995, but declined to 78 whales in 2001, prompting scientists to request protection under the Endangered Species Act. The southern resident killer whales are now listed as endangered in the U.S. As of 2011, the three pods contained 88 whales.

Several factors certainly have played a role in this decline. Because they are long-lived top-level predators, killer whales tend to concentrate environmental contaminants in their fatty tissue. The whales have frighteningly high levels of polychlorinated biphenyls (PCBs), flame retardants (PBDEs), dioxins, and other toxic chemicals. PCB levels in these orcas are among the highest ever found in whales, and PBDEs are found at high concentrations even in young whales.

Another problem is that their primary food source, salmon, has been on the decline, and half of the local salmon runs appear threatened with extinction. When the whales lack food, they consume stored blubber that contains PCBs, and these can cause reproductive and other problems.

During the 1960s and 1970s, some 48 young killer whales from this population were captured in Puget Sound for aquariums around the world; only one of these is still alive, an L-pod female known as Lolita, living in the Miami Seaquarium in Florida. This was a significant part of the population, and the loss of this 10-year age cohort of females is still being felt.

What role does whale-watching have in the whales' decline? This question comes immediately to mind if you've ever been on a whale-watching trip and discovered a flotilla of dozens of boats tailing the whales for hours at a stretch. Current research appears to show that the dramatic increase in vessel traffic (including whale-watching boats) in recent years may be causing the whales to compensate for boat noise in the way they communicate, adding stress to animals that have already been weakened by other factors. Boat noise can mask echolocation, possibly making it harder for killer whales to find what little food is available to them.

The Whale Museum in Friday Harbor recommends that people watch whales responsibly either from shore or with a whale watching company that belongs to the **Pacific Whale Watch Association** (www.pacificwhalewatch. org). The company should be one that hires professional naturalists and follows the Be Whale Wise guidelines. As a consumer, you can help by supporting habitat protection for salmon and limiting the use of chemicals.

pocket beach. Two north-end bodies of water, **Egg Lake** and **Sportsmans Lake,** are also popular with anglers in search of trout.

**Sunken Park** in Friday Harbor is a little pocket park with a gazebo, basketball court, and picnic area.

The **San Juan County Land Bank** (350 Court St., 360/378-4402, www.sjclandbank. org) maintains several hundred acres of protected lands on San Juan Island that are open to the public, including Westside Scenic Preserve and Limekiln Preserve.

## FARMS AND VINEYARDS

Several dozen small farms dot the San Juan Island landscape, producing such specialty products as cider apples, wines, miniature horses, alpacas, medicinal herbs, strawberries, goat cheese, organic vegetables, and rabbits (do they really need more of these?).

At **Heritage Farm** (360/378-2872, www. heritagefarmcsa.blogspot.com) along Cattle Point Road, owners Jim and Christina Sesby have a market garden, hay fields, chickens, and cows on this 39-acre traditional farm where sustainable agriculture is emphasized. Call ahead to set up a group tour ($25 for up to five people) providing opportunities to watch as cows are milked by hand, collect eggs in a chicken coop on wheels, taste unusual vegetables in the garden, pet the horses, and bottle-feed calves.

For a complete list of local agriculture, pick up the *San Juan Island Farm Products Guide* (http://sanjuan.wsu.edu) at the visitors center. Many local farm products are sold at the **San Juan Farmers Market** in Friday Harbor, held on summer Saturdays.

### Krystal Acres Ranch

Fans of the friendly alpaca will certainly want to visit Krystal Acres Ranch (3501 Valley Rd. 0.5 mile south of English Camp, 360/378-6125, www.krystalacres.com, 10 A.M.–5 P.M. daily Apr.–Dec., 11 A.M.–4 P.M. daily Jan.–Mar.), a picturesque 80-acre farm bordered

a beach at American Camp in San Juan Island National Historical Park

© DON PITCHER

© DON PITCHER

alpacas at Krystal Acres Ranch

by white picket fences. The multicolored herd is a favorite of photographers who happen by, and the teddy bear–faced alpacas are bound to elicit "I want one" from any child. A walking path leads between pastures containing more than 50 grazing alpacas—some worth many thousands of dollars as breeding stock. The gift shop (open daily year-round) sells alpaca yarn, stuffed animals, home furnishings, homemade jam, and Peruvian sweaters made from alpaca wool. Owners Kris and Albert Olson will be happy to tell you about alpacas and their immaculate ranch. The fur is sheared in May or June, so the alpacas will look closely cropped for a while after that.

## San Juan Vineyards

The award-winning San Juan Vineyards (3136 Roche Harbor Rd., 360/378-9463, www.sanjuanvineyards.com) is housed inside a restored one-room schoolhouse built in 1896 and originally located along Sportsmans Lake. The little six-acre vineyard grows Madeleine Angevine and Siegerrebe grapes. Winemaker Chris Primus produces a limited bottling of these—and they sell out quickly—but most of what he crafts comes from eastern Washington grapes, including chardonnay, cabernet, riesling, and syrah.

The Mona Vino is named for the friendly and much-photographed **dromedary camel** that lives across the road (he loves carrots, but watch your fingers). Drop by for wine-tasting ($1 per glass) daily 11 A.M.–5 P.M. in the summer, and on weekends in the spring and fall. Call for an appointment at other times. The second Saturday in June brings barrel tasting, with food and wine. Grapes are harvested in early October by local volunteers. Join them for the picking and partying fun. There's also a wine-tasting shop for San Juan Vineyards in Friday Harbor at 55 Spring Street.

## Westcott Bay Cider

Apples have a lengthy history on the San Juan Islands. Many orchards were planted by early settlers, and by 1900 this was perhaps the most important apple-producing region in the state. Eastern Washington apples have long taken over that crown, but apple and other fruit trees are again being planted on the San Juans. One sign of this resurgence is Westcott Bay Cider (12 Anderson Lane, 360/378-2606, www.westcottbaycider.com), located on the west side of the island near Roche Harbor. New orchards were planted here in 1996, and Westcott Bay Cider opened a few years later.

The winery produces and bottles traditional English-style ciders, from very dry to medium sweet using 16 different kinds of cider apples, including such heritage varieties as Yarlington Mill, Dabinett, Brown Snout, Sweet Coppin, Cox's Orange Pippins, and Kingston Black. You've probably never heard of these bittersweet little apples, with their high tannin and acidity, since they're grown for cider production, not eating. The juice is fermented to a 6.8 percent alcohol content.

In 2010, a brass pot still was added to distill apple brandy and gin. It's part of the same business, but is called **San Juan Island Distillery** (www.sjidistillery.com). Visitors can sample hard cider, apple brandy, and gin at the winery, and the tasting room is open Saturday 3–5 P.M. late May–early September, or by appointment at other times. Cider, brandy, and gin are available for purchase at the winery or from the state liquor store in Friday Harbor. Locals join in for a big apple harvest party each October.

## ◖ Pelindaba Lavender Farm

Pelindaba Lavender Farm (off Wold Rd. at 33 Hawthorne Lane, 360/378-4248 or 866/819-1911, www.pelindabalavender.com) grows these pungent flowers on 20 acres on the south side of the island. Owner Stephen Robins has 25,000 plants in production on his organic farm, plus a distillery to extract the oil. Organic lavender flowers and essential oils are used in a wide range of products, all of which are made here: body oil, eye pillows, sachets, lavender pepper, pet shampoo, and even a lavender-based product that kills pond algae. Lavender ice cream and lemonade are available in midsummer. A lavender

Pelindaba Lavender Farm

© DON PITCHER

## LAVENDER LEMONADE

- 2 cups water

- 6 sprigs fresh lavender spikes, or 2 tea-spoons dried Pelindaba Lavender

- juice of 3 lemons (about ½ cup)

- 1 quart water

- ½ cup sugar, or to taste, or ½ cup Pelindaba Lavender Syrup, or to taste

- additional lavender for garnish

Bring the 2 cups of water to a boil. Add lavender, cover the pan, and let it steep over very low heat for 30 minutes. Strain and reserve the liquid, which is the lavender tea you will use later.

Roll the lemons on a hard surface to help re-lease the juices. Cut and squeeze them, straining out the seeds. To the quart of water, add ⅓ cup of the lavender tea, lemon juice, and sugar or Lavender Syrup (to taste). Stir well to dissolve. Chill and serve over ice. Garnish with a fresh lav-ender spike. Makes 1 quart of lemonade.

*Recipe courtesy of Pelindaba Lavender Farm*

cookbook is available, and there's a cutting field if you're just looking for a fresh bouquet during the flowering season July–September; you'll see the most color in July. Pick up a brochure for a self-guided tour of the fields, drying racks, and distillery. There's even a webcam showing the current conditions on the farm.

The gift shop is open daily 9:30 A.M.–5:30 P.M. May–October, with limited hours the rest of the year. The farm also hosts a **Lavender Festival** the third weekend of July, with tours, distillation demonstrations, craft workshops, lavender-accented foods, and music.

# Entertainment and Events

## NIGHTLIFE

Friday Harbor's oldest bar—opened in 1943—is **Herb's** (80 1st St., 360/378-7076), with two pool tables, darts, a big selection of brews on draft, and decent bar food.

**Rumor Mill** (175 N. 1st St., 360/378-5555) serves a menu that rambles from seafoot to piz-zas, but is best known for the bar with 20-plus microbrews on tap, big-screen TVs showing sports, and live entertainment at least five eve-nings a week in the summer. It's a fun place to party late into the night.

**China Pearl Restaurant** (51 Spring St., 360/378-5254, www.chinapearldining.com) has open mic on Thursday nights and live bands Friday and Saturday nights, plus a big-screen TV, two pool tables, foosball, and Ping-

Pong. The bar is upstairs, with a harbor vista from the outdoor deck.

**Pablito's Tacqueria** (140A Spring St., 360/378-3317, www.pablitostaqueria.com) has no-cover live music—from funk to rock to accoustic—most Saturday nights all sum-mer. They clear out tables downstairs for danc-ing, and have an upstairs bar with beer, wine, horchatas, hard cider, and margaritas.

**Cask and Schooner** (1 Front St., 360/378-2922, www.caskandschooner.com) re-creates an English pub setting with nine beers on tap, including Guinness. Drop by on a weeknight for happy hour specials: $2.50 pint drafts and $5 nosh items. Belly up to the bar with the lo-cals or watch a game on the telly.

Over in Roche Harbor, **Madrona Bar &**

Grill (360/378-2155 or 800/451-8910, www. rocheharbor.com) has live music and dancing Friday and Saturday nights all summer.

Watch first-run and art films in downtown Friday Harbor at the two-screen **Palace Theatre** (209 Spring St., 360/378-5666).

## THEATER

The impressive **San Juan Community Theatre** (100 2nd St., 360/378-3210, www. sjtheatre.org) is a vital center for local performing arts, with year-round musical programs, plays, dance performances, chamber music, art shows, and more. Get your tickets early, as some events sell out. A local theater company, **Island Stage Left** (360/378-6767, www.islandstageleft.org) puts on free "Shakespeare Under the Stars" productions at the Roche Harbor amphitheater each July and August.

## FESTIVALS AND EVENTS

One of the most popular weekly island events is the **San Juan Farmers Market** (360/378-6301, www.sjifarmersmarket.com, 10 A.M.–1 P.M. Sat. late Apr.–mid-Oct.) that takes place at Brickworks Plaza (Nichols St. at Sunshine Alley). The market features organic fruits, delicious finger food, vegetables, berries, flowers, and more.

The first weekend of June brings the **Artists' Studio Tour** (www.sanjuanislandartists.com) at 20 or so studios around the island, along with the **Celebrity Golf Classic** at San Juan Island Golf & Country Club (360/378-2254, www.sanjuangolfclub.com); it's the county's biggest annual fundraising event.

**Fourth of July** features a variety of fun events, including a parade, "Rock the Dock" live music, Pig War picnic, 10K race, music, and dancing, plus evening fireworks above Friday Harbor. Over in Roche Harbor, the Fourth of July is the biggest event of the year, with a log-rolling contest, blind dinghy race,

and other events, topped off by an impressive fireworks display.

**A Splash of Summer Color,** held the third weekend of July, includes tours, demonstrations, lavender-accented foods, and a big Saturday picnic dinner at Pelindaba Lavender Farm (www. pelindaba.com), plus a summer arts fair in downtown Friday Harbor with art exhibits, food booths, and live music. Sailors should check out the **Shaw Island Classic,** a round-the-island race sponsored by the San Juan Island Yacht Club (www.sjiyc.com), held the first Saturday in August. Free **Music on the Lawn** concerts take place at the San Juan Historical Museum weekly in July and early August.

San Juan Island National Historical Park presents **Encampment** at English Camp (360/378-2240) the last weekend of July, when you'll meet 60 or so British and American "soldiers" and others in mid-19th-century period costume. Old-fashioned canvas tents are set up, and you can watch demonstrations on blacksmithing, woodworking, marching, and cookery. The highlight is a candlelight ball in the barracks building.

The four-day **San Juan County Fair** (360/378-4310, www.sanjuancountyfair.org) during the third week of August includes a sheep-to-shawl race, chicken and rabbit races, music, livestock judging, and, of course, carnival rides.

Held at San Juan Vineyards on the last Sunday in August, **Concours d'Elegance** (www.sanjuanconcours.org) attracts vintage car enthusiasts, with 90 or so classic cars, some dating back before 1920.

October is time for a monthlong festival called **Savor the San Juans,** including a variety of events; one of the most popular is **Artstock** on the first weekend of October.

Get ready for Christmas with an **Artisan's Holiday Marketplace** around Thanksgiving. The **Island Lights Fest** throughout December includes a tree lighting ceremony, caroling, and a lighted boat parade at Friday Harbor.

# Shopping

Downtown Friday Harbor is filled with interesting shops selling everything from Washington wines to bonsai trees. Browse the photos of homes for sale adorning the real estate offices, check out the toy shops for grandchild gifts, or sip a lavender tea at a coffee shop while surfing the web on your laptop.

In business since 1929, **Kings Market** (160 Spring St., 360/378-4505, www.kings-market. com, 7 A.M.–9 P.M. daily) is Friday Harbor's version of Wal-Mart, with a big gift and clothing shop, plus an upstairs marine center stocked with fishing tackle, boating supplies, charts, outdoor gear, and sea kayaks.

Find recycled clothing and much more at **Thrift House** (667 Mullis St., 360/378-8483, 9 A.M.–4 P.M. Mon.–Sat.).

## GALLERIES AND STUDIOS

Friday Harbor is home to several excellent art galleries, most of which are within a few blocks of the ferry landing. Just walk the streets to see what appeals to your taste. In addition to the galleries, you may want to drop by the library (1010 Guard St.) to see changing exhibits by local artists. During the **Artists' Studio Tour** (www.sanjuanislandartists.com) in early June, 20 or so San Juan Island studios are opened to the public; it's a great way to meet the folks behind the art.

Friday Harbor's don't-miss place is **Waterworks Gallery** (315 Argyle Ave., 360/378-3060, www.waterworksgallery.com), a fine-arts gallery with contemporary paintings, prints, watercolors, and sculpture by island and international artists. New exhibits are unveiled monthly.

One of the largest galleries in the San Juans, **Island Studios** (270 Spring St., 360/378-6550, www.islandstudios.com) has works from more than 250 local artists. You'll find paintings, photography, stained glass, jewelry, pottery, and lots more jammed into every square inch of space here. It's a fun place to spend time, with a mix of fine art and pieces that cross the line into kitsch. Don't miss the wonderful pottery garden out back, complete with a koi pond. Bring your newspaper to relax on a sunny afternoon.

**Arctic Raven Gallery** (130 S. 1st St., 360/378-3433, www.arcticravengallery.com) features quality art by Northwest Coast and Alaska Native Americans, including wood carvings, bentwood boxes, baskets, soapstone carvings, masks, art prints, and more.

**Gallery San Juan** (232 A St., 360/378-1376, www.gallerysanjuan.com) is a small gallery with paintings by Barbara and Matt Dollahite and other artists, along with changing monthly exhibits.

**San Juan Islands Museum of Art** (285 Spring St., 360/370-5050, www.sjima.org, 11 A.M.–5 P.M. Thurs.–Mon.) displays new exhibits by local and regional artists in a little Friday Harbor space. The museum also manages the sculpture park at Roche Harbor, and is officially known as the San Juan Islands Museum of Art & Sculpture Park, but is more commonly called simply IMA.

## BOOKSTORES

Friday Harbor has several good places to purchase books. **Griffin Bay Bookstore** (155 Spring St., 360/378-5511, www.griffinbaybook. com) is a book lovers' shop with both new and used books. Enjoy an espresso here and pull out your tablet or laptop for the free Wi-Fi.

Upstairs in Cannery Landing next to the ferry, **Harbor Bookstore** (360/378-7222, www.harborbookstore.com) has a nice selection of regional volumes, plus a comfortable corner where overstuffed chairs offer a bird's-eye view of the ferry action. Free Wi-Fi too.

Find an abundance of used titles—more than 48,000 books at last count—at the surprisingly well-organized **Serendipity Books** (223 A St., 360/378-2665). It's at the top of the ferry lanes.

SAN JUAN ISLAND

# Recreation

## BICYCLING

San Juan Island is very popular with cyclists, but it isn't as bike-friendly as slower-paced Lopez Island. The terrain is varied, with quiet lanes through rolling farm country, densely forested areas, wide-open grasslands and gorgeous beaches at American Camp, and stunning shorelines fronting Haro Strait. The hilly western shore of San Juan (rising to 400 feet) is especially inviting, highlighted by a whale-watching stop at Lime Kiln Point State Park. Friday Harbor has a good bike shop and all the other travel amenities, but traffic can get congested and drivers distracted, so use caution, particularly around the ferry loading area. The **San Juan Island Trails Committee** website (www.sanjuanislandtrails.org) provides route information showing bike turnouts and roads with wide shoulders. If you need a lift, both **San Juan Transit** (360/378-8887 or 800/887-8387, www.sanjuantransit.com) and **San Juan Taxi & Tours** (360/378-8294, www.378taxi.com) will haul your bike along.

### Bike Rentals and Tours

Rent bikes to cruise around San Juan Island from **Island Bicycles** (380 Argyle Ave., 360/378-4941, www.islandbicycles.com), a full-service shop just a few blocks from the ferry dock. Knowledgeable owner Paul Ahart has well-maintained, high-quality bikes, including mountain, cross, racing, tandem, and kids bicycles. Hybrid/cross bikes rent for $10/hour, $38/day, or $88 for three days; helmets and other essentials are included. The shop also rents bike trailers, Trail-A-Bikes, car racks, and baby strollers, and it is open year-round (daily in the summer). Reservations are strongly recommended in the summer months. Rental bikes are not for use on trails and cannot be taken off San Juan Island, so bring your own for trips to Stuart or other islands.

Bike rentals are also available at the Roche Harbor office of **Susie's Mopeds** (360/378-5244 or 800/532-0087, www.susiesmopeds.com, late June–early Sept., $10/hour or $40/day); bikes are provided by Island Bicycles. Find them across from IMA Sculpture Park as you come into Roche Harbor.

For San Juan Island cycling tours, contact one of the following companies: **Backroads** (510/527-1555 or 800/462-2848, www.backroads.com), **Bicycle Adventures** (425/250-5540 or 800/443-6060, www.bicycleadventures.com), or **Trek Travel** (608/441-8735 or 866/464-8735, www.trektravel.com).

## HIKING AND BIRDING

The island's finest hiking trails are within San Juan Island National Historical Park and Lime Kiln Point State Park. Other areas open to hiking include **Roche Harbor Trails** on the forested lands near Roche Harbor Resort. The trails are privately owned, but the public is welcome to traverse them. These trails connect Roche Harbor with miles of Park Service trails at English Camp and 320 acres of land at Mitchell Hill.

The **San Juan Island Trails Committee's** (www.sanjuanislandtrails.org) helpful website has downloadable maps for parks and other public areas on the island. Copies of these maps are also available at the San Juan Island Chamber of Commerce Visitor Center (135 Spring St.) in Friday Harbor.

The **San Juan Islands Audubon Society** website (www.sjiaudubon.org) lists recent sightings, upcoming bird walks, and other birding info. The group generally has San Juan Island birding walks twice a month (but not in July). Naturalist Barbara Jensen of **Bird the San Juans** (360/378-3068, www.birdthesanjuans.com) leads birding, natural history, and cultural history tours on San Juan Island; a three-hour trip for up to four people costs $135. For unusual bird sightings, visit the **Tweeters** website (www.scn.org/tweeters); click the "Latest Postings" link for recent sightings.

# ◖ SEA KAYAKING

Sea kayaking is exceptionally popular in the waters around San Juan Island, with local companies offering both day trips and multi-night tours. Each company has its own specialties, so ask around before deciding, particularly on a multi-day kayaking trip. Some companies take large groups, while others limit sizes and have a better guide-to-client ratio. Reservations are recommended for summer weekends. Most companies operate late April–September.

## Day Trips

A number of companies lead short sea-kayaking paddles from San Juan Island in the summer months. No experience is needed, but you should be in decent physical condition, and most don't allow young children. You aren't likely to get too far in such a short time, but this will at least provide a guided introduction to saltwater paddling under protected conditions. If you're looking for killer whales, go with a company whose trips begin from San Juan County Park; Friday Harbor and Roche

Harbor are fun but busy places to paddle. All companies provide free transportation from Friday Harbor.

**Discovery Sea Kayaks** (185 1st St., 360/378-2559 or 866/461-2559, www.discovery seakayaks.com) has some of the most experienced local guides, and the emphasis is on small groups—generally less than six. Discovery has the only kayak shop on San Juan Island and offers kayaking lessons. Day trips cover the west side of the island, departing from San Juan County Park; a six-hour trip is $90, and four-hour sunset paddles are $85. More unique are the nighttime bioluminescence trips (three hours for $99) to Griffin Bay during July and August. Marine dinoflagellates emit green light when the water is disturbed by paddles or kayaks, creating an otherworldly experience.

In business since 1986, **Outdoor Odysseys** (360/378-3533 or 800/647-4621, www.out-doorodysseys.com) has day trips ($89) departing from San Juan County Park. Kayakers spend four hours on the water (longer than other companies), and trips include a lunch,

© DON PITCHER

Sea kayaking is a favorite summertime activity in the waters around the San Juan Islands.

SAN JUAN ISLAND

something not offered by other operators. Guides are some of the most experienced around.

The largest kayaking company in the islands, **Crystal Seas Kayaking** (360/378-4223 or 877/732-7877, www.crystalseas.com) operates from Snug Harbor Marina on the west side, offering three-hour paddles ($79) for a quick sample, along with six-hour day trips ($99) that cover more coastline and increase your likelihood of viewing whales. Group sizes never exceed eight clients.

The nonprofit **Adventure Quest Expeditions** (360/378-5767 or 888/589-4253, www.sea-quest-kayak.com) leads day trips from San Juan County Park. Guides all have scientific backgrounds and emphasize natural history during their three-hour ($89) and six-hour ($85) trips. In addition to San Juan trips, Adventure Quest guides lead kayak trips to Baha and southeast Alaska.

**San Juan Outfitters** (360/378-1962 or 866/810-1483, www.sanjuanislandoutfitters. com) heads out daily from Roche Harbor and Friday Harbor in the summer. In addition to standard three-hour tours ($75) from both ports, San Juan Outfitters also has other tours, including five-hour "whale-sanctuary" paddles ($89) from Roche Harbor to San Juan County Park (or vice versa). The last of these provides a better chance of encountering whales.

## Multi-Day Kayak Tours

It takes time to really get a taste of the islands, and multi-day kayaking treks provide a fun way to explore places most visitors will never see.

At **San Juan Kayak Expeditions** (360/378-4436, www.sanjuankayak.com), owner-operator Tim Thomsen personally leads all trips—as he has for more than three decades. You won't find his brochures since he doesn't really need to advertise; word of mouth brings in the customers. He's even invented a unique sail that allows kayakers to take advantage of the winds when conditions are right. Three-day trips are $550, and four-day trips cost $650.

The highly experienced guides at **Discovery Sea Kayaks** (185 1st St., 360/378-2559 or 866/461-2559, www.discoveryseakayaks.com) lead all-inclusive three-to five-day adventures to the more remote parts of the archipelago, including Sucia, Patos, Matia, and Jones Islands. The price drops substantially if you provide your own food and camping equipment. Overnight trips have a maximum of just eight clients, and the itinerary is flexible. Also available are mothership adventures.

A respected kayak company with experienced guides, **Outdoor Odysseys** (360/378-3533 or 800/647-4621, www.outdoorodysseys. com) has three-day tours ($605) that depart San Juan Island for remote Stuart Island, and more leisurely four-day paddles ($759) to Stuart, Jones, and other islands. The company also offers women-only three-day trips ($619) twice each summer.

Another long-established company, **Adventure Quest Expeditions** (360/378-5767 or 888/589-4253, www.sea-quest-kayak. com) has multi-day trips to Stuart, Jones, Posey, Turn, and other islands. Group sizes are often larger than other companies.

**Crystal Seas Kayaking** (360/378-4223 or 877/732-7877, www.crystalseas.com) offers a wide variety of two- to six-day trips, including kayak-and-camping trips, inn-to-inn soft adventures, and multisport trips that combine kayaking, biking, and lodging at inns. A two-day, one-night trip is $780, while a six-day, five-night adventure costs $2,580. Groups are kept small—not more than eight people. In addition, the company leads kayak trips in Florida and Costa Rica.

In business since 1980, Seattle-based **Northwest Outdoor Center** (206/281-9694 or 800/683-0637, www.nwoc.com) leads three-day "whale search" trips a couple of times in the summer, with San Juan County Park as its camping base. The cost is $325 per person.

Multi-night kayak trips are also available from **San Juan Outfitters** (360/378-1962 or 866/810-1483, www.sanjuanislandoutfitters.com), with three-night trips to Jones and Stuart Islands for $579, including all meals and camping equipment.

## Kayak Rentals

On the waterfront below Downriggers Restaurant, **Friday Harbor Marine** (360/378-6702, www.sjimarine.com) has kayak rentals of all types, including a rather bizarre sit-on-top Mirage that uses foot pedals to turn a propeller. Also based in Friday Harbor, **San Juan Kayak Expeditions** (360/378-4436, www.sanjuan-kayak.com) rents double fiberglass kayaks with gear for $100 per day. Both companies charge lower rates for multi-day rentals.

**San Juan Outfitters** (360/378-1962 or 866/810-1483, www.sanjuanislandoutfitters.com) rents sit-on-top kayaks, paddle boards, and pedal-powered boats in Roche Harbor for playing around this hectic harbor.

**Lakedale Resort** (360/378-2350 or 800/617-2267, www.lakedale.com) rents canoes, paddleboats, and rowboats for use on Neva Lake, four miles from Friday Harbor on Roche Harbor Road.

Kayaks can be launched from the public dock just north of the Friday Harbor ferry landing ($10), but parking can be a challenge.

Other options include Shipyard Cove (0.5 mile from Friday Harbor), Pinedrona Cove (near Turn Island), Jacksons Beach, San Juan County Park ($7), Roche Harbor ($10), Snug Harbor ($10), American Camp, and English Camp. People planning their own kayak trip to the islands should get a copy of Randel Washburne's *Kayaking Puget Sound, the San Juans, and Gulf Islands* (The Mountaineers, www.mountaineers.org), with information on routes, safety issues, and more.

## 🄲 WHALE-WATCHING

For thousands of visitors, seeing a killer whale is *the* highlight of a trip to San Juan Island. Whale-watching has become a major business, particularly during June and July when a flotilla of boats and kayaks hovers around pods of orcas, trailing them as they move. Boat operators insist that they are not negatively impacting the whales, and most local companies are members of the **Northwest Whalewatch Operators Association** (www.nwwhalewatchers.org), which follows the "Be Whale Wise"

© DON PITCHER

A whale-watching boat spots several orcas.

# WHALE-WATCHING TRIPS

Guided whale-watching trips began in the early 1980s around the San Juan Islands and have exploded into a major business. Dozens of commercial operators run some 85 boats today. Some of these are based on San Juan and Orcas Islands, while many others make day trips from Victoria, Seattle, and other cities. The best viewing is usually in Haro Strait on the west side of San Juan Island from the shores of Lime Kiln Point State Park, but killer whales move almost constantly and may be seen elsewhere around the San Juans, particularly near Stuart and Waldron Islands northwest of Orcas Island.

Operated by The Whale Museum, the **Soundwatch Boater Education Program** works to protect the orcas from vessel impacts through education, along with a bit of verbal arm-twisting and "report cards" to commercial whale-watching companies. Flagrant violations are reported to the National Marine Fisheries Service and Fisheries & Oceans Canada, which may impose stiff fines for whale harassment. Boaters heading out on their own should pick up a copy of the *Be Whale Wise* guidelines from The Whale Museum in Friday Harbor or learn more at www.bewhalewise.org. Boaters and kayakers must stay at least 200 yards from killer whales and keep out of their path.

## WHERE ARE THE WHALES?

The best time to see killer whales is May and June, when salmon are moving into Puget Sound and killer whales are seen 90 percent of the time. The J pod is typically present year-round, while the K and L pods often head farther out to sea to hunt December through April, when most of the salmon are elsewhere. The Whale Museum's website has a monthly chart showing which pods have historically been seen in waters around the San Juans, plus webcams showing the current view from Lime Kiln Point State Park, along with live audio from underwater hydrophones just offshore.

## CHOOSING A TRIP

The least intrusive way to watch killer whales is from land at scenic **Lime Kiln Point State Park** (aka Whale Watch Park) on the west side of San Juan Island along Haro Strait. Other good spots to look for orcas are San Juan County Park and South Beach. The whales come in close to shore at times, though their arrival can't be predicted with certainty.

Many boat companies compete for your whale-viewing business, and their snazzy brochures fill the racks on ferries and tourist venues. Not all of these tours are created equally.

code of conduct to minimize disturbances to the whales.

The Whale Museum encourages folks to watch from shore, especially from such places as Lime Kiln Point State Park (aka Whale Watch Park) and American Camp. Drop by the museum to ask where whales have been reported that day and then take a bike, car, or shuttle bus over for the day. It's cheaper than a boat and you won't need to worry about impacting the whales.

Quite a few companies run scheduled whale-watching trips, and each has its advantages and disadvantages. Some companies promise "guaranteed whales" in their brochures. In reality,

the entire fleet knows where the whales are, so you're probably as likely to see them on one boat as another.

Some of the bigger outfits have flashy brochures and larger boats that pack folks on, while the small operators offer more intimate trips, though their boats may be slower and bounce around a lot (not good if you get seasick easily). Operators based on the west side of San Juan Island at Snug Harbor or Roche Harbor are often closer to the whales, but fast boats can get there from Friday Harbor, and the whales aren't always in that area. All the companies have hydrophones to listen in on whale conversations.

Some brag about their personalized trips aboard boats that hold just six passengers; some claim to be "closest to the whales"; others talk up their speedy boats, colorful captains, stable larger vessels, or hydrophones to listen underwater. From an environmental standpoint, larger boats may be better since this means fewer vessels bobbing around the whales, but you'll also hear complaints about the jam-'em-on whale-watching boats and the small inflatable Zodiac-type boats that come across from Victoria and buzz around the whales like angry bees. The latter have a bad reputation for "leapfrogging": intentionally positioning the boats where the whales are expected to surface. This makes for good photos and gives tourists a thrill, but is frowned upon by whale researchers and more reputable operators.

When choosing a whale-watching trip, take the time to learn more about the companies and how they operate. Be sure to ask about onboard naturalists' training and affiliated organizations. Companies listed in this book are all members of the **Northwest Whalewatch Operators Association** (www. nwwhalewatchers.org), which has a code of conduct that tries to minimize disturbances to the whales. A particularly good one – it's the oldest on the islands – is **Deer Harbor Charters** (360/376-5989 or 800/544-5758, www. deerharborcharters.com). Let the company know it is important to you that it follows the guidelines; it shows you have high standards. The Whale Museum does not lead trips; in fact, it encourages shore-based viewing instead. A local environmental group, **Orca Relief** (www.orcarelief.org) opposes boat-based whale-watching.

## LEARNING MORE

*Killer Whales*, by John K. B. Ford, Graeme M. Ellis, and Kenneth C. Balcomb (UBC Press, www.ubcpress.ca), is the definitive volume on these whales, with a detailed natural history and a genealogy of the British Columbia and Washington orcas. One of the authors, Dr. Kenneth Balcomb, heads the nonprofit **Center for Whale Research** (360/378-5835, www.whaleresearch.com) in Friday Harbor on San Juan Island. The center doesn't have facilities for visitors, but it does take volunteers for seasonal research projects in which the whales are photographed and identified.

For a hands-on chance to learn about killer whales and other marine mammals, be sure to visit another nonprofit organization, the excellent **The Whale Museum** (360/378-4710 or 800/946-7227, www.whalemuseum.org) in Friday Harbor.

Expect to pay $75–80 adults or $50 kids for a three- to four-hour (sometimes longer) trip, with half that time around the whales and the remainder in transit. In the peak season, be sure to make reservations for these very popular trips. Bring a warm jacket, snacks, drinks, camera, and binoculars.

In addition to killer whales, keep your eyes open for Dall's porpoises, harbor porpoises, harbor seals, Steller sea lions, bald eagles, and many species of seabirds. You might also spot an occasional minke or gray whale.

A good company operating out of Snug Harbor, **Maya's Whale Watch Charters** (360/378-7996, www.mayaswhalewatch.biz)

has a speedy little six-passenger boat for personalized trips at the same price as the bigger operators. Maya's heads out three times a day in the summer for three-hour trips.

Friday Harbor–based **Western Prince Cruises** (360/378-5315 or 800/757-6722, www.westernprince.com) uses a fast biodiesel-powered 46-foot boat with a maximum of 30 guests. Trips are around 3.5 hours. They also operate a 27-foot high-speed boat for those who don't mind wind in their faces; $99 for a 2.5-hour trip.

**San Juan Excursions** (360/378-6636 or 800/809-4253, www.watchwhales.com) operates the 65-foot *Odyssey,* a wooden boat with space for 97 passengers. Three tours depart from Friday Harbor and typically last 3.5 hours.

**San Juan Outfitters** (360/378-1962 or 866/810-1483, www.sanjuanislandoutfitters. com) has 3.5-hour trips out of Roche Harbor with a 24-passenger boat. Trips depart twice daily in midsummer.

Bill Carli of **Captain Carli's Charters** (360/378-0302 or 888/221-1331, www. carli-charters.com) has a fast, modern six-passenger boat with 3.5-hour trips from Friday Harbor twice daily. Custom trips to the outer islands are also available, including ones that combine hiking and whale-watching.

Maya's Whale Watch Charters heads out year-round; the other companies typically operate April–September when whales are more plentiful. Wintertime trips focus on bald eagles and other wildlife.

A number of companies lead **sea kayak trips** along the west coast of San Juan Island—through prime orca waters. Kayaks are quiet and don't leave behind the odor from exhaust fumes, but kayakers should raft up (stick close to each other) to minimize their impacts on the whales. Look for kayak companies that depart from San Juan County Park or Snug Harbor.

## BOATING

Sailing and powerboating are very big on San Juan Island, and the surrounding waters fill with a flotilla of watercraft on summer weekends. Two large marinas at Roche Harbor and Friday Harbor offer guest moorage, motorboat charters, sailboat rentals, sailing trips, fishing charters, and showers, with lodging, restaurants, and other amenities close by. Public boat launch ramps are located at San Juan County Park, Friday Harbor, Roche Harbor, Shipyard Cove Marina, Snug Harbor, and Jacksons Beach. A launch fee is charged at most of these locations.

Founded in 1964, the **San Juan Island Yacht Club** (273 Front St., 360/378-3434, www.sjiyc.com) sponsors a dozen or so local cruises for powerboats and sailboats each year, along with the biggest sailing event of the year, the Shaw Island Classic in early August.

© DON PITCHER

sailing past Cattle Point Lighthouse on the south end of San Juan Island

## Sailing

If you've ever dreamed of sailing the islands in a classic wooden boat, **Schooners North** (360/378-2224, www.schoonersnorth.com) is the way to go. Based in Friday Harbor, the company has two picture-perfect vessels available for day tours May–October. *The Sea Witch* is a 44-foot piece of art with space for six passengers. Even more impressive is the 80-foot *Spike Africa,* a gorgeous schooner with room for 33 guests. Built in 1974, the boat has appeared in TV shows and the Tom Hanks and Meg Ryan movie *Joe Versus the Volcano.* Schooners North offers a series of four-day trips, along with an extraordinary 11-day sail north to Desolation Sound. Groups can also charter one of the boats for a special occasion. If you're just looking for a day of sailing, join a three-hour trip for $45 per person, or a six-hour all-day sail for $85 including lunch. Call ahead for reservations if possible, especially for the evening sails. Highly recommended.

**San Juan Classic Day Sailing** (360/378-6700, www.sanjuanclassicdaysailing.com) has all-day sails for $199 per person, including lunch, plus two-day island circumnavigation cruises for $499 per person, including breakfast, two lunches, and berth. Hop onboard the 72-foot schooner *Dirigo II* for a wonderful day on the water. Built in 1939, the wooden boat has competed in international races and is now based in Friday Harbor. The company also has several other wooden boats for charter, and private charters are available.

Friday Harbor–based **Cap'n Howard's Sailing Charters** (360/378-3958, www.capnhoward.com, May–mid-Oct.) has sailing lessons, whale-watching, and charters. Join Howard Crowell for a 3.5-hour sail ($200 for up to six people) onboard the 35-foot *Capricious.* **Friday Harbor Marine** (360/378-6702, www.sjimarine.com) also provides lessons through an American Sailing Association–approved program.

## Motorboats

Built in 1925, the *Cutterhead* is a 36-foot wooden motor yacht operated by **Choice Charters** (360/472-0052, www.choicecharterscustomcruises.com). Personalized cruises can be of any length, and even in the moonlight. A two- or three-hour cruise is $225 for two people, up to $500 for six passengers. The boat is based in Roche Harbor and operated by Captain Bill West.

**Friday Harbor Marine** (360/378-6702, www.sjimarine.com) rents skiffs, odd electric-propelled launches (perfect for cruising around nearby Turn Island if you don't mind looking a bit foolish), sailboats, and other craft from their waterfront location at the foot of Spring Street in Friday Harbor. In addition, the company provides sailing lessons and kayak rentals.

Located on the northwest side of the island, **Mitchell Bay Landing/Friday Harbor Boats and RV** (2101 Mitchell Bay Rd., 360/378-9296, www.mitchellbaylanding.com) rents motorboats and sea kayaks, along with fishing gear and crab pots. The boats are on trailers so you can haul them to boat ramps around the island.

## Marinas

**Friday Harbor Marina** (360/378-2688, www.portfridayharbor.org) is at the center of the Friday Harbor action. This 500-slip marina has space for 150 visiting boats, plus a chandlery. Just about anything else you might need can be found within a few blocks, from whale-watching to gallery snooping. Charter boats and fishing trips are available, along with showers, laundry, pump-out service, and a launch ramp. It is also a U.S. Customs port of entry and seaplane base.

Busiest marina in the San Juans, **Roche Harbor** (360/378-2155 or 800/451-8910, www.rocheharbor.com) is a seasonal U.S. Customs port of entry for boaters arriving from Canada. Facilities include permanent and guest moorage for 350 boats, fuel, showers, laundry, and a launch ramp. Boat charters are through Adventure Charters Northwest. This full-service resort includes a grocery store, post office, tiny Catholic church, restaurants, bar, hotel, cabins, and a swimming pool. Whale-watching tours and guided kayak trips are popular summertime

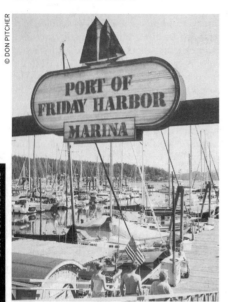

© DON PITCHER

SAN JUAN ISLAND

Friday Harbor Marina

diversions, and sit-on-top kayaks are available for rent through San Juan Outfitters (360/378-1962 or 866/810-1483, www.sanjuanislandoutfitters.com). Roche Harbor is one of the biggest attractions on San Juan Island. Oh yes, there's a free pump-out service called, creatively, the **M.V. Phecal Phreak,** whose motto is "We take crap from anyone."

## FISHING

Charter fishing for salmon (king, silver, and sockeye) is best in August and September, with bottom fish available year-round. For fishing and other boat charters from Friday Harbor, contact **Trophy Charters** (360/378-2110, www.fishthesanjuans.com), **Outer Island Expeditions** (360/376-3711, www.outer-islandx.com), and **North Shore Charters** (360/376-4855, www.orcasislandadventures.com). Expect to pay around $165 per person for an all-day fishing expedition.

Do-it-yourselfers can fish for trout at Egg Lake and Sportsmans Lake. Also popular is **Lakedale Resort** (4313 Roche Harbor Rd., 360/378-2350 or 800/617-2267, www.lakedale.com), where three lakes are stocked with widemouth bass, Kamloops trout, and rainbow trout.

## DIVING

Scuba diving is popular in the cold but amazingly productive waters off San Juan Island. Right on the harbor, **Friday Harbor Dive** (360/378-6702, www.fridayharbordiveservices.com) provides air, nitrox, and rental gear. Boat rentals are available through Friday Harbor Marine (same owners and location, www.sji-marine.com), but the nearest full dive shops are in Anacortes and Bellingham.

## HORSEBACK RIDING

Covering 66 acres off San Juan Valley Road, **Horseshu Ranch** (131 Gilbert Lane, 360/378-2298, www.horseshu.com) has 15 gentle horses and ponies. Even young children are welcome on the ponies (with parental help, of course). Hour-long rides through an old-growth forest cost $55, and Horseshu Ranch has an arena with riding lessons and horse boarding. This is a great family spot.

## ZIP LINING

The zip line phenomenon has reached the San Juan Islands. Located halfway between Friday Harbor and Roche Harbor, **Zip San Juan** (1959 Egg Lake Rd., 360/378-5947, www.zipsanjuan.com) has eight cable zip lines 15–50 feet above the ground in a forested setting—not nearly as impressive as the zip lines in Alaska or Costa Rica, but fun nevertheless. Tours last approximately three hours and cost $75 adults or $65 ages 8–14. Free round-trip transportation is provided from Friday Harbor.

## SWIMMING AND FITNESS

**Roche Harbor Resort** (360/378-2155 or 800/451-8910, www.rocheharbor.com, $7 adults, $5 kids, free for tots under age three) has a large outdoor pool and children's wading pool with a lifeguard on duty. It's open to the general public daily 10 A.M.–6 P.M. late June–early September (open mid-May through Sept.

for hotel and marina guests). This is the only heated public outdoor pool on the island.

Fitness fanatics may want to take advantage of one-day memberships ($15) to **San Juan Fitness** (435 Argyle Ave., 360/378-4449, www.sanjuanislandfitness.com). The lifeguard is only on duty one hour per day, and kids can swim during this time for $5. Although privately owned, the fitness center is viewed by most locals as a community resource akin to a YMCA. Facilities include an indoor 25-yard swimming pool and wading pool, kids' gym with climbing wall, racquetball courts, coed sauna, steam room, and hot tub, plus a cramped weight room. A variety of classes—from yoga to swimming lessons—are included at no extra charge. Open daily year-round.

**Lakedale Resort** (4313 Roche Harbor Rd., 360/378-2350 or 800/617-2267, www.lakedale.com) allows swimming and rents canoes, rowboats, and paddleboats at its mid-island private lakes. The water warms up by midsummer, providing perfect swimming. A day pass costs $7, and kids under 12 swim for free.

## SPAS

Looking to indulge yourself? Relax in **Afterglow Spa** at Roche Harbor Resort (360/378-9888 or 800/451-8910, www.

rocheharbor.com) or in Friday Harbor at **Lavendera Day Spa** (440 Spring St., 360/378-3637, www.lavenderadayspa.com). Both offer couples massage, hydrotherapy, manicures, pedicures, and more. **Mirabella** (425 Argyle Ave., 360/378-4250, www.mirabellaskincare.com) and **Spa d Bune** (669 Mullis St.,360/370-5027, www.spadbune.com) have facials, therapeutic massage, and skin care.

## GOLF AND TENNIS

Longest nine-hole course in the Northwest at 3,194 yards, the **San Juan Golf & Country Club** (2261 Golf Course Rd., 360/378-2254, www.sanjuangolfclub.com) overlooks Griffin Bay on the east side of San Juan Island. The course is open to the public and nine holes of golf costs $30; golf carts are an extra $15. Public **tennis courts** (45 Blair Ave.) are next to the high school.

## PARKS AND PLAYGROUNDS

Head out Argyle Avenue to the San Juan County Fairgrounds, where you'll find a **skateboard park** that's popular with BMX bikers, along with a playground for younger kids. Much more impressive is the **playground** at Roche Harbor Resort, where the adjacent **outdoor pool** and wading pool ($7 adults, $5 kids) are very popular in the summer.

# Accommodations

During the summer, it's a good idea to make reservations several months ahead of time to be assured of a bed on San Juan Island, particularly on weekends. All lodging prices quoted below are subject to an additional 9.8 percent tax.

## WEEKLY RENTALS

For weekly vacation rentals, both **Windermere Vacation Doorways** (360/378-3601 or 800/391-8190, www.vacationdoorways.com) and **San Juan Property Management** (360/378-2070 or 800/742-8210, www.sanjuanpm.com) have a big selection on San Juan

Island. These range from bungalows to luxurious waterfront villas with space for eight guests. Most require a one-week minimum in July and August, or three or four nights at other times. Prices are lower by the week and in the off-season.

Other companies offering vacation rentals include **San Juan Islands Dream Vacation Rentals** (360/378-5855 or 877/873-6160, www.sjidream.com), **San Juan Vacation Rentals** (360/317-6423, www.sanjuanrentals.net), **Friday Harbor Lights** (360/378-4317, www.fridayharborlights.com), **Dream**

**Vacation Rentals** (360/370-5855 or 877/873-6527, www.sjidream.com), and **Oak Ridge Vacation Home** (360/378-6184, www.oak-ridge.net). Most of San Juan Island's resorts, inns, guesthouses, and cottages are also available on a weekly basis.

For dozens of additional weekly rentals on San Juan Island, browse over to **VRBO** (www.vrbo.com), **CyberRentals** (www.cyberrentals.com), or **Homeaway** (www.homeaway.com). Also check out such websites as **Airbnb** (www.airbnb.com), **CouchSurfing** (www.couchsurfing.org) or **GlobalFreeloaders** (www.globalfreeloaders.com).

## APARTMENTS

Conveniently located just a few blocks from downtown Friday Harbor, **Sandpiper Condominiums** (570 Jenson Alley, 360/378-5610, www.sandpiper-condos.com) has six studio units and four one-bedroom apartments, all with fully equipped kitchens with dishes, plus access to a seasonal outdoor pool and hot tub, exercise room, and Wi-Fi, but no phones (use your cell instead). Apartments are priced at $89 per night for a studio ($550/week), or $119 per night for a one-bedroom unit ($675/week). Borrow an airbed to put kids on the living room floor. This may be the best bargain on the island for couples and small families, but most apartments in the complex are rented on a long-term basis, so you may contend with noise and cigarette smoke from adjoining units.

## HOSTELS

The only hostel on San Juan Island, **Wayfarers Rest** (35 Malcolm St., 360/378-6428, www.rockisland.com/~wayfarersrest) is an immaculate and quiet place with a flowery yard and a convenient location just four blocks from the Friday Harbor ferry. The ranch-style home has two dorm rooms with bunk beds ($35/person), along with two options for couples: a private room in the house, or two little cabins out back with space for two ($80) or three ($90). Children are welcome, but older kids pay the same rates as adults (free for kids under five). Linens are included, and travelers share a bath, two kitchens, a living room, dining room, and phone. The hostel is open year-round but is sometimes booked by groups in the summer, so make reservations as far ahead as you can, at least two weeks if possible for the peak of summer.

## HOTELS
### Best Western Friday Harbor Suites

Largest employer on the island, the sprawling Friday Harbor Suites (680 Spring St., 360/378-3031 or 800/752-5752, www.fridayharborsuites.com) is six blocks from downtown. The building was originally an assisted living center, and is a bit sterile compared to other local offerings. Fortunately, the 63 units are large, with well-maintained furnishings. This all-suites facility includes kitchenettes (full fridges, microwaves, and sinks), ceiling fans, Wi-Fi, and sitting rooms with large TVs; many also have gas fireplaces. Studio units are $240–250 d, one-bedroom suites cost $290–310 d, while two-bedroom suites are $350 d. Two-bedroom units sleep six, and all units have sliding glass doors leading to tiny patios or balconies. A couple of the rooms are wheelchair-accessible, and all guests are provided a filling hot breakfast and can relax in the covered hot tub or use the pool and exercise facility. A steak-and-seafood restaurant is on the premises. Ride the free shuttle to the ferry, airport, or around town.

### Bird Rock Hotel

Just a block from the water and right in the heart of town, Bird Rock Hotel (35 First St., 360/378-5848 or 800/352-2632, www.birdrockhotel.com) is close to restaurants and shops. This trendy 15-room hotel is the latest incarnation of one of the island's oldest buildings, dating from 1891. Inside, find luxurious accommodations, all with private baths, plasma TVs, a light breakfast, and Wi-Fi, plus afternoon tea and cookies. Standard rooms ($127–197 d) include queen-size beds, or step up to deluxe units ($227–267 d) with king-size beds and jetted tubs. A deluxe two-bedroom suite

($297) is the top option. Borrow a cruiser bike to explore, or pull out your laptop to take advantage of the Wi-Fi. On-street parking only, but guests are welcome to park at Earthbox Hotel (same owners) a couple of blocks up the street and use the indoor pool, hot tub, jacuzzi, and fitness center there.

## Earthbox Motel & Spa

This long-established 72-room motel underwent a transformation several years back, reemerging as Earthbox Motel & Spa (410 Spring St., 360/378-4000 or 800/793-4756, www.earthboxmotel.com, $197–257 d). Don't let the rather bland exterior fool you; the rooms are stylish and trendy (the larger $227 rooms are your best bet) with the flair of a European boutique hotel. Beds and linens are top-end, and all units contain mini-fridges, microwaves, hardwood floors, and Wi-Fi. A central building houses a small pool, hot tub, and sauna, and guests can borrow cruiser bikes to pedal around town. A separate two-bedroom house ($407) is also available. Lavendera Day Spa is adjacent, with massage and other pampering.

## Friday Harbor House

Located right along the harbor, Friday Harbor House (130 West St., 360/378-8455 or 866/722-7356, www.fridayharborhouse.com, $250–325 d) is one of the nicest and most romantic choices in town. The 23 rooms are chic, with gas fireplaces, large jetted tubs, queen-size beds, flat-screen TVs, fridges, and Wi-Fi. Most also feature ceiling-to-floor windows facing the harbor. A homemade continental breakfast is served in the dining room. Friday Harbor House is popular for meetings, retreats, and wedding parties. A two-night minimum is required for summer.

## Island Inn at 123 West

Friday Harbor's newest and swankest hotel, Island Inn at 123 West (123 West St., 360/378-4400 or 877/512-9262, www.123west.com) stair-steps up the hillside directly across from the harbor. Right in the heart of town, it encompasses six European-style guest rooms ($189–299 d) and seven penthouse units ($389–599 d); add $30 per person for additional guests. Guest rooms are stylish, with luxurious beds, flat-panel TVs, and Wi-Fi.

bikes for guests at Earthbox Motel & Spa

They face the hillside and share a comfortable lobby with harbor windows, a microwave, and fridge. Each penthouse has its own personality, but all include private decks, including three with rooftop decks. Other penthouse amenities are gourmet kitchens, space for up to six guests, and wonderful harbor vistas. Honeymooners and others looking for a romantic splurge will appreciate specialty packages that include in-room massage and champagne upon arrival. Two-night minimum for penthouses in the summer. Kids are welcome, and two units are pet-friendly. The hotel does not have an elevator.

## Orca Inn

Located near the airport in Friday Harbor, the 65-room Orca Inn (770 Mullis St., 360/378-2724 or 877/541-6722, www.orcainnwa.com, $64–99 d) has some of the lowest rates on the island. Motel rooms are cramped and not at all fancy, but they're clean and comfortable with fridges and microwaves. The least expensive units have one double bed, while others have two queens or a king bed.

## RESORTS
### Lakedale Resort

A modern and upscale place, Lakedale Resort (four miles from Friday Harbor at 4313 Roche Harbor Rd., 360/378-2350 or 800/617-2267, www.lakedale.com) sits on an 82-acre spread in the heart of San Juan Island. The rustically modern, 9,000-square-foot log lodge faces Neva Lake and features a great room with stone fireplace. Inside are 10 immaculate guest rooms, each with a fireplace, jetted tub, and private deck. Most rooms face the lake, and one is wheelchair-accessible, while a second is set up specifically for the hearing-impaired. Lodge rooms are $259–279 d, with additional guests at $35 per person; the rate includes a hot breakfast with waffles. No kids under 16 are permitted in the lodge, and a two-night minimum is required.

Six log cabins, also recently built, are situated along a lake or set beneath tall second-growth Douglas firs. Each includes two bedrooms, two baths, a full kitchen with dishes, a loft (great for children), fireplace, covered back porch, and DVD players. No television reception, but there's a big library of movies in the office. The cabins sleep up to six, and guests can use the central hot tub, or head to the lake to swim or fish for trout and bass; guests can also rent canoes and paddleboats. Cabins rent for $379–399 d, plus $35 per person for additional guests (kids free). No maid service at the housekeeping cabins. The most spacious option is a three-bedroom house with loft, kitchen, fireplace, and deck overlooking the lake; it rents for $579–599 for four guests. Call in January or February for peak season reservations since Lakedale books up early.

## Lonesome Cove Resort

This is what getting away from it all means. Lonesome Cove (416 Lonesome Cove Rd., 360/378-4477, www.lonesomecove.com) occupies the quiet north end of San Juan Island facing Spieden Channel. Get there by driving 0.5 mile down a narrow dirt road through tall trees before emerging onto the lovely grounds bordering Lonesome Cove and Spieden Channel—the passageway for ferries between Friday Harbor and Vancouver Island. The resort centers around an old apple orchard, small pond, and creek. Semi-tame deer wander through, and you're likely to see foxes and otters.

Lonesome Cove Resort is a favorite of the just-married crowd, but also remains popular with families. Guests stay in six charming waterfront log cabins, each with a double bed and futon, full kitchen with dishes, private bath, stone fireplace (with wood), and large deck just 40 feet from the beach. No phones, Internet, or TVs to disturb your time here. Nightly rates are $150 d or $190 for four people; kids are welcome but are charged the same as adults. A two-bedroom apartment suite sleeps six for $245.

Lonesome Cove is a delightful spot, but it was long ago discovered. You'll need to make reservations a year and a half in advance to be assured of space in the peak season; all the cabins are booked by the previous October! A five-night minimum is required June–August, with

© DON PITCHER

Lonesome Cove Resort

a two-night minimum at other times. During the summer, a 100-foot dock is available here, making this a fine base for boaters.

## Mar Vista Resort

Anyone with even rudimentary Spanish knows that Mar Vista (2005 False Bay Dr., 360/378-4448, www.marvistaresort.com, mid-Apr.–mid-Oct.) means "sea view." The name fits. Located on a remote corner of southern San Juan Island, this small resort occupies 40 acres of land along the Strait of Juan de Fuca. It has a total of eight beachfront cabins, all with kitchens and access to the private beach and tidepools. Orca whales, bald eagles, deer, and otters are all commonly seen. Nightly rates start at $120 d in one-bedroom units, up to $195 for a three-bedroom cabin that sleeps eight. There's a three-night minimum June–August (two nights at other times). Kids are welcome.

## € Roche Harbor Resort

On the National Register of Historic Places, Roche Harbor (360/378-2155 or 800/451-8910, www.rocheharbor.com) features impressive 19th-century buildings juxtaposed with attractive modern structures. In addition to a wide range of lodging options, resort facilities include a restaurant and café, general store, Wi-Fi, tennis and volleyball courts, bocce ball courts, a heated Olympic-size outdoor pool and wading pool, and a kids' playground (the best on San Juan Island), plus rentals of motorboats, bikes, mopeds, and sit-on-top kayaks. Whale-watching and sea-kayak tours depart from the harbor, a fascinating sculpture garden is just up the hill, and the lounge has live music and dancing on summer weekends.

Built in 1886, the classic **Hotel de Haro**—oldest hotel in Washington—fronts a gracious formal garden and marina. The hotel's downstairs lobby is worth a look even if you aren't staying here, with historic photos and a big fireplace. Rates at the hotel start at $130 d for an old-fashioned room (bath down the hall and no TV) with a double bed, up to the presidential suite ($350 d) with its own fireplace, private bath, and veranda facing the harbor. This one really is a presidential suite; Theodore Roosevelt slept here in 1906 and 1907, and John Wayne was a frequent visitor. The building has settled over the decades, leaving floors with a distinctive slope. Times have changed, and today's visitor expects more than even presidents received a century ago, so the hotel is not for everyone. If you're accustomed to modern hotels with all the accompanying luxuries, this will definitely not be to your taste, but those who enjoy slipping into the past in a gorgeous setting will love it. Be sure to check out the extra-long custom tub provided specifically for John Wayne.

Employees of the Roche Harbor Lime Company once occupied the resort's **Company Town Cottages,** which are now rented out for $400–450 per night. All of these have two bedrooms, full kitchens, and gas grills, and the more expensive ones face the water. The price is the same for up to six guests here. Also available are a number of gorgeous, newly built Victorian-style houses behind the hotel, starting at $550 for a two-bedroom place, up to $1,000 for one with four bedrooms. Less attractive are the 1970s-era

© DON PITCHER

rental houses at Roche Harbor Resort

condos that start at $295 for one-bedroom units, up to $600 for a three-bedroom condo. They're glaring eyesores in this historic and scenic place. One consolation: From their windows, you can't see them. A two-night minimum stay is required for the cottages, houses, and condos in the summer. Four **McMillin Suites,** located in an old harborside home, have wraparound covered decks, king-size beds, gas fireplaces, clawfoot tubs and radiant-heated floors in the bath, and tasteful furnishings. These cost $425–495 d and are a great splurge.

Luxurious accommodations can be found at **Quarryman Hall Suites,** each with 600 square feet of space (probably three times as much space as President Roosevelt's room!), heated tile floors, luxurious beds, separate sitting rooms with fireplaces, and private balconies facing the harbor for $375–495. A full-service spa is downstairs.

## GUESTHOUSES

In addition to the places listed below, you may want to consider **Nichols St. Suites** (85 Nichols St., 360/378-2638 or 866/374-4272, www.lodging-fridayharbor.com, $165–185 d), and **Courtyard Suites** (275 A St., 360/378-3033 or 800/378-1434, www.courtyard-suites-fridayharbor.com, $199–224 d).

### Friday Harbor Rentals

On the east side of town, Friday Harbor Rentals (595 Maple St., 360/376-7035, www.sleepingsea.com) has a comfortable house with two units, along with a cottage. The upstairs portion of the house contains two bedrooms, two baths, a large kitchen and living room, plus a deck with barbecue and hammock. It sleeps up to four for $295 on weekends or $250 weekdays; add $25 each for extra guests. Perfect for couples, the downstairs suite has a queen bed and private bath for $165 d on weekends or $150 d weekdays. The back cottage ($195 d weekends, $185 d weekdays) contains two bedrooms and a full kitchen, with a glass door opening to the garden. A two-night minimum is required. The units all have Wi-Fi, and pets are allowed (fee).

## Horseshu Hacienda

Less than two miles from town off San Juan Valley Road (131 Gilbert Lane, 360/378-2298, www.horseshu.com), this beautiful modern home is part of a 26-acre spread where pastures are filled with horses and ponies and trails lead into old-growth forests. The home contains a full kitchen, washer/dryer, jetted tub in the master bath, Wi-Fi, and a deck overlooking the pasture. It comfortably sleeps six for $340/night, with a two-night minimum; the price includes a horseback ride for two, but call well ahead for summer bookings. Horse boarding and trail rides are also available.

## ( Juniper Lane Guest House

Owner Juniper Maas took an ecocentric approach in constructing Juniper Lane Guest House (1312 Beaverton Valley Rd., 360/378-7761 or 888/397-2597, www.juniperlaneguesthouse.com), a cheery country home built largely from salvaged and recycled materials. This is one of the best deals on the island, with comfortable, reasonably priced rooms and a welcoming ambience. The main house contains five guest rooms ($85–135 d), private or shared baths, a stocked and stylish kitchen, and a relaxing common area, plus Wi-Fi throughout. Two rooms are perfect for families and groups, with a mix of queen- and twin-size beds. Wedding parties and groups can rent the entire house (it sleeps 15) for $745. A separate cabin ($185 d) has two bedrooms, a bath, and full kitchen, along with a deck looking across the grazing sheep and llamas in the fields of Beaverton Valley. Kids are welcome in the cabin, but no children under eight are allowed in the main house. Two-night minimum in the summer.

# BED-AND-BREAKFASTS

The **Bed & Breakfast Association of San Juan Island** produces a lodging brochure with brief listings and a map showing bed-and-breakfast locations. Pick one up onboard the ferry or in regional visitors centers. Call the hotline (360/378-3030 or 866/645-3030) for availability at 20 of the finest local bed-and-breakfasts, or head to www.san-juan-island.net for direct links to bed-and-breakfast homepages. Several of the places listed in *Hotels* and *Guesthouses* also provide a light breakfast for their guests.

## Argyle House B&B

A comfortable Craftsman-style home on an acre of land in Friday Harbor, Argyle House (685 Argyle Ave., 360/378-4084 or 800/624-3459, www.argylehouse.net) was built in 1910. Upstairs are three guest rooms ($165–170 d) with small private baths; two nicely appointed cottages ($210–225 d) provide more privacy. All guests have access to the backyard patio and hot tub. A filling breakfast is included, Wi-Fi is available, and children of all ages are welcome.

## Dragonfly Inn

Inspired by his years in Japan, co-owner Robert Butler constructed Dragonfly Inn (4770 Roche Harbor Rd., 360/378-4280 or 877/378-4280, www.thedragonflyinn.com, closed Nov.–Dec., $225 d) as a fusion of East and West. Located on 15 secluded acres, the home includes four guest rooms—each with unique air-massage tubs—along with unique Asian fusion breakfasts. This is a tranquil place to escape, so no kids under 17 are allowed.

## Harrison House Suites B&B

One of the nicest Friday Harbor lodging choices, Harrison House (235 C St., 360/378-3587 or 800/407-7933, www.harrisonhousesuites.com) offers the perfect blend of privacy and comfort, and it's just two blocks from the ferry landing. The main house was built in 1905, with a cottage added in the 1930s. Today, both have been lovingly transformed into six spacious apartment suites, each with a private entrance, full kitchen, and bath. The largest—1,600 square feet—encompasses three bedrooms, one-and-a-half baths with a jetted tub, hardwood floors, a piano and woodstove, plus a large private deck and sunroom. It can sleep 10 and goes for $400 d. The other suites (one has its own hot tub) sleep 2–8 and rent for $205–335 d. Additional adults are $25/person in any of the rooms. Guests will appreciate the four-course breakfasts, outdoor hot tub, flower-filled grounds, plus use of mountain bikes and sea kayaks for no extra charge. Children are welcome and cribs are available, making this a fine option for families and wedding parties. Pets are accepted for an additional $20 fee. A two-night minimum stay is required in the summer. Owners Anna Maria DeFreitas and David Pass also run the adjacent Tucker House B&B, and together the two properties provide space for 60 guests—room for all your family and friends.

### Highland Inn

Set on a wooded hillside on the west side of San Juan with spectacular view of Mount Baker, Highland Inn (360/378-9450 or 888/400-9850, www.highlandinn.com, $275 d) offers some of the finest and most private lodging on the island. The two elegantly appointed suites each have a king-size bed, down comforter, steam shower, jetted tub, wood-burning fireplace, and small fridge. Sliding-glass doors open onto a covered deck that runs the length of the house, providing knock-your-hat-off views across Haro Strait. It's a killer place to watch for killer whales on a summer day, or to hear them at night as they blow and splash.

A fine breakfast is served each morning on the veranda (or in your room), along with afternoon tea and fresh cookies (you'll want her recipe). Guests are welcome to use the outdoor hot tub. Owner Helen King has a reputation for graciousness, and she really goes all out to make your visit a pleasure. Be sure to ask about her world-record 270-pound Pacific tuna mounted in the foyer. A two-night minimum stay is required on weekends. This bed-and-breakfast is not for children because of the high decks. Free Wi-Fi is available here; check out the live web views from the website.

### Hillside House B&B

A spacious contemporary dwelling, Hillside House (365 Carter Ave., 360/378-4730 or 800/232-4730, www.hillsidehouse.com, $139–189 d) occupies an acre of wooded land less than a mile from the ferry. There are views of Friday Harbor, the islands, and Mount Baker

## MRS. KING'S COOKIES

2 cups butter
2 cups brown sugar
2 cups white sugar

Blend the above until creamy and add:
4 eggs
2 teaspoons vanilla
grated rind and juice of one orange

Beat until well mixed.
Sift together:
4 cups flour
2 teaspoons baking powder
2 teaspoons salt
2 teaspoons baking soda

Stir into the egg and butter mixture and mix until just blended, then add:
2 cups white chocolate chips
2 cups semisweet chocolate chips
3 cups raisins
3 cups chopped nuts
2 cups old-fashioned rolled oats
3 cups orange-almond granola, or any good granola

When well mixed, shape into Ping-Pong-size balls and bake on an ungreased cookie sheet at 350°F for 8-10 minutes or until just turning brown around the edges. The cookies are best when warm from the oven. This recipe makes 12 dozen cookies. Dough keeps refrigerated or frozen. Bake them fresh as needed.

*Recipe courtesy of Highland Inn*

from the deck, and the grounds feature an ornamental pond and atrium. Covering 4,000 square feet, this is one of the larger bed-and-breakfasts on San Juan, with seven guest rooms offering private baths and Wi-Fi. One room ($239 d) takes up the entire third floor with a king-size bed, jetted tub, fireplace, and private balcony. A big buffet breakfast is offered each morning. Children under age 10 are not permitted, and there is no minimum stay.

## Inn to the Woods B&B

A luxurious hillside bed-and-breakfast, Inn to the Woods (46 Elena Dr., 360/378-3367 or 888/291-9502, www.inntothewoods.com, $165–235) is surrounded by serene Douglas firs four miles northwest of Friday Harbor and directly across the road from Sportsmans Lake. The four guest rooms have private baths, Wi-Fi, and filling breakfasts. Three of these rooms feature private outdoor hot tubs. The B&B isn't really for children, and a two-night minimum stay is required during July and August.

## Kirk House B&B

A lovely and romantic Craftsman home, Kirk House (595 Park St. in Friday Harbor, 360/378-3757 or 800/639-2762, www.kirkhouse.net, closed Oct.–Apr., $195–250 d) was built in 1907 as a summer retreat for industrialist Peter Kirk, the namesake of Kirkland, Washington. Four inviting guest rooms have private entrances and baths. The two nicest rooms each contain king-size beds; one room features a wood-burning fireplace, while the other has a big jetted tub. A full vegetarian breakfast is included. No children under 15 are allowed.

## Longhouse B&B

Located on the west side of the island, Longhouse B&B (2387 Mitchell Bay Rd., 360/378-2568, www.sanjuanlonghouse.com) is an eclectic, modern waterfront home with a fine view from the great room. Two spacious bedrooms ($120–130 d) are available, both with private baths. Co-owner Patty Rasmussen once owned a restaurant, and her kitchen skills come to the fore each morning with gourmet breakfasts. A quaint cottage ($135 d or $150 for three; breakfast not included) has a kitchen with a wraparound deck along Mitchell Bay. Kids are allowed in the small cottage, which dates back more than 125 years. Guests can rent kayaks or take whale-watching trips from the adjacent Snug Harbor Marina. A two-night minimum stay is required in the summer.

## ◖ Olympic Lights B&B

Located in the open meadows on the south end of the island, Olympic Lights (146 Starlight

**SAN JUAN ISLAND**

© DON PITCHER

Olympic Lights B&B

Way, 360/378-3186 or 888/211-6195, www.olympiclights.com, $155–165 d) is one of the more remote bed-and-breakfasts on the island. Hosts Christian and Lea Andrale discovered the old Johnson farmhouse when they were on vacation in 1985 and opened it as a bed-and-breakfast the following year. This beautifully maintained Victorian farmhouse was built in 1895, and contains four guest rooms with king- or queen-size beds, down comforters, and private baths. A side garden becomes a riot of flowers in the summer, and the big lawn is a fine place for a game of croquet or to listen to singing birds.

Guests are served a full vegetarian breakfast that typically includes fresh eggs from resident hens, scones or biscuits, fruit juice smoothies, and more. The grassy parklands of American Camp are an easy after-breakfast walk, or you can saunter down to the shore at nearby Eagle Cove for a view of the Olympic Mountains. A two-night minimum is required in the summer and on holiday weekends, and children are not allowed.

## States Inn & Ranch

States Inn (2687 West Valley Rd., 360/378-6240 or 866/602-2737, www.statesinn.com, $100–180 d) began life as a grade school in 1910, but the building was later moved across the island. The bed-and-breakfast, located seven miles northwest of Friday Harbor, is on a working 60-acre ranch with horses, sheep, chickens, and alpacas. All eight guest rooms include private baths and Wi-Fi, and a three-room suite ($260 for up to four) works well for families or couples traveling together. Add $20 for each additional person. All guests share the large sunroom and are served a filling country breakfast made with local organic produce. Guests are welcome to feed and pet the alpacas and sheep or help collect eggs from the chickens. Kids are accepted in the suite.

## ◖ Trumpeter Inn B&B

A contemporary two-story home, Trumpeter Inn B&B (318 Trumpeter Way, 360/378-3884 or 800/826-7926, www.trumpeterinn.

com, open Apr.–Oct., $169–199 d) overlooks five pastoral acres 1.5 miles southwest of Friday Harbor. Horses and cattle graze in the adjoining fields. The pond is perfect for bird-watching; a small orchard has plum, apple, and pear trees; and the gardens are filled with summertime flowers. Six luxurious guest room are available (one is wheelchair accessible), all with private baths, Wi-Fi, and access to the gardenside hot tub; the two nicest units include fireplaces and private decks. Owners Geoff and Shaun Andres serve a gourmet breakfast each morning, and a guest computer is available. No children under 12 are permitted, but dogs are okay with prior notice.

## Tucker House B&B

Just a couple of blocks from the ferry, Tucker House B&B (260 B St., 360/378-2783 or 800/965-0123, www.tuckerhouse.com) offers a variety of lodging options. A total of 11 units—most with jetted tubs—are located within a simple Victorian home built in 1898 and an adjacent home dating from 1910. Rooms rent for $245–280 d, and two suites (one sleeps six) cost $325–400 d. Three cottages ($185–285 d) also contain kitchenettes and woodstoves, and welcome both kids and pets. One of these is rather plain, but the other is a modern and attractive log cabin that's perfect for families. Add $25 per person for extra guests, $20 for pets. The B&B is adjacent to Harrison House Suites, and the two properties have the same owners, sharing a café for filling breakfasts. Guests from both can use the outdoor hot tub and borrow a bike or sea kayak.

## Wharfside B&B

One lodging place on San Juan Island isn't really on the island—it's in the water. Wharfside B&B (360/378-5661, www.slowseason.com) is a gracious 60-foot sailboat, the *Slow Season*, docked at the Friday Harbor Marina, Slip K-13. Two diminutive staterooms rent for $175–195 d, including a hot breakfast. Originally from Vienna, owners Ilse and Helmut Komnen are fluent in German and Italian. No kids under 12 are allowed. Kenmore Air floatplanes land nearby, so travelers can fly from Seattle and step into their accommodations without even touching the shore!

## Wildwood Manor

Set atop a high knoll, Wildwood Manor (5335 Roche Harbor Rd., 360/378-3447 or 877/298-1144, www.wildwoodmanor.com) is a lavish Queen Anne–style home surrounded by 11 acres of forest, with manicured grounds and a view across San Juan Channel to Vancouver Island. Owners John Gallagher and Michael Bitterman provide three tastefully decorated guest rooms ($210 d) and a two-room suite ($280 d), all with private baths, fine linens, and an extraordinary three-course breakfast feast. Relax in the great room or step outside to watch the semi-tame deer that visit each morning. The B&B has gained an international reputation, and in 2011 was voted one of the top 10 B&Bs in the world by TripAdvisor! A two-night minimum stay is required in summer, and the home isn't appropriate for children under 12. Reserve by May if you plan a July or August visit.

© DON PITCHER

library inside Wildwood Manor

## CAMPING

Camping options on San Juan Island are limited and fill fast, so make reservations as far in advance as you can. **Coin-operated showers** are available at the Friday Harbor Marina and Roche Harbor Marina.

### San Juan County Park

Pitch a tent at one of 20 campsites at the 12-acre San Juan County Park (360/378-8420, www.sanjuanco.com/parks, year-round, $30–45), a mile north of Lime Kiln Point State Park along West Side Road. Cyclist or kayaker sites are $10 per person. Because this is essentially the only public campground on the island, you'll need to reserve months ahead for the summer season. Reservations ($7 extra) can be made between five days and three months ahead of time through the park website. You may find last-minute space on a summer weekday, but weekends are almost always fully reserved, especially in August. The park has a boat ramp, drinking water, ice, picnic tables, and shelters, plus flush toilets, but no RV hookups.

### Griffin Bay Marine State Park

This small boat-in-only campsite is on the southeast end of the island just north of American Camp. The 15-acre state park (360/378-2044, www.parks.wa.gov, $12–28) has four campsites, along with picnic tables and pit toilets. You'll need to bring your own water. Griffin Bay is a popular destination for quick overnight kayak trips out of Friday Harbor and has a pleasant gravelly beach, but you're limited to the immediate area by fences that block access to adjacent private property. The park is a fine stopping point for kayakers circumnavigating San Juan or Lopez Islands. Note, however, that nearby Cattle Pass can be extremely treacherous under certain tide and wind conditions.

### Lakedale Resort

Located in a peaceful setting with open fields, small lakes, and forests, Lakedale Resort (4313 Roche Harbor Rd., 360/378-2350 or 800/617-2267, www.lakedale.com, May–Oct.) has a hundred or so attractive campsites along two small lakes near the center of San Juan Island, four miles from Friday Harbor. Car campers with tents pay $33–49, and sites for hikers, bicyclists, and motorcyclists are a reasonable $21–25 d. More unique are the resort's surprisingly comfortable **canvas tent cabins,** complete with cots, chairs, and a table; $149–159 for four people (two-night minimum on weekends). There's even an over-the-top canvas cottage with space for four at an over-the-top price of $259. It has a king bed, bathroom, electricity, and even a chandelier! Canvas cabin guests also get a complimentary continental breakfast. (By the way, the pseudo-official term for this is *glamping,* as in glamorous camping.) Also available are two vintage Airstream trailers with space for four at $229. All campers share a central bathhouse

and porta-potties, and the little store sells basic supplies. Reservations are advised, but there is usually space for tents (except over 4th of July weekend). The resort also has rooms and cottages and rents out rowboats, canoes, paddleboats, and fishing poles. Wi-Fi is available around the lodge and store, but your cell phone probably won't work at Lakedale.

## Mitchell Bay Landing

Located on the northwest end of the island, Mitchell Bay Landing (2101 Mitchell Bay Rd., 360/378-9296, www.mitchellbaylanding.com) is a small campground with tent sites on the lawn for $25, and RV sites with hookups for $55–65. No showers (the nearest ones are at Roche Harbor), but portable toilets and bottled water are available. Guests can rent boats, kayaks, and crab pots.

# Food

San Juan Island has a wide range of restaurants and eateries, including some real gems. Unless otherwise noted, all of these restaurants are in the town of Friday Harbor.

## BREAKFAST AND LUNCH

A favorite of both locals and visitors, **Rocky Bay Café** (225 Spring St., 360/378-5051, $8–10) serves enormous portions in a simple diner setting. Brunch covers all the basics, plus breakfast burritos, crab omelets, sweet potato fries, and daily specials. The café often has a long line, so you may need to wait up to an hour on a summer weekend.

At **KO's Sub Shop** (180 1st St., 360/370-5496, 9:30 A.M.–5 P.M. daily, $6–8), Kenny Oberreit offers variations on the standard theme, adding thinly sliced cabbage, onions, banana peppers, and oregano to his subs. Count on fresh breads and quality meats and cheeses too. The tiny shop is just up from the ferry for a quick last bite before you sail away.

In a cozy historic home off the main drag, **Garden Path Café** (135 2nd St., 360/378-6255,

www.gardenpathcafe.com, 8:30 A.M.–3 P.M. Mon.–Fri., $6–10) has classic breakfasts, plus homemade soups, salads, hot and cold sandwiches, burgers, and wraps for lunch. Order and pay at the counter.

Tiny **Market Chef** (225 A St., 360/378-4546, 10 A.M.–4 P.M. Mon.–Fri., $8–9) is a wonderful deli next to the ferry lanes in Friday Harbor. Owner/chef Laurie Paul creates mouthwatering sandwiches (especially the roast beef), daily soups, and salads in the open kitchen. She uses island produce and meats whenever possible, and locals rave about the crab cakes—featured in *Gourmet Magazine*—and house-smoked meats. Call a day ahead to get a boxed picnic lunch to go, but you're probably better off picking your favorites from the day's creations in the deli case. All menu items are worth every penny. Market Chef is closed on weekends (lots of weddings to cater).

## CAFÉS

**San Juan Coffee Roasting Company** (18 Cannery Landing, 360/378-4443 or 800/624-

© DON PITCHER

Friday's Crabhouse faces the busy ferry dock.

4119, www.rockisland.com/~sjcoffee, 9:30 A.M.–5 P.M. daily) specializes in full- and dark-roasted coffees, and sells them from its shop. You can get espresso drinks there, but I prefer **The Doctor's Office** (85 Front St., 360/378-8865, 4:30 A.M.–8 P.M. daily, till 10 P.M. June–Aug., $3–8), inside the lime-green Queen Anne–style building adjacent to the ferry lines. This place also uses San Juan Coffee Roasting beans and has a walk-up window so you don't miss the boat, along with a juice bar, sandwiches, soups, sweets, and homemade ice cream. Over in one corner is a computer where you can check email or surf the web. Many, if not most, of the other Friday Harbor cafés also serve mochas, lattes, and the other de rigueur Washington coffee drinks.

Step inside **The Bean Café** (150B 1st St., 360/370-5858, 7 A.M.–5 P.M. Sun.–Thurs., 7 A.M.–8 P.M. Fri.–Sat. in summer, 7 A.M.–5 P.M. daily in the off-season) for a steaming mug of organic, shade-grown espresso. The café serves brunch fare, including breakfast paninis, salads, and their signature chicken salad and tomato wrap. Scan the display case for fresh-baked goods, including the "supreme" with chocolate chips, coconut, and macadamia nuts. Big windows and seating both indoors and out make this a great hang-out spot. Free Wi-Fi, and the video monitor provides a view of the nearby ferry lanes to see when your ship comes in.

## QUICK BITES

One of the most popular eating establishments on San Juan Island is **Friday's Crabhouse** (360/378-8801, www.fridayscrabhouse.com, 11:30 A.M.–8 P.M. daily late May–Sept., weekends only Apr. and May), directly across from the ferry. Open seasonally, this is *the* place for finger-lickin' fish and chips, homemade crab cakes, fish tacos, shrimp cocktails, grilled salmon, or pan-fried oysters, along with faji-tas, hamburgers, and veggie burgers—mostly under $12. Service is fast, making this an ex-cellent last-minute stop. The multi-level eat-ery is primarily alfresco dining at picnic tables topped by big umbrellas, but a covered space is also available.

Another simple family place is **Hungry Clam** (250 A St., 360/378-3474, 5 A.M.–9 P.M. daily in summer, 5 A.M.–7 P.M. the rest of the year), where you will find cheap, greasy, and quite good cod fish and chips served in a basket. The fries are fresh and crunchy. Also on the menu are such staples as clam chowder, Canadian bacon cheeseburgers, and grilled chicken sandwiches. The diner is open for the early ferry crowd, and breakfast is available till 1 P.M.

If you're in search of a great all-American burger, fries, and shake—mostly under $9— head up the hill to **Vic's Drive-In** (25 2nd St., 360/378-8427, 11 A.M.–7 P.M. Mon.–Fri., 8 A.M.–2 P.M. Sat.). Breakfast is only available on Saturdays, and the drive-in is closed Sundays.

Locals also wax enthusiastic about **Herb's** (80 1st St., 360/378-7076, 11 A.M.–2 A.M. daily), an old-timey downtown bar famous for burgers. Fish and chips, hot dogs, and chicken wings round out the pub menu.

## FINE DINING

Dinner reservations are strongly suggested for any of San Juan Island's better restaurants, particularly on weekends and during the summer.

Just two blocks from the ferry, **Backdoor Kitchen** (400 A St., 360/378-9540, www.backdoorkitchen.com, 5–10 P.M. Wed.–Mon. July–Aug., 5–9 P.M. Wed.–Sat. Sept.–June, closed Christmas–Feb), is a hidden gem known to locals and wandering tourists who happen upon it (or read this book); find it behind a nondescript warehouse near Mi Casita Restaurant. Step through the gate into a small garden area with a handful of teak tables for open-air dining. There's additional seating inside the restaurant, and dinner includes inspired ethnic fare such as Mediterranean lamb sirloin or pan-seared sea scallops, but also check the daily specials. The full bar serves unusual specialty drinks and a lighter menu, and be sure to try

the coconut cream pie for dessert. Reservations are advised, especially for rainy days.

One of Friday Harbor's most romantic dining places **Coho Restaurant** (120 Nichols St., 360/378-6330, www.cohorestaurant.com, 5–9 P.M. Mon.–Sat. mid-June–Sept., 5–9 P.M. Tues.–Sat. Oct. and Apr.–mid-June, 5–9 P.M. Wed.–Sat. Nov.–Mar., closed Sun., $25–30 entrées) is housed in a cozy little side-street house. Reservations are recommended, not just because the restaurant only has nine tables, but more importantly because of its popularity with locals. The menu changes seasonally, with a focus on Pacific Northwest cuisine, much of it from local sources. Everything is made on the premises, from bread and pasta to ice cream. Seafood is featured on the menu— especially a sesame-crusted salmon with mirin sauce (recipe available on Coho's website)—but also might include risotto with wild prawns, house-smoked duck breast, flat-iron steak, and other adventurous dishes. Can't choose a dessert? Get a sampler trio of mini desserts. The owners also operate two nearby B&Bs: Tucker House Inn and Harrison Suites.

Open for dinner only, **The Place Restaurant and Bar** (1 Spring St., 360/378-8707, www.theplacefridayharbor.com, $25–33 entrées) gets rave reviews from locals who come here for the friendly service, from-scratch gourmet fare, and sophisticated atmosphere. The name should give you a clue to its location: on pilings over the water, with windows facing the ferry and marina. It's perfect for a warmly romantic evening. The menu changes seasonally but typically features a mushroom sauté appetizer with shiitake mushrooms and herbed goat cheese, along with fresh Alaskan weathervane scallops, New Zealand lamb chops, and even a vegan stir fry called Evil Jungle Prince. Be sure to save room for the warm chocolate pudding cake with toffee sauce. Get there for happy hour (weekdays 6 P.M.) to taste locally famous Cuban pork sandwiches and small pizzas.

Housed within Friday Harbor House, **The Bluff Restaurant** (130 West St., 360/378-8455 or 866/722-7356, www.fridayharborhouse.com,

4–9 P.M. Thurs.–Mon., $24–36 entrées) is another San Juan Island favorite. Chef Kyle Nicholson changes his menu often, emphasizing ultra-fresh local produce and seafood, along with beef short ribs and chard-wrapped summer vegetables. There's an extensive wine selection available by the glass and in flights of wine, too. The food is exquisite, and the setting is upscale and fashionable, with a central fireplace and tall windows overlooking the harbor. Call ahead to request a window table. Patio dining is available in the summer, and kids are welcome.

**Vinny's Ristorante** (165 West St., 360/378-1934, www.vinnysfridayharbor.com, 4–9:30 P.M. daily June–Oct., 4–9 P.M. Tues.–Sat. Nov.–May) is a casually elegant Italian restaurant where the air is deliciously redolent and the tables are draped in white linen. The menu encompasses all the standard favorites, including veal marsala, shrimp scampi, and lasagna, along with "pasta from hell" for those who like it hot: pasta with garlic, pine nuts, raisins, mushrooms, and peppers in a fiery habanera and curry cream sauce. Prices start at $14 for a simple spaghetti with marinara sauce, up to $33 for rack of lamb. Unfortunately, the restaurant's hilltop vista is now blocked by recently constructed penthouses.

Five miles north of Friday Harbor on Roche Harbor Rd., **Duck Soup Inn** (360/378-4878, www.ducksoupinn.com, 5–10 P.M. Tues.–Sun. July–early Sept., 5–10 P.M. Fri.–Sun. spring and fall, closed Nov.–Mar., $27–35 entrées) specializes in superbly prepared local seafood and meats, along with a changing and eclectic menu with an international bent. Roasted duck breast is always on the menu, and recommended. The country setting and woodsy interior add to the relaxed and romantic atmosphere. This is where locals go for a celebration night. Reservations are recommended.

Three places serve meals at **Roche Harbor Resort** (360/378-2155 or 800/451-8910, www.rocheharbor.com). Busy **Madrona Bar & Grill** (11 A.M.–midnight Sun.–Thurs., 11 A.M.–2 A.M.

Fri.–Sat., no food after 10 P.M., reduced winter hours, $11–20 entrées) has waterside patio dining with 10-inch kiln-fired pizzas, delicious fish and chips, burgers, and much more, along with live music on summer evenings. The bar has a fine beer selection, along with wine by the glass, mojitos, and margaritas. Visit upscale **McMillin's Dining Room** (5–10 P.M. daily, $22–39 dinner entrées) for consistently good prime rib, seafood, steaks, and chicken. The four-course chef's tasting menu ($38) is always an excellent option. On the wharf, **Lime Kiln Café** (7 A.M.–8 P.M. daily, $7–12) serves a breakfast and lunch menu with burgers, deli sandwiches, salads, and housemade soups.

## INTERNATIONAL

Friday Harbor has one standout spot for Asian meals: **Golden Triangle** (140 1st St. in Friday Harbor, 360/378-1917, 11 A.M.–2:30 P.M. Mon.–Fri., 5–8 P.M. Mon.–Sat., closed Sun.), where Laotian owner Avon Mangala serves Vietnamese pho, Japanese teriyaki, Thai curry dishes and spring rolls, Laotian noodles, and other fast Asian treats in an eat-in or takeaway setting.

An unexpected find, **Maloula's** (1 Front St., 360/378-8485, www.maloula.com, 11:30 A.M.–3 P.M., 5:30–9 P.M. Thurs.–Tues. Apr.–Sept., closed in winter, $19–29) serves Mediterranean food on a flower-filled rooftop deck. Just follow the wonderful smells to this quiet spot with gracious hosts and a broad harbor view. Maloula's menu includes grilled lamb, beef, poultry, and vegetarian specialties. You'll find *kibbeh* (a traditional Syrian dish), kabobs, gyros, and other Mediterranean cuisine using hormone-free beef and organic vegetables. Especially good are the Greek salad and homemade baklava.

## PUBS

**Cask and Schooner** (1 Front St., 360/378-2922, www.caskandschooner.com, 11 A.M.–11 P.M. daily Apr.–Oct., noon–9 P.M. Mon.–Thurs., noon–10 P.M. Fri., 10 A.M.–10 P.M. Sat., 10 A.M.–9 P.M. Sun. the rest of the year) occupies a busy corner at the base of Front Street right across from the harbor. Newly opened in 2011, Cask and Schooner is something of a cross between an English pub and the deck of an old schooner (no Johnny Depp, alas). The food and drink—not surprisingly—follow a similar theme, with a menu featuring meat pie, fish and chips (the house specialty), bangers and mash, oyster stew, and other upscale pub grub for $9–14. Fries are fresh cut daily, bread is baked in-house, and greens and meats are locally sourced when possible. The restaurant also has full dinners ($24–38), from Dungeness crab with corn risotto, to ribeye steaks. Not a lot of meat-free options, but the restaurant does serve a grilled eggplant sandwich and even a delicious gluten-free razor clam chowder (not vegetarian, of course). On draft are nine beers—including Guinness—along with martinis and a fair wine selection. Brunch items are all $11, and include Scotch eggs, frittatas, biscuits and gravy, hobo scramble, and corned beef hash; they're available 10 A.M.–2 P.M. on weekends. A take-out window—open mornings for espresso and pastries—is here if you want to eat outside.

## MEXICAN

Reasonably priced **Mi Casita** (95 Nichols St., 360/378-6103, 5–8:30 P.M. Mon.–Sat.) occupies a yellow Victorian-style house behind Sunken Park in Friday Harbor. The interior is festive and inviting, and the menu encompasses all the standards, including tacos, fajitas, burritos, enchiladas, and tostadas, along with homemade salsa. House specialties include relleno del mar (chile relleno filled with crab, shrimp, scallops, and vegetables), carnitas (roast pork with onions, cilantro, tomatoes, and guacamole), and zarapes (steak-filled enchiladas). Portion sizes are substantial, so be ready to waddle away from the table. Full combination plates are around $13, but you can get a filling tostada or burrito for $9.

Next to Golden Triangle on a little alley off 1st Street, **Pablito's Tacqueria** (140A Spring St., 360/378-3317, www.

pablitostaqueria.com, 11:30 A.M.–3 P.M. Mon.–Fri., 5–8 P.M. Thurs.–Sun.) is an open, two-story place to get a quick meal. The "gringo loco" food here is delicious, filling, and varied; not at all like your standard Mexican restaurant. Ordering is a bit confusing. Choose two items from the menu—coffee-braised pork tacos or chorizo, kale, and roasted garlic empenadas are great choices—and then add a side of beans and rice to your order. Head to the salsa bar for added flavor and up the stairs for a beer or margarita. Daily lunches are around $10, with dinner specials (these change weekly) for $13–15. There's live music on summer Saturdays, and Pablito's has a booth at the Saturday market. Highly recommended!

## SEAFOOD

A tiny floating shop surrounded by the cruise and fishing fleet at the Friday Harbor Marina, **Friday Harbor Seafood** (360/378-5779, www.interisland.net/fishcreek) sells fresh salmon, halibut, and snapper, along with live mussels, clams, Dungeness crab, scallops, and prawns.

In business since 1978, **Westcott Bay Sea Farms** (904 Westcott Dr., 360/378-2489, www.westcottbay.com, 11 A.M.–5 P.M. daily, late May–early Sept.) raises petite oysters, Manila clams, and Mediterranean mussels. A 400-foot dock extends into peaceful Westcott Bay, a mile east of Roche Harbor. The aquaculture farm cultivates shellfish in lantern nets suspended in deep water, and is primarily a wholesale operation. Westcott Bay oysters are served locally at Friday Harbor House, Duck Soup Inn, Vinny's, Roche Harbor, Cask and Schooner, and Willows Lodge. Visit the farm to select ultra-fresh oysters from the flow-through tanks. The smallest ones—perfect for cocktails—are the most expensive at $10 per pound. Baking-size oysters are $6 per pound. You can pick your own oysters off the beach for just $1 per oyster on several days each summer when the tides are lowest. Even if you aren't a fan of oysters, do take a visit to

© DON PITCHER

dining at Roche Harbor Resort

this old-fashioned operation in a very special place. When this book was written, the 77-acre property—adjacent to national park land at English Camp—was for sale, and the long-term survival of the oyster farm was in doubt. Hopefully, the land and oyster farm will be preserved by a local group instead of being sold to a wealthy individual who puts up a gate and builds a waterfront mansion.

## MARKETS AND BAKERIES

For a real taste of the islands, head to the **San Juan Farmers Market** (360/378-6301, www.sjifarmersmarket.com, 10 A.M.–1 P.M. Sat. late Apr.–mid-Oct.). It takes place at Brickworks Plaza (Nichols St. at Sunshine Alley) and features organic fruits, delicious finger food, vegetables, berries, flowers, and more.

**Kings Market** (160 Spring St., 360/378-4505, www.kings-market.com, 7 A.M.–9 P.M. daily) is the primary grocer on San Juan. You'll find fresh meats and fish, gourmet foods and wines, plus a fine deli with tasty sandwiches. Also here is a gift shop and marine supply center.

**Friday Harbor Market Place** (515 Market St.) is a larger grocery out near the airport. There's no sign out front, no deli, and even the phone number is unlisted—I'm surprised it isn't painted in camouflage. It's owned by Kings Market, but often has lower prices. Locals all know about it, but most travelers don't—except you, of course.

Dolled up in pink trim and flower boxes, **The Sweet Retreat & Espresso** (264 Spring St., 360/378-1957, www.sweetretreatespresso.com, $4–8) is a busy takeaway spot for ice-cream cones (20 or so flavors), sundaes, lemonade, Hawaiian shave ice, malts, and ice-blended coffee drinks. Breakfast sandwiches here consist of a biscuit with egg, cheese, and bacon; surprisingly good lunches include sandwiches, jumbo hot dogs, and burgers.

You'll find excellent pastries at **Café Demeter** (80 Nichols St., 360/370-5443, 7 A.M.–3 P.M. Tues.–Sat., under $6), but be

SAN JUAN ISLAND

© DON PITCHER

Westcott Bay Sea Farms grows a variety of oysters.

prepared for a wait at this very popular bakery. Stop by to check out the fresh baguettes, bagels, and breads, old-world-style pastries (brioche, Danish, sweet cinnamon rolls, chocolate croissants, flaky turnovers, and more), along with soups, sandwiches, pizza slices, and fine coffee.

**Bakery San Juan** (775 Mullis St., 360/378-5810, www.bakerysanjuan.com, 11 A.M.–6 P.M. Mon.–Fri., 2–7 P.M. Sat.) bakes several breads daily, has fantastic sandwiches, cookies, lemon tarts, honey pecan buns,

and pizza by the slice ($5) or pie ($18–20). Definitely off the beaten path—the bakery is next to the airport south of town—but worth the drive or bike ride!

## WINE

**Island Wine Company** (360/378-3229 or 800/248-9463, www.sanjuancellars.com, 9:30 A.M.–7 P.M. daily late May–early Sept., 10 A.M.–6 P.M. daily the rest of the year) is a cozy shop in Cannery Landing, adjacent to the Friday Harbor ferry dock. Owners Dave Baughn and Kathryn Kerr have their own **San Juan Cellars** label, produced from eastern Washington grapes and bottled under contract, and you're welcome to sample any of their eight wines, which are only available here. The riesling is especially notable. In addition to these, the shop also has a range of upper-end Northwestern wines, including vintages you won't find in Seattle wine shops. Grace, the resident black lab, loves to be petted.

The **San Juan Vineyards** (360/378-9462 or 888/983-9463, www.sanjuanvineyards.com, $1 per taste) tasting room at 55 Spring St. is open daily 11 A.M.–6 P.M. A good selection of their wines are available for tasting or to purchase. Be sure to also visit the vineyard at 3136 Roche Harbor Road.

A mile or so from Roche Harbor, **Westcott Bay Cider/San Juan Island Distillery** (360/378-2606, www.westcottbaycider.com) produces award-winning hard cider, along with apple brandy and gin. Visit the tasting room at 12 Anderson Lane on Saturdays 3–5 P.M. or by appointment.

# Information and Services

The friendly **San Juan Island Chamber of Commerce Visitor Center** (135 Spring St., 360/378-5240, www.sanjuanisland.org, 10 A.M.–4 P.M. daily Apr.–Dec., often till 5:30 P.M. in the summer, 10 A.M.–4 P.M. Mon.–Sat. the rest of the year). Helpful private websites for San Juan Island are **San Juan Island Update** (www.sanjuanupdate.com) and **San Juan Island Directory** (www.sanjuandirectory.com). For other information, visit the **Town of Friday Harbor** offices (60 2nd St., 360/378-2810, www.fridayharbor.org).

## LAUNDRY

**Blue Sky Laundromat** (210 Nichols St., no phone) is the only coin-op laundry on the island. Although primarily a dry cleaners, **Sunshine Laundries** (80 Web St., 360/378-7223) has a fluff-and-fold service that takes a day or so; $15 for a 10-pound load.

## KIDS' STUFF

Forgot your stroller for that out-of-control three-year-old? **Island Bicycles** (380 Argyle Ave. in Friday Harbor, 360/378-4941, www.islandbicycles.com) rents them and also has children's bikes and other cycling gear.

## LIBRARY AND INTERNET ACCESS

Spacious **San Juan Island Library** (1010 Guard St., 360/378-2798, www.sjlib.org, 10 A.M.–6 P.M. Mon., Wed., and Fri., 10 A.M.–8 P.M. Tues. and Thurs., 10 A.M.–5 P.M. Sat., 1–5 P.M. Sun.) is a pleasant rainy-day spot and a good place to check your email on the computers or use your laptop with Wi-Fi. Families will appreciate the lap-sit book sessions and preschool story time.

Pop open your laptop and you'll find free Wi-Fi hotspots around town, including **The Bean Café** (150 1st St., 360/370-5858), **Blue Water Bar & Grill** (7 Spring St., 360/378-2245, www.bluewaterbarandgrill.com), **Griffin Bay Bookstore** (155 Spring St., 360/378-5511, www.griffinbaybook.com), and **China Pearl Restaurant** (51 Spring St., 360/378-5254). **The Computer Place** (435 Argyle Ave., 360/378-8488, www.compplace.com, 9 A.M.–5 P.M. Mon.–Fri., 10 A.M.–4 P.M. Sat.) has computer rentals and Wi-Fi access for a fee. Espresso too.

## BANKING AND MAIL

Friday Harbor's four banks all have ATMs: **Wells Fargo** (305 Argyle Ave., 360/378-2128, www.wellsfargo.com), **Islanders Bank** (225 Blair Ave., 360/378-2265 or 800/843-5441, www.islandersbank.com), **Key Bank** (95 2nd St. S, 360/378-2111, www.keybank.com), and **Whidbey Island Bank** (535 Market St., 360/370-5641 or 800/290-6508, www.wibank.com). You can also get cash back from an ATM purchase at Kings Market. Find other ATMs at Roche Harbor Grocery and Hotel de Haro in Roche Harbor, along with several Friday Harbor stores.

There are **post offices** in Friday Harbor (220 Blair Av., 360/378-4511) and in Roche Harbor (195 Reuben Memorial Dr., 360/378-2155), inside the Company Store. Head to **Post San Juan** (685 Spring St., 360/378-2400, www.rockisland.com/~postsanj) for FedEx, UPS, and other shipping needs.

## MEDICAL CARE

Brand new in 2012, **Peace Island Medical Center** (1049 San Juan Valley Rd., 360/378-2141, www.peaceislandmedicalcenter.org) is the only hospital on the San Juan Islands. Built to stringent "green" standards, the building is said to be the nation's first carbon-neutral hospital. Services include primary care, critical care, a 24-hour emergency department, imaging and diagnostic equipment, and 10 beds for short-stay inpatient care; the hospital does not have surgery, obstetrics, and other complex medical services. The closest full hospital is in Anacortes.

**San Juan Healthcare Associates** (689 Airport Center, 360/378-1338, www.sanjuanhealthcare.org, Mon.–Fri.) has three doctors and a nurse practitioner on staff. Fill prescriptions at **Friday Harbor Drug** (210 Spring St., 360/378-4421).

## VETERINARY CARE

Take sick or injured pets to **Islands Veterinary Clinic** (700 Mullis St., 360/378-2333) or **Harbor Veterinary Services** (849 Spring St., 360/378-3959, www.harborvetclinic.com). **Animal Inn** (25 Boyce Rd., 360/378-4735, www.animalinnwellness.com) has a kennel for dogs, cats, birds, and other critters.

# Getting There and Around

Friday Harbor has a serious parking problem in the summer, and the city *strictly* enforces a two-hour downtown parking limit. Get back to your car three minutes late and you'll probably have a $20 ticket pasted on your windshield. Meters are checked Monday–Saturday 8 A.M.–5 P.M., and officers stop marking cars after 3 P.M., so you're probably OK to park anytime after that.

Eight-hour on-street parking is available at the north end of 1st Street near San Juan Community Theatre, and along Web Street (off Argyle Ave.). Seventy-two-hour parking spaces are up Spring Street beyond the junction with Argyle Avenue (a five-minute walk from the center of town).

## WASHINGTON STATE FERRIES

The Washington State Ferries (360/378-8665 for the Friday Harbor terminal, 206/464-6400 or 888/808-7977 for general information, www.wsdot.wa.gov/ferries) stop right in Friday Harbor. Find all the details—including current ferry wait times—on the website, or get a visual of the action at www.ferrycam.net/fridayhrbr.html. Credit cards are accepted.

Peak season fares from Anacortes to Friday Harbor are $11.50 for passengers and walk-ons, or $53.80 for a car and driver. Bikes are $4 extra, and kayaks cost $17.50 more. There is no charge for eastbound travel by vehicles or passengers from Friday Harbor to Orcas, Shaw, Lopez, or Anacortes, but reservations are not available for these runs so you'll need to get in

line well ahead of time. Vehicle reservations *are,* however, highly recommended (at least 24 hours in advance) if you're heading west on the runs from San Juan Island to Sidney, British Columbia. These one-way tickets to Vancouver Island cost $29 for a car and driver or $6.30 for passengers or walk-ons.

## PRIVATE FERRIES

Clipper Vacations operates the passenger-only *Victoria Clipper* (206/448-5000 or 800/888-2535, www.clippervacations.com, daily mid-May–early Sept., weekends only the rest of Sept.), a high-speed catamaran with day trips between Seattle and Friday Harbor. If you book at least one day ahead, adult rates are $70 round-trip and kids under 12 are free, or pay $80 adults, $40 kids if you wait till the last minute. Combine transportation from Seattle with a 2.5-hour whale-watching trip for $30–40 extra. The company has a multitude of other travel options in the Northwest, including packages that add a night's lodging on San Juan Island, or a three-day/two-night visit to San Juan Island and Victoria. You can also use this as transportation to the islands from Seattle, traveling north one day and returning at a later date.

**Puget Sound Express** (360/385-5288, www.pugetsoundexpress.com) provides passenger-only service between Port Townsend and Friday Harbor. The boat leaves Port Townsend daily May–October, staying in Friday Harbor long enough for a quick three-hour visit, or you can overnight and return to Port Townsend

Washington State Ferries make frequent trips to Friday Harbor.

later. The round-trip charge is $89 adults, $49 kids ages 2–10, and $15 extra for bikes and kayaks. This isn't a whale-watching trip, but it isn't uncommon to sight orcas en route.

## WATER TAXIS

Operating from Friday Harbor, **Captain Carli's Charters** (360/378-0302 or 888/221-1331, www.carlicharters.com) focuses on whale-watching trips, but also offers custom charters to Jones, Yellow, Turn, and Stuart Islands for an hourly rate. The speedy C-Dory boat holds six passengers, making for a personalized tour.

Also based in Friday Harbor, **San Juan Islands Water Taxi** (360/317-5475, www.sji-watertaxi.net) can transport six passengers anywhere in the San Juan Islands. Captain Gunnar Wickman has sailed all over the world, and his boat spent many years fishing in Alaska. It isn't fast, but it is comfortable, with space for bikes or kayaks. **Friday Harbor Marine** (360/378-6702, www.sjimarine.com) also sets up water taxi service to other islands.

**North Shore Charters** (360/376-4855,

www.orcasislandadventures.com) is based on Orcas Island, but can pick up passengers anywhere in the San Juans for an hourly rate. **Humpback Hauling** (360/317-7433, www.humpbackhauling.com) provides passenger and freight service throughout the San Juans on a large landing craft, with a smaller boat (Roche Harbor Water Taxi) also available.

## BY AIR

Taking off from Lake Union in Seattle, **Kenmore Air** (425/486-1257 or 866/435-9524, www.kenmoreair.com) has daily scheduled floatplane flights to Friday Harbor and Roche Harbor. A 24-pound baggage weight limit is in effect on these flights. The company also offers wheeled-plane flights between Boeing Field in Seattle and **Friday Harbor Airport** (360/378-4724, www.portfridayharbor.org/fridayharborairport), immediately south of town. Wheeled-plane flights have a 70-pound baggage limit.

**San Juan Airlines** (360/293-4691 or 800/874-4434, www.sanjuanairlines.com) has

## SAN JUAN ISLAND MILEAGE

| | Friday Harbor | American Camp | English Camp | Roche Harbor | San Juan County Park | Lime Kiln Point State Park |
|---|---|---|---|---|---|---|
| American Camp | 6 | | | | | |
| English Camp | 9 | 13 | | | | |
| Roche Harbor | 10 | 16 | 4 | | | |
| San Juan County Park | 10 | 12 | 5 | 9 | | |
| Lime Kiln Point State Park | 9 | 9 | 7 | 12 | 3 | |
| Cattle Point | 9 | 4 | 20 | 24 | 15 | 13 |

scheduled daily wheeled-plane service to San Juan Island from Anacortes and Bellingham, plus connecting service to Orcas, Lopez, Decatur, and Blakely Islands from Friday Harbor and Roche Harbor. Air charters are available to the outer islands or to Victoria, Vancouver, or to Seattle. A half-hour flightseeing trip costs $250 for up to five passengers.

**Island Air** (360/378-2376 or 888/378-2376, www.sanjuan-islandair.com) runs charter flights and flightseeing out of Friday Harbor Airport. It is the only company actually based in the San Juans. The experienced local pilots can take you virtually anywhere in the region, including north to British Columbia or south to Portland.

**San Juan Air Tours** (360/378-7717, www.scenic-flights.com, summer only) and **Westwind Aviation** (360/378-6991, www.westwindav.com) offer flightseeing trips and air charters.

**Northwest Sky Ferry** (360/696-9999, www.nwskyferry.com) has twice-daily flights from Bellingham to San Juan, Orcas, and Lopez Islands, with flightpooling charters to other destinations throughout the San Juan Islands.

## BUSES AND TOURS

**Island Airporter** (360/378-7438, www.islandairporter.com) provides direct van service daily from Sea-Tac to San Juan Island. The bus departs the airport and heads straight to the Anacortes ferry, where it drives on for San Juan Island, and then continues to Friday Harbor ($50) and Roche Harbor ($60). You'll need to add the ferry fare, but it's approximately half the standard rate since you're on a bus. Vans operate once a day in each direction Monday–Saturday in summer and Monday–Friday in winter.

### San Juan Transit

You really don't need a car to get around San Juan Island. San Juan Transit (360/378-8887 or 800/887-8387, www.sanjuantransit.com) operates shuttle buses between the ferry landing in Friday Harbor and Roche Harbor, with stops at San Juan Vineyards, Lakedale Resort, Krystal Acres Alpaca Ranch, English Camp (by reservation only), and the IMA Sculpture Park. Buses run mid-May–early September, with hourly service 10 A.M.–6 P.M.) every midsummer day, and on weekends only for the first half of May and throughout September.

A second route departs Friday Harbor for Pelindaba Lavender Farm and Lime Kiln Point State Park (whale-watching), with hourly service 11 A.M.–4 P.M. The later buses operate on weekends till early June, with daily service the rest of the summer. No scheduled service to American Camp, but charters are a year-round option. The buses can carry bikes and luggage, and fares are $5 each way ($2 for kids under 12), or $15 for an all-day pass ($5 kids). These passes are a great deal, letting you get off and on along the way. The San Juan Transit office is in the Cannery Landing building adjacent to the ferry dock.

## CAR AND MOPED RENTALS

Rent cars from **M&W Auto Rentals** (360/378-2886 or 800/323-6037, www.sanjuanauto.com) near the airport. They'll pick you up from the airport or ferry terminal. Rentals are $50 per day for a compact or $70 per day for an SUV. If you just need a vehicle for a short time, M&W also provides four-hour rentals for $10 less.

**Susie's Mopeds** (125 Nichols St., 360/378-5244 or 800/532-0087, www.susiesmopeds.com, Mar.–mid-Oct.) rents all sorts of unusual vehicles, including mopeds (starting at $30/hour or $65/day), two-person Jetson's-like Scootcoupes ($70/hour or $150/day), and four-person Chevy Trackers ($32/hour or $96/day) from its shop at the top of the ferry lanes in Friday Harbor. Call a couple of days ahead for reservations on summer weekends. Susie's also rents mopeds, scootcars, and bikes next to the IMA Sculpture Park in Roche Harbor late June–early September.

## TAXIS

Call **Bob's Taxi & Tours** (360/378-6777), **Classic Cab Co.** (360/378-7519), or **Friday Harbor Taxi** (360/298-4434, www.friday-harbortaxi.com) for local rides and island tours. **San Juan Taxi & Tours** (360/378-8294, www.378taxi.com) has seven-passenger minivans with racks for bikes and kayaks. Friday Harbor to Roche Harbor (or most other places on the island) costs around $20 for two people.

# ORCAS ISLAND

Known as "The Gem of the San Juans," Orcas Island is considered by many the most beautiful island in the archipelago. It is definitely the hilliest—drive, hike, or bike to the top of 2,409-foot Mount Constitution for a panoramic view from Vancouver, British Columbia, to Mount Rainier. The island is home to around 4,500 people and has one of the only real towns in the archipelago, Eastsound.

Orcas is the largest island in the San Juans, covering 57 square miles. Locals jokingly refer to it as Orcapulco in the hectic summer season, or Orcatraz when winter doldrums make it an isolated rock. Orcas is home to a handful of celebrities who appreciate the relative anonymity of island life: cartoonist Gary Larson (creator of *The Far Side*), Richard Donner (director of *Free Willy, Lethal Weapon,* and *Superman*) and his wife, Lauren Shuler Donner (producer of *X-Men, Pretty in Pink, You've Got Mail,* and *Any Given Sunday*), Warren Miller (adventure ski filmmaker), author Richard Bach (*Jonathan Livingston Seagull*), astronaut Bill Anders (Apollo 8), and singer Susan Osborn (of Paul Winter Consort).

From the air, Orcas Island looks like either a giant horseshoe or a misshapen M, with two long inlets cutting in from the south. Washington State Ferries dock on the south end of the island at **Orcas Village** (also called Orcas Landing or simply Orcas), where you'll find a cluster of cafés and gift shops centering on a Victorian gem, the Orcas Hotel.

**East Sound** is the longest channel, nearly splitting the island into two pieces. The village of **Eastsound** (note that the village is rendered

© DON PITCHER

# HIGHLIGHTS

◖ **Moran State Park:** Acclaimed as one of the best state parks in Washington, this one has it all: more than 5,200 acres of wild country, a road-accessible lookout tower atop 2,409-foot Mount Constitution, many miles of hiking trails, abundant campsites, and a great swimming lake (page 164).

◖ **Rosario Resort:** This well-known resort centers on the mansion built for industrialist Robert Moran a century ago (page 166).

◖ **Eastsound:** The largest settlement on Orcas, Eastsound has the look and feel of a town along the coast of Maine. Its central location, good shopping, delectable meals, and upmarket lodging choices add to the appeal (page 167).

◖ **Howe Art Gallery:** Welded-metal mobiles and other kinetic art pieces by artist Tony Howe dot this big field of a gallery. Guaranteed to bring a smile to your child's face (page 172).

◖ **Orcas Island Artworks:** Out of the way, but worth the drive, this cooperative art gallery is one of the oldest in the region. The café serves delicious lunches (page 172).

◖ **Orcas Island Pottery:** Step through the gate to discover hundreds of pieces of pottery strewn across a large lawn. Enjoy a million-dollar view across President Channel from one of the benches out back (page 173).

◖ **Orcas Island Skateboard Park:** Most visitors to Orcas are unaware that the island has one of the finest skateboard parks in the Pacific Northwest (page 175).

◖ **The Funhouse:** Although ostensibly for kids, this hands-on science discovery center is a blast for all ages, with musical instruments, arts and crafts, a climbing wall, games, and all sorts of other fun activities (page 175).

**ORCAS ISLAND**

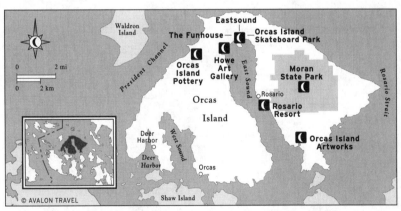

LOOK FOR ◖ TO FIND RECOMMENDED SIGHTS, ACTIVITIES, DINING, AND LODGING.

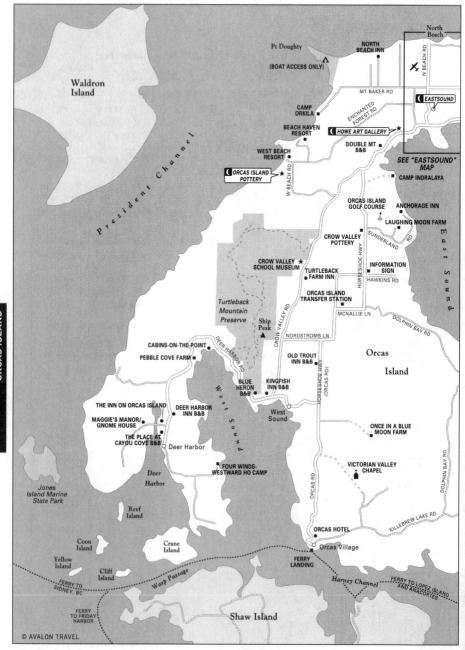

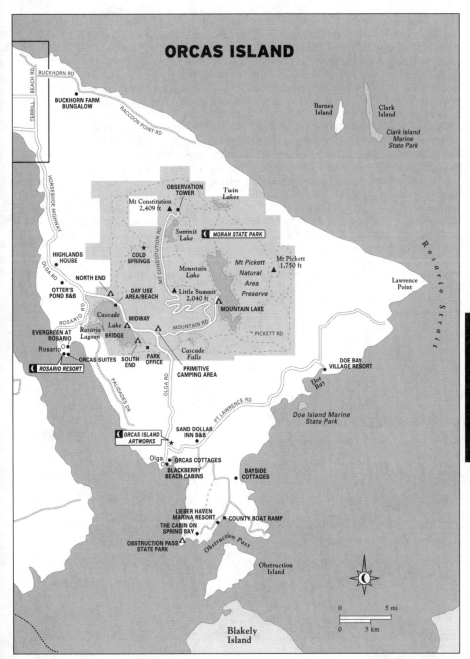

# ORCAS ISLAND

BUCKHORN RD

TERRILL BEACH RD

BUCKHORN FARM
BUNGALOW

RACCOON POINT RD

Barnes
Island

Clark
Island

Clark Island
Marine
State Park

OBSERVATION
TOWER

Twin
Lakes

Mt Constitution
2,409 ft

Summit
Lake

**MORAN STATE PARK**

HORSESHOE HIGHWAY

HIGHLANDS
HOUSE

COLD
SPRINGS

Mountain
Lake

Mt Pickett
Natural
Area
Preserve

Mt Pickett
1,750 ft

Lawrence
Point

OLGA RD

NORTH END

OTTER'S
POND B&B

DAY USE
AREA/BEACH

Little Summit
2,040 ft

MT CONSTITUTION RD

MOUNTAIN LAKE

*R o s a r i o   S t r a i t*

ROSARIO RD

Cascade
Lake

MIDWAY

MOUNTAIN RD

EVERGREEN AT
ROSARIO

Rosario
Lagoon

BRIDGE

PICKETT RD

Rosario

ORCAS SUITES

SOUTH
END

PARK
OFFICE

Cascade
Falls

DOE BAY
VILLAGE RESORT

**ROSARIO RESORT**

OLGA RD

PRIMITIVE
CAMPING AREA

Doe
Bay

PALISADES DR

PT LAWRENCE RD

Doe Island Marine
State Park

**ORCAS ISLAND
ARTWORKS**

SAND DOLLAR
INN B&B

Olga

ORCAS COTTAGES

BLACKBERRY
BEACH CABINS

BAYSIDE
COTTAGES

LIEBER HAVEN
MARINA RESORT

THE CABIN ON
SPRING BAY

COUNTY BOAT RAMP

OBSTRUCTION PASS
STATE PARK

*Obstruction Pass*

Obstruction
Island

Blakely
Island

0        5 mi

0        5 km

ORCAS ISLAND

as one word, unlike the body of water) occupies the head of this sound and is 10 miles from the ferry. Although unincorporated, this is the primary village on the island, and *the* place to go for groceries, gas, and a wide choice of gift shops, cafés, and galleries. It also probably has more lounging cats per shop than any other town in the Pacific Northwest!

The easternmost lobe of Orcas Island delivers the most rugged terrain anywhere in the San Juans, including the half-mile-high summit of Mount Constitution within famous **Moran State Park.** Not far away is **Rosario Resort,** an equally famous historic mansion and resort.

Smaller than East Sound, **West Sound** is home to the predictably named little settlement of West Sound. It is eight miles northwest of the ferry landing and has a marina, a homey little café, and a couple of lodgings. Approximately four miles west of here is another gathering place for boaters and others, **Deer Harbor,** with its substantial marina, plus bed-and-breakfasts, a restaurant, charter

sailboats, and kayak rentals. It's appropriately named for the many black-tailed deer in the area (and throughout the San Juans).

## HISTORY

Orcas Island is apparently named for a viceroy of Mexico, Don Juan Vicente de Guemes Pacheco Pedilla Horcasitas y Aguayo, Conde de Revilla Gigedo. Fortunately, his name was shortened rather substantially, with "Horcasitas" becoming "Orcas." (Variations on his name also ended up on nearby Guemes Island and Padilla Bay, along with southeast Alaska's Revillagigedo Island.) The Spanish explorer Francisco Eliza named Orcas Island during his 1791 visit, and some scholars believe he actually named the island after his schooner of the same name. More imaginative folks claim the name came from the word *orca,* a Spanish term for the mammals still often seen here, killer whales or orcas.

Place names within West Sound highlight the area's sometimes violent history: Haida Point, Indian Point, Massacre Bay, Skull Island, and

farm on Orcas Island

© DON PITCHER

Victim Island. All of these names originated from Haida raids on the peaceful Coast Salish people who lived here for centuries. Many Salish men were murdered during these attacks, and surviving women and children were typically hauled away as slaves. Both Skull and Victim Islands are marine state parks.

Early white settlers on Orcas Island hunted deer, logged, farmed, and fished. Louis Cayou came to the island in 1859 as a market hunter for the Hudson's Bay Company, but he settled down with a Salish woman and raised a family. He is regarded as the first white settler. Other folks trickled in over the next 15 years, and by 1873 the island was home to 40 or so white settlers. Within a few years, the population grew rapidly as farmers discovered that Orcas was perfect for growing apples, pears, and Italian plums. In the 1880s and onward, thousands of fruit trees were planted across the island for the Orcas Island Fruit Company. A major recession in 1890 forced the company into bankruptcy, but the trees kept producing and growers found other outlets. Competition from farmers in eastern Washington spelled the end to commercial fruit growing by the 1930s, but many of these small orchards still produce fruit more than a century after they were planted.

## PLANNING YOUR TIME

Because of its size, unusual shape, and rugged topography, Orcas Island takes longer to get around than other islands in the San Juans. It's approximately 25 miles by road from the easternmost end of the island to the western end at Deer Harbor, and that takes an hour or more to drive (if you don't speed). Yes, you can "see" the main sights in a single day, but why bother? If you can, plan to spend at least three or four days on Orcas.

Because of its central location and abundant amenities, many travelers choose to base their travels in the Eastsound area. Even those staying at Doe Bay Resort or Deer Harbor, however, can easily get to the main island attractions if they set aside a bit of time. A pair of don't-miss sights are the legacy of Robert Moran: ostentatious **Rosario Resort** and nearby **Moran State Park,** with its winding road up Mount Constitution.

The beauty of Orcas Island has provided inspiration for countless artists, whose works are displayed in shops and galleries throughout the island. A few miles south of the park is a low building that houses one of the oldest artist-owned cooperatives in the Northwest, **Orcas Island Artworks.** North of the park and just before you reach Eastsound is **Lambiel Museum,** with hundreds of locally produced pieces on display. Just west of Eastsound, a dirt road leads to **Howe Art Gallery,** where Tony Howe's delightful kinetic sculptures fill a big field, bringing smiles to all who discover them.

**Orcas Island Pottery**—famous for its pottery-filled yard—hugs the western shore of the island, while historic **Crow Valley Pottery** lies right on the main road southwest of Eastsound.

The town of Eastsound is home to not just shops, restaurants, and lodgings, but also to two kid-friendly places: **The Funhouse,** with its mix of science and play, and the surprising **Skateboard Park** along Mt. Baker Road.

# Sights

## ◖ MORAN STATE PARK

Near Eastsound, 5,252-acre Moran State Park (360/376-2326, www.parks.wa.gov) is best known for its steep paved road to the 2,409-foot summit of **Mount Constitution.** The mountain is crowned by a 52-foot **stone observation tower** constructed by the Civilian Conservation Corps (CCC) in 1936 and patterned after the 12th-century watchtowers of Russia's Caucasus Mountains. This is the highest point anywhere in the San Juans and offers a commanding view, from Mount Rainier to British Columbia. The park is 14 miles by car from the Orcas ferry landing and occupies much of Orcas Island's eastern appendage. It is open year-round for both day use and camping.

Moran State Park was the creation of Robert Moran—a shipbuilder, former mayor of Seattle, and builder of the mansion that is now Rosario Resort. Moran was working as chief engineer on an Alaskan steamer, the *Cassiar,*

when he met famed naturalist John Muir. The two became close friends, and that friendship opened Moran's eyes to the natural world. In later years, Moran prospered financially, but this appreciation for nature inspired him to do something beneficial with his wealth.

In 1911, he tried to donate 2,700 acres on Orcas Island to establish a state park just uphill from his mansion at Rosario. The offer was turned down, and it wasn't until 1921 that the state finally accepted the land and created Moran State Park. Eventually, Moran would donate nearly 4,000 acres for the park. He later constructed the distinctive concrete entrance arch and the road up Mount Constitution. During the 1930s, the CCC built most of the park's trails, bridges, shelters, and other structures, using sandstone from a local quarry and wood from area forests.

Moran State Park is a heavily wooded area, with old-growth forests of Douglas fir (some six feet in diameter), western hemlock, western

© DON PITCHER

**view from Mount Constitution in Moran State Park**

red cedar, and Pacific yew in the lower elevations, plus hardy stands of shore pine (a subspecies of lodgepole) higher up the slopes. The windswept summit of Mount Constitution has grassy openings accented by lilies, asters, stonecrop, and other flowers in the summer. Black-tailed deer are relatively common, along with river otters, muskrats, raccoons, bald eagles, and many other species.

## Park Information

Drop by the park registration booth (10:30 A.M.–9 P.M. daily late May–early Sept.) for maps and other information. You can also visit the park office (9 A.M.–5 P.M. Tues.–Sat.) near the north end of Cascade Lake. A small **Summit Shop** atop Mount Constitution (360/376-3111, 11 A.M.–4 P.M. daily May–Sept., 11 A.M.–4 P.M. Sat.–Sun. in the off-season) sells maps, books, postcards, and a few gifts. Get additional park information at 360/376-2326, www.parks.wa.gov. Parking requires a $10 day-use pass, or get an annual Discover Pass for all Washington parks for $30. Interested in helping the park's preservation efforts? Join the nonprofit **Friends of Moran State Park** (www.friendsofmoran.com).

## Hiking Trails

Moran State Park has 38 miles of hiking trails, from short nature loops to remote and rugged out-of-the-way hikes. The CCC constructed most of these trails during the 1930s. Get a park map for details on the various routes, or see Ken Wilcox's *Hiking the San Juan Islands* (Northwest Wild Books).

The easiest path is 0.3-mile **Moran State Park Nature Trail,** which takes off from the day-use area along Cascade Lake, with signs identifying plants along the way. Only slightly more challenging is the 0.25-mile trail to **Cascade Falls,** where Cascade Creek plummets into a pool 75 feet below. The path begins from a parking area 0.25 mile up Mount Constitution Road and drops downhill to the falls, a 10-minute walk. Come here in spring for the most dramatic show. You can also continue downstream to two smaller waterfalls.

A longer path, the **Cascade Creek Trail,** begins near the park office on Cascade Lake and follows the creek uphill (with a detour to Cascade Falls) to the picnic area at Mountain Lake, a distance of three miles with a gain of 700 feet. You'll encounter enormous old-growth Douglas firs along the way. From the lake, you can hike back or catch a ride downhill along Mount Constitution Road.

Cascade Lake is a busy place in midsummer, with three oft-full campgrounds, a popular picnic area, rowboat and paddleboat rentals, and a great swimming beach. Orcas Road parallels its northeast shore. For a nearly level walk, follow the **Cascade Lake Loop Trail** for 2.7 miles around the lake, past tall trees drooping over the water and across a picturesque arched wooden bridge at Rosario Lagoon, known for good fishing. Several side trails offer tantalizing options, including one that switchbacks 300 feet uphill over 0.75 mile to **Sunrise Rock.** The vistas encompass Cascade Lake below, with the Cascades themselves in the distance on a clear day.

Another relatively easy round-the-lake hike is the **Mountain Lake Loop Trail,** a four-mile path that offers a chance to see black-tailed deer, particularly in the morning and early evening, and passes enormous old Douglas firs. Circle the lake counterclockwise for the best vistas.

The summit of **Mount Constitution** is readily accessible by car via a paved road, but to really appreciate the views, there's nothing like climbing it yourself. A number of trails ascend the mountain from various sides, but one of the best begins from Mountain Lake Landing (accessible by car). From here, you follow the lakeshore to the north end and continue uphill to **Twin Lakes.** Ascend sharply up a series of switchbacks to the summit, where you'll suddenly be surrounded by the hoi polloi who drove here. Finally, climb the old CCC viewing tower for a panoramic of northern Puget Sound and the San Juans. It's 3.7 miles to the top of Mount Constitution from Mountain Lake. For variety on the way back, take the trail to **Little Summit,** which leads through stands of shore pine before dropping into dense forests of western hemlock and Douglas fir. The return is 3.3 miles long, for a round-trip hike of seven miles, with a 1,500-foot elevation gain (and loss) en route. You can, of course, save your legs by catching a ride to the top and hiking downhill instead.

The western portion of Moran State Park encompasses **Mount Pickett Natural Area Preserve,** the largest contiguous tract of unlogged forest remaining in Puget Sound. It is closed to all off-trail hiking or other uses, but trails circle its margins, providing a woodsy 6.5-mile loop hike if you start at Mountain Lake Landing. Mount Pickett itself is a 1,750-foot summit with limited views from the trail.

## Water Sports

During the summer, the beach at Cascade Lake is an exceptionally popular family destination, with a roped-off **swimming area** (no lifeguard) that has a shallow sandy bottom and relatively warm water June–August. There's a delightful playground and a snack bar (daily mid-June–early Sept.) selling hot dogs, sodas, microwave pizzas, other fast food, and ice. The boathouse (360/376-3411, www.outerislandx.com) rents rowboats, kayaks, canoes, and paddleboats late May–early September. Rowboats are also available at Mountain Lake, but you'll need to reserve them at Cascade Lake. Both of these lakes have boat ramps, but motorboats are prohibited. Anglers have fun casting about for rainbow, cutthroat, and kokanee trout; Cascade Lake is stocked annually by the Washington Department of Fish and Wildlife.

## Cycling

Moran is the most challenging cycling destination in the San Juans, with trails (and a paved road) leading from Cascade Lake to the summit of Mount Constitution, a gain of 2,100 feet in elevation. It's a fast and exhilarating ride back down! Eleven miles of park trails are open year-round to cyclists, and September 15–May 15, there are 25 miles open to mountain-bike use. Before heading out, purchase a *Local Knowledge Trail Map* for Mount Constitution

at Wildlife Cycles in Eastsound. This helpful map includes tips for the various trails and roads, along with difficulty ratings and seasonal closings. Cyclists must yield to hikers and horses. Never ride off-trail within the park.

## Other Park Activities

The park has five kitchen shelters—most available on a first-come, first-served basis—plus a multitude of picnic tables. A spacious log kitchen shelter next to the Cascade Lake swim area can be reserved (888/226-7688, www.parks.wa.gov). It holds up to 100 people and includes a stone fireplace, wood grill, sink, electrical outlets, and lights.

Equestrians will appreciate the six miles of trails open to **horseback riding** within the park; see the park's official map for details.

## ◖ ROSARIO RESORT

One of the most historic resorts in the San Juans, Rosario Resort & Spa (1400 Rosario Rd., 360/376-2222 or 800/562-8820, www.rosarioresort.com) is five miles south of Eastsound along the protected Cascade Harbor. This famous getaway is well worth a look even if you can't afford to stay here, with a picture-perfect setting that is popular for outdoor (and indoor) weddings.

Now on the National Register of Historic Places, the ostentatious mansion at Rosario Resort was built more than a century ago by Robert Moran, a shipbuilder and two-term Seattle mayor who—on doctors' orders—came here to retire.

Moran sold his mansion in 1938 to Donald Rheem, the son of Standard Oil Company founder William S. Rheem and a major shareholder in Paramount Studios. Donald Rheem spent $400,000 improving the mansion, but it was his wife who is best remembered today. Some say he bought Rosario to keep her out of sight, but she certainly didn't stay out of sight on the island. Alice Goodfellow Rheem cut a wild swath, drinking and playing cards with the locals, zooming around the island on a motorcycle in a bright red nightgown, and playing host to military personnel while her husband was in California. She died in 1956 after falling from the library balcony into the Rosario music room below; some believed it was a suicide. Employees tell of a ghost who wears high heels and skimpy clothing, and of erotic moans coming from her old bedroom late at night. Aficionados say her presence is particularly strong around Christmas, when she died. After Alice's death, the mansion was sold a couple of times, and in 1960 it became Rosario Resort.

The historic mansion at Rosario Resort is open to the public. Visitors are welcome to tour the grounds and check out the antiques-filled rooms, distinctive furnishings, parquet floors crafted from Indian teak, and walls paneled in Honduran mahogany.

Head upstairs to the vaulted ballroom with its heavy doors, stained-glass window, Tiffany chandelier, and ornate 1909 Steinway grand piano, which is dwarfed by the 1,972-pipe Aeolian organ. A horseshoe-shaped balcony hides the organ itself, which plays from musical rolls, much like a player piano. Moran had absolutely no musical talent, but he often pretended to play the organ and none of his guests were the wiser. The organ was later modified, adding a keyboard to allow it to be played. Today, a gifted local musician—**Christopher Peacock**—puts on one-hour performances that include music on the organ and piano, along with a slide show about the life of Moran and the resort's rich history. These free performances are open to the public and take place most afternoons at 4 P.M. mid-June–mid-September.

Also upstairs is a small free museum with original furnishings and Moran's impressive library just as he left it. Historical photos line the walls, and there's even a model of the U.S.S. *Washington,* one of the ships built by Moran's company. An upscale restaurant and lounge are downstairs, and the basement houses a gift shop, pool, and spa. Outside are manicured grounds and a veranda overlooking Cascade Harbor's bobbing boats. The anchor chain from the U.S.S. *Nebraska* and a beautifully carved figurehead from the clipper ship

*America* are in front of the mansion. Lodging is available in newer buildings surrounding Moran's historic home, but not in the mansion itself.

For more about the life of Robert Moran, pick up *Rosario Yesterdays: A Pictorial History* by Christopher Peacock (Rosario Productions); the book is sold at Rosario and in local bookstores.

# **⟨ EASTSOUND**

Located at the north end of Orcas Island near its narrowest point, the settlement of Eastsound is the primary village on the island. Here you'll discover a mix of gift shops, top-end restaurants, comfortable inns, grocery stores, and kayak outfitters, not to mention the kids' science center, skateboard park, and historical museum.

## **Orcas Island Historical Museum**

The Orcas Island Historical Society began in the 1940s as a small group of individuals dedicated to protecting and preserving the island's history. The organization's first museum consisted of artifacts displayed on the front porch of a pioneer family's home. In the 1950s and 1960s, island families donated six original homestead cabins built on Orcas between the 1870s and 1890s. Volunteers reconstructed and linked the structures to create the main museum building. These cedar cabins not only house the collections, but are considered important historical artifacts in themselves.

The collection at the Orcas Island Historical Museum (181 North Beach Rd. in Eastsound, 360/376-4849, www.orcasmuseum.org, 11 A.M.–4 P.M. Wed.–Mon. July–Sept., 11 A.M.–4 P.M. Wed.–Sun. June, 10 A.M.–3 P.M. Sat. the rest of the year, $5 adults, $4 seniors, $3 students, free for kids under 13) has displays covering relics, life stories, and historical photos from 1880s farms and homesteads, early stores and post offices, fruit farming, and the Coast Salish people. Be sure to see the bison bones found at peat bogs around Orcas. Cut marks on the bones were caused by human hunters,

# ROBERT MORAN AND ROSARIO RESORT

Two of Orcas Island's most famous destinations – Moran State Park and Rosario Resort – were the creations of Robert Moran, a self-made millionaire who turned his back on success in the business world. Born in 1857 to a New York family of 10 children, Robert Moran left home at age 14 to become an apprentice machinist. Three years later, in 1875, he decided that his future lay westward. After walking all the way to Cincinnati, he got a summer job at an iron mill and made enough money to return to New York and book passage on a ship for San Francisco. He arrived in the midst of an economic depression, and after failing to find a job, spent his last $15 on a steerage ticket to Seattle.

Moran stepped onto Yesler's Wharf in the Seattle rain with just $0.10 left in his pocket. A hungry belly led him to the aroma of pork sausage and flapjacks at a little eatery called Our House, run by Big Bill Gross. Gross took pity on Moran and offered him breakfast on credit, and later helped him get a job as a cook at a logging camp. Moran's cooking was so bad that the men threatened revolt and he had to hightail it back to Seattle, where Gross found him yet another job, this time as a deckhand on a steamer running between Seattle and Bellingham. Finally, Moran was in his element. Over the next few years, he studied mathematics, drafting, and engineering under the tutelage of an experienced ship captain, gradually moving up the ranks to become chief engineer on the steamer *Cassiar*, sailing in southeast Alaska.

## BOOM TIMES

In 1881 Moran married Melissa Paul, and together they raised five children. He paid $500 for his mother, five younger brothers, and two sisters to sail from New York to Seattle. Shortly after their arrival, the brothers set up a marine repair shop and Robert also took over management of the adjacent Seattle Drydock and Shipbuilding Company. Within a few years, Moran was on the city council, and in 1888 was elected the Republican mayor of Seattle. Within a year of taking office, a huge

fire swept through downtown, leaving 30 city blocks in ruins – including the Moran brothers' machine shop. Moran moved quickly to rebuild the city after the fire, and within six months, Seattle's population had actually doubled.

The Moran Brothers Company wasted no time in rebuilding; the new shop was open 10 days after the old one had burned to the ground! The company established an international reputation and within a few years began getting contracts to build ships for the U.S. Navy.

The 1897 discovery of gold in the Klondike transformed Seattle. Thousands of gold-crazed men flooded the town, intent on getting north as quickly as possible. Ships were needed to haul them there (and the gold out), and Moran Brothers began building stern-wheelers at a furious pace. Eighteen of these – each 175 feet long – were completed in 1898, and Robert Moran himself led the flotilla, starting at Roche Harbor on San Juan Island and sailing all the way to St. Michael at the mouth of the Yukon River, a distance of 4,000 treacherous miles. Only one of the 18 steamers was lost along the way, and it was insured. The Morans were on a roll.

During Robert Moran's two terms as Seattle mayor, he made business contacts in Washington DC and impressed the U.S. Navy with his design expertise. In 1900 the shipyard – then the Northwest's largest – landed a contract to build the U.S.S. *Nebraska,* one of a new class of battleships. It was a huge event for Seattle, and more than 55,000 people watched the launching ceremony. The ship became a favorite of naval officers and remained in service through World War I.

## SHOWPIECE OF THE SAN JUANS

The mental and physical stresses of business took a severe toll on Robert Moran, making him, in his own words, "a nervous wreck." Specialists from Europe told him that he was destined to soon gain "permanent residence in Lakeview Cemetery, Seattle, for the reason that they predicted that I had organic heart disease." He retired in 1905 at the age of 49, turning the shipyard over to his brothers. In 32 years, he had gone from a boy with one dime in his pocket to one of the wealthiest men in the Pacific Northwest. The Moran Brothers Company was sold in 1906 to, and later became part of, Todd Shipyards, a large Seattle operation that still flourishes.

Shortly after retiring, Robert Moran took a pleasure cruise in the San Juan Islands and fell in love with Orcas Island. It was his paradise, and he described it thus:

> In the lower reaches of Puget Sound and the Gulf of Georgia, looking out through the Strait of Juan de Fuca, toward the indles and lands of romance on the chief trade routes of the world's future commerce, lies a land unique and apart from anything else in the Western Hemisphere – the San Juan Islands! .... It is a wonderful place in which to forget one's troubles and worries and get back to Nature in her happiest moods; a delightful place in which to regain health – physical, mental, and spiritual.

He purchased 7,800 acres on Orcas Island and began work on a retirement home he called Rosario, after nearby Rosario Strait. But this was no simple waterfront cottage. He hired the finest shipwrights of the day (many of them former employees of Moran Brothers Company) to create a 54-room mansion covering 35,000 square feet. It cost $1.5 million in 1905 dollars and took four years to complete. Much of the ironwork – including butterfly hinges, nautical-style lamps, and door fasteners – was wrought at an on-site machine shop. Other touches included an indoor pool (with Italian marble) and bowling alley, a large veranda, beautifully landscaped grounds with a figure-eight-shaped lagoon, and a small hydroelectric plant to supply electricity; it still operates. The home was furnished in custom-made Mission-style pieces of teak and leather.

## MORAN DEPARTS

In 1932 – at the height of the Great Depression – Moran put his estate up for sale. His wife had died two years earlier, his brothers and sisters had also passed away, and his children had other interests. Despite ads in prominent national magazines, there were no takers. The mansion was finally sold in 1938 to a wealthy Californian, Donald Rheem, who paid just $50,000 for the mansion and 1,339 acres of surrounding land. Moran moved to much simpler quarters near the Orcas ferry landing. He died on his beloved Orcas Island on March 27, 1943, at the age of 86, and is buried in the same Lake View Cemetery in Seattle that the doctors had warned him about 37 years earlier. He probably outlived most of those doctors by many years.

For the complete story of Robert Moran and Rosario, read *Rosario Yesterdays: A Pictorial History* by Christopher Peacock.

© DON PITCHER

**Rosario Resort**

ORCAS ISLAND

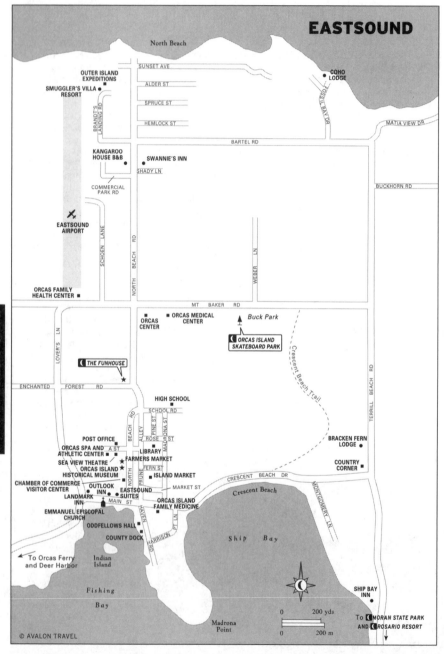

# EASTSOUND

North Beach

SUNSET AVE

ALDER ST

SPRUCE ST

HEMLOCK ST

BARTEL RD

OUTER ISLAND
EXPEDITIONS

SMUGGLER'S VILLA
RESORT

BRANDT'S LANDING RD

COHO
LODGE

FOSSIL BAY DR

MATIA VIEW DR

KANGAROO
HOUSE B&B

SWANNIE'S INN

SHADY LN

COMMERCIAL
PARK RD

BUCKHORN RD

EASTSOUND
AIRPORT

SCHOEN LANE

NORTH BEACH RD

WEBER LN

ORCAS FAMILY
HEALTH CENTER

MT BAKER RD

Buck Park

ORCAS
CENTER

ORCAS MEDICAL
CENTER

ORCAS ISLAND
SKATEBOARD PARK

Crescent Beach Trail

TERRILL BEACH RD

LOVER'S LN

THE FUNHOUSE

ENCHANTED FOREST RD

HIGH SCHOOL

SCHOOL RD

BEACH RD

PINE ST

MADRONA ST

BRACKEN FERN
LODGE

ALLEY

ROSE

COUNTRY
CORNER

POST OFFICE

ORCAS SPA AND
ATHLETIC CENTER

A ST

LIBRARY

FERN ST

SEA VIEW THEATRE

FARMERS MARKET

ORCAS ISLAND
HISTORICAL MUSEUM

NORTH

PRUNE

ISLAND MARKET

CRESCENT BEACH DR

CHAMBER OF COMMERCE
VISITOR CENTER

MARKET ST

Crescent Beach

OUTLOOK
INN

EASTSOUND
SUITES

LANDMARK
INN

MAIN ST

ORCAS ISLAND
FAMILY MEDICINE

MONTGOMERY LN

EMMANUEL EPISCOPAL
CHURCH

ODDFELLOWS HALL

HAVEN

HARRISON DR

COUNTY DOCK

Ship Bay

To Orcas Ferry
and Deer Harbor

Indian
Island

SHIP BAY
INN

Fishing
Bay

N

200 yds

To MORAN STATE PARK
AND ROSARIO RESORT

Madrona
Point

0        200 m

© AVALON TRAVEL

providing evidence that people have been on the islands for nearly 14,000 years!

## CROW VALLEY SCHOOL MUSEUM

This small museum, three miles southwest of Eastsound (2274 Crow Valley Rd., 360/376-4260, noon–4 p.m. Wed. and Sat. July–early Sept.) is in a quiet spot surrounded by tall trees, and makes a pleasant stop during a cycling tour of the island. Built in 1888, the classic one-room school houses old desks and a collection of memorabilia that includes school photos, report cards, school clothes, toys, and other items from a bygone era.

## VICTORIAN VALLEY CHAPEL

Hidden in an out-of-the-way part of the island, this picture-perfect chapel is surrounded by lush pastures and woods. From the Orcas ferry landing, drive north 1.5 miles on Orcas Road, turn right onto the easy-to-miss Victorian Valley Road, and continue 0.75 mile to the chapel. Built in 1974, Victorian Valley Chapel (360/376-3289, www.victorianvalleychapel.com) was intended as the centerpiece for a village of Victorian-style homes. Although the village never materialized, the little white chapel, with its quaint setting, historic stained-glass windows, and lovely wood interior, has become a favorite nondenominational place for candlelit weddings and other gatherings throughout the year. Book well ahead for summer weddings. In December, the chapel hosts a series of Christmas concerts by renowned singer—and Orcas resident—Susan Osborn (www.susanosborn.com).

## HISTORIC BUILDINGS

Both Deer Harbor and Olga contain a number of buildings dating from the late 1800s, including the Olga Store, the former Deer Harbor Store (1893), and the Deer Harbor Post Office (1893). The last of these is worth a visit, if only for its blue and yellow stained-glass windows. The quaint and beautifully situated **Emmanuel**

**Episcopal Church** (242 Main St., 360/376-2352, www.orcasepiscopal.org) faces the water in downtown Eastsound. Built in 1886 and modeled after an English country church, it is also the site for Thursday brown-bag concerts all summer. The church was built on land that was originally intended for a saloon. The owner started clearing land here but was so harassed by temperance movement women that he finally gave up and left town. The land was later donated to the church.

Located between Orcas Village and Eastsound, **Crow Valley Pottery** (2274 Orcas Rd., 360/376-4260, www.crowvalley.com) is housed in the oldest building on Orcas Island, an 1866 log cabin. It's well worth a stop. There is a second shop in the heart of Eastsound.

## LAMBIEL MUSEUM

An eccentric patron of the arts, Leo Lambiel (360/376-4544, www.lambielmuseum.org) has spent more than three decades collecting hundreds of the finest works by 200 San Juan County artists. The pieces cover a wide array of media: paintings, drawings, sculpture, murals, glasswork, photography, and ceramics, with some dating back to 1915. This private collection is housed in Lambiel's gracious home/museum, located 1.5 miles from Eastsound on Olga Road. The walls are lined with art, and you'll even find pieces inside the closet doors! The collection includes 135 etchings by Helen Loggie (1895–1976), the best-known artist to emerge from the San Juans. On the grounds are various sculptures, along with a couple of fantasy structures: a three-room grotto (with humorous and grotesque pieces) and a "ruined" Greek Doric temple. Exceptionally detailed two-hour tours of this nonprofit museum are given year-round for a $20 per person suggested donation; call for an appointment (required). Anyone with an appreciation for the arts will certainly enjoy a visit to this fascinating private museum, but I'd advise getting a drink first. This is not a gallery, and the works are not for sale.

ORCAS ISLAND

# Shopping

## BOOKS

**Darvill's Bookstore** (296 Main St. in Eastsound, 360/376-2135, www.darvillsbookstore.com, 9:30 A.M.–5:30 P.M. daily) has the finest selection of books on Orcas, with a knowledgeable staff and many regional titles. The little coffee stand in the back cranks out some of the finest espresso on the island.

## ART GALLERIES AND STUDIOS

Orcas Island has a well-deserved reputation as an arts mecca. Nearly 10 percent of locals list "artist" as their profession, and the island's diverse beauty is reflected in galleries dotting the landscape, selling everything from traditional oils to whimsical sculptures.

### ( Howe Art Gallery

As visitors approach Eastsound from the ferry, they are surprised to see several tall silvery sculptures twirling in the wind alongside the road. Just a quarter mile from town is the turnoff to Howe Art Gallery & Kinetic Sculpture Garden (360/376-2945, www. howeart.net, Wed.–Sun. late May–early Sept., by appointment the rest of the year). Follow Double Hill Road uphill to the home of Tony Howe, a transplant from the New York City art scene. Many of his whimsically playful welded-metal mobiles and kinetic art pieces fill the grounds and an adjacent gallery. Don't miss this place!

### ( Orcas Island Artworks

The barnlike structure that houses Orcas Island Artworks (Horseshoe Hwy. and Doe Bay Rd., 360/376-4408, www.orcasartworks.com, 10 A.M.–6 P.M. daily Apr.–Oct., 10 A.M.–5 P.M. daily spring and fall, closed Jan.–mid-Feb.) was built in 1938 and originally served as a processing plant for strawberries picked on nearby farms. The gallery has been here since 1982, making this one of the oldest artist-owned cooperatives in the Pacific Northwest. More than 40 artists and crafts workers display their pieces on two levels (painter and musician James Hardman's works are featured upstairs), and the back corner houses the popular Café Olga. The gallery is approximately eight miles south of Eastsound and two miles beyond Moran State Park.

### Studio 4:20

Head a mile east of Orcas Island Artworks to find Studio 4:20 (1179 Point Lawrence Rd., 360/376-3622, www.studio420orcasisland. com), a whimsical little spot with pottery, candles, leather, and jewelry, and an honor system for payment. The date 4/20—April 20—has become a holiday of sorts for those promoting the decriminalization of marijuana. This may or may not have anything to do with the gallery's name, but the shop's bumper stickers might provide a hint. One says "Studio 420: We smoke the competition."

© DON PITCHER

metal sculptures at Howe Art Gallery

## Crow Valley Pottery

Housed within the oldest building on the island, an 1866 log cabin, tiny Crow Valley Pottery (2274 Orcas Rd., 360/376-4260, www.crowvalley.com) contains works by four local potters, plus paintings, jewelry, sculpture, cards, baskets, and glass from regional artists. The studio has been here since 1959 and mounts four different exhibits throughout the summer. It is located along the main road connecting Orcas Village and Eastsound. A second, larger shop (360/376-5260) is right in the heart of Eastsound at 296 Main Street, with art spilling through several rooms. Both shops are open daily in the summer, and the in-town gallery stays open all year.

## ◖ Orcas Island Pottery

This out-of-the-way studio should not be missed. The oldest pottery studio in the Northwest—it opened in 1945—Orcas Island Pottery (360/376-2813, www.orcasislandpottery.com) sits atop a high bluff overlooking President Channel and is a 0.25-mile drive

© DON PITCHER

Orcas Island Pottery

through tall Douglas firs off West Beach Road. The inspiring setting alone makes it worth the side trip, but the wheel-thrown and hand-built pottery is equally notable. This is a laid-back and friendly place, and you're welcome to bring a picnic lunch and relax on the benches or have your kids climb into the tree house or try out the swings with a million-dollar view. Two rustic log buildings feature the works of 15 potters—many of whom fire their pieces here—along with four bronze artists. Dozens of colorful plates and pots sit outside on the grounds, filling with water when it rains.

## Olga Pottery

Located in a quiet corner of the island near the village of Olga, Olga Pottery (360/376-4648, www.olgapottery.com, daily year-round) exhibits the works of Jerry Weatherman. A potter since 1973, he exhibits a variety of styles that include colorful decorative porcelain. Drop by to watch him at work.

## The Right Place

Trudy Erwin runs The Right Place (2915 Enchanted Forest Rd., 360/376-4023, www.rightplacepottery.com), a small and seasonal Westside pottery studio near West Beach Resort. She owned Orcas Island Pottery for many years—it's now run by her daughter and grandson—and continues to produce an assortment of local crafts, from personalized plates to blown glass. In the summer, she'll introduce you to the potter's wheel with make-it-yourself pieces for a mere $10; the process requires three firings. They're a longtime Orcas tradition and always a hit with children.

## Other Galleries

Other galleries worth a visit are **Peter C. Fisher Gallery** (138 North Beach Rd. in Eastsound, 360/376-5955 or 800/920-8918, www.petercfisher.com) for fine art nature photos, **Mary Jane Ceramics** (269 Main St. in Eastsound, 360/376-7602, www.maryjaneceramics.com), and **Jillery** (310 Main St. in Eastsound, 360/376-5522).

ORCAS ISLAND

# Entertainment and Events

The **Orcas Center** (917 Mt. Baker Rd. in Eastsound, 360/376-2281, www.orcascenter. org) hosts a variety of events year-round, from concerts by nationally known musicians like Taj Mahal, Buckwheat Zydeco, or Wynton Marsalis to local theatrical performances and kid productions. There's also a monthly gallery show by local artists. Surprisingly, the theater was constructed solely from local contributions, not government grants.

Check out the latest movies at **Sea View Theatre** (A St., 360/376-5724) in Eastsound.

Anyone coming to Orcas for the nightlife will find slim pickings, though you might find the occasional weekend band in the summer at **The Lower Tavern** (Prune Alley, 360/376-4848). The bar also has karaoke on Friday nights and open-mic Tuesdays. Thursday night brings open-mic sessions at **Doe Bay Café** (107 Doe Bay Rd., 360/376-2291, www.doebay.com). There's also blues or jazz on Friday nights at **Octavia's Bistro** (360/376-4300 or 888/672-2792, www.orcashotel.com) in the Orcas Hotel at the ferry landing, plus classical or piano music Sundays at **Deer Harbor Inn** (360/376-4110 or 877/377-4110, www.deerharborinn.com).

See the Orcas Island Chamber's website (www.orcasislandchamber.com) for information on upcoming island events. Start the summer off with the **Bite of Orcas** on Memorial Day weekend, a great chance to taste foods prepared by local restaurants to benefit Wolf Hollow Wildlife Rehabilitation Center. Don't miss the fun parade of pets.

Don't miss the **Orcas Island Farmers Market** (360/317-8342, www.orcasislandfarmersmarket.org, 11 A.M.–2 P.M. Sat. May–Nov.). It takes place next to the Orcas Island Historical Museum on North Beach Road. You'll find everything from locally grown flowers and fresh veggies to artwork and tempting food.

A **Summer Solstice** parade takes place in Eastsound on the Saturday closest to June 21. Every Thursday at noon during July and August, head to the waterside Emmanuel Episcopal Church in Eastsound for a free **Brown Bag Concert.** Over in **Deer Harbor Marina,** find live music on the pier 4–7 P.M. on summer Saturdays. The **Orcas Island Garden Tour** takes place the last weekend of June.

Eastsound—like nearly every small town in the United States—has a fun parade on the Saturday nearest the **Fourth of July.** Other holiday weekend festivities include a community band concert, a pancake breakfast, and a salmon barbecue in Eastsound, plus fireworks at Eastsound on the 4th and at Deer Harbor on the 3rd of July.

The first weekend of August brings the popular **Orcas Island Fly-In** (www.portoforcas.com) featuring many antique planes and a classic car show. It's followed on the second Saturday of August by the **Library Fair** (360/376-4985, www.orcaslibrary.org), a big arts and crafts fair and book sale.

In mid-August, **Doe Bay Fest** (www.doebayfest.com) features three days of live rock music from up-and-coming musicians. Held at Doe Bay Resort, it's limited to just 1,000 people and typically sells out within minutes of the official announcement in May! Good luck getting a ticket for this one, but if you do, you're in for a treat.

The always-sold-out **Orcas Island Chamber Music Festival** (360/376-6636 or 866/492-0003, www.oicmf.org) takes place over the last two weeks in August. You'll hear the works of Mozart, Bach, Schubert, Rachmaninoff, Gershwin, Copland, Brahms, Tchaikovsky, and others.

Labor Day weekend brings the **Steve Braun Memorial Triathlon.** In early September, the **Wooden Boats Rendezvous** (360/376-3037, www.deerharbormarina.com) exhibits handcrafted boats and features a sailing race and live music at Deer Harbor.

# Recreation

## ◖ ORCAS ISLAND SKATEBOARD PARK

Head out Mt. Baker Road past the medical clinic and just before the cemetery (there must be a reason for their proximity) to Orcas Island Skateboard Park (www.skateorcas.org), recognized as one of the finest skate parks in the Northwest. It was funded in part by Warren Miller, the guru of extreme skiing, and contains 15,000 square feet of bumps and curving concrete that attract both locals and off-island skaters. No bikes are allowed, and helmets are required. The skateboard park is a part of **Buck Park,** which also contains tennis courts and baseball fields.

## ◖ THE FUNHOUSE

Founded by Jim Bredouw, who spent more than $1 million of his own money on the project, The Funhouse (30 Pea Patch Lane, 360/376-7177, www.thefunhouse.org, 11 A.M.–5 P.M. Mon.–Sat. mid-June–Sept., 3–5:30 P.M. Mon.–Fri. the rest of the year, teens-only sessions 6–11 P.M. Fri.–Sat., $5/person or $25/family, no charge for kids under four) is an impressive nonprofit spot for kids. It provides a place to learn with other children and acts as an after-school hangout and teen center on weekend evenings. With science exhibits that challenge and interest all ages, The Funhouse isn't just for the youngsters. It includes a music studio (guitar, drums, and keyboard), climbing wall, pitching cage with speed gun, art studio, pool table, foosball, Ping-Pong, air hockey, Karaoke system, Wii and Xbox games, science exhibits, Internet access, library, and kid videos. Outside is a fun playground and grassy lawn. This is a great place to drop your kids when they're bored on a rainy day.

## HIKING

The best hiking on Orcas is found within Moran State Park, but a handful of other trail options exist. Get a copy of *Hiking the San Juan Islands* by Ken Wilcox (Northwest Wild Books) or *San Juan Islands: A Guide to Exploring the Great Outdoors* by Dave Wortman (FalconGuides) for detailed descriptions of Orcas trails. **Olga Community Park** contains picnic tables and a playground next to the community hall in Olga.

### Guided Hikes

Natalie (Nat) Herner of **Gnat's Nature Hikes** (360/376-6629, www.orcasislandhikes.com, $35/person) leads morning nature walks that emphasize both human and natural history, along with wild edible and medicinal plants. The cost includes pickup and return to your hotel or bed-and-breakfast, plus two or three hours exploring Moran State Park trails. The pace is set to your abilities. She also offers customized half-day boat-and-hike trips to the marine state parks, including Jones Island and The Nature Conservancy preserve on Yellow Island. There's a two-person minimum for the Moran hikes and a three-person minimum (and a six-person maximum) for the boat trips. Natalie has a background in environmental studies along with more than a decade of experience as a naturalist and guide on whale-watching boats.

### Indian Island

**Eastsound Waterfront Park** is a little grassy picnic area across from the intersection of Lovers Lane and Horseshoe Highway. At low tide, a sandy spit emerges, providing access to tiny Indian Island. Tidepools here are alive with fish, sea stars, crabs, anemones, mollusks, and marine creatures, along with black oystercatchers and other birds. When visiting the island, be careful to watch where you step and avoid nesting birds.

### Madrona Point

For ease of access, it's hard to beat Madrona Point, just a few blocks from downtown Eastsound. This small peninsula of land now belongs to the Lummi Indian Nation (the federal government bought it from developers in the 1980s and gave it to the Lummi) but is open to the public. Get here by following Haven Road south from Eastsound past the Odd Fellows Hall to the park, where you will also find a county dock for launching boats and kayaks. Madrona Point is aptly named, with tall and colorful Pacific madrone (aka madrona) trees, along with graceful Douglas firs framing the view across the water to Eastsound and the rest of Orcas Island. A meadow on the point contains camas plants; the bulbs of the purple great camas were a prized food source for the Coast Salish.

## Crescent Beach

Owned by the San Juan County Land Bank (360/378-4402, www.sjclandbank.org), the Crescent Beach Preserve includes shoreline along this shallow bay (popular with kayakers) and 140 acres of nearby woods. A nearly level 0.5-mile trail starts at Crescent Beach in Eastsound and continues through the woods to Mt. Baker Road. A few parking spaces are available on both ends of this path. The usually placid bay at Crescent Beach is home to an oyster farm, a salmon hatchery, starfish along Madrona Point, and **thousands of colorful sand dollars.**

## Obstruction Pass State Park

Obstruction Pass (360/376-2326, www. parks.wa.gov) is an 80-acre park at the end of a one-mile dirt road off Obstruction Pass Road. It is approximately 2.5 miles southeast of Olga and 20 road miles from the ferry dock. A woodsy (and sometimes muddy) trail leads 0.5 mile from the parking lot to a small beach facing nearby Obstruction and Blakely Islands. Nine campsites are just back from the beach, and a side trail leads to a second beach looking west to Olga and the setting sun. Obstruction Pass is a favorite destination for sea kayakers, who can put in for free at the nearby county boat ramp and dock. No bikes allowed on park trails, but several campsites are available.

## Turtleback Mountain Preserve

This 1,576-acre preserve was purchased in 2006 after local citizens raised an astounding $18.5 million to prevent its development. Shaped like a tortoise—hence the name—Turtleback Mountain is accessed from trailheads on two sides. The north entrance is via a gravel road (look for the Turtleback Mountain sign) just south of Crow Valley Schoolhouse on Crow Valley Road. The south entrance is 2.4 miles west from West Sound along Deer Harbor Road. No sign for the preserve here, so look on the right (north) side for Wild Rose Lane. The south side trailhead is a few hundred feet up this lane.

Hiking trails loop for more than five miles through second-growth forests (logged in the 1920s and 1930s), with overlooks on both ends of the mountain; the best views are from the south side, where a path climbs 1.3 miles to 931-foot Ship Peak overlook, where you can stand atop rocky outcrops overlooking Crow Valley. The 1,519-foot summit of Turtleback Mountain is second highest in the San Juan

© DON PITCHER

**Turtleback Mountain Preserve has miles of beautiful trails.**

Islands (after Mount Constitution). Get additional info on the preserve—including a downloadable map—from the **San Juan County Land Bank** (360/378-4402, www.sjclandbank.org). The preserve is open for day use only, with no developed facilities or camping. Horses and bikes are allowed on north-end trailheads only, with bikes on even calendar days and horses on odd calendar days.

## Point Doughty Marine State Park

Popular with kayakers, this small peninsula extends from the northwest edge of Orcas near YMCA's Camp Orkila. Access by larger boats is very difficult, and kayakers may contend with wind and waves at this exposed site. The point contains tall cliffs and a forest of Douglas fir and madrone. Nearby waters are a favorite of scuba divers, and harbor porpoises are common sights in rips just off the point.

Only the four acres at the very tip of Point Doughty are open to the public; the rest is a natural area preserve where trespassing is prohibited. There are no trails in this little park, and no easements to allow access from nearby roads, so you'll need a kayak to visit. Point Doughty's four primitive campsites are part of the Cascadia Marine Trail. No drinking water is available, but vault toilets are provided.

## Frank Richardson Wildlife Preserve

Located close to Deer Harbor, this 20-acre freshwater marsh is a premier birding area, with red-winged blackbirds, wood ducks, hooded mergansers, Canada geese, mallards, widgeons, scaups, buffleheads, teal, rails, marsh wrens, and many other species. It is named for a University of Washington professor of zoology (and birder) who lived nearby. After his death in 1985, the land was saved through the efforts of the San Juan Preservation Trust. Get here by driving to Deer Harbor, turning right on Channel Road just before you reach the harbor itself. Cross the bridge and continue uphill for 0.75 mile. The marsh is on the right.

# BICYCLING

Orcas has a great diversity of cycling conditions, from easy valley rides to a difficult five-mile climb (and worth it!) to the summit of Mount Constitution within Moran State Park. The island's 82 miles of county roads tend to be narrow, hilly, and winding, making this the most challenging of the islands for cyclists. Always travel in single file. Be sure to pull well off the road when you stop, and watch out for long lines of traffic heading up the road when a ferry has just docked at Orcas Village. Get a helpful cycling map of Orcas from Wildlife Cycles.

## Rentals and Tours

Orcas Island's only bike shop, **Wildlife Cycles** (350 North Beach Rd. in Eastsound, 360/376-4708, www.wildlifecycles.com, daily in the summer, $35–50/day) rents high-quality mountain bikes, road bikes, hybrids, baby joggers, trailers, panniers, and other biking gear. This is where you'll meet the hardcore local cyclists for organized rides. Guided bike tours are available for groups heading to Moran State Park. Stop by Wildlife Cycles for a map of park trails open to cyclists. You can also rent basic mountain bikes at **Deer Harbor Marina** (360/376-3037, www.deerharbormarina.com).

For Orcas Island **cycling tours,** contact **Backroads** (510/527-1555 or 800/462-2848, www.backroads.com) or **Trek Travel** (608/441-8735 or 866/464-8735, www.trektravel.com).

# SEA KAYAKING

Orcas Island is an excellent launching point for day trips and multi-day paddles. Several of the most popular kayaking destinations—including Jones, Sucia, Patos, and Matia Islands—are within a few miles of Orcas.

## Tours

Established in 1982, **Shearwater Adventures** (138 North Beach Rd. in Eastsound, 360/376-4699, www.shearwaterkayaks.com) has a variety of kayak tours that depart daily from Rosario Resort, Deer Harbor Resort, West Beach Resort, and Doe Bay Resort & Retreat.

Three-hour paddles—including popular sunset tours—cost $69 per person and are led by experienced guides. All-day trips ($159) provide a chance to explore beautiful Sucia Island off Orcas at a leisurely pace. In addition, Shearwater staff members set up custom tours, and the Eastsound shop sells kayaks, along with quality paddling and camping gear, books, videos, and more.

Located at the ferry landing, **Orcas Outdoors** (360/376-4611, www.orcasoutdoors.com, May–mid-Oct.) specializes in short paddles that entice folks waiting in line for the ferry. A one-hour trip is just $30 per person, with a three-hour tour for $65. Longer trips (including overnights) are also available. No reservations are necessary.

Based at Smuggler's Villa Resort on the north side of Orcas, **Outer Island Expeditions** (360/376-3711, www.outerislandx.com) provides kayak tours to beautiful Sucia Island. A five-hour trip ($159 adults or $99 kids) includes a water taxi to Sucia and guided kayaking in the convoluted bays of this unique island. A shorter three-hour paddle from Point Doughty on the northwest side of Orcas is $79 adults or $49 kids.

At **Spring Bay Kayak Tours** (360/376-5531, www.springbayonorcas.com), owners Carl Burger and Sandy Playa guide two-hour paddles around the waters of Obstruction Pass. Twice-daily tours are just $35 per person. (Guests at the cabin get a free kayak tour included with their stay.) The remote location, reasonable price, knowledgeable guides, and relatively protected waters make this an excellent option. No age limits and a triple kayak is available, making these perfect for families.

Teenagers may be interested in the 7- to 14-day sea-kayaking trips offered by the YMCA's **Camp Orkila** (360/376-2678 or 206/382-5009, www.camporkila.org).

## Kayak Rentals

Do-it-yourselfers can rent sea kayaks from several places on Orcas: **Outer Island Expeditions** (360/376-3711, www.outerislandx.com, $75/day for doubles, $50/day for singles), **Lieber Haven Resort & Marina** (360/376-2472, www.lieberhavenresort.com), **West Beach Resort** (360/376-2240 or 877/937-8224, www.westbeachresort.com), and funky **Crescent Beach Kayaks** (at Crescent Beach in Eastsound, 360/376-2464, www.crescentbeachkayaks.com, $50/person for a half-day, including a short lesson). The last of these has all sorts of kayaks—including sit-on-top versions and kayaks with extra space for children.

If you're planning on launching your own kayak, be forewarned that you may be subject to a launching fee ($5 at Deer Harbor) if you aren't on public lands, and may be charged for overnight parking. **North Beach** near Eastsound is the primary launch point for kayakers heading to the very popular trio of Sucia, Matia, and Patos Islands. Unfortunately, parking is limited and the spaces are quickly filled on summer weekends. You can also launch kayaks for free at the county dock near Madrona Point in Eastsound, or use the dock at Coho Lodge on the north end of the island for $10. On the southern edge of the island, kayakers put in at Obstruction Pass, where the county maintains the only public boat ramp. Across the road is **Lieber Haven Resort & Marina** (360/376-2472, www.lieberhavenresort.com) with a wonderful beach that's open to the public and doesn't charge for launching kayaks.

## WHALE-WATCHING

Two respected companies provide whale-watching trips from Orcas Island. Note, however, that killer whales are most often found in Haro Strait west of San Juan Island, so trips starting from Orcas require a bit more time en route than those out of Roche Harbor on San Juan Island. Reservations are advised.

Established in 1990 and highly recommended, **Deer Harbor Charters** (360/376-5989 or 800/544-5758, www.deerharborcharters.com, closed Nov.–Jan.) is the oldest whale-watching business on Orcas. Owner Tom Averna has a background in marine science and keeps professional naturalists aboard his two boats (one holds a maximum of

© DON PITCHER

**boat-watching on Orcas Island**

20, and the other up to 32 passengers). Four-hour trips depart from Deer Harbor Resort and Rosario Resort daily in the summer in search of orcas and minke whales, and cost $75 adults, $49 kids under 14. Wildlife cruises ($62 adults, $39 kids) are available in the off-season.

**Orcas Island Eclipse Charters** (360/376-6566 or 800/376-6566, www.orcasisland-whales.com, May–mid-Oct., $75 adults, $45 kids) has a spacious 48-passenger boat with an upstairs deck and a heated cabin. Trips last 3.5 hours, head out from Orcas Village (next to the ferry) and are timed to meet ferry departures, which is advantageous if you're in a hurry but might mean a shorter trip if you aren't. For something different, join a **lighthouse tour** through Eclipse Charters. These four-hour voyages take place once or twice a month April–August and cost $89 adults, $59 kids. Some are entirely water-based, with visits to lighthouses at Turn Point (Stuart Island), Patos Island, and two on San Juan Island: Lime Kiln and Cattle Point. Other tours include time on-shore at Turn Point or Patos Island.

Former park ranger Beau Brandow runs **Outer Island Expeditions** (360/376-3711, www.outerislandx.com), providing twice-daily trips ($99 adults, $79 kids) that include whale-watching, crabbing, and time to explore the more remote islands in the San Juans. A better bet is an afternoon trip (six hours for $199 adults or $169 kids), with time to visit Sucia or Stuart Islands and enjoy a big steak and seafood dinner. The fast boat (top speed 45 knots) makes it possible to cover a lot of water in a short time. The boat is based in Brant's Landing on the north side of Orcas near Eastsound.

## BOATING
### Marinas

Located on the southwest end of Orcas Island, picturesque **Deer Harbor Marina** (360/376-3037, www.deerharbormarina.com) is a busy place in the summer. Flowers drape the docks, and you'll find boat rentals, fishing (North Shore Charters), sailing charters, water taxis (North Shore Charters and Orcas Boat Rentals), sea-kayak tours (Shearwater Adventures), daily floatplane flights to Seattle (Kenmore Air), whale-watching trips (Deer Harbor Charters), mountain bike rentals, showers, laundry, nature tours (Gnat's Nature Hikes), moorage, an ATM, boat gas and diesel (also for cars in an emergency), and a tiny year-round market. The small sandy beach here is a great diversion for kids. Lodging, a post office, and a restaurant (Deer Harbor Inn) are just up the road.

Scan Deer Harbor for the luxury yacht **Apogee,** owned by former astronaut Bill Anders. As the lunar module pilot for Apollo 8, he was onboard the first spaceflight to leave earth's orbit en route to the moon, and the first to see the entire sphere of the earth from outer space. Earthrise, a photo taken by Anders on Christmas Eve 1968, is one of most famous images ever taken; it shows a blue and white earth rising over a desolate moonscape. The late photographer Gelen Rowell called Earthrise, "the most influential environmental photograph ever taken."

ORCAS ISLAND

Historic Rosario Resort is the base for **Rosario Resort Marina** (360/376-2222 or 800/562-8820, www.rosarioresort.com), with moorage, fuel, showers, and a seasonal store with supplies on Cascade Bay near Moran State Park. There's direct Kenmore Air floatplane service to the marina from Seattle, and you can take sea-kayaking and whale-watching trips or go sailing with a pro. The resort itself houses a full-service spa.

Located three miles west of Eastsound off Enchanted Forest Road, **West Beach Resort** (360/376-2240 or 877/937-8224, www.westbeachresort.com) has a pier and summer-only marina. You can rent motorboats, canoes, and sea kayaks, or take a guided kayak tour through Shearwater Kayaks; a sunset tour costs $69. Only cabin guests and campers staying at the resort are allowed to launch boats or kayaks at the resort's private beach.

Orcas Island's largest marina is **West Sound Marina** (360/376-2314, www.westsoundmarina.net, year-round) on the northeast side of West Sound. Here you will find guest moorage, showers, a waste pump-out, fuel dock, marine repair facility, and chandlery.

Friendly **Lieber Haven Resort & Marina** (360/376-2472, www.lieberhavenresort.com) is a small marina where you can rent kayaks and rowboats, or go along on whale-watching trips, sea-kayak tours, or fishing charters. They even have loaner fishing poles. A little store sells fishing supplies and snacks, and public moorage is available, along with free Wi-Fi. It is located along Obstruction Pass on the southeast end of the island. Across the road is the **Obstruction Pass Boat Ramp,** the only public ramp on Orcas.

## Sailing

Deer Harbor (www.deerharbormarina.com) is the primary center for sailboat charters on Orcas Island. Skipper Ward Fay of **Northwest Classic Day Sails** (360/376-5581, www.classicdaysails.com) sails a meticulously maintained cedar sloop, the 33-foot *Aura.* Three-hour trips depart Deer Harbor daily on this beautiful 1940s sailboat ($70 per adult, $55 per child).

Also based at Deer Harbor, **Emerald Isle Sailing Charters** (360/376-3472 or 866/714-6611, www.emeraldislesailing.com) has both six-hour day trips ($135/person with a two-person minimum) and multi-day San Juan Islands skippered charter trips, starting at $997 per person for a three-day voyage. Longer trips head up British Columbia's Inside Passage all the way to Ketchikan, Alaska. The boat, an immaculate 54-foot pilothouse ketch, is called *Nawalak,* a name that means "spirit of nature" in the Kwakwaka'wakw language.

Skipper Ben Booth operates **Orcas Island Sailing** (360/376-2113, www.orcassailing.com) from Lieber Haven Resort & Marina on the east side of the island. In addition to skippered charters, he provides sailing instruction and bareboat charters onboard 19- to 26-foot boats.

At Rosario Resort, Captain Tony Lee of **Morning Star Sailing Charters** (360/376-2099, www.orcascharters.com) sails a classic 56-foot Chesapeake "Bugeye" with space for up to 25 passengers. It's available for groups (and perfect for an onboard wedding) at $350 for a two-hour cruise.

## Motorboats

Located at Deer Harbor Marina, **Orcas Boat Rentals** (360/376-7616, www.orcasboats.com, daily June–Sept., by reservation Apr. and May) rents a variety of boats, including 16-foot Runabouts ($300/day) and 19-foot Habercrafts with 90-horse engines ($375/day). The staff also provides water-taxi service to nearby islands.

**West Beach Resort** (three miles west of Eastsound, 360/376-2240 or 877/937-8224, www.westbeachresort.com) rents 16-foot skiffs ($199/day), along with canoes and sea kayaks ($12–18/hour).

Based on the north side of Orcas Island, **Cruise Control** (360/927-8216, www.cruisecontrolweb.com) has a beautiful 45-foot motor yacht with space for six. Captain Robin Watson provides dinner cruises to Sucia Island ($400 for four people on a four-hour evening). Guests can go ashore to explore this island park.

## Fishing

Fishing charters—primarily for salmon and halibut—are offered by **Outer Island Expeditions** (360/376-3711, www.outer-islandx.com) and **North Shore Charters** (360/376-4855, www.orcasislandadventures.com). Expect to pay around $165 per person for an all-day fishing expedition.

## SWIMMING AND FITNESS

The YMCA's **Camp Orkila** (360/376-2678 or 206/382-5009, www.camporkila.org) has a large heated outdoor swimming pool open to the public in the summer daily 1–2 P.M. (except Sat.) for just $1 per person. The wonderful beachside location is two miles from Eastsound at the western end of Mt. Baker Road. Families staying on Orcas for a week or more should be sure to get details on the Y's youth swim lessons, offered four days a week late June–mid-August.

Three Moran State Park lakes—**Mountain Lake, Cascade Lake,** and **Twin Lake**—are popular summertime swimming destinations, but there are no lifeguards. Cascade Lake is the center of the action and a favorite for families. It has a roped-off swimming area and shallow water that warms up to swimmable June–August. A snack bar is nearby, along with a playground and boathouse that rents rowboats and paddleboats. Rowboats are also available at Mountain Lake.

There are no public pools on Orcas, but you can pay $15 for a day pass and use the indoor pool at **Orcas Spa & Athletics** (188 A St. in Eastsound, 360/376-6361 or 888/894-8881, www.orcasspaandathletics.com). This full-service athletic club also includes a hot tub, dry sauna, free weights, cardio machines, racquetball, and various classes. The spa offers massage, aromatherapy, facials, mud masks, and other body treats.

**Rosario Resort Spa** (360/376-2222 or 800/562-8820, www.rosarioresort.com) includes outdoor and indoor pools, a children's pool, exercise facility, sauna, and hot tub. Pay $20 adults or $5 kids for an all-day pass to the spa and pools.

ORCAS ISLAND

© DON PITCHER

the beach at Cascade Lake in Moran State Park

## SPAS AND YOGA

Several places provide massage and other creature comforts on the island, including **Orcas Spa & Athletics** (188 A St. in Eastsound, 360/376-6361 or 888/894-8881, www.orcasspaandathletics.com), **Healing Arts Center** (353 North Beach Rd., 360/376-4002, www.healingartsonline.com), and **Island Massage Studio** (365 North Beach Rd., 360/376-1434).

**Rosario Resort Spa** (360/376-2152 or 800/562-8820, www.rosarioresort.com, $20/day) is open to those who aren't staying at the resort. The day fee provides access to an indoor pool, an outdoor pool, hot tub, sauna, exercise equipment, towels, and showers. A full range of spa options are also available, including fitness classes, professional massage, aromatherapy, body wrap, facial, manicure, and pedicure.

For less pretentious facilities, head a few miles beyond Rosario to **Doe Bay Resort & Retreat** (360/376-2291, www.doebay.com, $15 for a day pass), with its au naturel sauna and hot tubs. Children under six are not allowed and no minors are allowed after 6 P.M. The resort offers weeklong Ayurvedic yoga retreats throughout the year.

**Orcas Mandala Yoga Studio** (138 North Beach Rd., 360/298-0218, www.orcasmandala.com) has yoga classes most days for all levels of ability, and drop-ins are welcome.

## GOLF AND TENNIS

Golfers will enjoy a round at **Orcas Island Country Golf Club** (360/376-4400, www.golforcas.com, Apr.–Oct., $25) a nine-hole, par-36 public course on Orcas Road southwest of Eastsound. Built in 1962 and reminiscent of Scottish country clubs, the course challenges with gently rolling hills, cantankerous water

hazards, and a quaint setting. It's easily the most interesting course in the San Juans. The pro shop rents clubs, pull carts, and electric carts.

**Buck Park,** just north of Eastsound along Mt. Baker Rd., has public tennis courts, baseball diamonds, and a big skateboard park.

## HORSES AND ALPACAS

**Orcas Island Trail Rides** (360/376-2134, www.orcastrailrides.com) leads rides along trails within Moran State Park. These are for all abilities (ages 7 and up), starting with a 1.5-hour horseback ride ($79) that's perfect for novices. Their most popular trip ($119) lasts 2.5 hours and covers remote mountain terrain along the park boundary. Trail rides depart from a campground at the south end of Cascade Lake within the park. Call ahead for reservations.

On the west flank of Turtleback Mountain, **Turtlehead Trails** (360/376-3649, www.turtleheadfarm.com) leads guided horseback rides on 750 acres of land adjacent to the preserve. Some trails lead to dramatic hilltop and waterside vistas. These are private guided rides, customized for your ability and interests, making them perfect for families. The cost is $62 for a one-hour ride; available for ages 8 and up. Horse boarding, horsemanship camps, and farmstays are also available.

A favorite of kids and weavers, **Orcas Moon Alpacas** (329 Dolphin Bay Rd., 360/376-2707, www.orcasmoonalpacas.com, noon–2 P.M. Wed.–Sat. late May–early Sept.) has 20 or so of these adorable furry animals. Stop by to take a tour (donation) or feed the friendly alpacas and miniature donkeys. The farm stand sells produce, alpaca yarn, and eggs—all from this 20-acre farm.

# Summer Camps and Retreats

Orcas is a delightful spot for summer camps, with three very different options available. Camp Orkila and Four Winds-Westward Ho Camp are the definitive summer camps you probably remember from childhood, with a fun mix of activities and challenges. Each has its own advantages—Orkila is very reasonable but also large, while Four Winds-Westward Ho is chummier but more expensive. Camp Indralaya serves as a retreat center for members of the Theosophical Society, but the general public is welcome. With its eco-ethics, we-are-all-one philosophy, and budget pricing, Indralaya is a place to get in touch with your spiritual center.

## CAMP ORKILA

Operated by the Seattle YMCA, Camp Orkila (360/376-2678 or 206/382-5009, www.camp-orkila.org) covers 280 acres of forests and shoreline on Orcas Island. The camp first opened in 1906—more than a century ago—when 30 boys from Seattle spent a month on waterfront land belonging to Laurence Colman. The property was deeded to the Y in 1938. Located on the northwest shore of Orcas Island, with a spectacular sunset view across President Channel to the Gulf Islands of British Columbia, the camp is one of seven run by the Y in Washington. Forested grounds slope gently down to the water, with a half mile of private beach and an ideal setting for outdoor activities.

Featured camp attractions include a large heated outdoor pool, marine life touch tanks, a 150-foot dock, sea kayaks, BMX track, sailboats, rowboats, canoes, a 44-passenger powerboat, large climbing tower, zip lines, ropes courses, sports fields, a craft center, pottery studio, horses and riding arena, and a vegetable garden. The Y also owns a mountain camp at Twin Lakes on the edge of Moran State Park, along with the 107-acre Satellite Island, a favorite overnight boating trip for campers.

## Summer Camp

Camp Orkila is the ideal place for an old-time summer camp, available for youths in grades 3–12. Depending on their age and abilities, kids can join in a wide range of activities, including sports, crafts, swimming, nature study, archery, wilderness camping, skateboarding, high-ropes training, horseback riding, bicycling, rock climbing, canoeing, marine biology, and kayaking. Campers choose from a variety of skill clinics, sports, crafts, and activities each day. Younger kids take part in traditional summer camp sessions, while older youths enjoy more focused sessions.

Lodging is in rustic open-air Adirondack-style cabins with bathroom facilities a short walk away. Filling meals are served family style. Prices are on a three-tier system based upon your ability to pay; most camps run $680–730 per week for tier 1, up to $850–1,050 for tier 3. Camp spaces go fast, so make reservations early for your child—in January for the most popular programs.

Special teen expedition programs focus on building self-confidence and leadership skills through biking, sea-kayaking, and sailing treks. These last 1–4 weeks each and vary in cost, starting around $730 for a one-week kayaking camp.

### Family Camps and Retreats

Camp Orkila isn't just for kids, offering both family camps and women's wellness retreats six weekends a year. The cost for family camps varies seasonally, with the highest rates over Labor Day: $232 for adults and $191 for ages 4–12; free for kids under four. Lodging is in rustic cabins that accommodate two or three families, with bathrooms a short walk away. Your fee includes lodging, meals, and activities. If you want to stay in something nicer, the camp also has a half-dozen deluxe four-plex cabins, but these cost an extra $236 for a family of four over Labor Day weekend.

Family camp activities include hikes, archery, arts and crafts, pottery, rowboats, climbing wall, campfires, games, horseback rides, swimming, and more. There's a small extra fee to use

ORCAS ISLAND

the sea kayaks or to try out the daredevil high-ropes course. The women's wellness weekends provide time away from husbands, kids, dogs, phones, and mortgages in mid-March and late October, with yoga, massage, sea kayaking, archery, climbing, crafts, and other activities. These cost $142–198; visit www.camporkila.org or call 360/376-2678 for the complete story.

### Day Camps

If you're bringing school-age children on vacation, this may be the hottest tip you'll find in this book. Camp Orkila operates an outstanding community day camp (8:45 A.M.–4:45 P.M. Mon.–Fri. July>–Aug., starting at $170/week) that is open to anyone with kids in grades 1–6. The program includes swimming, arts and crafts, archery, games, field trips, and much more. Call 360/376-2678 several weeks ahead of your visit to Orcas to be assured of space in the day-camp program.

## FOUR WINDS-WESTWARD HO CAMP

In 1927, a young teacher named Ruth Brown established Four Winds Camp for girls at Four

Winds Bay on Orcas Island. Five years later, she created Westward Ho Camp for boys on the opposite side of the bay. She ran the camp for many years, and in 1967 deeded the 150 acres of land, facilities, and equipment to a nonprofit foundation called Four Winds, Inc. (360/376-2277, www.fourwindscamp.org).

### Camp Life

Today, all Four Winds–Westward Ho Camp activities are coed, but the boys and girls are still housed on separate sides of Four Winds Bay—to the relief of parents of teenage girls. The camp houses 170 kids at a time, with one counselor for every 4–6 children. Everyone wears a uniform (polo-style shirts and khaki shorts for the boys and decidedly old-fashioned middies and bloomers for the girls) to cut down on teen fashion jealousies and make it easier to manage the laundry. Girls live in simple cedar cabins and wall tents, while boys stay in wall tents.

During their stay, campers learn horseback riding (20 horses, and both Western- and English-style riding classes), sailing, tennis, archery, soccer, photography, arts and crafts, poetry, and many other activities. No candy,

sign at Four Winds-Westward Ho Camp

cell phones, laptop or tablet computers, or electronic games are allowed, but music is a big part of camp life. In addition to dinghies and sailboats, the camp has a 61-foot yawl to train older kids in the art of sailing. The sailboat, canoes, and kayaks are used for multi-night trips away from camp as kids explore the San Juan Islands.

Two one-month sessions are offered each summer for kids entering grades 4–10, followed by a one-week session that introduces younger children (grades 2–5) to the wonders of camp life. These aren't cheap: $4,250 for the one-month sessions (June 24–July 21 and July 24–Aug. 20) or $975 for the one-week camps (Aug. 23–29). Families without that kind of money can apply for a scholarship, and the staff strives to make this a noncompetitive experience that brings together campers from various racial, economic, and social backgrounds. Approximately 20 percent of the kids attend on scholarships, and a few partial scholarships are available for middle-income families. Most of those who attend Four Winds–Westward Ho Camp come from San Francisco, Los Angeles, and Seattle—including quite a few children from famous families. Free transportation is provided from Sea-Tac Airport, Seattle, and Anacortes. In addition, a separate counselor-training program is available, giving young people the chance to take on greater responsibilities as they mature.

Four Winds–Westward Ho Camp is located along the southern end of West Sound, a mile from Deer Harbor.

## CAMP INDRALAYA

This is a camp unlike any other in the San Juan Islands. The camp was founded in 1927 by members of the Theosophical Society (www.theosophical.org), a religion that shares philosophical similarities with Buddhism. The guiding principles of theosophy are that the universe and all within it are all one, and that everyone finds his or her own truth. There's a strong sense of community at this peaceful spot, where you might learn about environmental ethics one week and the Koran the next.

Indralaya (360/376-4526, www.indralaya. org) is one of just four Theosophical retreat centers in America; the others are in Arkansas, California, and New York. The 78-acre camp is on the northwest end of East Sound, just two miles from the village of Eastsound. The name Indralaya is derived from Sanskrit and means "a home for the spiritual forces in nature," and the setting is sublime, with 1.5 miles of shoreline, 3 miles of wooded hiking trails, and an abundance of deer, almost-tame rabbits, and other critters.

Many types of programs are offered, particularly in the summer, when the facilities are almost always busy. The camp is open to all, so you don't need to be a member of the Theosophical Society. Campers stay in simple rustic cabins (bring your own bedding or rent it) with wood-burning stoves and separate bathhouses. Vegetarian meals are served in the dining hall, and all participants join in the cleanup. Indralaya also has a substantial metaphysical library and a small bookstore.

All sorts of classes and workshops take place here: silent meditations, deep singing, family gatherings, therapeutic touch classes, yoga, and much more. Program fees are amazingly inexpensive: lodging in simple cabins with a shared bathhouse is just $47 per person per night, $68–70 per person per night in cabins with baths, or $35 per night if you stay in a tent, with discounts for anyone under 25. Incredibly, these rates include three meals a day. Indralaya also welcomes volunteers willing to trade work for camping and meals. Day visitors can attend programs and activities at Indralaya for a small charge.

# Accommodations

Anyone planning to stay on Orcas in the summer—particularly on weekends—should make reservations several months ahead of time. Note that all lodging prices quoted below are subject to an additional 9.8 percent tax.

The Orcas Island Chamber of Commerce website (www.orcasislandchamber.com) provides an online listing of available lodging; just enter your dates to see what's available. The **Orcas Island Lodging Association** (www.orcas-lodging.com) has links to a dozen local places and a calendar listing availability at the various bed-and-breakfasts, cottages, and inns.

## WEEKLY RENTALS

If you plan to spend more than a few nights on Orcas, the best deal is often a vacation rental, especially for families needing space to spread out or folks looking to save money by cooking their own meals. **Cherie Lindholm Real Estate** (360/376-2204, www.orcashomes.com) offers 40 or more rental homes on Orcas Island. Most are two- or three-bedroom homes costing $1,200–1,500 per week, but a number of modest places can be found for under $900 per week. The most elaborate waterfront mansions cost $2,400 or more weekly. Many homes go early, so book several months ahead if possible. Off-season (Sept.–May) rates are typically lower.

**Windermere Vacation Doorways** (360/378-3601 or 800/391-8190, www.vacationdoorways.com) typically has 35 or more homes on Orcas, plus additional rentals on San Juan and Lopez Islands. There's a one-week minimum mid-June–mid-September, and three nights at other times. Many of the resorts, inns, cottages, and bed-and-breakfasts described in this section also offer weekly rates; call for specifics.

For additional weekly rentals on Orcas, browse over to **VRBO** (www.vrbo.com), **CyberRentals** (www.cyberrentals.com), or **Homeaway** (www.homeaway.com). More adventurous souls may want to check out websites such as **Airbnb** (www.airbnb.com), **CouchSurfing** (www.couchsurfing.org), or **GlobalFreeloaders** (www.globalfreeloaders.com).

## HOSTELS

Find affordable lodging just a 20-minute walk from Eastsound at **Bracken Fern Lodge** (32 Bracken Fern Lane, 360/376-4090, www.brackenfernlodge.com). Owner Dave Page provides a friendly, clean, and comfortable home with a shared kitchen and bathrooms, plus a covered deck and backyard hammock. The shared dorm room ($25/person) has four bunk beds; one private room ($60) has two single beds; the other private room ($70) has a queen bed. Tent camping is $40, with full access to the house. Families are welcome, and the hostel is open year-round.

For a truly unique hostel, head to laid-back **Doe Bay Resort & Retreat** (107 Doe Bay Rd., 360/376-2291, www.doebay.com) on the east end of the island, 20 miles from the ferry dock. A six-bed coed hostel costs $55 per person in a large room, or $90 d for a private room.

## HOTELS AND INNS
### Coho Lodge

Off the beaten path amid a small luxury home development northeast of Eastsound, Coho Lodge (178 Fossil Bay Dr., 360/376-2242, www.coholodgeorcas.com, $105–145 d) is a weather-beaten beachfront hotel with four guest rooms containing small fridges and microwaves. Kids are welcome. Amenities include tennis courts, a boat launch, and private moorage for guests. Cormorants often sit on the pier out front.

### Inn at Ship Bay

Just 1.5 miles out of Eastsound, Inn at Ship Bay (326 Olga Rd., 360/376-3933 or 877/276-7296, www.innatshipbay.com) houses one of the finest and most popular restaurants on Orcas. Behind the restaurant and facing the waters of Eastsound are modern units containing 10 comfortable staterooms ($195 d) and an executive suite ($295 d), all with king-size beds, covered balconies, gas fireplaces, and fridges. Rates include a continental breakfast, and one room is disabled-accessible. The busy restaurant brings considerable traffic most evenings, but mornings are quiet. Kids are welcome, but only three guests (including children) are permitted per room.

## Landmark Inn

Landmark Inn (67 Main St. in Eastsound, 360/376-2423 or 800/622-4758, www.landmarkinn.net) has 15 recently constructed, well-maintained condo units, all with private decks, fireplaces, kitchens, and Wi-Fi. Rates are $194–249 d for two-bedroom units that can sleep four, and $229–254 d in three-bedroom condos that can sleep six; add $20 per person for additional guests. Kids are welcome, pets are $25 extra, and a two-night stay is required in the summer.

## Orcas Hotel

For classic lodging and friendly owners, stay at Orcas Hotel (360/376-4300 or 888/672-2792; www.orcashotel.com), a 12-room Victorian inn overlooking the ferry landing in Orcas. Rates are just $125–185 d for small, nicely furnished old-style rooms with private baths. The two finest rooms ($218 d) have decks and jetted tubs, and two tiny rooms with a bath down the hall are just $89–92 d. Room 9 on the third floor is reputed to be haunted by the ghost of Octavia Van Moorhem, who operated the hotel from its opening in 1904 until her death in 1933. The staff and visitors relate many tales of strange noises and ghostly appearances near this room. For ease of access, Orcas Hotel's location can't be beat; just step off the ferry and you're there. The hotel is also an extremely popular place for weddings, family reunions, and office parties, though it isn't a quiet place due to the constant ferry traffic. Free Wi-Fi.

## Orcas Suites at Rosario

Next to Rosario Resort, Orcas Suites (1600 Rosario Rd., 360/376-6262 or 866/986-6262, www.orcassuites.com) has a variety of units, all of which face the harbor. Guest rooms are $149 d, and king studios with fireplaces and jetted tubs are $199 d. One bedroom suites ($279 d) and two-bedroom suites ($349 d) feature

© DON PITCHER

Orcas Hotel

balconies, fireplaces, jetted tubs, and kitchens, plus a seasonal outdoor pool. Add $20 for each additional guest. Two-night minimum stay.

## Outlook Inn

Outlook Inn (360/376-2200 or 888/688-5665, www.outlookinn.com) is a superbly restored 1888 hotel right in Eastsound with its own private beach. The historic main building features comfortable upstairs rooms with sinks and phones in the rooms (no TVs) and baths down the hall. They aren't spacious but offer old-time hospitality for a budget price: $94 d. Larger rooms with private baths and TVs are $199 d, and the newest building contains 16 exceptional suites with king-size beds, jetted tubs, radiant floor heat, kitchenettes, small balconies overlooking the bay, and mini-bars for $329 d. Kids are welcome, and two rooms are wheelchair-accessible. New Leaf Café is on the premises, serving Northwest-style gourmet fare.

## RESORTS
### Beach Haven Resort

One of the hidden treasures in the San Juans, Beach Haven Resort (684 Beach Haven Rd., 360/376-2288, www.beach-haven.com) has a peaceful setting, old-time cabins, and reasonable prices. Located on the northwest side of Orcas Island three miles from Eastsound, the resort consists of 11 log cabins—all built in the 1940s—along with a couple of newer units. Cabins front a long pebble beach (dramatic sunsets are a high point) and nestle beneath an old-growth forest of cedar and Douglas fir. Seals and Canada geese are common sights. Don't expect TVs, radios, phones, cell phone service, Wi-Fi, or the latest furnishings; the one- to four-bedroom cabins have rustic decor, full kitchens with dishes, woodstoves with firewood, private baths with showers, and decks with picnic tables and barbecues. There's a one-week minimum stay mid-June–early September, with a three-night minimum the remainder of September and winter holidays, and a two-night minimum in winter.

One-bedroom cabins are $1,015 per week for two guests, two-bedroom cabins cost $1,225 per week for up to five guests, and three-bedroom cabins are $1,435 per week for eight. The resort's largest cabin holds up to 10 people in

Outlook Inn

© DON PITCHER

four bedrooms for $2,100 per week and has tall picture windows, a fireplace, and a large deck facing the bay. Also available is a modern honeymoon cottage ($1,050 d/week) with a jetted tub and heated tile floor, along with two apartments with waterfront decks. The smaller one sleeps two for $875 d per week, while the larger unit has space for six at $1,295 per week. Children are welcome in most of Beach Haven Resort's cabins, and they will love the delightful playground, Ping-Pong table, and beach. Guests can also rent canoes, rowboats, and sit-on-top kayaks, or hike the 1.5-mile wooded nature trail.

Don't tell anyone else about this place and maybe it'll stay a secret just between us. Sorry, but that was wishful thinking, since Beach Haven has been discovered for decades. Anyone looking for a cabin July–mid-September should look elsewhere; families return each year and the resort doesn't even take reservations for July and August; they quit when the waiting list hits 10 pages! Space is, however, available at other times of the year, especially in the winter when prices are lower and fellow travelers are scarce.

### ◖ Doe Bay Resort & Retreat

Located on a 30-acre spread along a peaceful cove, Doe Bay Resort & Retreat (107 Doe Bay Rd., 360/376-2291, www.doebay.com) is 20 miles from the ferry terminal. Don't let the "Resort" in the name fool you; this is an unpretentious place with cabins (many of which are prefab units), yurts, a hostel, and tent sites. The emphasis is on relaxation. Doe Bay attracts the Gen-X/30-something/greenie/vegetarian/Subaru-driving/espresso-swigging/NPR crowd. It's the sort of place you'd expect to see featured in *Yoga Journal,* but it's also a fun spot for families and couples. You can sit inside the wood-fired sauna, and then head to one of three covered soaking tubs right on a pretty creek with a waterfall that drops into Doe Bay. The clothing-optional sauna and tubs are open daily 8 A.M.–10 P.M. (11 A.M.–6 P.M. for families; adults only after 6 P.M.) and cost $15 if you aren't a guest.

hot tubs at Doe Bay Resort & Retreat

© DON PITCHER

The six-bed coed **hostel** charges $55 per person in a large room, or $90 d for a private room. Also at the budget end are summer-only tent spaces ($55 d), minuscule units ($90 d) with simple furnishings, and in-the-trees yurts and domes ($120 d; unheated and no water so not recommended in winter). These share a central shower house and communal kitchen. Somewhat nicer are 20 or so cabins ($125–275) with full baths and kitchens, and the two-story retreat house for groups ($650 for up to 18 guests). A two-night minimum stay is required at Doe Bay, and one unit is wheelchair-accessible. Add $20 per person for more than two guests in the cabins and yurts.

Resort headquarters is the historic Doe Bay General Store, built in 1908 and now home to a little store, a game room/library, and the Doe Bay Café, serving mostly vegetarian fare three meals a day year-round. Watch feature-length films in the café on Monday nights, or join one of the yoga sessions ($10) each summer morning. Guided sea-kayaking trips and massage are also available (but no bike rentals). Free Wi-Fi is available throughout the resort, along with a variety of outdoor activities: horseshoes, croquet, bocce, and volleyball.

## Lieber Haven Resort & Marina

A small, out-of-the-way place, Lieber Haven Resort & Marina (360/376-2472, www.lieberhavenresort.com) occupies a quiet and protected cove on the southern edge of Orcas Island near Obstruction Pass. A county boat ramp and dock are right across the road, and one of the only sandy beaches on the island is out front—it stretches for nearly a mile. Lodging is in a dozen simple studio units and one- and two-bedroom cottages that are popular for families on a budget. This old-school resort (no massage or facials here!) opened in the 1950s and retains a down-home feel that isn't for everyone. Friendly owners Dave and Kittie Baxter provide nightly beach fires in the summer along with a variety of lodging options. Most units have a small kitchen (with dishes, pots, and pans), queen-size bed, and sofa bed, along with a deck just a few steps from the water. Simple sleeping rooms cost $135 d, studio units are $145 d, apartments run $155 d, and one- and two-bedroom cottages cost $165–175. No minimum stay, and the owners welcome sailors and kayakers. A little store sells snacks, and you can check out the collection of nautical antiques, rent kayaks and rowboats at the marina, or go along on whale-watching and sailing trips. Free Wi-Fi is available, and the resort is open year-round.

## North Beach Inn

A mile west of Eastsound, North Beach Inn (650 Gibson Rd., 360/376-2660, www.northbeachinn.com) is something of a misnomer, since this is actually a quaint family resort where 13 housekeeping cottages face a very private beach. Most date from the 1930s and 1940s, and each unit contains a full kitchen, fireplace, Adirondack chairs, and barbecue. The furnishings are showing their age. Kids are welcome and so are dogs ($70/week).

Older studio cabins are $960 d per week, and two-bedroom cottages cost $1,320 per week for four people. The resort has three more recently built, larger cottages—one even has a loft—that go for $1,800 per week for four guests; add $130 per person per week for additional guests. Reserve far ahead for any of these popular cottages where many people return year after year; try to book in September for the following summer. A one-week minimum stay is required in July and August, but you might find a few shorter openings at the last minute. The resort is closed late November–mid-February.

## Rosario Resort & Spa

Built between 1905 and 1909 and now on the National Register of Historic Places, famous Rosario Resort (1400 Rosario Rd., 360/376-2222 or 800/562-8820, www.rosarioresort.com) is five miles south of Eastsound near Moran State Park. The striking mansion at the center of Rosario was once the home of Robert Moran, a shipping magnate, Seattle mayor, and philanthropist; he donated the land for nearby Moran State Park.

This is the largest lodging place on Orcas, with 55 guest rooms. Moran's grand white mansion serves as a centerpiece for the resort and is a great place to explore even if you aren't staying here. Free organ concerts and tours are given most days at 4 P.M. mid-June–mid-September in the grand music room, or you can take a self-guided tour at other times. The lush grounds and sprawling veranda, backdropped by boat-filled Cascade Bay, are popular for summer weddings. The mansion also houses a restaurant, along with a fascinating collection of historical items and photos. Downstairs is a full-service spa with massage, body wraps, facials, manicures, and pedicures, plus an indoor pool, hot tub, sauna, exercise equipment, and daily yoga and fitness classes.

On the 30 acres of lovingly manicured grounds and flower gardens, you'll find a large outdoor pool facing the harbor and a separate pool for kids, plus tennis courts, horseshoes, croquet, shuffleboard, bocce, and other lawn games. Head to the marina for sea kayaking (through Shearwater Adventures), sailboat

© DON PITCHER

**hotel room at Rosario Resort & Spa**

charters, and whale-watching trips (through Deer Harbor Charters). A concierge and gift shop are available. Scheduled floatplane flights directly to Rosario are provided by Kenmore Air out of Seattle's Lake Union.

Rosario rooms vary greatly in size and amenities, but following years of deterioration and bad management, new owners have made enormous strides in returning the resort to its glory days. Visitors consistently give the resort high marks. The least expensive rooms cost $129 d, while spacious suites start at $229 d. Two of the finest options ($299 d) are the luxurious Cliffhouse honeymoon suite and the unique Roundhouse Suite built as a playground for Thomas Moran's children. The latter has a king sleigh bed, waterside location, and separate living room. All guests have free access to the pools, spa, and other facilities.

## Smuggler's Villa Resort

Located on the north side of Orcas Island along Haro Strait, Smuggler's Villa Resort (360/376-2297 or 800/488-2097, www.smuggler.com,

$279–325/night) consists of two-bedroom townhouses and apartments with full kitchens and gas fireplaces. Some units can sleep six for no additional charge. Amenities at Smuggler's Villa include a year-round outdoor pool, two hot tubs, a sauna, tennis and basketball courts, playground, moorage, and a private pebble beach. Kids are welcome at this pleasant waterfront resort. A four-night minimum is required in the summer.

## West Beach Resort

A busy waterside spot, West Beach Resort (three miles west of Eastsound off Enchanted Forest Rd., 360/376-2240 or 877/937-8224, www.westbeachresort.com) opened in 1939 and remains popular with families today. Cabins face west along a gravelly beach, offering sunset vistas in a peaceful setting. Several types of cottages are available, and guests appreciate the central hot tub, general store, and free Wi-Fi.

Most of the 21 cottages are right along the shore—we're talking 20 feet to the water—and

© DON PITCHER

cabins at West Beach Resort

have one or two bedrooms with double beds, full kitchens, woodstoves, private baths with showers, hide-a-bed sofas, and covered porches with barbecue grills. Many of these are plain older units with a mismatched and funky decor that isn't for everyone, but several modern ones are nicer and have large decks. Cabins are normally available only on a weekly basis in the summer, with a two-night minimum in spring and fall, plus on weekends year-round. Call ahead, however, since one-night stays are occasionally available.

The cottages rent for $1,225–1,785 per week for up to four guests, plus $126 per week for each additional guest. Two modern cabins (numbers 18 and 19; $1,785–1,890) and a remodeled 1930s farmhouse ($2,205) are ideal for groups and family gatherings of six or more people. An adorable little honeymoon cottage (number 17; $1,680 d) faces a small pond, and the Madrona cabin ($1,785 d) is perfect for those looking for privacy. In addition, West Beach Resort has tent and RV spaces, and a small store selling limited supplies, espresso,

and gas. The marina rents skiffs, kayaks, and canoes, and kayak tours are available.

None of the West Beach cottages include phones and most lack TVs, though you can rent TV/VCRs to watch videos. The resort caters to families and offers an array of kid activities daily in the summer, along with evening bonfires. Cribs are also available, and pets are allowed in some of the cottages for an extra $126 per week. West Beach Resort is open year-round.

## GUESTHOUSES AND COTTAGES

A number of bed-and-breakfasts also have guest cottages available, including Deer Harbor Inn and Old Trout Inn B&B.

### Abigail's on the Water

Located on the north shore of Orcas near Eastsound, Abigail's (360/376-7035, www.sleepingsea.com, closed Jan.–Feb., $165–225 d) has four suites, each with a queen bed, private bath, flat-screen TV, and Wi-Fi. A boardwalk extends over wetlands in front of the house to a lovely private beach. There's a two-night minimum stay. Owner Shana Lloyd also runs Once in a Blue Moon Farm.

## All Dream Cottages

Consisting of five units scattered around the west side of Orcas Island, All Dream Cottages (360/376-2500, www.alldreamcottages.com) are shoreside retreats from the stresses of life. Least expensive is the Tree House Suite ($217 d), with a small deck facing President Channel. Smallest is the romantic Isle Dream Cottage ($257 d), where a deck encompasses the cottage on three sides, and guests can follow the path to a private beach with a hammock and dock. Day Dream Farm Cottage ($217 d, $257 for five) has two bedrooms, an open floor plan, a queen-size bed along the bay window, and a small kitchen area. Sea Dream Cottage ($277 d) is a beachfront one-bedroom place with a magical location on the west side of Orcas. Watch the sunset over an array of islands spreading across the horizon. Mariner's Dream Cottage ($297 for four) has a dramatic waterside setting near the ferry terminal, large deck, hot tub, woodstove, and full kitchen. A two-night minimum stay is required, or three nights in summer. Children are welcome at three of the cottages. Both Sea Dream and Isle Dream have been featured in national magazines.

## Bayside Cottages

Bayside Cottages (65 Willis Lane, 360/376-4330, www.orcas1.com) consists of nine vacation cottages and houses on 14 waterfront acres near the village of Olga. All include full kitchens and baths, with access to a private beach and fine views east to Mount Baker. The cottages range from a nicely appointed loft in the upper level of a converted barn ($185 d) to a recently built 2,000-square-foot three-bedroom home that sleeps six for $375. Also available is a small cottage ($185 for up to five) in the heart of Eastsound that's fine for families. The least expensive option is a nicely restored 1950s-era four-unit motel in

Eastsound ($125 d). Weekly rates are available, and kids are welcome. A two-night minimum is required in the summer.

## Blackberry Beach Cabins

Located in tranquil Olga on the east side of the island, Blackberry Beach Cabins (360/376-2845, www.blackberrybeach.com) consists of two comfortable cabins, both with queen-size beds, private baths, and kitchens. The waterfront cabin ($150 d) has a picture window and an outdoor hot tub overlooking Buck Bay, and the modest garden cabin ($110 d) is a reasonably priced option. This is a place to kick back, so you won't find TVs or Wi-Fi. Four-night stays are generally required in the summer (two nights in the off-season). No credit cards.

## Boardwalk Waterfront Cottages

Right next to the busy Orcas ferry landing, Boardwalk Waterfront Cottages (360/376-2971 or 877/376-2971, www.orcasislandboardwalk.com) consists of two small cottages with fridges and microwaves ($180 d), and two others that have separate bedrooms and full kitchens ($250–290 d). Kids are welcome in one of the units, and Wi-Fi is available.

## Buckhorn Farm Bungalow

If you're looking for a place that exemplifies island living, be sure to check out Buckhorn Farm Bungalow (17 Jensen Rd., 360/376-2298, www.buckhornfarm.com, $150 d, $10/person for additional guests), a cute one-bedroom cottage on the north side of Orcas near Eastsound. Step inside to find a full kitchen, woodstove, and private bath. Step outside to take in the peaceful orchard setting. There's a two-night minimum in the summer, and kids are welcome, but book early for this popular spot.

## ◖ The Cabin on Spring Bay

A secluded waterside retreat adjacent to Obstruction Pass State Park, The Cabin on Spring Bay (360/376-5531, www.springbay-inn.com, maximum three guests for $240/night) provides comfortable accommodations in a gorgeous setting. The cabin is surrounded by 57 acres of private woods, with five miles of hiking trails and a covered deck a stone's throw from Spring Bay. There's even an active eagle nest nearby. The cabin has queen and twin beds, a kitchenette, barbecue grill, DVD player, and bath, along with a waterside hot tub and kayaks. Former park rangers Carl Burger and Sandy Playa live just up the hill, bringing a strong knowledge of the outdoors to this slice of heaven. They lead daily **two-hour sea-kayak paddles**—all equipment provided—for no extra charge. (Non-guests pay $35/person.) During the off-season (Oct.–Apr.), your second night is free at the cabin. Reserve well ahead for summertime stays.

### ❢ Cabins-on-the-Point

Cabins-on-the-Point (360/376-4114, www.cabinsonthepoint.com) consists of Cape Cod–style cabins facing Massacre Bay and West Sound from a rocky point of land. It's a wonderful spot for weddings or yoga retreats. Three cabins are available, each with a woodstove (wood provided) and full kitchen. The Heather Cabin ($285 for up to three) is a premier choice, with windows just a few feet from the water (no TV here). Nearby, the Primrose Cabin ($250 d) features skylights, French doors into the sitting room, and a little garden. Willow ($285 for up to five) is a two-bedroom cottage with a sun porch that fronts the bay. Guests at Heather and Primrose have access to the outdoor hot tub and Wi-Fi, and all cabin guests can use a private beach where kayaks are available at no additional charge. The trailhead for Turtleback Mountain Preserve is just a short walk from the cabins, and deer are frequent visitors.

Owner Jennifer Johnson is a good source for information and recommendations—she'll even set up restaurant reservations. Also offered are three family-friendly lodging options around Orcas. **Highlands House** is a large two-bedroom, two-bath hilltop home that includes a great room with cathedral ceiling and fireplace, an open kitchen, and a deck affording stunning vistas across East Sound from the hot tub. The house is near Moran State Park

and costs $325 d for up to six guests. One of the most private places on the island, the house works well for two couples. **Sunset House** is a large waterside home close to Eastsound with three bedrooms and two baths, a big deck, floor-to-ceiling windows, and a full kitchen—all in a woodsy setting. It sleeps up to six comfortably for $420. **Westsound House** ($325 for up to four guests) is a 1940s-era home just 100 feet from the water. Amenities include a king bed, full kitchen, beach access, kayaks, French doors, Ping-Pong table, spacious lawns, and Wi-Fi.

These cabins and houses get repeat customers, so make reservations before March for a peak-season rental. Many guests book for a one-week stay, and a five-night summertime minimum is required at Willow, Highlands House, Westsound House, and Sunset House, with a three-night minimum at the others. Off-season, there's a two-night minimum. Kids are welcome in the houses and cottages, and pets are also allowed in some units with prior arrangement.

### Camp Moran Vacation House

Beneath tall trees on the south end of Cascade Lake within Moran State Park, Camp Moran Vacation House (360/360-4240 or 800/360-4240, www.parks.wa.gov/vacationhouses) sleeps up to eight guests for an amazingly reasonable $123. Inside this wheelchair-accessible structure are two bedrooms with a mix of full-size and bunk beds (bring your own linens and towels), a bathroom, a full kitchen with utensils, and a spacious living room with TV/VCR. Guests have access to a dock on the lake (not open to general park users). This is a fine base from which to explore the park, and can be reserved up to one year in advance. Two-night minimum stay is required.

### Eastsound Suites

Find luxurious rooms in the heart of town at Eastsound Suites (269 Main St., 360/376-2887, www.eastsoundsuites.com), with spacious one-bedroom units ($295 d) that can be combined into a two-bedroom suite ($365 d). Each has a gas fireplace, jetted tub, full kitchen, washer/dryer, Wi-Fi, and small deck facing the water. There is a two-night minimum stay, and kids are welcome. The suites are upstairs above Moon Glow Arts & Crafts.

### Evergreen Cottage at Rosario

A recently built A-frame home with an open floor plan and high windows, Evergreen Cottage at Rosario (415/806-9455 or 877/328-2303, www.evergreenatrosario.com, $250 for up to six) sits beneath tall trees just a short drive from Moran State Park. Inside are two bedrooms, a full kitchen, living room, loft, two baths, and Wi-Fi, while the wraparound deck has a hot tub. Two-night minimum stay is required.

### Heartwood House

A beautiful handcrafted post-and-beam home, Heartwood House (360/317-8220, www.heartwoodhouse.com) is just a short walk from Eastsound. Inside are three bedrooms and two baths, a full kitchen, two woodstoves, and a large deck with a hot tub. It can sleep eight and rents for $2,950 per week, with nightly rates in the off-season. This distinctive home is popular for weddings and family reunions.

### Laughing Moon Farm

On the shore of East Sound, and within walking distance of the golf course, Laughing Moon Farm (451 Osprey Lane, 360/376-7879, www.laughingmoonfarm.com) is a woodsy retreat with two recently constructed cottages. Each unit contains a full kitchen and bath, and the largest includes two bedrooms and a loft—plenty of space for a family gathering. The two smaller cottages sleep four and are available at $225 per night with a two-night minimum, or $1,200 per week. The largest unit is $285 per night with a four-night minimum, or $1,400 per week for up to six; nightly rates may be available with a three-night minimum. Guests always enjoy meeting the sheep and llama, and watching the nesting eagles.

### Maggie's Manor and Gnome House

Maggie's Manor (Deer Harbor, 360/376-4223, www.orcas-island-rentals.com) is a pretty waterfront home on a 110-acre estate. The front porch and outdoor hot tub provide picture-postcard vistas, while inside are four bedrooms and baths, a large kitchen, and a living room with a concert grand piano. The house rents for $2,250 per week and sleeps up to eight. Nightly stays are also available, starting at $375 d, with a two-night summer minimum.

Also on the estate is a unique little place called the Gnome House, a handcrafted cottage that looks like it belongs in a fairy tale. It's a delightful honeymoon spot. You'll find a spiral staircase, sleigh bed, sunken tub bath, full kitchen, and a bay window facing the surrounding flower gardens. Outside is a private hot tub. The Gnome House rents for $225 d ($275 for four people) or $1,230 per week. A two-night summertime minimum is required.

### Meadowlark Guest House

An antiques-filled home, Meadowlark Guest House (440 Point Lawrence Rd. in Olga, 360/376-3224, www.meadowlarkguesthouse.com, $169 for up to four) provides a quiet country setting facing Buck Bay. The bedroom has a queen-size bed, with a pullout sofa in the living room, private bath, full kitchen, washer/dryer, Wi-Fi, and a deck where you can watch the ferries pass. Children and dogs are welcome, and there's a two-night summer minimum. The owner also has a small garden-level apartment-style unit for just $85 d.

### Once in a Blue Moon Farm

On the south end of Orcas, a couple of miles from the ferry dock, Once in a Blue Moon Farm (412 Eastman Rd., 360/376-7035, www.onceinabluemoonfarm.com) is a peaceful 35-acre farm featuring guest rooms with private baths and Wi-Fi. The farm is popular with agri-tourists and families who appreciate the menagerie of horses, goats, alpacas, and chickens—not to mention the wild deer

ORCAS ISLAND

and rabbits—plus an orchard with heirloom varieties of fruit (apple, plum, quince, cherry, kiwi, peach, and pear) and an organic garden that produces all sorts of berries, herbs, and flowers. Kids love the chance to pet animals and feed the chickens, and a brief farm tour is provided to arriving guests. Lodging rates are $165 d weekends or $150 d weekdays, or $225 d weekends or $195 weekdays for units with full kitchens. Pets are allowed for a fee. Once in a Blue Moon added "glamping" spaces in 2012 for those who want to rough it in style. These luxury camping cabins ($125 d) are in the woods, but have electricity and Wi-Fi. The owners also operate Abigail's Beach House, which rents by the week.

## Orcas Cottages

Right in Olga Village, Orcas Cottages (360/779-1296, www.orcascottages.com) are two charming places with panoramic water views. Most impressive is the Island Cottage, which is actually a comfortable home built in 1884. It includes three bedrooms, a full kitchen, and views of Rosario Strait and costs $200 nightly for up to six people. Smaller but still delightful is a second cottage that runs $115 d. A two-night minimum stay is required.

## Swannie's Inn

On the north end of the island near Eastsound, Swannie's (24 Shady Lane, 360/376-5686, www.swanniesinn.com, $95 d) is a one-bedroom suite in a century-old home with a private entrance, fridge, microwave, bath, and patio. Kids are accepted, but a two-night minimum is required.

# BED-AND-BREAKFASTS

Orcas has quite a few luxurious bed-and-breakfasts for discriminating travelers looking for a sanctuary from the hustle and bustle. Be sure to book several months ahead for summertime rooms.

## Anchorage Inn

Anchorage Inn (249 Bronson Way, east of the Orcas golf course, 360/376-8282, www.anchorageonorcas.com, closed Oct.–Apr., $195 d) is well out of the way, hidden among tall Douglas firs along East Sound at the end of a dirt road. Three modern townhouse-style units are available on a 16-acre parcel with a pebbly beach out front—perfect for launching kayaks—and a bluff-top hot tub to enjoy those romantic starry nights. Bald eagles nest close by, and you may also see herons, seals, deer, ospreys, otters, loons, and other critters. Each unit has a private stairway and entrance, queen-size bed, bath, fireplace, kitchenette, small cedar deck, and Wi-Fi. The fridge is stocked with fixins for a make-it-yourself breakfast, and a decanter of port awaits. No children are allowed, and a two-night minimum stay is required in the summer. Check in with owners Dick and Sandra Bronson, who live in the house next door.

## Blue Heron B&B

Built in 1910 and surrounded by madrone trees along West Sound, Blue Heron B&B (982 Deer Harbor Rd., 360/376-4198, www.orcasblueheron.com, $130–180 d) features four upstairs guest rooms, all with private baths, decks, a full hot breakfast, and Wi-Fi. This is one of the few B&Bs where both kids and pets are welcome ($15 extra for kids or pets); owners Bogdan and Carol Kulminski have a friendly dog and cat. A private beach is directly across the road.

## Deer Harbor Inn

A variety of lodging options exist at Deer Harbor Inn (360/376-4110 or 877/377-4110, www.deerharborinn.com), located eight miles west of the ferry dock and just above Deer Harbor. The inn buildings surround an old apple orchard (Gravenstein and King varieties) and pear and plum trees that were planted in 1906. A contemporary log lodge contains eight comfy but rather small rooms ($149 d) with tables, chairs, queen beds, and other furnishings crafted from lodgepole logs. Each also has a fridge and private bath. No TVs in the rooms, but a central sitting area has sofas, a woodstove, and a television.

Four attractive, modern cottages costing $239–350 d ($20 for additional guests) are also on the grounds. Each is a bit different: The largest (1,100 square feet, with room for eight people) has two bedrooms, a full kitchen, and covered deck, while the other three units are smaller but have gas fireplaces, fridges, microwaves, TVs, log furnishings, and decks with private Jacuzzis. Pets are $25 extra in the cottages. Across the road is a small remodeled house ($385 for up to eight guests) with a king-size bed in one of the three bedrooms, plus a log fireplace, full kitchen, hot tub, and barbecue grill on the wraparound deck, and even a telescope for spying on boats in the harbor.

All guests at Deer Harbor Inn (including those staying in the lodge) can hop in the hot tub behind the lodge, but it can get a bit busy. Massage is also available, and all rooms have free Wi-Fi. A two-night minimum stay is required in the summer, and no young kids are allowed in the lodge, though they're welcome in the cottages and house. Deer Harbor Inn is also home to a fine restaurant, run by the owners' sons and housed in a farmhouse built in 1915.

## Double Mountain B&B

Enjoy a panoramic view of the San Juans from the deck of Double Mountain B&B (Double Hill Rd., 360/376-4570, www.doublemountainbandb.com), a contemporary home atop a 500-foot hill, two miles out of Eastsound. Inside are two guest rooms ($95–135 d) and a two-room suite ($160 d or $230 for four) with its own kitchen and entrance. All rooms have private baths, and a full country breakfast is served. No kids under 10 are permitted, and a two-night minimum is required in July and August.

## ◖ The Inn on Orcas Island

Nestled along a marsh at the head of Deer Harbor, The Inn on Orcas Island (114 Channel Rd., 360/376-5227 or 888/886-1661, www.theinnonorcasisland.com) is one of the newest and most unusual lodgings on Orcas. Former owners of a Santa Barbara art gallery, John

ORCAS ISLAND

© DON PITCHER

The Inn on Orcas Island

Gibbs and Jeremy Trumble have filled the walls of their graceful home with a remarkable collection of 19th- and 20th-century English paintings. Catering to couples in search of a romantic escape (no kids allowed), it's an art gallery masquerading as a luxury inn. Most rooms have gas fireplaces, and all include jetted tubs, indulgent beds, Wi-Fi, and balconies overlooking a pristine landscape. Borrow a bike to pedal around Deer Harbor, or take the canoe out on the lagoon to watch birds. Guest are treated to a multi-course gourmet breakfast. Rooms start at $215 d for a queen-size bed with water view, up to $265 d for a king suite. Two cottages ($285 d and $325 d) provide more private luxury; one has a full kitchen. A two-night minimum stay is required in the summer and on holiday weekends.

## Kangaroo House B&B

Kangaroo House (just north of Eastsound, 360/376-2175 or 888/371-2175, www.kangaroohouse.com, $165–195 d) was built in 1907 and bought in the 1930s by a sea captain, Harold Ferris, who picked up a young female kangaroo on one of his Australian voyages. The kangaroo is long gone, but the name remains on this attractive old home with a big fireplace, antique furnishings, decks, Wi-Fi, and a garden hot tub. The five guest rooms and suites all have king- or queen-size beds and private baths. There's a memorable multi-course organic breakfast each morning, and bird-watchers will appreciate the many species that come to the backyard feeders. Kids are generally accepted, but call ahead for specifics. Owners Charles Toxey and Jill Johnson also manage **Artsmith** (www.orcasartsmith.org), a nonprofit literary organization with occasional writers' retreats and public readings at the B&B.

## Kingfish Inn B&B

Built around 1915, Kingfish Inn (Deer Harbor and Crow Valley Rds., 360/376-2500, www.kingfishinn.com, $197 d) sits directly across the road from West Sound. The four small but nicely remodeled guest rooms exhibit a Victorian charm. Each has a private bath, TV, and VCR, and two contain king-size beds. The building also houses justifiably popular West Sound Café, where a continental breakfast is served each morning. Kids are accepted.

## Old Trout Inn B&B

For a bit of France on Orcas, stay at Old Trout Inn (5272 Orcas Rd., 360/376-7474, www.oldtroutinn.com), an elegant country home just three miles from the ferry dock. The pond out back attracts birds, and you can fish (catch-and-release only) for trout, carp, or bluegills. Inside the house are a large guest room ($125 d) with private bath and two suites ($185–220 d) with private baths and hot tubs, minifridges, and separate entrances; the larger suite features a fireplace and deck facing the pond. A separate cottage ($205 d) is next door, with a full kitchen, gas fireplace, private bath, covered porch, and hot tub along the pond. Extra guests are $25 each. Owners Henri and Nicole de Marval once ran a French restaurant and offer two-night stays with a three-course dinner for $290–480 d (depending upon the room). Because of the unfenced pond, young children aren't allowed.

## Otters Pond B&B

A modern country home near Moran State Park, Otters Pond B&B (360/376-8844 or 888/893-9680, www.otterspond.com, $125–235 d) sits alongside a 20-acre pond. Five elegantly furnished rooms have private baths, access to the shoji screen–enclosed hot tub, and Wi-Fi. The more expensive rooms are quite spacious, with king-size beds and skylights; the Swan Room ($235 d) has a gas fireplace, clawfoot tub, and pond view, while the Goldfinch Room ($235 d) features a gas fireplace and TV. The little Chickadee Room ($160 d) is equally popular, with a clawfoot tub and views of the pond. Tiny Blue Heron Room ($125 d; summer only) is fine for one person, but might be a bit claustrophobic for couples. Innkeepers Carl and Susan Silvernail are delightful hosts who create a five-course breakfast that's certain to please. Behind the home are a large deck,

## APPLE WALNUT GORGONZOLA OMELET

This makes 1 serving.

1 ounce gorgonzola or blue cheese
1 tablespoon sour cream
2 tablespoons toasted walnuts, coarsely chopped and bounced around in a sieve to remove skin
2 eggs
2 drops Tabasco sauce
2 teaspoons cold water
4 or 5 thin slices of apple, about ¼ of an apple
2 teaspoons butter
2 tablespoons cooked crumbled bacon (1 piece per serving)

Mix the cheese, sour cream, and walnuts together to make the filling and set aside. Beat eggs with Tabasco and water until blended. Heat an 8-inch omelet pan, melt butter, and pour egg mixture into pan when butter is sizzling. When eggs begin to firm up, place apple slices along one side and cook at medium heat. When eggs are no longer liquid, add filling. Fold omelet in half and top with crumbled bacon.

*Recipe courtesy of Otters Pond B&B*

dahlia garden, and several bird feeders that attract a flittering crowd most mornings. The pond is home to nesting mallards and wood ducks in the summer, and migrating flocks at other times. This is a place to escape, so young children are not allowed.

### Pebble Cove Farm

Overlooking a grassy lawn along Massacre Bay, Pebble Cove Farm (3341 Deer Harbor Rd., 360/376-6161, www.pebblecovefarm.com) has two suites ($185 d) and a cottage ($250 d), each with private deck, bath, kitchenette, hardwood floors, barbecue grill, and Wi-Fi. The cottage sleeps four and includes a separate bedroom. An organic continental breakfast is provided

each morning, and children will love the goats, chickens, and pony, not to mention the zip line, trampoline, and rowboat. Bring a kayak to paddle out from the private beach. A two-night minimum is required on weekends.

### ◖ The Place at Cayou Cove

Find inviting accommodations and a peaceful waterside setting at The Place at Cayou Cove (161 Olympic Lodge Lane in Deer Harbor, 360/376-3199 or 888/596-7222, www.cayou-cove.com, closed Dec.–mid-Mar., $325–425 d). Guests stay in three luxurious private cottages, each with a full kitchen, wood-burning fireplace, flat-screen TVs, and Wi-Fi. Wine and hors d'oeuvres are served on summer evenings. Each cottage has a private hot tub where you can relax as the sun sets behind a harbor filled with bobbing boats, or you can saunter to the private beach. A two-night minimum stay is required, three nights on holidays. Children and dogs are welcome (additional charge).

### Sand Dollar Inn B&B

Sand Dollar Inn B&B (445 Point Lawrence Rd. near Olga, 360/376-5696, www.sdollar.com, $120 d) is a 1920s home with three large upstairs rooms, all with private baths and sweeping views of Buck Bay, Lopez Island, and the Olympic Mountains. Moran State Park is just up the road, making this a good base for hiking and biking. The house is furnished with Japanese antiques and woodblock prints, and a full breakfast is served, with Wi-Fi available. No kids under 14.

### ◖ Turtleback Farm Inn

Orcas Island's most famous bed-and-breakfast, Turtleback Farm Inn (1981 Crow Valley Rd., 360/376-4914 or 800/376-4914, www.turtle-backinn.com) began life as a simple 1910 farmhouse in the shadow of Turtleback Mountain. Innkeepers Susan and Bill Fletcher bought the run-down old farmhouse, restored and expanded the building, added hardwood floors, and then opened the doors to Orcas Island's first B&B. The inn is approximately six miles from the ferry landing near the center of Orcas,

**ORCAS ISLAND**

# WARM CHOCOLATE-ESPRESSO PUDDING CAKES

¾ cup butter or margarine
6 ounces bittersweet chocolate, chopped
2 teaspoons freeze-dried espresso powder, or 2 tablespoons hot espresso
4½ tablespoons unbleached white flour
2 tablespoons unsweetened cocoa
5 large eggs, separated
⅓ cup sugar
1½ tablespoons Kahlua
½ teaspoon vanilla

Preheat oven to 375°F.

In a small pan, combine butter and chocolate. Heat over low flame until melted and smoothly mixed. Add espresso and mix. Mix together flour and cocoa. In a large bowl, beat the 5 egg whites until they become white. Beat in sugar, 1 tablespoon at a time, until the eggs hold stiff and shiny, but not dry, peaks.

Blend together the yolks, liqueur, vanilla, and the cocoa and flour mixture, then add the chocolate and butter mixture. Gently fold in the egg whites.

Pour about ½ cup batter into each of 8 buttered ramekins or custard cups. For ease of handling, place the ramekins on a cookie sheet before placing in the oven to bake. Bake until the edges begin to firm but the center is still soft when pressed, 11-12 minutes. Let cool for a few minutes, then invert onto serving plates. Serve with coffee ice cream.

*Recipe courtesy of Turtleback Farm Inn*

minuscule room, barely big enough for the double bed and your shoes, is an inexpensive ($125 d) option and has a small private bath. The others are substantially larger, with queen-size beds and clawfoot tubs in the private baths for $165–195 d. Nicest is the Valley Room, with antique furnishings and a private deck overlooking the farm. The emphasis is on relaxation and getting away from it all, so no televisions or phone, but Wi-Fi is available. Kids over eight are welcome in the house. A substantial breakfast is served downstairs each morning, or on the deck when weather permits. End the day sipping sherry by the fireplace.

Adjacent to the historic farmhouse is the **Orchard House,** a cedar barnlike structure where the emphasis is on privacy. Each of the four plush guest rooms has a king-size bed, gas fireplace, private deck, sitting area, Wi-Fi, bath with clawfoot tub, and separate shower. Breakfast is delivered to your room, making this spot popular with couples who just want to be alone for a quiet morning. It's perfect for honeymooners, but families with children are also welcome. One of the rooms has been set up to accommodate travelers with disabilities; it's the most popular room. Orchard House rooms go for $260 d. All rooms at Turtleback Farm require a two-night minimum in the summer and on many weekends and holidays at other times.

## CAMPING

Orcas Island has the vast majority of public campsites on the San Juans, nearly all of which are in Moran State Park on the east end of the island.

Find **showers** in Moran State Park and the marinas at Deer Harbor, Rosario, and West Sound.

### ◖ Moran State Park

One of the most popular camping areas in Washington, Moran State Park (360/376-2326, www.parks.wa.gov) has 151 campsites scattered across three campgrounds along Cascade Lake, with a fourth along Mountain Lake, and a separate bike-in area. These represent some of the

and its two-level back deck overlooks a bucolic pasture, part of this 80-acre farm. Cows and sheep graze below, and a crowing rooster might wake you in the morning. Bird-watchers will enjoy exploring the farm's half-dozen ponds.

The farmhouse's seven guest rooms are furnished with a Victorian-inspired decor that deftly balances luxury and comfort. One finest camping opportunities in the San Juans, and they fill early during July and August. Tent sites cost $21–25 (maximum eight people/site), including hot showers. No RV hookups, though there is a dump station. The four standard campgrounds all accommodate trailer campers and RVs, but some campsites will not fit large motor homes. Camping is not allowed outside established park campgrounds.

**North End Campground** is across the road from the swimming beach area, and several of these sites are quite private. **Midway Campground** is near the Cascade Lake boat launch, and its most popular sites are right on the lakeshore (but also next to the sometimes noisy road). **South End Campground** is the park's most popular (and justly so), with almost all of the sites right along the shore. This premier area has a wheelchair-accessible campsite and restroom. **Mountain Lake Campground** is one mile up Mount Constitution Road on the shores of Mountain Lake, the park's largest lake. In addition, for those who arrive by bicycle or on foot, 15 primitive campsites ($12) are located in a small site on the road to Mount Constitution.

Due to Moran State Park's popularity, camping reservations are highly advised in July and August, when the sites are perpetually full seven days a week. (You may find a space without a reservation, but get there early if you want to risk it.) All sites are pre-assigned in the summer, so check in at the pay station across from Cascade Lake when you arrive. Campground reservations can be made as little as two days in advance, or as much as nine months ahead. Make reservations ($9 extra) at 888/226-7688 or the park website (which also includes a campsite availability map). Mid-September–mid-May, camping is on a first-come, first-served basis with no reservations. At least one of the campgrounds remains open year-round.

## Obstruction Pass State Park

This 80-acre park sits on the south end of Orcas Island, 2.5 miles southeast of Olga and 17 road miles from the ferry dock. A 1-mile

dirt road heads off Obstruction Pass Road and ends at a parking lot where a pleasant 0.5-mile hike takes you to four campsites (360/376-2326, www.parks.wa.gov, $14) with pit toilets. The location is very scenic, with sites facing nearby Obstruction and Blakely Islands, but there's no vehicle access, reservations, or potable water. Campsites fill fast, and it's illegal to camp elsewhere nearby, so get there early on summer weekends to be sure of a space following your hike. Avoid the crowds by coming in midweek or the off-season. A county boat ramp is available at Obstruction Pass, and it's just a short paddle to privately owned Obstruction Island.

## Point Doughty Marine State Park

Located on the northeast end of Orcas, this 60-acre park has four primitive water-accessible Cascadia Marine Trail campsites ($14). There's no drinking water, but vault toilets are provided. You'll need a kayak to camp here since there's no road or trail access. The point faces west to British Columbia's Gulf Islands, making for magnificent sunsets. Only the four acres at the very tip of Point Doughty are open to the public.

## Doe Bay Resort & Retreat

Funky Doe Bay Resort (107 Doe Bay Rd., 360/376-2291, www.doebay.com, open for camping May–Nov., $55 d) is a couple of miles east of Olga and 20 miles from the ferry terminal. It has tent sites (no RV hookups) with access to a guest kitchen and bathhouse. Drive-up sites are in a field, but walk-in tent spaces sit atop a wooded bluff overlooking Doe Bay. Campers can join other resort guests in the popular creekside hot tubs at no extra charge, take a kayak tour, or enjoy a fine vegetarian meal in the café. A two-night minimum stay is required at the campground. Free Wi-Fi.

## West Beach Resort

A cozy family place, West Beach Resort (three miles west of Eastsound off Enchanted Forest Rd., 360/376-2240 or 877/937-8224, www. westbeachresort.com) has both lodging and campsites in a setting that serves up great sunsets over President Channel. Tent spaces are $32–37 for up to three people, while RV sites with water and electricity cost $42–49 for up to three. Five recently built canvas tent cabins ($109 d; $12 for extra guests) are furnished with queen beds, futons, tables and chairs, plus small decks and picnic tables (but no water or electricity). A shower house is nearby, and pets are an extra $7. Kid activities are offered most days, and parents will appreciate the big hot tub ($5/person; free if you're staying in the tent cabins), along with free Wi-Fi.

The store sells firewood, groceries, ice cream on homemade waffle cones, and limited supplies, while the marina rents motorboats, rowboats, canoes, and kayaks and offers seakayaking tours. Guest moorage is available ($25) for campers. Reservations are highly advised for July and August and on holidays and busy weekends. If you show up without a reservation in the peak summer season, you may well be out of luck. Call two weeks ahead of your visit if you're bringing an RV, and a year ahead for the ocean-view sites near the beach! The tent cabins are open April–September, while the RV and tent spaces are available year-round.

### Once in a Blue Moon Farm
On the south end of Orcas, a couple of miles from the ferry dock, Once in a Blue Moon Farm (412 Eastman Rd., 360/376-7035, www.onceinabluemoonfarm.com) is a peaceful 35-acre farm. In addition to traditional lodging, the farm has added luxurious camping cabins (glamping) for $125 d. These are in the woods, but have electricity and Wi-Fi.

# Food

Eastsound, the "big city" on Orcas, has the best choice of food on the island, though you'll find a scattering of fine restaurants and cafés elsewhere.

One rather odd summertime phenomenon in Eastsound is the presence of pesky **yellow jackets.** These annoying wasps occasionally swarm around folks dining outside and do a bit of their own dining on your food, so be aware that your wonderful deck meal with a water view may be interrupted by an angry buzz and wasps chomping on your roast duck.

## EASTSOUND AREA
### Breakfast and Lunch
Eastsound's old firehouse has been thoroughly transformed into a bright and delightful deli-restaurant called ( **Roses Bakery Café** (382 Prune Alley, 360/376-5805, 8:20 A.M.–4 P.M. Mon.–Sat. for the café, bakery till 6 P.M., both closed Sun.). The café serves some of the best local espresso coffees and creative morning meals ($4–12), including baked eggs with gruyère, breakfast egg sandwich, or a simple baguette with butter and jam—the perfect complement to a latte. Lunch (starting at 11 A.M., $8–18) brings out the crowds for an ever-changing menu of made-to-order sandwiches (including a popular salami, provolone, roasted red bell pepper, and tapenade on baguette), three daily soups, salads, and thin-crust pizzas from the wood-burning oven. The adjacent deli sells wines, rustic artisan breads (try the garlic parsley walnut), pastries, cobblers, and gourmet cheeses, and has a freezer packed with homemade soups, potpies, and fruit pies to take home. You'll never go wrong with a meal at Roses!

Friendly Swiss owner Heinz Brand brings a European sensibility to **Enzo's Caffè** (365 North Beach Rd., 360/376-3732, 7 A.M.–6 P.M. Mon.–Sat., 8 A.M.–4 P.M. Sun., $7–10) in the heart of Eastsound. The café attracts a loyal following with made-to-order crepes (try the Italian sausage savory crepe or one with fresh strawberries and blueberries), bagels with lox and cream cheese, grilled panini, homemade gelato (a big hit with the kids), baked goods, and espresso, plus Wi-Fi and a guest computer. A few outside tables fill on sunny mornings.

A great little breakfast and lunch destination, **Mia's Café** (360/376-6427, 8 A.M.–3 P.M. Mon.–Sat., 8 A.M.–1 P.M. Sun., $8–14) hides in an off-street set of shops at 109 North Beach Road. Owner Mia Kartiganer's breakfasts include lemon blueberry blintzes, chorizo scramble, and red flannel hash (bacon, beets, onions, and potatoes). For lunch, try her surprisingly good fried egg sandwich with bacon, pesto, cheddar, tomato, and lettuce. Check the blackboard for daily specials; there's always a lunchtime pizza and three soups from which to choose.

Eastsound's best latte destinations are Roses, Enzo's, and **Strait Shots** (360/376-2177) inside Darvill's Bookstore (296 Main St., 360/376-2177, www.darvillsbookstore.com).

## Burgers and Pizza

A good spot for finger food is **The Lower Tavern** (Prune Alley, 360/376-4848, 11 A.M.–10 P.M. Sun.–Thurs., 11 A.M.–11 P.M. Fri.–Sat. for food, till 2 A.M. for drinks), where bar meals include the best fish and chips in town, along with specialty burgers (including a popular bacon cheeseburger) and soups. This is a tavern (10 beers on tap), so you must be 21 to enter. There's outside seating and a pool table, and the TVs are tuned to sports action, making this a popular rainy-day retreat.

At **Madrona Bar & Grill** (310 Main St., 360/376-7171, www.madronabarandgrill.com, breakfast 8:30–11:30 A.M. Sat.–Sun., lunch 11:30 A.M.–4:30 P.M. daily, dinner 4:30–8:30 P.M. Sun.–Thurs.), it's all about the location, with a large back deck right on Fishing Bay in downtown Eastsound. Steaks, seafood, sandwiches, burgers, and salads are served ($12–29), but service can be spotty. The bar has a selection of microbrews and sports on the TVs; it's open weekdays till 11 P.M., and weekends till 1 A.M.

Get pizzas, along with focaccia, sandwiches, and salads at **Portofino Pizzeria** (A St., 360/376-2085, 11:30 A.M.–5 P.M. Wed.–Mon., closed Tues.). This noisy, kid-friendly

spot is upstairs behind the Village Stop convenience store, and the second-floor deck affords a view across Eastsound. A large cheese pizza costs $13, and the lunch special includes a large slice of pizza plus soda for $5. Far better pizzas can be found at Roses Bakery Café, described above, or on summer Sunday afternoons from Inn at Ship Bay, described below.

## International Food

Get quick Asian-influenced takeaway fare—including hot and sour soup, wraps, potstickers, fried tofu with sesame rice cakes, and teriyaki chicken—at **The Kitchen** (249 Prune Alley, 360/376-6958, www.thekitchenorcas.com, 11 A.M.–7 P.M. Mon.–Sat. late May–early Sept., 11 A.M.–3 P.M. Mon.–Fri. the rest of the year). Many items are under $10 (simple teriyaki and rice is just $6) at this tiny walk-up lunch spot popular with locals. A few covered picnic tables sit next to a flower-filled yard.

If you visited Orcas Island sometime in the last 30 years, there's a good chance you ate at least one meal at Bilbo's Festivo. The restaurant changed hands and deteriorated in recent years, and eventually folded. In 2011, former owner Julie Fraser reopened a new variation on the Mexican theme, **Chilada's** (310 A St., 360/376-6722, www.chiladas.com, 4–9 P.M. daily, $11–20 entrées). House favorites include mesquite grilled carne asada, pork and plantain tacos, local oysters with salsa verde, and daily specials, plus traditional desserts such as sopapillas and flan. The salsa is made in-house, a diversity of margaritas await, and there's an outdoor seating area accented by shade trees and handcrafted tables. Reservations are advised. Daily happy hour is 4–6 P.M. in the courtyard.

Chef Bill Patterson has gained a loyal following of travelers and locals at **Chimayo Restaurant** (123 North Beach Rd., 360/376-6394, 11 A.M.–3 P.M., 5–9 P.M. Mon.–Sat., closed Sun.). Hidden in a cluster of shops near the museum, the restaurant has a schizophrenic personality. Lunches ($7–10) emphasize Tex-Mex tacos, tostadas, burritos, chili, enchiladas, and a very popular redemption salad with greens, avocado, pumpkin seeds, tomato, rice, black beans, and cheese. At dinner, Chimayo morphs into an Italian bistro serving pappardelle with artichokes, eggplant involtini, and Dungeness crab ravioli. Organic local meats and vegetables are used, and the pasta is made fresh daily.

## Fine Dining

Ask locals where they go for special occasions and you're certain to hear one place at the top of everyone's list: **( Inn at Ship Bay** (326 Olga Rd., 360/376-5886, www.innatshipbay.com, 5:30–9 P.M. or later Tues.–Sat., closed Dec.–mid-Feb., $21–29 entrées). Chef/owner Geddes Martin prepares a variety of fresh-from-the-sea specials—including Judd Cove oysters harvested that morning—and uses fresh organic greens from the garden, along with plums, apples, and pears from the orchard out front. The owners even have a pig or two to help recycle scraps, and you might find mangalista pork on the menu later. The menu is updated frequently, and there's an impressive wine list. Located a mile east of Eastsound at an old farmhouse, this comfortably upscale restaurant is the sort of place where the knowledgeable staff stays year after year. Inn at Ship Bay has attracted the likes of Al Gore and Conan O'Brien in the past, so check nearby tables for a recognizable face, and be sure to call ahead for reservations. A bar menu includes lighter meals. The restaurant is closed December–mid-February and is always closed on Sunday and Monday. The restaurant itself may be closed, but on sunny Sundays in summer, the owners light their outdoor wood-fired oven to craft small pizzas ($10–12), salads ($5), and desserts ($5). They're served on picnic tables next to the garden noon–8 P.M., and pizzas are also available to go.

Housed within Outlook Inn, **( New Leaf Café** (360/376-2200, www.newleafcafeorcas.com, 8 A.M.–1:30 P.M., 5–8:30 P.M. daily late June–mid-Sept., reduced spring and fall hours, closed mid-Nov.–Jan.) is easily one of the finest restaurants on Orcas. Killer

brunches ($10–18) include seafood omelets, Monte Cristo sandwiches, duck confit hash, and a memorable smoked salmon Benedict. Pacific Northwest fusion seafood is the dinnertime focus ($20–34 entrées), including a Northwest shellfish pot of clams, mussels, crab, and shrimp, or pan-seared salmon with a pear-ginger glaze. Every seat has a water view, and a special late-night menu (8:30–9:30 P.M.) features Kobe beef sliders, duck mac and cheese, and Dungeness crab cakes for $8–16. The "regional-centric" wine list has a fine choice of pinot noirs, and signature cocktails such as the New Leaf Manhattan are a treat. Join locals for weeknight happy hours in the lounge. Reservations are recommended.

Head up a set of 22 narrow steps to one of the top dining places on the island, **Allium** (310 Main St., 360/376-4904, www.alliumonorcas.com, brunch 10 A.M.–2 P.M. Sat.–Sun., 5:30–9 P.M. dinner Wed.–Mon., closed Tues., $24–38 entrées). Chef/owner Lisa Nakamura is best known for her caramelized sea scallops with a foie gras and Madeira butter, daily gnocchi with white truffle oil, and creamy polenta with asparagus and goat cheese. Seating is limited, but there's a wonderful back deck overlooking Fishing Bay. Meals come with a basket of sourdough bread and scrumptious caramelized onion jam. Weekend brunch ($9–15) delivers crepes with orange peach sauce and other delights. Allium is pricy, but worth it.

## Sweets

**Katheryn Taylor Chocolates** (109 North Beach Rd., 360/376-1030, www.ktchocolates.com) will send chocoloholics into a coma. Whimsically decorated bonbons are filled with local pears, berries, plums, hazelnuts, lavender, rhubarb, and other flavors. Pastries, quiche, fruit tarts, and breads change daily. Owned by accomplished chef Ted Taylor and his wife, Kathryn Taylor Aspinall, the shop is named for their young daughter, Katheryn. It's easy to miss this little place, tucked behind Mia's Café in Eastsound Square.

Downstairs from Allium Restaurant—one

of the culinary highlights on Orcas—is its sister, **Lily** (310 Main St., 360/376-4904, www.lilyonorcas.com, 10 A.M.–5 P.M. Thurs.–Sun.), dishing up 15 or so flavors of Lopez Creamery ice cream. A double-scoop waffle cone is $6, or drop by on Saturday mornings for fresh cinnamon rolls.

**Enzo's Caffé** (365 North Beach Rd., 360/376-3732) serves homemade gelato in a variety of flavors. A bit out of the way—it's three miles west of Eastsound—the little store at **West Beach Resort** (360/376-2240 or 877/937-8224, www.westbeachresort.com) serves ice cream in homemade waffle cones, plus tasty milkshakes.

A little Eastsound shop, **Passionate for Pies** (460 Main St., 360/376-7437, www.passionateforpies.com, 10 A.M.–6 P.M. Wed.–Sat., 11 A.M.–5 P.M. Sun., closed Oct.–Apr., $6 per slice) bakes pies, savory tarts, potpies, pasties, and pizzas by the slice. The house favorite is a jumbleberry crumb pie, and all are made using unrefined sweeteners (such as agave nectar) and butter. Wi-Fi is available.

## Markets and Bakeries

For groceries, film, and other essentials, stop by **Orcas Island Market** (469 Market St., 360/376-6000, 8 A.M.–9 P.M. Mon.–Sat., 10 A.M.–8 P.M. Sun.). Largest market in the San Juans, it houses an in-store bakery, deli, ATM, and video rentals.

**Homegrown Market** (138 North Beach Rd., 360/376-2009, www.orcashomegrownmarket.com, 9 A.M.–7:30 P.M. daily) has natural foods and a deli with daily specials and salads, plus fresh crab and salmon in season. This is the place to buy ultra-fresh Judd Cove oysters harvested at nearby Crescent Beach; it costs $8 for a dozen big ones.

The **Orcas Island Farmers Market** (360/317-8342, www.orcasislandfarmersmarket.org, 10 A.M.–3 P.M. Sat. May–Nov.) takes place at Eastsound's Village Square, with local produce, flowers, crafts, photography, pottery, clothing, and tasty food. In October and November, the market moves indoors to the Odd Fellows Hall on Madrona Point.

For the finest breads, cheeses, and gourmet

© DON PITCHER

Orcas Island Farmers Market

deli foods, don't miss **Roses Bakery Café** (382 Prune Alley, 360/376-5805, 8:20 A.M.–4 P.M. Mon.–Sat. for the café, bakery till 6 P.M., both closed Sun.).

**Country Corner** (837 Crescent Beach Dr., 360/376-6900, www.countrycornerorcas.net, 6 A.M.–11 P.M. daily) is a Chevron gas station and convenience store with a deli, decent take-out pizzas, wine, and beer.

## THE WEST END
### Orcas Village

When you step off the ferry at Orcas, the grand old Orcas Hotel faces you. Inside is **Octavia's Bistro** (360/376-4300 or 888/672-2792, www.orcashotel.com, 5–8:30 P.M. daily for dinner, breakfast 8 A.M.–noon Sun.), where chef Ryan Houser has gained a regional reputation for island fusion cuisine. Evening entrée ($15–24) highlights include seafood, lamb, ribs, and more. For just $15, try the crispy batter cod and tiger prawns, served with a unique side of pressed red potatoes—think of it as fish and chips gone gourmet. Outdoor seating is available. By the way, the restaurant is named for a one-time owner of the hotel whose ghost reportedly haunts the room where she died. Also here is **Orcas Hotel Café,** serving tasty breakfasts (quiche, baked goods, and croissant sandwiches) starting at 6 A.M., along with lunchtime salmon fillet sandwiches, burgers, fish and chips, salads, and wraps. Everything is made in-house using local ingredients whenever possible. Get a Starbucks iced mocha on a warm afternoon. Eat inside or on the covered patio. A computer is available to check your email, and free Wi-Fi is also available. Pub night is Friday, when local musicians perform jazz or blues tunes.

Right next to the ferry landing is **Orcas Village Store** (360/376-8860, www.orcasvillagestore.com, 6 A.M.–8 P.M. daily year-round), with a good selection of groceries and a deli that makes pre-made and made-to-order sandwiches, salads, chowder, and lattes. Fresh pastries and cookies are prepared daily, with homemade soups in winter. Stop here for a last-

enjoying a sunny afternoon on the porch at Orcas Hotel Café

© DON PITCHER

minute take-aboard lunch ($8) before walking on the ferry.

**Mamie's Restaurant at The Boardwalk** (360/376-2971 or 877/376-2971, www.orcasislandboardwalk.com, 7 A.M.–5 P.M. Mon.–Sat., 7:30 A.M.–5 P.M. Sun., reduced winter hours) serves breakfast omelets, along with lunchtime burgers, halibut and chips, and other fare, but is best known for the stand out front serving Lopez Creamery ice cream.

### Deer Harbor

Housed in a 1915 farmhouse, **Deer Harbor Inn** (Deer Harbor, 360/376-4110 or 877/377-4110, www.deerharborinn.com, 5–9 P.M. daily in summer, 5–8 P.M. Fri.–Sun. the rest of the year) is a spacious and comfortable place with fine meals. It's a bit off the beaten path if you're staying near Eastsound, but worth the drive. You can get something as simple as freshly baked bread, salad, and homemade soup for $12, or choose a full dinner ($22–38 entrées) from the blackboard listing the day's specials. Meals come with a large soup, bread, salad, and veggies. There's always grilled seafood, steaks, enormous salads (try the New York steak and blue cheese salad for $17), and a vegetarian choice, along with a full bar. Homemade apple pie à la mode is made from apples picked in the century-old orchard out front, and greens come from the adjacent garden. A large wraparound deck opens seasonally for al fresco dining, where you can hear classical or piano music on summer Sundays. Two generations of the Carpenter family have owned Deer Harbor Inn since 1982. Reservations are advised.

Homey ◖ **West Sound Café** (360/376-4440, www.westsoundcafe.com, 8:30–11:30 A.M. Wed.–Fri., 8:30 A.M.–noon Sat.–Sun., 5–9 P.M. Wed.–Sun.) occupies a historic waterside building at the intersection of Crow Valley and Deer Harbor Roads. This is the real deal, with wonderful food, a classic setting, and friendly service. Dinner chef Joe Cain has a rather surprising background, spending a decade as an NFL linebacker for the Seattle Seahawks, Chicago Bears, and Minnesota Vikings. Entrées such as prawn pasta puttanesca, flat-iron steak, and fish tacos are reasonably priced ($15–19), and be sure to order the Buck Bay steamer clams appetizer. Dinner reservations are required, though you might get lucky without one if they have a cancellation. For breakfast, try the hang town fry omelet (with oysters, bacon, and chives) or a wonderful baked cinnamon apple French toast. Outside seating is available on a little deck facing West Sound.

## THE EAST END

Housed within the historic Orcas Island Artworks building at the intersection of Horseshoe Highway and Doe Bay Road, **Café Olga** (360/376-5098, www.orcasartworks.com, 8 A.M.–4 P.M. Thurs.–Tues., reduced hours in fall and winter, closed Wed. and Jan.–mid-Feb., $10–15 lunch) is a pleasant breakfast and lunch stop. In addition to sandwiches and salads, the restaurant serves daily seafood specials, vegetarian items, and espresso, but save room for the justly famous blackberry pie. One of their monster cinnamon rolls could feed a small nation. The out-of-the-way location keeps the crowds at bay.

Famous **Rosario Resort & Spa** (downhill from Moran State Park, 360/376-2152 or 800/562-8820, www.rosarioresort.com) has spectacular views and romantic dining in a historic building five miles south of Eastsound. The Mansion Restaurant (breakfast 8 A.M.–5 P.M., dinner 5–10 P.M. daily, $13–26 dinner entrées) features a seafood menu that ranges from fish tacos to Penn Cove mussels and Manila clams. Reservations are recommended on Friday and Saturday nights. For something less formal, head to the marina, where Cascade Bay Grill (7 A.M.–9 P.M. daily late May–early Sept.) has pizzas, burgers, and beer on draft.

Located at Doe Bay Resort & Retreat, ◖ **Doe Bay Café** (107 Doe Bay Rd., 360/376-8059, www.doebay.com, 8 A.M.–2 P.M., 5–9 P.M. daily June–Aug., 8 A.M.–2 P.M. Sat.–Sun. and 5–9 P.M. Fri.–Mon. the rest of the year) serves delicious vegetarian and seafood meals in an inviting, out-of-the-way location. Tables are set against large bayside windows at this peaceful spot where dreadlocks and nose rings are still in vogue. Brunch specials ($8–12) include caramelized pumpkin brioche French toast, huevos rancheros, and espresso. Dinner entrées ($14–28) change, so check the board for chef Abigael Birrell's specials, but the menu usually includes pan-roasted king salmon and island harvest bowl—with local organic vegetables and rice noodles with ginger-sesame sauce. There's a good selection of wines, along with several beers on draft. After your meal, head up the creek for a soak in the hot tubs ($15 for a day pass if you aren't a guest). Thursday nights bring 10-inch pizzas and open-mic music, and there's always free Wi-Fi.

# Information and Services

Get island information from the helpful **Orcas Island Chamber of Commerce Visitor Center** (360/376-2273, www.orcasislandchamber.com, 10 A.M.–4 P.M. Mon.–Sat. year-round), located in Eastsound at 65 North Beach Road. Two helpful private websites—www.orcasisle.com and www.orcasisland.org—have links to many local businesses.

## LAUNDRY AND WASTE DISPOSAL

**Country Corner Laundry** (837 Crescent Beach Dr., 360/376-6900, www.countrycorner-orcas.com) is a half mile east of Eastsound. Additional washers and dryers are at Rosario Resort Marina and Deer Harbor Marina, and both of these have **coin-op showers.**

If you're staying in a rental house on the island, you'll need to haul garbage to the **Orcas Island Transfer Station** (3398 Orcas Rd., 360/376-4089, www.sanjuanco.com, 10 A.M.–4 P.M. Fri.–Sun.) on the west side of the island. You can recycle many items here, including mixed paper, tin cans, aluminum, plastic bottles, cardboard, and newspapers, but don't bother to sort your recyclables; they all go in one bin to be sorted later. Dumping garbage costs $12 per bag.

## KIDS' STUFF

Weekday child care is available on a drop-in basis at **Orcas Island Children's House** (36 Peapatch Lane, 360/376-4744, www.oich.org) and **Kaleidoscope** (1292 North Beach Rd., 360/376-2484, www.ourkaleidoscopekids.org). You'll need to provide a copy of your child's immunization records. Call ahead for age requirements and to make sure they have space.

## LIBRARY

Eastsound is home to the attractive **Orcas Island Library** (500 Rose St., 360/376-4985, www.orcaslibrary.org, 10 A.M.–7 P.M. Mon.–Thurs., 10 A.M.–5 P.M. Fri.–Sat., noon–3 P.M. Sun.), a great place to relax on a drizzly afternoon. The public is welcome at the preschool story hour every Thursday and Saturday. A half-dozen computers are available to surf the web or check your email, but you may need to wait for a machine. Non-locals pay $10 for a 30-day library card if you want to check something out. Free Wi-Fi, and it's even available if you're sitting outside the library when they're closed!

## COMMUNICATIONS

In addition to the free computers and Wi-Fi at the library, **Orcas Online** (254 North Beach Rd. in Eastsound, 360/376-4124, www.orcasonline.com, $5 for 30 min.) lets you surf the web. The company also provides mobile hotspots at Eastsound and the ferry landing for $8 per day.

Cell phone service can be surprisingly spotty on the east side of Orcas Island, and from the west side your phone may use Canadian cell towers; this could potentially add a roaming charge to your bill.

## BANKING AND MAIL

Find ATM machines at **Islanders Bank** (475 Fern St. in Eastsound, 360/376-2265 or 800/843-5441, www.islandersbank.com) and **Key Bank** (487 Main St. in Eastsound, 360/376-2211, www.keybank.com), inside the Orcas Island Market and Ray's Pharmacy in Eastsound, and the Orcas Village Store at the ferry landing.

**Post offices** can be found on A Street in Eastsound (360/376-4121), and at Deer Harbor (360/376-2548), Olga (360/376-4236), and Orcas (360/376-4254).

## MEDICAL CARE

Several options are available if you need medical care while on the island: **Orcas Medical Center** (7 Deye Lane, 360/376-2561, www.orcasmedicalcenter.com), **Orcas Island Family Medicine** (33 Urner St., 360/376-4949), and the nonprofit **Orcas Family Health Center**

(1286 Mt. Baker Rd., 360/376-7778, www.orcasfamilyhealthcenter.org). All three facilities can provide urgent care and lab tests and are open weekdays, with a physician on call after hours. Orcas Island has a paramedic system, but the closest hospital is in Anacortes, and serious medical problems require a Medevac flight to Seattle. Get prescription medicines from **Ray's Pharmacy** in Eastsound (Templin Center, 360/376-2230, 9 A.M.–6 P.M. Mon.–Sat.; after-hour emergencies call 360/376-3693).

For a New Age take on health—including a naturopath, massage therapists, acupuncture, life coaching, and intuitive counselors—visit **Healing Arts Center** (453 North Beach Rd., 360/376-4002, www.healingartsonline.com).

## VETERINARY CARE

Take sick or injured pets to **Orcas Veterinary Service** (450 North Beach Rd. in Eastsound, 360/376-6373, www.orcasveterinary.com), or board your dog or cat at **Eastsound Kennels** (186 Dolphin Bay Rd., 360/376-2410). **Pawki's Pet Boutique** (199 Main St., 360/376-3648, www.pawkis.com) sells pet supplies in Eastsound.

# Getting There and Around

## WASHINGTON STATE FERRIES

**Washington State Ferries** (360/376-6253 for the Orcas ferry terminal, 206/464-6400 or 888/808-7977 for general info) dock at Orcas Village on the south end of the island. Find all the details—including current ferry wait times—at www.wsdot.wa.gov/ferries, or view current waits at www.ferrycam.net/orcas.html. Credit cards are accepted.

The high-season fare for a car and driver from Orcas to Friday Harbor is $23.50; walk-ons and passengers ride free. Vehicles and passengers traveling east from Orcas to Shaw, Lopez, or Anacortes do not need tickets and there is no charge. Peak-season fares from Anacortes to Orcas are $11.50 for passengers and walk-ons, $45.30 for a car and driver. Bikes are $4 extra, and kayaks cost $15.80 more. Reservations are not available for any

ORCAS ISLAND

## ORCAS ISLAND MILEAGE

|  | Orcas Village Ferry Dock | Deer Harbor | Doe Bay | Eastsound | Moran State Park | Olga |
|---|---|---|---|---|---|---|
| Deer Harbor | 8 | | | | | |
| Doe Bay | 20 | 22 | | | | |
| Eastsound | 9 | 11 | 11 | | | |
| Moran State Park | 14 | 15 | 7 | 4 | | |
| Olga | 17 | 18 | 3 | 8 | 4 | |
| West Sound Marina | 4 | 4 | 18 | 7 | 12 | 15 |

© DON PITCHER

**waiting for the ferry**

of these runs, so you'll need to get in line and wait. Vehicle reservations *are,* however, highly recommended (at least 24 hours in advance) if you're heading west on the runs from Orcas Island to Sidney, British Columbia. These tickets to Vancouver Island cost $29 for a car and driver or $16.85 for passengers or walk-ons.

## WATER TAXIS
Marty Mead of **North Shore Charters** (360/376-4855, www.orcasislandadventures. com) provides water-taxi service to state marine parks on Stuart, Sucia, Matia, Patos, and other islands—even to Victoria, Vancouver, and the Gulf Islands in Canada. Rates are around $195 per hour for up to six people, with trips departing Deer Harbor Marina. There's also space for kayaks and bikes.

Operating from Deer Harbor Marina, **Orcas Boat Rentals** (360/376-7616, www. orcasboats.com) provides water-taxi service to nearby Jones and Yellow Islands ($100 round-trip), and also serves other islands in the San Juans.

Based on the north side of Orcas near the Eastsound Airport, **Outer Island Expeditions** (360/376-3711, www.outerislandx.com) leads daily summertime shuttles to nearby Sucia Island ($45/person round-trip), where they also have kayaks available for rent. Beau Brandow, a former park ranger, manages the company. In addition, Outer Island Expeditions has lighthouse tours to Stuart and Patos Islands, water-taxi service throughout the San Juans and to Bellingham and Anacortes, plus whale-watching, charter fishing, and guided kayak trips.

## BY AIR
Operating out of Lake Union in Seattle, **Kenmore Air** (425/486-1257 or 866/435-9524, www.kenmoreair.com) has daily scheduled floatplane flights to Rosario Resort, Deer Harbor, and West Sound on Orcas Island. A 24-pound baggage weight limit is in effect on these flights, and excess baggage costs $1 per pound. They also fly wheeled planes between Seattle's Boeing Field and Eastsound Airport daily; there's a 70-pound weight limit on these flights.

**San Juan Airlines** (360/376-4176 or 800/874-4434, www.sanjuanairlines.com) has daily scheduled wheeled-plane service to Eastsound Airport from Anacortes and Bellingham, plus connecting service to San Juan, Lopez, Decatur, and Blakely Islands. Flightseeing is available; a half-hour flight for up to five people costs $250. For point-to-point service, book a charter to Victoria, Seattle, Vancouver, or other destinations.

**Northwest Sky Ferry** (360/696-9999, www.nwskyferry.com) has twice-daily flights from Bellingham to Orcas, San Juan, and Lopez Islands, with flightpooling charters to other destinations throughout the San Juan Islands.

### Biplane Rides
For a ride into the past, hop aboard the gorgeous biplane flown by effusive Rod Magner, an ex-Navy pilot who has flown since age 14. His **Magic Air Tours** (360/376-2733 or 800/376-1929, www.magicair.com) depart

from Eastsound Airport. The plane is officially a 1929 TravelAir (one of just 40 still flying), but only a few pieces remain from the original fuselage. Rebuilt from the ground up in 1984, the plane looks brand new and is decked out in glistening red and yellow, bringing out the "wow" factor. Rod compares a flightseeing trip to "flying in an old Buick convertible." There's room for two in the open front cockpit, and he narrates the sights along the way. The cost for two people is $300 for a half-hour flight, including leather helmets, goggles, and headsets. Flights take place May–September and are available for anyone; he's flown 18-month-old babies and 93-year-old seniors! Even if you aren't planning to fly, you may want to check out his plane at the airport. His old-fashioned hangar, filled with flying memorabilia, is fun to see, and the plane itself is a stunner. Kids love to play on his pedal planes, one of which is an exact copy of the TravelAir.

## CAR RENTALS

Located just up from the Orcas Village ferry landing, **Orcas Mopeds** (360/376-5266, www.orcasmopeds.com) has year-round car rentals, starting at $60 per day for an economy car. Mopeds ($65–71 for all day), scootcars ($110/day), and two-person scoot coups ($155/day) are available April–mid-October.

Gas is available at two stations east of Eastsound along Crescent Beach Drive, but prices are slightly cheaper at the hardware store at the junction of West Beach Road and Crow Valley Road. In a pinch, you can also get fuel from the various boat harbors, including West Beach Resort and Deer Harbor Marina. Fuel prices are a rip-off on Orcas, so fill up on the mainland before you get on the ferry or get ready to add at least $1 a gallon.

## TAXIS

**Orcas Island Taxi** (360/376-8294 or 800/942-1926, www.orcasislandtaxi.com) and **Orcas Taxi Cab** (360/298-1639) provide service from the ferry terminal to Eastsound ($27), Moran State Park ($40), Rosario Resort ($40), Doe Bay ($55), and other places on the island. Rates are for two people; add $5 each for additional people.

ORCAS ISLAND

# LOPEZ ISLAND

If you're venturing out to the San Juans from Anacortes, Lopez Island (population 2,200) is the first place the ferry stops. The third largest island in the archipelago, it covers almost 30 square miles. Pastoral farmland and water vistas predominate, especially on the southern end of the island.

Because of its lack of both steep hills and traffic, Lopez is very popular with cyclists, including many groups of touring bikers. The roads are mostly paved, and views of the surrounding islands and mountains to the east and west jut out from every turn.

Along the west side of Lopez just north of Fisherman Bay is the island's quaint business center, little **Lopez Village.** Here you'll find a scattering of cafés and shops; a museum, grocery store with gas, post office, pharmacy, and medical clinic; and a few real estate offices. Islandale Store is on the south end of the island, and a few more businesses cluster along pretty **Fisherman Bay,** filled with sailboats and other craft, but the rest of Lopez Island is rural. Many Lopez businesses are shuttered during the winter.

Often called "The Friendly Isle" or "Slowpez," Lopez is an easygoing place with gently rolling terrain, old farms with buildings in various states of disrepair, shaggy black dogs, and a famously friendly populace. Waving to passing cars and bicycles is a time-honored local custom, and failure to wave back will label you a tourist as surely as a camera around your neck and rubber flip-flops.

Lopezians are an odd amalgamation of carpenters, retirees, back-to-the-land organic

© DON PITCHER

# HIGHLIGHTS

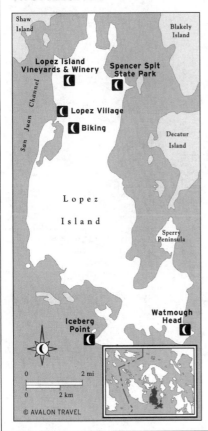

**⟪ Lopez Village:** The center of commerce on Lopez, this little business center has a small museum, galleries, good food, and more (page 215).

**⟪ Lopez Island Vineyards & Winery:** This little six-acre farm eschews pesticides in the production of its Madeleine Angevine and Siegerrebe wines. Locals pick the grapes each fall in a harvest party (page 216).

**⟪ Spencer Spit State Park:** Excellent camping, kayaking, beachcombing, and clamming attract the crowds to this park on the east side of Lopez (page 217).

**⟪ Iceberg Point:** An easy half-mile hike leads through forest and grasslands to this extraordinary rocky point (page 219).

**⟪ Watmough Head:** This out-of-the-way spot on the south end of Lopez features a pebbly beach facing the snowy summit of Mount Baker (page 220).

**⟪ Biking:** Cycling the 30-mile loop is a favorite form of recreation and a perfect way to explore the farms, fields, forests, and bays of Lopez (page 222).

LOOK FOR ⟪ TO FIND RECOMMENDED SIGHTS, ACTIVITIES, DINING, AND LODGING.

farmers, commercial fishers, artists and musicians, bed-and-breakfast owners, and more than a few eccentrics. This is the kind of place where bumper stickers poke fun at the NRA ("National Waffle Association") and conservative Christians (a fish-shaped symbol surrounding the word *gefilte*). Microsoft billionaire Paul Allen owns a home on Lopez; his purchase of Sperry Peninsula for a private, guarded estate in the 1990s forced Camp Nor'wester to move to Johns Island.

## HISTORY

Lopez is named in honor of Lopez Gonzales de Haro, the first European to discover the San Juans. He served as sailing master during the 1791 expedition of explorer Francisco Eliza. Haro Strait is another of his namesakes.

The Coast Salish people occupied Lopez Island for thousands of years, and the coastline is littered with archaeological sites. Whites first settled the island in the 1850s. They found incredible forests covering a rich land that would

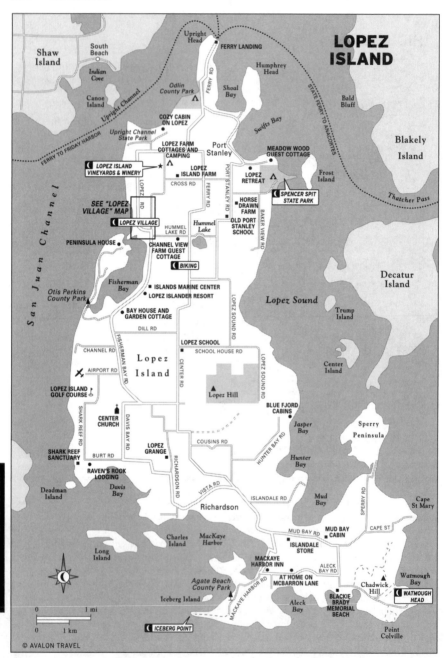

# LOPEZ ISLAND

Shaw Island

South Beach

Indian Cove

Canoe Island

Upright Head

FERRY LANDING

Humphrey Head

Shoal Bay

Swifts Bay

Blakely Island

Bald Bluff

Frost Island

Thatcher Pass

Odlin County Park

COZY CABIN ON LOPEZ

Upright Channel State Park

LOPEZ FARM COTTAGES AND CAMPING

Port Stanley

MEADOW WOOD GUEST COTTAGE

LOPEZ RETREAT

LOPEZ ISLAND VINEYARDS & WINERY

LOPEZ ISLAND FARM

CROSS RD

SEE "LOPEZ VILLAGE" MAP

SPENCER SPIT STATE PARK

HORSE DRAWN FARM

LOPEZ VILLAGE

HUMMEL LAKE RD

Hummel Lake

OLD PORT STANLEY SCHOOL

PENINSULA HOUSE

CHANNEL VIEW FARM GUEST COTTAGE

BIKING

Fisherman Bay

ISLANDS MARINE CENTER

LOPEZ ISLANDER RESORT

Decatur Island

Lopez Sound

Trump Island

Otis Perkins County Park

BAY HOUSE AND GARDEN COTTAGE

DILL RD

CHANNEL RD

LOPEZ SCHOOL

SCHOOL HOUSE RD

Center Island

Lopez Island

AIRPORT RD

LOPEZ ISLAND GOLF COURSE

Lopez Hill

BLUE FJORD CABINS

Jasper Bay

Sperry Peninsula

CENTER CHURCH

LOPEZ GRANGE

COUSINS RD

Hunter Bay

SHARK REEF SANCTUARY

RAVEN'S ROCK LODGING

Deadman Island

Davis Bay

ISLANDALE RD

Mud Bay

Cape St Mary

Richardson

Charles Island

MacKaye Harbor

MUD BAY RD

MUD BAY CABIN

CAPE ST

Long Island

ISLANDALE STORE

MACKAYE HARBOR INN

AT HOME ON MCBARRON LANE

ALECK BAY RD

Watmough Bay

Chadwick Hill

WATMOUGH HEAD

Agate Beach County Park

BLACKIE BRADY MEMORIAL BEACH

Iceberg Island

Aleck Bay

Point Colville

ICEBERG POINT

0    1 mi

0    1 km

San Juan Channel

Upright Channel

FERRY TO FRIDAY HARBOR

STATE FERRY TO ANACORTES

FERRY RD

PORT STANLEY RD

FERRY RD

LOPEZ RD

BAKER VIEW RD

CENTER RD

LOPEZ SOUND RD

LOPEZ SOUND RD

FISHERMAN BAY RD

SHARK REEF RD

DAVIS BAY RD

BURT RD

RICHARDSON RD

VISTA RD

HUNTER BAY RD

SPERRY RD

MACKAYE HARBOR RD

© AVALON TRAVEL

prove perfect for farming, a heritage that continues today. By the middle of the 20th century, Lopez was known as the Guernsey Island, and more than 130 farms produced milk, eggs, poultry, veal, pork, peas, vetch, oats, barley, and wheat. Nearly all of the big farms are gone, but agriculture is still important. Today, the farms are smaller and more specialized, offering everything from organic beef to cut flowers.

## PLANNING YOUR TIME

Lopez reaches 17 miles north to south, and approximately 4 miles across. Flat or gently rolling terrain, open country, and relatively straight roads make it easy to cover the island in a day—even on a bike. It's the first ferry stop heading west from Anacortes and has a couple of campgrounds near the ferry landing on the north end, making it perfect for relatively short visits, such as a weekend.

Because it's so easy to get around, you can stay almost anywhere on the island and still be just a few miles from the main settlement of **Lopez Village.** There aren't a lot of "sights" to discover, but the rural, farming island is a perfect place to explore by bicycle. Most of the land is privately owned, but a handful of small parks and preserves remain in public hands, including **Spencer Spit State Park** on the northern end of the island. This park is popular not only for beachcombing, camping, and picnicking, but also as a launching point for sea kayaks. A number of mooring buoys are just offshore. **Iceberg Point** is an especially scenic spot on the south end of the island, and other small but interesting wild areas include **Hummel Lake Preserve, Shark Reef Park, Odlin County Park,** and **Agate Beach County Park.**

One of the few commercial places in Washington that grows pesticide-free grapes, **Lopez Island Vineyards & Winery** has Madeleine Angevine and Siegerrebe plants and a small winery where locals pitch in for the fall harvest.

# Sights

Lopez's main attraction is its pastoral countryside. The long stretches of hills, fields, orchards, and woods could just as well be rural Vermont, complete with contented cows. You might even see flocks of sheep being driven along local roads. Bucolic Lopez Island is a delightful place to explore, but unfortunately, much of the shoreline and many of the beaches are privately owned and closed to the public.

Picturesque **Fisherman Bay** is the boating center for Lopez, with two marinas and a small fleet of commercial fishing boats, including a few distinctive reefnet boats unique to this area.

## ◖ LOPEZ VILLAGE

This small settlement near Fisherman Bay is as developed as things get on Lopez, with all the "necessities" of life: restaurants, fresh baked goods, espresso, video rentals, art galleries, books, a farmers market, and hot dogs. Like

© DON PITCHER

historic water tower in Lopez Village

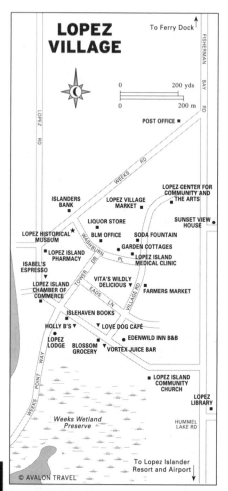

**LOPEZ VILLAGE**

To Ferry Dock

FISHERMAN BAY RD

0      200 yds
0      200 m

LOPEZ RD

POST OFFICE ■

WEEKS RD

LOPEZ CENTER FOR COMMUNITY AND THE ARTS ■

ISLANDERS BANK ■

LOPEZ VILLAGE MARKET ■

LIQUOR STORE ■

SUNSET VIEW HOUSE ●

LOPEZ HISTORICAL MUSEUM ★

BLM OFFICE ■

SODA FOUNTAIN ●

WASHBURN PL

■ LOPEZ ISLAND PHARMACY

GARDEN COTTAGES ●

● LOPEZ ISLAND MEDICAL CLINIC

ISABEL'S ESPRESSO ▼

VITA'S WILDLY DELICIOUS ▼

LOPEZ ISLAND CHAMBER OF COMMERCE ■

FARMERS MARKET ■

TOWER RD

EADS LN

VILLAGE RD

ISLEHAVEN BOOKS ■

HOLLY B'S ▼

▼ LOVE DOG CAFÉ

LOPEZ LODGE ■

BLOSSOM GROCERY ■

▼ VORTEX JUICE BAR

● EDENWILD INN B&B

WEEKS POINT WAY

■ LOPEZ ISLAND COMMUNITY CHURCH

LOPEZ LIBRARY ■

Weeks Wetland Preserve

HUMMEL LAKE RD

To Lopez Islander Resort and Airport

© AVALON TRAVEL

---

the rest of the island, it's laid back, and stores may or may not open at the posted hours.

## Lopez Historical Museum

The Lopez Historical Museum (on Weeks Road in Lopez Village, 360/468-2049, www.lopezmuseum.org, noon–4 P.M. Wed.–Sun. May–Sept., by appointment only Oct.–Apr., $2) contains local flotsam and jetsam: old farm equipment, a stuffed albino red-tailed hawk, historical photos, and changing exhibits.

Outside, find a reefnet fishing boat, a gillnetter, and an aging tractor.

## Historic Buildings

A number of other buildings are worth a gander around the island. Pick up a historical landmark tour brochure from the museum for all the details. The white New England–style **Lopez Island Community Church** in Lopez Village was built in 1904 and is notable for its steeple, which splits into four cupolas. **Center Church,** built in 1887, is a simple white structure surrounded by a picket fence and next to a hilltop cemetery. The church is home to both Catholics and Lutherans (what would Martin Luther say?) and is about two miles south of Lopez Village on Fisherman Bay Road. It's a favorite spot for island weddings.

The **Lopez Library** (just east of Lopez Village) is housed in a bright red-and-white building that began life in 1894 as a schoolhouse. Built in 1917 and used until 1940, the restored **Port Stanley School** is on Port Stanley Road near Hummel Lake; call the museum at 360/468-2049 for tours. Also of interest is the **Lopez Grange** (built in 1908) on the south end of the island along Richardson Road.

## ◖ LOPEZ ISLAND VINEYARDS & WINERY

Head a mile north of Lopez Village on Fisherman Bay Road to Lopez Island Vineyards & Winery (724 B Fisherman Bay Rd., 360/468-3644, www.lopezislandvineyards.com), a family operation that grows pesticide-free grapes on six acres of land. The grapes grown here are Madeleine Angevine (a white-wine grape from the Loire Valley of northern France) and Siegerrebe (a cross between Madeleine Angevine and Gewürztraminer). In addition to producing award-winning wines from local grapes, winemaker Brent Charnley, trained in enology at the University of California Davis, uses grapes from Washington's hot and dry Yakima Valley for his chardonnay, merlot, and cabernet sauvignon-merlot wines. Lopez Island Winery also produces several fruit wines—primarily from locally grown organic fruits—including raspberry, blackberry, and apple-pear wines. Lopezians harvest all the grapes by hand at a community picking party in early October.

The winery's **tasting room** is in Lopez Village (265 Lopez Rd., 360/468-4888, noon–6 P.M. Wed.–Sun. July–Aug., reduced hours in fall and spring, closed Jan.–Mar.) across from Isabel's Espresso. The vineyards themselves are open during twice-weekly events in July and August, with classical music on Saturday afternoons and jazz Thursday evenings ($5 cover). There's a large tent for inclement weather or to get out of the sun, and wine tasting. Buy a glass or bottle of wine and bring your picnic lunch to enjoy surrounded by landscaped gardens. See Lopez Island Vineyards' Facebook page or website for upcoming music and events.

## FARMS

Several dozen farms dot the Lopez Island landscape, producing such specialty products as blackberry jams, mohair yarn, Asian pears, organic garlic, Nubian goats, heirloom tomatoes, Kobe beef, and cut flowers, and even Navajo Churro sheep. One of the most interesting is **Horse Drawn Farm** (2823 Port Stanley Rd., 360/468-3486), where vegetables, lamb, pork, and beef are raised—primarily with animal power. You might even see someone plowing a field with oxen. Tours are available by appointment. Also worth a visit is **Lopez Island Farm** (193 Cross Rd., 360/468-4620, www.lopezislandfarm.com), raising sheep and pasture-raised pigs.

For a complete list of island farms, pick up the *Lopez Island Farm Products Guide* (360/378-4414, http://sanjuan.wsu.edu) at the museum or chamber of commerce office. Farm stands pop up in the summer, and many local farm products are sold at the Lopez Island Farmers Market, held on summer Saturdays in Lopez Village.

## PARKS

The **Bureau of Land Management** maintains a small office (360/468-3754) next to the liquor store in Lopez Village. The one lonely staff person is often out working on trails, so hours can be haphazard, but there's a rack out front with maps and brochures describing local BLM lands, including Watmough Head and Iceberg Point on Lopez, plus Patos and Stuart Islands. **San Juan Islands Preservation Trust** (360/468-3202, www.sjpt.org) has offices on Fisherman Bay Road.

The **Lopez Bicycle Alliance** (www.members.shaw.ca/lopezbeaches) produces a helpful map that details publicly accessible beaches on Lopez; paper copies are available at the chamber of commerce.

### ◀ Spencer Spit State Park

On the east side of Lopez Island, the 130-acre Spencer Spit State Park (360/468-2251, www.parks.wa.gov, Mar.–Oct.) has a half-mile beach with good clamming, beachcombing, hiking, and picnicking. The sandy shoreline is strewn with driftwood, and a reconstructed cabin—part of an old homestead belonging to

© DON PITCHER

Navajo-Churro sheep like this one can be found on Lopez Island farms.

© DON PITCHER

beach at Spencer Spit State Park

the Spencer family—sits at the end of the spit. The spit points like an arrow to nearby **Frost Island,** less than a hundred feet from its tip. Frost is private and rocky, with a handful of homes. Spencer Spit hems in a brackish lagoon that frequently hosts ducks, herons, gulls, and shorebirds. Rabbits and black-tailed deer are common evening sights in the park. Day use of the park costs $10 per vehicle.

Spencer Spit State Park has excellent campsites, but if you're pitching a tent here, you won't be the first person to do so. Not only is it a very popular destination today, but the Coast Salish people also used it for at least 3,000 years as a seasonal fish camp. In addition to camping, park facilities include 12 very popular mooring buoys ($10), drinking water, restrooms, and an RV dump station. Spencer Spit doesn't have a boat ramp or dock, but the beach is a launching spot for sea kayaks; ask at the park office for access via a service road so you don't have to carry your kayaks and gear too far. Kayak and bike rentals are available from a beachside kiosk. Kayakers heading out overnight will need to get a parking permit ($10/day).

## Odlin County Park

Located on the north end of Lopez just a mile from the ferry landing, Odlin County Park (360/468-2496, www.co.san-juan.wa.us/parks) has a sandy beach along Upright Channel with views of nearby Shaw Island.

Two short paths provide a bit of diversion here: **Big Tree Trail** leads through a stand of giant old-growth Douglas firs and **Little Bird Trail** offers up bluff-top viewpoints. Campsites, picnic areas, a boat launch, and a baseball field are also in the park, and the abundant rabbits are a treat for kids.

## Upright Channel State Park

This 20-acre park is accessible from a parking area on Military Road. A short, wooded walk takes you to four picnic tables on the beach, but public access is limited to the immediate area since adjacent beaches are private property. Four mooring buoys are just offshore.

## Agate Beach County Park

Very few of Lopez's beaches are open to the public. One exceptional exception is Agate Beach, on the south end of the island at the end of MacKaye Harbor Road. Across the road from the beach are a few parking spaces, a picnic area, and outhouses. The pebbly beach is filled with colorful wave-rounded stones. I've never found agates here, but persistent rock hounds might find a few. At low tide you can walk to the tiny island just offshore.

## ◖ Iceberg Point

Located on the southern end of the island, picture-perfect Iceberg Point is accessed from the parking lot at Agate Beach County Park. Walk south up MacKaye Harbor Road past signs noting End of County Road and Private Road for 100 yards or so, before turning right at the small Iceberg Point sign. A trail (no bikes) leads 0.5 mile through the bird-filled forest (look for salmonberries in early summer) to open grassy slopes and rocks at the end of the point. On a clear day you'll be treated

Agate Beach

to vistas of Mount Baker and the Cascade Range to the east, with the Olympics rising to the southwest. The land is managed by the Bureau of Land Management; get a map from its Lopez Village office to make sure you're not trespassing. Do not drive on the private road. The **Iceberg Point Project** (www.icebergpointproject.org) is conducting ongoing bird studies here.

## Lopez Hill

Managed by San Juan County Land Bank (360/378-4402, www.sjclandbank.org), Lopez Hill is a 400-acre parcel of wooded land near the center of the island with access from Lopez Sound Road. A maze of trails provides several miles of fun hiking, horseback riding, and mountain biking. The **Friends of Lopez Hill** produces a helpful map showing hiking trails and access; get a copy from the chamber of commerce or download one at www.lopezhill.org.

## Shark Reef Park

A fine small natural area is Shark Reef Park, at the end of Shark Reef Road on the southwest side of Lopez. An easy 0.5-mile path takes you through one of the few old-growth stands of trees (including Douglas fir, lodgepole pine, and Pacific yews) left on the island. It ends at a rocky coastline, a good place to look for harbor seals and sea lions sunning on nearby rocks, while bald eagles wheel through the sky and black oystercatchers call from the rocks. Less than a mile away is the southern end of San Juan Island, with the grassy slopes of American Camp capped by Cattle Point Lighthouse. The narrow passage frequently develops turbulent flows when the tide is changing. Tiny **Deadman Island**—just offshore south of Shark Reef—is owned by The Nature Conservancy (206/343-4344, www.tnc-washington.org); no public access.

## Weeks Wetland Preserve

This 22-acre saltwater marsh is on the north end of Fisherman Bay and adjacent to Lopez Village. A short loop trail leads to an observation deck overlooking this important resting

© DON PITCHER

LOPEZ ISLAND

Shark Reef Park

© DON PITCHER

area for migrating birds, and interpretive signs describe the animals and plants that live here.

## Otis Perkins County Park and The Spit

The scenic beach at Otis Perkins County Park—one of the longest on the islands—is located along Bayshore Road on the south end of Fisherman Bay. The west-facing location makes this a fine sunset stroll, with San Juan Island and the Olympic Mountains accenting the horizon. A couple of picnic tables are also here. The beach (day use only) is public north from the parking area, but to the south it becomes private property.

The north end of the peninsula is a 29-acre preserve called The Spit. Trails cut through tall grass to the shore overlooking bucolic Fisherman Bay and Lopez Village.

## ◖ Watmough Head

The Bureau of Land Management owns several easily accessible natural areas on the southeast end of Lopez Island off Watmough Head Road.

Access to this area is confusing, and local landowners sometimes have No Trespassing signs posted on public land, so contact the BLM office in Lopez Village for a detailed map and specific directions. No motorized vehicles or camping are allowed, and please follow the leave-no-trace ethic to preserve these environmentally significant places.

The most accessible area is **Watmough Bay;** look for the Watmough Bay sign on the left at the bottom of a hill in the woods. The road leads to a parking area where a 0.25-mile trail continues to a protected beach, hemmed in by rocky cliffs, a marsh, and dense woods. On a clear day, Mount Baker stands front-and-center from the pebbly shore. Don't be surprised if you see a bit of skin; nobody seems to care at this de facto nude beach. Take the trail south from the east end of the beach to a wooded ridge along **Watmough Head,** or scramble up steep slopes to nearby **Chadwick Hill** (470 feet) from the parking lot. The hill can also be accessed from an unmarked trail off Watmough Head Road.

**Point Colville** is farther out Watmough Bay Road (a rough dirt road), with access 0.25 mile beyond the sign that marks the end of county maintenance. There's a small parking area where the gate blocks the road to public access. Follow the one-mile loop trail south to the shore along the Strait of Juan de Fuca, where a small section of the beach is public land.

### Hummel Lake Preserve

A pleasant trail passes through the woods to a tiny dock along this lake near the middle of Lopez. The path starts off Center Road, where you'll find picnic tables and an outhouse. This 79-acre preserve is one of many areas protected by the San Juan County Land Bank (360/378-4402, www.sjclandbank.org).

### Blackie Brady Memorial Beach

Find this little county-owned beach on the south end of Lopez along Hughes Bay; turn right on Huggins Road off Aleck Bay Road. Huggins ends at a couple of parking spaces with stairs leading to this gorgeous cove. It's a fine, out-of-the-way place to escape.

# Entertainment and Events

The modern **Lopez Center for Community and the Arts** (204 Village Rd., 360/468-2203, www.lopezcenter.com) was built entirely with local funding and is used for concerts, art exhibitions, theatrical productions, and other activities. Outdoor pavilion concerts are a staple in the summer months here.

Located at Lopez Islander Resort (2864 Fisherman Bay Rd., 360/468-2233 or 800/736-3434, www.lopezfun.com), **Tiki Cocktail Lounge** has two pool tables and occasional live music on summer weekends. **Galley Restaurant and Lounge** (3365 Fisherman Bay Rd., 360/468-2713, www.galleylopez.com) has a pool table and live music on an irregular basis.

Held the last Saturday of April, the **Tour de Lopez** is a non-competitive 5-, 10-, 18-, or 31-mile ride around the island, with a big community barbecue lunch afterward. This is a great family event with a maximum of 750 people. Register online at www.lopezisland.

com/tourdelopez.htm by mid-January to be assured of a space.

The big event in Lopez Village comes, not surprisingly, on the **Fourth of July,** with a corny parade, fun run, salmon barbecue, live music, arts fair, library book sale, and a big display of fireworks (www.lopezfireworks.com) over Fisherman Bay. It's said to be the largest private fireworks display in Washington, attracting multitudes of people to the island.

The popular **Lopez Island Studio Tour** (www.lopezisland.com/studiotour) takes place over Labor Day weekend, with 30 or so artists participating.

You can also join in the fun at the annual **Harvest Festival** at Lopez Island Vineyards & Winery (360/468-3644, www.lopezislandvineyards.com) in early October. It's a combination party and community grape harvest. Held the Friday after Thanksgiving, **Winter Village Gathering** brings holiday lights, decorations, bonfires, Christmas carols, and other traditions.

**LOPEZ ISLAND**

# Shopping

Note that many Lopez businesses are closed Monday (and some also on Tuesday) in the summer and some aren't open at all in the winter.

Get books and cards from cozy **Islehaven Books** (Lopez Village, 360/468-2132, www.islehavenbooks.com). **Paper Scissors on the Rock** (131 Weeks Rd., 360/468-2294) is a stationery and arts and crafts shop that also has a good selection of cards, gifts, and toys.

For fashion on the cheap, head to the **Lopez Thrift Shop** at 83 Weeks Point Way.

## GALLERIES

The **Lopez Artist Guild** website (www.lopezartistguild.com) provides descriptions of local artists. Don't miss **Chimera Gallery** (Lopez Village Plaza, 360/468-3265, www.chimeragallery.com), a cooperatively run gallery with unusual blown-glass pieces, etchings, ceramics, watercolors, pottery, sweaters, cedar baskets, and jewelry. Also of interest in the village is **Gallery 10 Fine Art** (265 Lopez Rd., 360/468-4910), offering works from local artists and a little boutique for clothing and accessories. Next door is **Lo-Co** (360/468-3818), short for Lopez Island's Co-op of Fine Crafters, with a variety of island crafts, jewelry, photography, and pottery.

**Colin Goode Gallery** (95 Village Rd., 360/468-4715) has a small shop showing regional artists; it's across from the farmers market. Farther afield—on the north end of the island—is **Christa Malay Studio** (341 Shoal Bay Lane, 360/468-2159, www.christamalay.com), which exhibits her bright watercolor, oil, and pastel paintings. Open by appointment only. Renowned painter Steven Hill exhibits his pastels at **Windswept Studios** (783 Port Stanley Rd., 360/468-2557, www.windsweptstudios.com).

# Recreation

The **Lopez Island Family Resource Center** (360/468-4117, www.lifrc.org) puts on a wide range of activities open to the general public, from sailing lessons to kayaking and watercolor classes.

## ◖ BIKING

A favorite local activity is pedaling the 30-mile loop around Lopez Island. Once you get beyond the steep initial climb from the ferry dock, the rest of the island consists of gently rolling hills, making Lopez ideal for family rides. Center Road is relatively busy and best avoided, but most of the other roads don't see a lot of traffic.

In business since 1978, **Lopez Bicycle Works** (at Lopez Islander Resort, 2864 Fisherman Bay Rd., 360/468-2847, www.lopezbicycleworks.com) is the oldest bike shop on the San Juans. Mountain bikes rent for $7 per hour or $30 per day, including a helmet. Tandem, road bikes, children's bikes, recumbent bikes, trailer carts, and panniers are also available. Reservations are recommended, especially for midsummer weekends. The shop is open daily late May–early September, but bikes may be available in the off-season if you call ahead. The shop can drop off or pick up bikes at your lodging place or the ferry early in the morning for a small fee. No tours are offered, but the island is easy enough for almost anyone, and it's hard to get lost.

A full-service bike shop in the heart of Lopez Village, **Village Cycles** (9 Old Post Rd., 360/469-4013, www.villagecycles.net, Mar.–Oct.) rents hybrids, road, and mountain bikes, plus child bikes, tagalongs, and bike trailers. Standard bikes start at $7 per hour or $45 per

© DON PITCHER

cyclists on Lopez Island

day; add $5 for delivery to the ferry terminal. Tours start at $55 for a two-hour ride, everything provided.

Seasonal mountain bike rentals are also available from a small kiosk within Spencer Spit State Park operated by **Outdoor Adventures Center** (425/883-9039 or 800/282-4043, www.outdooradventurecenter.com) for $5 per hour or $25 per day.

For Lopez Island **cycling tours,** contact **Backroads** (510/527-1555 or 800/462-2848, www.backroads.com) or **Bicycle Adventures** (360/786-0989 or 800/443-6060, www.bicycleadventures.com).

## SEA KAYAKING

If you're taking your kayak on the ferry to Lopez, note that you can't access the water near the ferry terminal. The closest put-in is Odlin County Park, a mile away. Other commonly used places to put your kayak in the water include Spencer Spit State Park, the marinas on Fisherman Bay, and boat ramps at MacKaye Harbor and Hunter Bay.

On the grounds of Lopez Islander Resort, **Lopez Kayaks** (2845 Fisherman Bay Rd., 360/468-2847, www.lopezkayaks.com, late May–Sept.) rents and sells sea kayaks from its beach location along Fisherman Bay. Double plastic kayaks go for $60 per day ($70/day for fiberglass touring doubles), and guided day trips may also be available. Lopez Bicycle Works has a shop right next door; they're father-and-son operations.

Adjacent to Vortex Juice Bar in Lopez Village, **Cascadia Kayak Tours** (360/468-3008, www.cascadiakayaktours.com) leads a variety of professionally guided trips, including a half-day paddle for $69, and full-day tours for $99 with a gourmet lunch. Two-day trips take you to Jones Island for $330.

The **Outdoor Adventures Center** (425/883-9039 or 800/282-4043, www.outdooradventurecenter.com) rents sea kayaks and bikes from a kiosk at Spencer Spit State Park. It's open daily in the summer and weekends through September, with singles, doubles, and triples available by the hour. Rent a kayak to

**LOPEZ ISLAND**

paddle across to James Island or to explore the nearby shoreline. The company also has various tours from Spencer Spit, from a three-hour guided paddle up to multi-night explorations of the San Juans.

## BOATING, FISHING, AND WHALE-WATCHING

Lopez's two marinas are next to each other along Fisherman Bay. Both offer guest moorage, boat launching ramps, and restrooms with showers. It's less than a mile from the marinas to "downtown" Lopez Village. **Islands Marine Center** (360/468-3377, www.islandsmarinecenter.com) has a 100-slip marina and the largest marine repair operation in the San Juans, plus a chandlery, marine supplies, fishing licenses, boat launch ramp, showers, and apartment rentals. Immediately to the south is **Lopez Islander Resort and Marina** (360/468-2233 or 800/736-3434, www.lopezfun.com), with a 64-slip marina, boat fuel, propane, laundry, and groceries, plus a small resort with lodging, camping, RV sites, a restaurant, gift shop, and lounge. Just down the road is a dock and transient slips for boaters visiting Galley Restaurant and Lounge.

Patrick Cotton of **Harmony Charters** (360/468-3310, www.harmonycharters.com) rents a luxurious 65-foot motor yacht, the *Countess,* for $425 per person per day including meals and crew. The boat is based in Fisherman Bay, and there's a four-person minimum, with a maximum of six.

You'll find public boat-launch ramps at Odlin County Park on the north end of the island, and at MacKaye Harbor and Hunter Bay on the south end.

Fishing charters—primarily for salmon and halibut—are offered by **Outer Island Expeditions** (360/376-3711, www.outer-islandx.com) and **North Shore Charters** (360/376-4855, www.orcasislandadventures. com). Expect to pay around $165 per person for an all-day fishing expedition. Join Outer Island for a 3–5 hour **whale watching** tour; these depart Lopez Islander Resort and cost $109 adults or $89 kids.

Anglers may want to drop a line at **Hummel Lake,** just a mile east of Lopez Village along Hummel Lake Road. The largest freshwater lake on Lopez, this is also a pleasant spot for a picnic lunch if you're cycling around the island. A trail leads into a small cedar grove and eventually winds up at the floating dock.

## GOLF AND FITNESS

**Lopez Island Golf Club** (360/468-2679, www.lopezislandgolf.com, year-round, $25) is a nine-hole, par-35 public course along Airport Road.

Housed within Lopez Islander Resort, **Lopez Islander Gym** (2864 Fisherman Bay Rd., 360/468-4911, www.lopezfun.com) has exercise equipment and tanning booths. A $6 day pass includes access to the seasonal outdoor pool and year-round hot tub, $10 also gets you in the gym.

# Accommodations

Only 80 or so rooms are available on Lopez Island, so it's a good idea to make reservations a month or more ahead of time to be assured of a space, particularly on summer weekends. If you want to stay at a specific place, make reservations in January or February for a midsummer date. Many of the resorts, inns, and cottages also offer weekly rates. The Lopez Chamber of Commerce website (www.lopezisland.com) has links to local lodgings. All lodging prices quoted below are subject to an additional 9.8 percent tax.

## WEEKLY RENTALS

For furnished homes on a weekly basis, contact **Lopez Village Properties** (360/468-5055 or 888/772-9735, www.lopezisproperties.com) with more than 65 vacation rental properties on Lopez. These vary greatly, starting at $750 per week for a cozy cabin to $3,000 for a four-bedroom waterfront estate with its own mooring buoy. **Windermere Vacation Doorways** (360/378-3601 or 800/391-8190, www.vacationdoorways.com) and **Lopez Islander Resort** (360/468-2233 or 800/736-3434, www.lopezfun.com) also have weekly rentals around Lopez. Some of these may be available for shorter (three days and up) rentals.

For additional weekly rentals on Lopez, browse over to **VRBO** (www.vrbo.com), **CyberRentals** (www.cyberrentals.com), or **Homeaway** (www.homeaway.com). Also check out such websites as **Airbnb** (www.airbnb.com), **CouchSurfing** (www.couchsurfing.org), or **GlobalFreeloaders** (www.globalfreeloaders.com).

## RESORTS
### Lopez Islander Resort

Less than a mile south of Lopez Village, Lopez Islander Resort (2864 Fisherman Bay Rd., 360/468-2233 or 800/736-3434, www.lopezfun.com) is an unpretentious, family-friendly spot. Small motel-style units ($139–189 d) have queen- or king-size beds, mini-fridges, and microwaves; upstairs rooms include decks facing the water. There's a two-night minimum on summer weekends, or three nights over holiday weekends. Also available are two modern and spacious family suites with three bedrooms, full kitchens (with dishes, utensils, and pans), and gas fireplaces for $289–299 per night or $1,500–1,600 per week for up to eight guests. A three-night minimum is required for the suites. Three nearby guesthouses provide plenty of room for families and groups; $275–325 per night or $1,200–1,900 per week. All lodging rates are approximately 15 percent lower Sunday–Thursday nights. Also at the resort are a very popular seasonal outdoor pool (only one on the island), year-round hot tub, volleyball court, horseshoes, marina, restaurant, lounge, and limited Wi-Fi. Catch the free shuttle from the ferry or airport; Kenmore Air has direct floatplane flights from Seattle. This is a favorite place for boaters to pull in and dry out awhile.

## GUESTHOUSES AND COTTAGES
### At Home on McBarron Lane

One of the most unique places on Lopez Island, At Home on McBarron Lane (109 McBarron Lane, 206/329-3914, www.nowakhouse.com, $198 d) was built in 2008 by Seattle glass artist James Nowak. Given its heritage, the enormous front windows shouldn't be a surprise, and the interior has a European elegance accented by the artist's blown-glass pieces. There's a loft bedroom, modern kitchen, living room with gas stove, bath with Italian tiles, flat-screen TV, Wi-Fi, and a large patio. The house faces a big meadow and MacKaye Harbor. There's a two-night minimum and no children.

### ( Bay House and Garden Cottages

Two different options are available at Bay House and Garden Cottages (360/468-4889, www.interisland.net/cc). A two-bedroom house ($200 d plus $25 per person for additional guests) on Fisherman Bay has a full kitchen and stone fireplace, with an outside deck facing across the channel to San Juan Island. Two delightful guest cottages ($150 d) are right in the heart of Lopez Village on a beautifully accented and flower-filled yard (the owners are professional landscapers). Cottages include a queen-size bed, skylights, kitchen, and woodstove. Kids ($25 extra) and dogs ($35) are welcome.

## Blue Fjord Cabins

Blue Fjord Cabins (862 Elliot Rd., 360/468-2749 or 888/633-0401, www.bluefjord.com, $150 d, mid-June–mid-Sept.) consists of two secluded chalet-style log cabins in a quiet, wooded setting on the east side of the island. Each has a queen-size bed, full kitchen, skylight, covered deck, and TV/VCR. A short walk away is a gazebo set on the shore of pristine Jasper Cove, and a barred owl nests nearby. This is a fine place to relax and soak up the quietude; guests sometimes liken it to staying in an adult treehouse. A three-night minimum is required.

## Channel View Farm Guest Cottage

Surrounded by colorful perennial gardens, Channel View Farm Guest Cottage (444 Hummel Lake Rd., 360/468-4415, www.channelviewfarm.com, $135 d) overlooks a five-acre meadow. Inside, find a queen-size bed, sitting area, bath, full kitchen, and sleeping loft with twin beds. Channel View is within walking distance of Lopez Village. A two-night minimum is required, and no children under 12 are allowed because of the loft.

## Cozy Cabin on Lopez Island

Find simple, woodsy accommodations at Cozy Cabin (244 Shady Lane, 360/468-3347, www.cozycabinonlopezisland.com, $120 d), with a queen-size bed, bath, dining area, and deck. The cabin is on the north end of the island near Upright Channel State Park. A three-night summertime minimum is required, two nights the rest of the year. Closed December–January.

## Islands Marine Center

Islands Marine Center (360/468-3377, www.islandsmarinecenter.com) is the boating hub for Lopez, but it also rents out two apartments over the store and right across the road from Fisherman Bay. Each has a full kitchen with dishes, private bath, woodstove, TV, and VCR. The smaller unit rents for $85 d, and the larger one goes for $95 d. A third room can be combined with either apartment for an additional $35, and extra guests are $10 each. This is a good deal for families and groups, since doors open between all the apartments, creating a unit that includes three bedrooms, two kitchens, two baths, and two living rooms; it can sleep up to 13 guests at once! A barbecue pit and picnic tables are out front, and Lopez Islander Resort is next door.

## Lopez Lodge

Three options are available at Lopez Lodge (Weeks Point Rd., 360/468-2816, www.lopezlodge.com) in the heart of Lopez Village: a studio apartment and two motel-style rooms with Wi-Fi and TVs. The studio ($145 for up to four) includes two queen-size beds and a full kitchen, while the rooms ($75–100 d) are simpler, with a bath, fridge, and microwave.

## Lopez Retreat

A charming two-bedroom vacation home, Lopez Retreat (1795 Port Stanley Rd., 360/410-9149, www.lopezretreat.com) faces Swifts Bay close to Spencer Spit State Park. You'll find all the amenities, including a full kitchen, two baths, wraparound deck, tall windows, washer and dryer, Wi-Fi, and even a mooring buoy at this attractive home. It is primarily offered on a weekly basis ($1,200), but space may be available for shorter stays ($200/night with a three-day minimum). Book early if you plan to visit in July and August.

## Meadow Wood Cottage

Set on a quiet five-acre spread near Spencer Spit, Meadow Wood Cottage (360/468-4023 or 406/728-1777, www.rockisland.com/~joann, $145 d) is a two-bedroom, two-bath home with a full kitchen and deck. There's a four-night minimum stay in summer, three nights in winter.

## Mud Bay Cabin

A fine budget option on the south end of the island, Mud Bay Cabin (4055 Mud Bay Rd., 360/468-3726, www.interisland.net/kpatrick, $100 d) has a cozy bedroom, kitchenette, and bath, but no phone. Outside is a deck with gas barbecue plus a little hillside garden. The cabin is in the woods, but not far from the beach at Mud Bay.

## Raven's Rook Lodging

A unique in-the-trees option, Raven's Rook Lodging (58 Wild Rose Lane, 360/468-2838 or 877/321-2493, www.ravensrooklodging. com) is just a short hike from Shark Reef Park on the south end of Lopez. Inside this post-and-beam cabin ($135 d) you'll find skylights, two queen-size beds, a full kitchen, and bath. A two-night minimum stay is required. Families are welcome, but no toddlers. Two bikes are available if you want to explore the island. Not far away is a lovely octagonal home with gardens, large skylights, two queen bedrooms, and a full kitchen. There's a four-night minimum at $215 per night or $1,350 per week for four guests. No children in the main house, and it is only available mid-June–September.

## Sunset View House

An airy contemporary farmhouse, Sunset View House (43 Navarre Lane, 530/753-0841, www. sunsetviewhouse.com) is a three-bedroom, two-bath home with a full kitchen and space for up to nine guests. Weekend rates are $260 for up to four; add $17 for extra guests. The home is just a couple of blocks from Lopez Village. A minimum three-night stay is enforced during July and August. Kids are welcome.

## View Cabin on Lopez

Located on the southern part of the island, View Cabin on Lopez (1005 Richardson Rd., 360/468-2088, www.rockisland.com/-stonem, $125 d) is a good spot for a weekend escape.

High windows and a large deck provide a view west to the lights of Victoria, and the cabin has two queen-size beds, a TV, and kitchen, but no phone. There's a three-night minimum in the summer and over holidays, or two nights at other times. Kids are welcome.

## BED-AND-BREAKFASTS

### ◖ Edenwild Inn B&B

Edenwild Inn (132 Lopez Rd., 360/468-3238 or 800/606-0662, www.edenwildinn.com, $170–195 d) is a modern and elegant Victorian-style inn in the heart of Lopez Village. Rose arbors and floral gardens fill the yard, and the home itself features eight spacious and distinctive rooms, all with private baths. One room is wheelchair-accessible, and three of them have fireplaces that actually burn wood (a rarity in our turn-on-the-gas era). A filling European-style breakfast buffet is included. There are no kids under 12, TVs, or phones to disturb your relaxation, but Wi-Fi is available.

### ◖ Lopez Farm Cottages and Tent Camping

For delightful in-the-country lodging, stay at the fairy-tale Lopez Farm Cottages (555 Fisherman Bay Rd., 360/468-3555 or 800/440-3556, www.lopezfarmcottages.com, $180–190 d) just up the way from Lopez Island Vineyards. These four immaculate little cottages include kitchenettes, gas fireplaces, a continental breakfast basket, private baths with dual showerheads, and a delightful outdoor hot tub. Guests walk in the last 100 yards or so, and the intentional lack of phones, TVs, and Wi-Fi—not to mention children (kids must be 14 or older)—helps preserve the quiet character. The adjacent pasture has several sheep, and you're almost guaranteed to see rabbits hopping around the grounds in the morning. Also here is a fifth cottage that is larger and more luxurious, with a king-size bed and private outdoor hot tub ($215 d). You can drive up to this one, and it's wheelchair-accessible. Lopez Farm Cottages are especially popular with honeymooners and couples celebrating anniversaries.

© DON PITCHER

Edenwild Inn B&B

### ( MacKaye Harbor Inn

This stately white farmhouse sits near the southernmost end of Lopez, directly across the road from protected Barlow Bay. Originally constructed in 1904, MacKaye Harbor Inn (949 MacKaye Harbor Rd., 360/468-2253 or 888/314-6140, www.mackayeharborinn.com) was the first place on Lopez to have electric lights. Today, four guest rooms ($175–195 d) and a lovely suite ($235 d) are available, all with private baths. The suite features a fireplace, private covered deck facing the setting sun, antique Italian furnishings, and a bath. The inn is just a stone's throw from a sandy beach where seals, otters, and eagles are common sights. Rent sea kayaks ($25/day) to explore nearby waters, or borrow a mountain bike to ride around the island. Guests are served a filling hot breakfast, along with port and chocolates in the evening. Children 12 and up are welcome, and Wi-Fi is available. The inn is a dozen miles from the restaurants in Lopez Village, though the Islandale Store is relatively close for groceries and deli meals.

## CAMPING

Camping is available at four places on Lopez, but the two public campgrounds do not have showers. Coin-operated showers are available at the public restrooms near Lopez Village Market and the marinas on Fisherman Bay.

### Odlin County Park

Just a mile south of the ferry landing, Odlin County Park (360/378-8420, www.sanjuanco.com/parks) has year-round waterfront campsites ($25), wooded sites ($22), and walk-in ($20) or shared hike-in/bike-in sites ($8). There are no RV hookups or showers, but the park does have a boat ramp, mooring buoy ($10), a sandy beach, and hiking trails. Make reservations ($7 extra) online only through the park website. Reservations are available April–October, and can be made five days to three months ahead; they're a wise idea on summer weekends.

### ( Spencer Spit State Park

Spencer Spit State Park (360/468-2251, www.parks.wa.gov, open Mar.–Oct.), five miles from

# FINNISH PANCAKES (PANNUKAKKU)

8 eggs
¼ cup honey
½ teaspoon salt
2½ cups milk
⅔ cup flour
4 tablespoons butter

Blend all ingredients except butter in a blender, alternating flour and milk last. Melt 4 tablespoons of butter in a large baking dish or pan (9 by 13 inches). Pour blended mixture into this dish and bake at 425°F for 20-25 minutes until puffed and golden. Drizzle with hot jam or sprinkle with nutmeg or powered sugar. Serves 6-8 people. This recipe is almost like having custard for breakfast, something gentle for the awakening tummy and tongue.

*Recipe courtesy of MacKaye Harbor Inn*

the ferry landing on the east end of Baker View Road, has standard campsites ($21–26) and bike/hike sites ($12), along with Adirondack-style shelters ($26) for groups. No showers or RV hookups, but there are restrooms and a dump station. The delightful sandy spit is a short walk from the campground. All sites fill early on summer weekends, so make reservations in advance ($10 fee) at 888/226-7688 or through the park website. The separate Cascadia Marine Trail campsite ($12) within

the park is accessible by kayak or other beach-able boat only.

## ◖ Lopez Farm Cottages and Tent Camping

Located on a 30-acre spread, Lopez Farm Cottages and Tent Camping (555 Fisherman Bay Rd., 360/468-3555 or 800/440-3556, www.lopezfarmcottages.com, $45 d, $10 for each additional guest, open late May–Sept.) has 13 nicely designed walk-in "gourmet" campsites in the woods with hammocks, Adirondack chairs, barbecues, fireplaces, croquet, and badminton, plus a central building for cooking and showers. Tent sites are ideal for couples and families, but no RVs are allowed. Don't want to bring a tent and sleeping bags? One site has been set up as a "camp nest": The tent is already set up on a carpeted platform, with a queen-size futon bed made up inside and a cooler outside for $85 d. All you need is a toothbrush and bath towel. Parking is in a separate location to cut down on noise and nighttime headlights.

### Lopez Islander Resort

Less than a mile from Lopez Village, this centrally located resort (2864 Fisherman Bay Rd., 360/468-2233 or 800/736-3434, www.lopezfun.com) has an abundance of in-the-open tent sites ($25) on the lawn, along with woodsy RV sites ($35 with water and electricity). The shower house is next to a seasonal pool and year-round hot tub ($6 for a day pass), volleyball, and horseshoes. Kayak and bike rentals are available at the resort, which also has a full-service marina, motel, and restaurant.

LOPEZ ISLAND

# Food

Dining choices on Lopez are good but a bit limited, particularly in the winter when many places are shuttered. Get there on a Tuesday evening in November and you'll find only a couple of places open. In addition, local restaurants have a tough time finding workers so may not be open for breakfast and lunch. The island's premier fine dining place for 25 years, The Bay Café, closed in 2012, but locals are hoping a new restaurant will open in its location.

Lopez Island's most famous product—ice cream—is no longer made on the island. Established in 1993, **Lopez Island Creamery** (www.lopezislandcreamery.com) is regionally famous for ultra-creamy (16 percent milk fat) gourmet ice creams, including wild blackberry, cappuccino chunk, and lemon raspberry swirl. In 2010 the creamery moved from Lopez to Anacortes to be closer to regional markets. Today, Lopez Island Creamery sells its ice cream by the pint throughout western Washington.

## BAKERIES, CAFÉS, AND SWEETS

**⟨ Holly B's Bakery** (Lopez Village, 360/468-2133, www.hollybsbakery.com, 7 A.M.–5 P.M. Wed.–Sat., 7 A.M.–4 P.M. Sun., closed Dec.–Mar., $3–5), begun by Holly Bower in 1978, is *the* place to go for great breads, cookies, almond butterhorns, raspberry scones, gruyere croissants, and enormous cinnamon rolls, plus focaccia and pizza by the slice. Check out the "Holly's Buns Are Best" T-shirts. Holly is the author of *With Love and Butter,* a beautiful cookbook–*cum*–island history.

Next door is **⟨ Caffé la Boheme** (360/468-3533, 7 A.M.–4 P.M. Mon.–Sat., 7 A.M.–2 P.M. Sun., $3–5), where owner Robert Hermann serves the finest—bar none—espresso anywhere in the San Juans. He'll also fill you in on the latest in island politics and gossip. Just up the road, **Isabel's Espresso** (360/468-4114, 7:30 A.M.–5 P.M. daily) is a relaxed hangout with a large outdoors deck that attracts locals.

Also in the village—and just steps from Holly B's—is **Bucky's Lopez Island Grill** (360/468-2595, 11:30 A.M.–8 P.M. daily Apr.–Sept., $9–10). Check the board for today's lunch or dinner specials, or try one of the justly famous fish tacos. The black and bleu burger (with Cajun spices and blue cheese) is another favorite. Dine inside, or on the waterside deck.

## QUICK BITES

Located in the Homestead Building within Lopez Village, **Vortex Juice Bar** (360/468-4740, www.vortexjuicebarandcafe.com, 10 A.M.–7 P.M. Mon.–Sat., till 6 P.M. in winter, $4–11) serves healthy food using organic produce and ingredients whenever possible. On the menu are burritos, wraps, salads, daily soups, smoothies, housemade chai tea, and a big choice of fruit and vegetable juice combinations. Faves include the black beans and corn wrap, and the salmon, cream cheese, and feta version. For something different, try the green juice, blended from greens, celery, cucumber, and parsley. There are a few indoor seats, plus a couple of tables outside on the deck facing the old apple orchard.

Open for wildly delicious lunches and dinners to go, **⟨ Vita's Wildly Delicious** (77 Village Rd., 360/468-4268, www.vitaswildlydelicious.com, 11 A.M.–5 P.M. Mon.–Sat., May–Sept., 11 A.M.–5 P.M. Sat. only Oct.–Apr.) is right across from the farmers market on Village Road North. Check the chalkboard for today's gourmet paninis ($9), or scan the deli for other favorites, including chicken satay, meatloaf, shrimp cakes with chipotle sauce, Lopez lamb pies, salads, and a delectable green-chili chicken breast. One side of the shop is devoted to an extraordinary selection of organic wines and small-production wines you'll never find at Safeway. Wine is also available by the

Vita's Wildly Delicious

glass. Seating is limited inside, but colorful picnic tables are on the front patio. Service can be slow, so don't come here in a hurry.

## AMERICAN

In business since 1971, **Galley Restaurant and Lounge** (3365 Fisherman Bay Rd., 360/468-2713, www.galleylopez.com) is right across the street from Fisherman Bay; there's even a dock for customers' boats. The working-class restaurant is open three meals daily, covering the basics with seafood, steaks, pasta, Mexican specialties, and double-size bacon cheeseburgers. The food is surprisingly consistent, hence the always-packed parking lot out front. There's a bar with a half-dozen beers on tap, along with a pool table and sports on the television. The restaurant is open daily 8 A.M.–9 P.M., but the bar stays open much later. If you visit Lopez on a weekday in the off-season, this may be the only restaurant open in the evening.

If you're looking for a real slice of life on the "rock," drop by **Lopez Island Soda Fountain** (157 Village Rd. in Lopez Village, 360/468-4511, www.lopezislandpharmacy.com, 7:30 A.M.–5 P.M. Mon.–Sat.). The old-fashioned soda fountain fills at lunch, serving soups, sandwiches, malts, sundaes, ice cream sodas, and banana splits. Breakfast is available till 11 A.M., and they'll put together a box lunch if you call ahead.

Housed within Lopez Islander Resort, **Islander Restaurant & Tiki Lounge** (2864 Fisherman Bay Rd., 360/468-2233 or 800/736-3434, www.lopezfun.com, $17–24 entrées) serves prime rib and seafood dinners, but it also opens for lunch daily and breakfast on weekends. The main attraction here isn't so much the food as the view from the harborside patio, out back. It' a great spot for a sunset drink.

## MARKETS

Get groceries and general merchandise from **Lopez Village Market** (162 Weeks Rd., 360/468-2266, www.lopezvillagemarket.com, 7:30 A.M.–8 P.M. daily year-round). The store moved and greatly expanded several years ago, and features a deli, bakery, ATM, fresh produce, seafood, meats, bulk foods, wine, beer, firewood, and general merchandise. The deli

LOPEZ ISLAND

© DON PITCHER

serves everything from fried chicken and burgers to pizza slices and pies.

**Lopez Liquor Store** (Lopez Village, 360/468-2407, Tues.–Sat.) sells the hard stuff, along with beer and wine.

In the heart of Lopez Village, **Blossom Grocery** (360/468-2204, www.blossomgrocery.com, 9 A.M.–7 P.M. Mon.–Sat., 10 A.M.–5 P.M. Sun.) focuses on organic fare, including cheeses, milk, bulk foods, nuts, herbs, and local produce, along with island-raised lamb, beef, and pork.

On the south end of the island, the **Islandale Store** (3024 Mud Bay Rd., 360/468-2315, 7 A.M.–7 P.M. Mon.–Fri., 8 A.M.–7 P.M. Sat., 9 A.M.–5 P.M. Sun.) has a fair choice of groceries, supplies, beer, wine, and gas. In the rear of the store, **South Island Bistro** (360/468-3566, www.lopezislandcatering.com, 11 A.M.–2 P.M. Tues.–Sat., closed Sun.–Mon.) cranks out burgers, deli sandwiches, pizzas, and quiche, plus breakfasts—including biscuits and gravy. The back deck and lawn are fun on a summer afternoon.

The popular **Lopez Island Farmers Market** (www.lopezfarmersmarket.com, 10 A.M.–2 P.M. Sat. mid-May–early Sept.) in the village has fresh garden produce, flowers, preserves, plants, and eggs, along with arts and crafts.

# Information and Services

Get local information at the helpful **Lopez Island Chamber of Commerce** (265 Lopez Rd., 360/468-4664, www.lopezisland.com, 11 A.M.–3 P.M. Tues.–Sat. late May–early Sept., 11 A.M.–3 P.M. Tues., Thurs.–Sat. fall and spring, 10 A.M.–2 P.M. Tues., Thurs.–Sat. Nov.–Mar.). It's in Lopez Village across from Isabel's. Be sure to pick up the free *Map and Guide of Lopez Island* here or at the museum.

Quaint **Lopez Island Library** (Fisherman Bay and Hummel Lake Rds., 360/468-2265, www.lopezlibrary.org, 10 A.M.–5 P.M. Mon. and Sat., 10 A.M.–6 P.M. Tues., Thurs., and Fri., 10 A.M.–9 P.M. Wed., closed Sun.) is close to Lopez Village. Use the computers here to check your email or surf the web; free Wi-Fi. This library gets more usage per capita than any other in Washington.

## LAUNDRY

Wash clothes at the self-service **Keep It Clean Laundry** (865 Fisherman Bay Rd., 360/468-3466), a mile north of Lopez Village; it's open daily.

## LOPEZ ISLAND MILEAGE

|  | Ferry Landing | Spencer Spit State Park | Lopez Village | Agate Beach | Islandale Store |
|---|---|---|---|---|---|
| Spencer Spit State Park | 3 |  |  |  |  |
| Lopez Village | 4 | 4 |  |  |  |
| Agate Beach | 15 | 10 | 11 |  |  |
| Islandale Store | 14 | 15 | 12 | 7 |  |
| Shark Reef | 9 | 19 | 6 | 5 | 5 |

## KIDS' STUFF

Activities for kids are mostly do-it-yourself on Lopez, though they will certainly appreciate the downtown hot dog stand and the old-fashioned soda fountain. Lopez Elementary School has a **playground,** and **Lopez Children's Center** (160 Village Rd., 360/468-3896, www.lopezchildrenscenter.com) provides day care on a space-available basis in a wonderful setting. The island's beaches, bike routes, and wooded trails provide popular family activities.

## BANKING AND MAIL

Get cash from ATMs at **Islanders Bank** (45 Weeks Rd., 360/468-2295 or 800/843-5441, www.islandersbank.com) or **Lopez Village Market** (162 Weeks Rd., 360/468-2266, www.lopezvillagemarket.com).

Take care of your mailing needs at the **Lopez Post Office** (Weeks Rd., 360/468-2282) in Lopez Village.

## MEDICAL AND VETERINARY CARE

**Lopez Island Medical Clinic** in Lopez Village (157 Village Rd., 360/468-2245, www.lopezislandmedical.org, 9 A.M.–5 P.M. Mon.–Fri.) has a physician or nurse practitioner on duty, along with a lab and X-ray services. The clinic is open for primary care and emergencies. The closest hospital is in Anacortes. Fill your prescriptions at **Lopez Island Pharmacy** (352 Lopez Rd., 360/468-2616, www.lopezislandpharmacy.com, 9 A.M.–6 P.M. Mon.–Fri.).

For pet care, contact **Ark Veterinary Clinic** (262 Weeks Rd., 360/468-2477).

# Getting There and Around

There is no bus service, car rentals, or taxi service on Lopez. Hitchhiking is not uncommon on Lopez Island, but you might end up in the back of a pickup atop a load of hay. It's relatively easy to get a ride from the ferry to Lopez Village if a ferry is off-loading.

## WASHINGTON STATE FERRIES

Washington State Ferries (360/468-4095 for the Lopez ferry terminal, 206/464-6400 or 888/808-7977 for general info) dock at the north end of Lopez Island at Upright Head, about four miles from Lopez Village. Credit cards are accepted at the Lopez ferry terminal. Find all the details—including current ferry wait times—at www.wsdot.wa.gov/ferries.

Tickets are needed if you're heading west from Lopez to Shaw, Orcas, or San Juan Islands, but not for travel east to Anacortes (even with a vehicle). Peak-season fares from Anacortes to Lopez are $11.50 for passengers and walk-ons, or $37.75 for a car and driver. Bikes are $4 extra, and kayaks cost $14.25 more. The fare for a car and driver to any of the other islands is $23.50; walk-ons and passengers ride free between the islands. Reservations are not available for any of these runs, so you'll need to get in line and wait. Vehicle reservations *are,* however, recommended at least 24 hours in advance if you're heading west on the runs from Lopez Island to Sidney, British Columbia. These tickets to Vancouver Island cost $29 for a car and driver or $6.30 for passengers and walk-ons.

Here's a somewhat confusing tip that isn't widely publicized: If you're planning a short stop on Shaw Island or Orcas Island and then continuing westward to another island within 24 hours, request a **free vehicle transfer** before leaving the Lopez terminal. This is useful if you're on Lopez and heading to Friday Harbor (free stops at Shaw and Orcas), or going from Lopez to Orcas (free stop at Shaw). It saves you $23.50 for each stop, but you must ask for it on Lopez. Note that you cannot stop for more than 24 hours when using a vehicle transfer.

LOPEZ ISLAND

Lopez Island ferry dock

## BY AIR

Operating out of Seattle's Lake Union, **Kenmore Air** (425/486-1257 or 866/435-9524, www.kenmoreair.com) has daily scheduled floatplane flights to the Lopez Islander Resort Marina. A 24-pound baggage weight limit is in effect on these flights, and excess baggage costs $1 per pound.

**San Juan Airlines** (360/293-4691 or 800/874-4434, www.sanjuanairlines.com) has scheduled daily service to Lopez Airport from Anacortes and Bellingham, with connecting flights to San Juan, Orcas, Decatur, and Blakely Islands. Flightseeing and air charters are also available.

**Northwest Sky Ferry** (360/696-9999, www.nwskyferry.com) has twice-daily flights from Bellingham to Lopez, San Juan, and Orcas Islands, with flightpooling charters to other destinations throughout the San Juan Islands.

# OTHER SAN JUAN ISLANDS

In addition to the three main islands, the San Juan archipelago contains a myriad of smaller ones, including some islets that only appear at low tide. Shaw Island is served by the ferry system but has limited services. Lummi Island is just a short distance from the mainland and is served by an hourly ferry. Of the remaining islands, only Blakely and Decatur Islands have stores. The rest are either marine state parks, part of the San Juan Islands National Wildlife Refuge, or dominated by private property.

This chapter begins with coverage of Shaw and Lummi Islands, followed by descriptions of the various marine state parks and private islands, places often called the "outer islands." Even though these islands are not widely known outside the region, many still see large numbers of boat-in visitors, especially on summer weekends. This is particularly true for the marine state parks on Clark, James, Jones, Matia, Patos, Stuart, Sucia, and Turn Islands, where the campsites fill quickly and protected coves are dotted with motor yachts and sailboats.

The **San Juan Islands National Wildlife Refuge** encompasses 83 islands, islets, and reefs within the archipelago. The largest, Matia Island, covers 145 acres, while many more are just tiny rocky points. These islands are vital nesting areas for bald eagles and seabirds, including pelagic and double-crested cormorants, pigeon guillemots, rhinoceros auklets, black oystercatchers, and glaucous-winged gulls. Tufted puffins are also present in these waters, but they only breed on

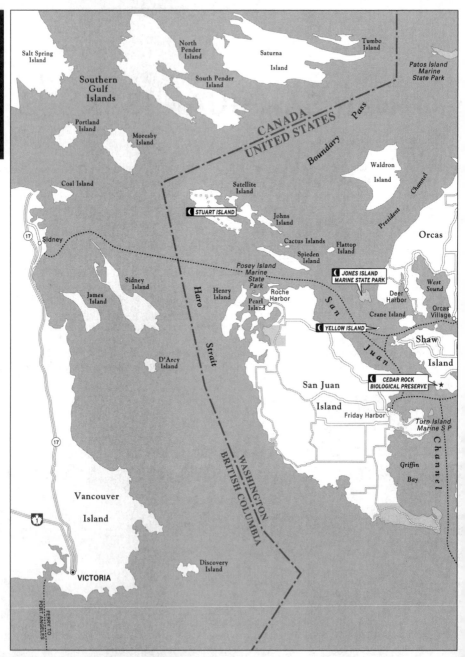

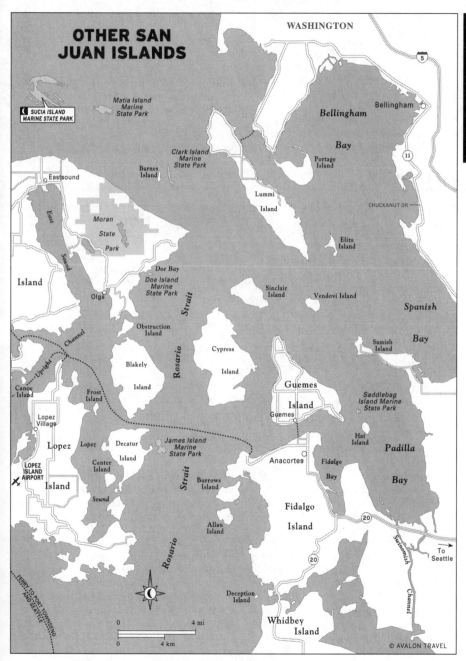

# OTHER SAN JUAN ISLANDS

WASHINGTON

Sucia Island Marine State Park

Matia Island Marine State Park

Clark Island Marine State Park

Barnes Island

Eastsound

East Sound

Moran State Park

Olga

Doe Bay

Doe Island Marine State Park

Island

Strait

Rosario

Obstruction Island

Blakely Island

Cypress Island

Frost Island

Canoe Island

Lopez Village

LOPEZ ISLAND AIRPORT

Lopez

Decatur Island

Center Island

James Island Marine State Park

Burrows Island

Sound

Island

Allan Island

Rosario

Strait

Rosario

FERRY TO PORT TOWNSEND AND SEATTLE

0        4 mi
0        4 km

Bellingham

Bellingham Bay

Portage Island

Lummi Island

CHUCKANUT DR

Eliza Island

Sinclair Island

Vendovi Island

Spanish

Samish Island

Bay

Saddlebag Island Marine State Park

Guemes Island

Guemes

Hat Island

Padilla Bay

Anacortes

Fidalgo Bay

Fidalgo Island

20

20

Swinomish Channel

To Seattle

Deception Island

Whidbey Island

© AVALON TRAVEL

# HIGHLIGHTS

🌓 **Cedar Rock Biological Preserve:**
Owned by the University of Washington, this little-known gem is located on the south side of Shaw Island (page 242).

🌓 **Jones Island Marine State Park:** A quick water-taxi ride from Orcas Island, this easily accessible marine park has fun hikes, tall trees, and a gorgeous shoreline (page 254).

🌓 **Stuart Island:** Take a water taxi from Friday Harbor to this island, where you can hike

to one of the most picturesque lighthouses in the San Juans (page 259).

🌓 **Sucia Island Marine State Park:** An exceptionally popular marine park, this diverse island is a favorite of kayakers, sailboaters, campers, and hikers (page 262).

🌓 **Yellow Island Preserve:** The Nature Conservancy allows daytime access to this 11-acre jewel, where more than 150 species of flowers bloom each spring (page 272).

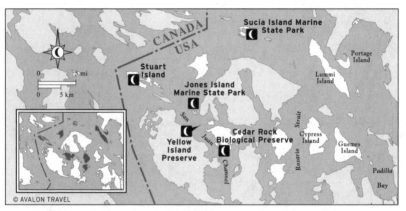

© AVALON TRAVEL

LOOK FOR 🌓 TO FIND RECOMMENDED SIGHTS, ACTIVITIES, DINING, AND LODGING.

one undisclosed island in the San Juans. The NWR islands are also used as haul-outs for harbor seals, California and Steller sea lions, elephant seals, and other animals.

Boaters—including sea kayakers—must stay at least 200 yards offshore from these islands, and no landings are permitted except at designated areas on Turn and Matia Islands. The U.S. Fish & Wildlife Service office (Port Angeles, 360/457-8451, http://pacific.fws.gov) manages the refuge and can provide a small map of the islands. Marine navigation charts also denote islands within the refuge.

## PLANNING YOUR TIME

Most travelers to the San Juans don't get beyond the three main islands: San Juan, Orcas, and Lopez, but the lesser-known islands also have much to offer, especially for those who love wild places. These less-visited islands are scattered across the archipelago and include a mix of public and private lands.

Best known of these "other islands"—and the only one visited by the state ferry system—is **Shaw Island,** home to a little country store, many well-heeled landowners, and a couple of natural areas: **Cedar Rock Biological**

Preserve, with day use only, and **Shaw Island County Park,** with a handful of campsites.

**Lummi Island** is just west of Bellingham, with access via a county-run ferry. The island has very little public land, but comfortable lodging and cafés are available.

Quite a few of the more remote islands in the San Juans are marine state parks. They are popular with boaters, kayakers, campers, and day hikers, and are accessible by water taxi from the main islands, Anacortes, or Bellingham. **Jones Island Marine State Park** is a short boat ride from Deer Harbor on Orcas Island and features good mooring, camping, and easy hikes. **Stuart Island** lies northwest of San Juan Island. Much of the island is privately owned, but the main harbors are public, and a pleasant day hike takes you to a lighthouse overlooking Boundary Pass.

**Sucia Island Marine State Park** is north of Orcas Island, with protected coves, miles of hiking and biking trails, good campsites, and a couple of sandy beaches. It's an especially popular place for sailboats to drop anchor.

A scattering of islands in the San Juans are privately owned or have only limited public access. Two of the islands (Canoe and Johns) have summer camps open to the public, and two others (Blakely and Decatur) have general stores and limited access or lodging. Sinclair Island has a boat dock and dirt roads leading to a 35-acre public park. The Nature Conservancy owns several San Juan Islands, the best known being tiny **Yellow Island,** a short water-taxi ride from Friday Harbor or Orcas Island. It's famous for springtime floral displays and is open to the public during the day.

# Shaw Island

Smallest and least visited of the ferry-served islands, Shaw is a primarily residential island where locals jealously guard their privacy. Around 200 people live here year-round, with two or three times that in the summer. Covering a bit less than eight square miles, it is the fifth largest of the San Juans (after Orcas, San Juan, Lopez, and Cypress). It sits at the center of the San Juan archipelago, with the Orcas ferry landing just a mile and a half away from the Shaw ferry dock. A number of well-known and wealthy business leaders have homes on the island, including Bill Gates Sr., members of the Kaiser family, and executives from Boeing and the *Seattle Times.* Bill Gates Jr. also owns hundreds of acres of land on Shaw and may or may not have a house here.

Shaw Island received its appellation during the 1841 Wilkes Expedition, and was named for U.S. naval captain John Shaw, who fought against the Barbary pirate states in 1815. The island was home to the Coast Salish people for thousands of years; one archaeological site at

Blind Bay is 9,000 years old. The island supported far more people than now live here, with almost 750 Native Americans living here in the 1700s. Many of them died from diseases brought by Europeans or from raids by the Haidas, but some remained on the island. A few Salish women married American settlers.

Shaw Island remains essentially undeveloped, with second-growth forests, old orchards, and pastures covering most of the land. Prominently posted No Trespassing signs limit access to all but a few beaches. To outsiders, Shaw Islanders appear insular (guess that shouldn't be surprising, given their location) and anxious to keep the rest of the world—and you in particular—away. Too bad they couldn't take a few lessons from their friendly Lopez Island neighbors! But Shaw Islanders really don't care what the rest of the world does. They relish their peaceful and slow-paced life, the lush landscape, and a grade school where the teacher-to-student ratio is 1:6. The island has a general store, one lodging place, a little

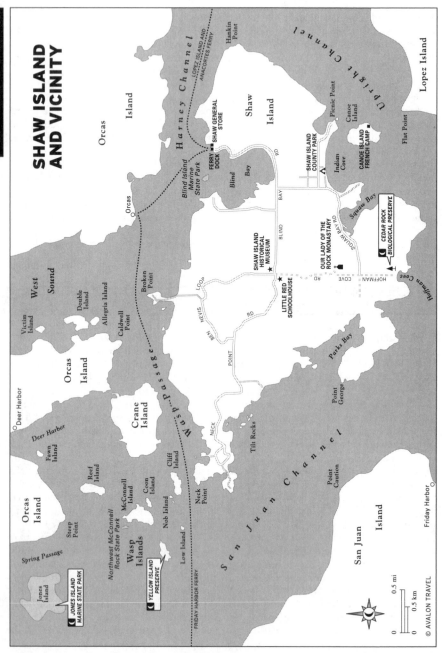

# SHAW ISLAND AND VICINITY

Orcas Island

Harney Channel

LOPEZ ISLAND AND ANACORTES FERRY

Hankin Point

SHAW GENERAL STORE

Shaw Island

FERRY DOCK

Blind Island Marine State Park

Orcas

Blind Bay

Picnic Point

Upright Channel

Lopez Island

SHAW ISLAND COUNTY PARK

Indian Cove

Canoe Island

CANOE ISLAND FRENCH CAMP

Flat Point

BAY RD

BLIND BAY RD

West Sound

SHAW ISLAND HISTORICAL MUSEUM

OUR LADY OF THE ROCK MONASTARY

SQUAW BAY RD

Squaw Bay

CEDAR ROCK BIOLOGICAL PRESERVE

Double Island

Allegria Island

Caldwell Point

Broken Point

LITTLE RED SCHOOLHOUSE

COVE RD

HOFFMAN COVE RD

Hoffman Cove

Victim Island

Orcas Island

LOOP

NEVIS

BEN

POINT

RD

Parks Bay

Deer Harbor

Crane Island

Point George

Fawn Island

Reef Island

McConnell Island

Coon Island

Northwest McConnell Rock State Park

Cliff Island

Nob Island

NECK

Neck Point

Tilt Rocks

Point Caution

San Juan Channel

San Juan Island

Steep Point

Wasp Islands

Wasp Passage

Low Island

FRIDAY HARBOR FERRY

Friday Harbor

Spring Passage

Jones Island

JONES ISLAND MARINE STATE PARK

YELLOW ISLAND PRESERVE

0   0.5 mi

0   0.5 km

© AVALON TRAVEL

post office, and two private airstrips, but no medical facility. The only other commercial business headquartered on Shaw Island is **Northwest Marine Technology** (www.nmt. us), the manufacturer of fish tags used all over the world.

There are no bike rental shops, kayak companies, B&Bs, or galleries on Shaw, and none are likely to appear. When kayakers started launching from a dock next to the ferry landing, Shaw Islanders purchased the land and posted signs to keep commercial kayak companies away. Sky-high land prices, minimal turnover, and locals who snatch up whatever comes on the market make it virtually impossible to buy property or a house on Shaw.

**Independence Day** on July 4th brings a little parade across the island and a potluck dinner. In early August, the **Round Shaw Row** (www.soundrowers.org) hosts rowboats, kayakers, and canoeists in a fun race around the island; the record is 1 hour and 39 minutes. On the first Saturday of August, a popular sailing race circumnavigates the island, the **Shaw Island Classic** (www.sjiyc.com).

## SIGHTS AND RECREATION

Besides the preserve and county park, nearly all of Shaw is a look-only place. Despite this, the roads are quiet and the countryside is very scenic, making Shaw a wonderful place to explore by bicycle. You'll find old orchards, some beautiful homes, and peaceful vistas of nearby islands. From the ferry, Blind Bay Road follows the shore of this pasture-and-forest-bordered bay, with **Blind Island Marine State Park** in the middle. The westernmost end of Shaw Island, **Neck Point,** is especially picturesque, with the road passing over a slender peninsula where waves lap on both sides.

### Shaw General Store

"Downtown" Shaw consists of the ferry dock, the Shaw General Store (360/468-2288, www. shawgeneralstore.com, 9 A.M.–6 P.M. daily late May–early Sept., 10 A.M.–5 P.M. Mon.–Sat. the rest of the year), and a couple of adjacent buildings. For almost three decades, the island's

claim to fame was the Franciscan Catholic nuns who operated the ferry dock and store. They left in 2004 when the nuns grew too aged to continue their work. Today, the store and adjacent ferry terminal are run by friendly Steve and Terri Mason and their kids. Step inside the store for basic supplies and gifts, local produce and eggs, and items made at Our Lady of the Rock Monastery: mustards, vinegars, teas, and spices. The store's **Silver Bay Café** in back serves lattes, wraps, deli sandwiches, clam chowder, freshly baked muffins, croissants, and cinnamon rolls, plus ice cream and take-and-bake pizzas. You'll find picnic tables and restrooms nearby, and the little marina has a couple of slots for guest mooring.

The owners of Shaw General Store rent out a charming 1900s **waterside cottage** close to the ferry dock; find it at www.vrbo. com/334848. This nicely restored two-bedroom, one-bath cottage with a full kitchen, Wi-Fi, a glassed-in "wheelhouse," and a magnificent location along Harney Channel sleeps 4–6 guests for $2,800/month, and shorter stays may be available; call 360/468-2288 for details.

### Our Lady of the Rock Monastery

The store sells Mother Prisca's Hot Mustard, herbal vinegars, and spices made by a Catholic order called Our Lady of the Rock Monastery (360/468-2321, www.ourladyoftherock.com). Founded in 1977, the monastery is home to eight Benedictine nuns who live on an immaculate 300-acre spread of forests and farmland. The nuns are sometimes called the "spinning nuns," and you might see them spinning and weaving hand-dyed yarn on the ferry to Shaw. Guest mistress Mother Hildegard George has a Ph.D. in child and adolescent psychology and is a leader in the field of animal-assisted therapy. Not surprisingly, the priory raises long-haired Scottish Highlands cattle, black Cotswold sheep, Kerry cattle, llamas, alpacas, and a menagerie of pigs, turkeys, chickens, geese, ducks, peacocks, and other critters—all of which have names. The farm's state-licensed raw milk is sold to folks on Shaw and Orcas but is not available in the store. Tours of Our Lady of the Rock may be available, but call a day in advance. The order also has a small guesthouse for religious retreats.

## Shaw Island Historical Museum

This tiny museum (360/468-4068, 2–4 P.M. Tues., 11 A.M.–1 P.M. Thurs., 11 A.M.–1 P.M. and 2–4 P.M. Sat., free) is housed in a log cabin two miles from the ferry landing at the intersection of Blind Bay and Hoffman Cove Roads. Inside are historical photos and various farming and fishing implements, along with arrowheads and other Coast Salish artifacts. Out front is a reefnet fishing boat like those still used to fish for salmon in nearby waters. Next door is **Shaw Island Library** (360/468-4068), which keeps the same hours. If the museum is locked, ask for a key from the librarian.

## Little Red Schoolhouse

Across the intersection from the museum and library is a red one-room grade school (www.shaw.k12.wa.us) that is now on the National Register of Historic Places. It's still in use today, with 20 or so students in grades K–8; a second building has been added in the back. Shaw's count-them-on-one-hand high-school students commute by ferry to Orcas or San Juan Islands.

## Shaw Island County Park

Also known as South Beach County Park (360/378-8420, www.sanjuanco.com/parks) this 65-acre park is one of the few public spots on the Shaw shoreline. It is two miles south of the ferry landing off Squaw Bay Road and faces Canoe Island, home to a French-language summer camp. The park is best known for its beautiful sandy beach—one of the best in the islands—where you'll sometimes find sand dollars. By midsummer, the shallow waters of Indian Cove are warm enough for a swim, and a picnic area and boat launch are available, along with outhouses.

The park includes six waterfront ($20) and five in-the-trees ($15) campsites, along with a shared hiker/biker site ($8), and one Cascadia

Scottish Highlands cattle at Our Lady of the Rock Monastery

© DON PITCHER

Marine Trail site for kayakers ($8). The campground has a cooking shelter and seasonal drinking water, but no showers. There are no other camping options on Shaw, so reserve ahead for peak-season weekends unless you want to catch the next ferry back to Anacortes. Visit the park website for campground reservations ($7 extra); you can reserve from 5 days to 90 days in advance. The campground is open year-round.

## ( Cedar Rock Biological Preserve

The University of Washington's Cedar Rock Biological Preserve (owned by the University of Washington Friday Harbor Laboratories, 360/378-2165, http://depts.washington.edu/fhl) is a quiet off-the-beaten-path place on the south side of Shaw along Hoffman Cove. Open to the public, it covers approximately 370 acres with rocky shorelines and forests dominated by stately Pacific madrones and Douglas firs. (The land was donated by Robert Ellis, and an adjacent 579-acre parcel was set aside by his

© DON PITCHER

Cedar Rock Biological Preserve

brother Frederick and Marilyn Ellis. The latter—on the west side of the road—is for preservation and biological research only, with no public access.)

Get to Cedar Rock from the ferry by following Blind Bay Road to the schoolhouse and turning left (south) on the gravel Hoffman Cove Road. The road ends near the water's edge at the preserve, but parking is almost nonexistent, so bikes are a better way to get here. Sign in at the entrance box and head up the path to an old field with several homestead buildings and out to a small rocky point. Stop awhile to soak up the view across San Juan Channel and to watch the ferries steaming into Friday Harbor. From here, a rough path continues east along the shore to small coves with gravelly beaches, through pristine forests with periodic openings, and up rocky knolls. The route dwindles away, becoming little more than a game trail, but ambitious hikers could continue along the shore 1.5 miles to Squaw Bay, where you run into private land again. Most folks turn back before this, but even a

short hike at Cedar Rock offers a relaxing respite. You may want to time your hike to coincide with low tide, making it easier to walk the beaches.

## Kayaking, Boating, and Biking

The relatively protected waters and undeveloped shores of Shaw Island are very popular with sea kayakers. Randel Washburne's *Kayaking Puget Sound, the San Juans, and Gulf Islands* (The Mountaineers, www.mountaineers.org) has details on a 14-mile circumnavigation of Shaw Island. Unfortunately, you can't launch sea kayaks from the Shaw Island ferry landing; the closest place to do so is Shaw Island County Park, two miles away, or from Odlin County Park on Lopez Island.

The island's shoreline is also popular with sailors and motorboaters, and each August the **Shaw Island Classic** (www.sjiyc.com) yacht race circles the island.

Shaw Island, with its paved roads, bucolic country, and paucity of cars, is a delight for cyclists. Unfortunately, even Shaw can get busy in midsummer, particularly when large touring groups of cyclists roll off the ferry. Because of the island's small size, some cyclists arrive in the morning, pedal around, take a lunch break, and are off on another island when it comes time to pitch their tents.

## GETTING THERE

Washington State Ferries (360/468-2142 for Shaw ferry terminal, 206/464-6400 for general info, or 888/808-7977 in Washington and British Columbia, www.wsdot.wa.gov/ferries) ply the waters around Shaw almost constantly, en route to Anacortes, Lopez Island, Orcas Island, San Juan Island, or Vancouver Island. Quite a few of these also stop at Shaw Island's little dock. Peak-season interisland service costs $23.50 for a car and driver if you're heading west to Orcas Village or Friday Harbor; eastbound service to Lopez or Anacortes is free. There's never a charge for walk-on passengers commuting between the islands. Peak-season fares from Anacortes to Shaw Island are $11.50 for passengers and walk-ons, or $45.30 for a car and driver. Bikes are $4 extra, and kayaks cost $15.80 more. Reservations are not available—just get in the line and wait.

If you're on Shaw and want to take a short look around Orcas Island before continuing to Friday Harbor, be sure to request a **free vehicle transfer.** These are good for up to 24 hours, and getting one saves you $23.50, but you must ask for it on Shaw Island before getting on the ferry.

**Northwest Sky Ferry** (360/696-9999, www.nwskyferry.com) offers flightpooling from Bellingham to Shaw Island. Flightpooling is similar to carpooling, where travelers are put together to fly at a reduced rate.

# Lummi Island

Lummi (pronounced LUM-ee, as in tummy) is only an eight-minute ferry ride from the mainland, but since it is some distance from the other islands in the San Juans, it doesn't get a lot of attention. Lummi Island lies within Whatcom County, not San Juan County, and many people do not consider it part of the archipelago. At the peanut-shaped island's southern end is a steeply wooded mountain that slopes down abruptly to flatter land on the north end, which is where nearly all the residents live. The 800 or so locals are a diverse lot, with tony homes and dramatic waterside vistas just up the road from hardscrabble mobile homes where rusting trucks serve as lawn ornaments.

Lummi is a quiet island, home primarily to artists, weekenders, and a few salmon fishers, some of whom fish with reefnets. Most of the island is private property with no public access, and the undeveloped mountainous southern end of the island is off-limits, but you can ride the roads to a few public areas: in front of the Beach Store Café just north of the ferry dock, and a side road off West Shore Drive. Stop for a photo of reefnet boats along Legoe Bay and

© DON PITCHER

Lummi Island

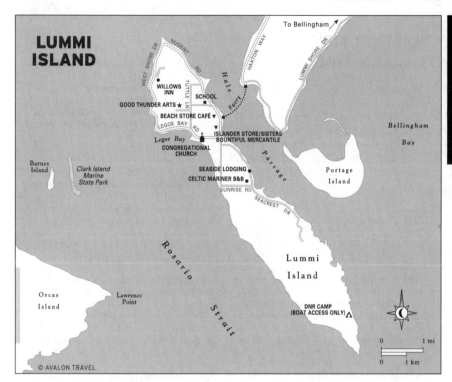

the charming **Lummi Island Congregational Church** (www.lummichurch.com) just up the road. The church has been here since 1903.

The Lummi people were the first inhabitants of the island, but they abandoned it after Haidas raided their village to capture slaves. By the time the first whites arrived in the 1870s, the Lummi had moved to the mainland. Today, 600 Lummi people live in scattered homes on the 13,000-acre Lummi Reservation at Gooseberry Point, where the ferry departs for the island.

## ENTERTAINMENT AND EVENTS

One corner of the The Islander grocery store has been transformed into **Sisters Bountiful Mercantile** (2106 South Nugent Rd., 360/758-2190, www.islandergrocery. com, 6 A.M.–10:30 P.M. daily), selling island arts and crafts. Also check out **Good Thunder Arts** (2307 Tuttle Lane, 360/758-7121). Call ahead to see one of the more interesting local places, **Sculpture Woods,** where Ann Morris (360/758-2143, www.annmorrisbronze.com) has positioned 16 large bronze pieces that appear to be emerging from the earth. **Lummi Island Artists' Studio Tours** (360/758-7121) are popular events over Memorial Day and Labor Day weekends, and the first weekend of December.

Held on the Lummi Reservation, the **Lummi Stommish Water Festival** (360/384-1489, www.stommish.com) in mid-June features competitive war-canoe races over a five-mile course, with up to 11 people per canoe. Other activities include arts and crafts sales, Native American dancing, and a salmon bake.

# REEFNET FISHING

*When we went out there and put in those reef nets, we caught fish right off starting the first day and the white fishermen never had one to eat. They didn't know how to catch them. They didn't know how to use a reef net. Every night when we'd go home, you could go down and sit on the beach and see them out there measuring our reef net and copying it.*

Herman Olsen, *Lummi Elders Speak,*
edited by Ann Nugent

This unique and ingenious way to catch salmon originated with the Coast Salish people around the San Juans. Today, fewer than a dozen commercial reefnet operations remain in Washington, all run by non-Native Americans. Each summer, salmon return from the Pacific Ocean to spawn in British Columbia's Fraser River. Their migration takes them past the San Juan Islands, where reefnet fishers work from a pair of small scows with a net strung between them. (The Salish originally used large dugout canoes for this purpose.) Salmon are directed into the net through an artificial reef covered with plastic ribbons that simulate reef grasses. The open end of the "reef" is held on the bottom by heavy con-crete anchors, and at the back is a 50-foot-long windsock-shaped net.

Each boat has a tall ladder that allows spotters to see salmon as they enter the net and to alert crew members below to close the net. Timing is tricky, and precautions must be taken to keep from spooking the salmon. Within 15–30 seconds the net is winched up, pulling the boats together and forcing the fish into a pocket. The fish are lifted onboard and dumped into a water-filled tank called a live box. They remain in the tank until sold to a fish buyer, who selects the salmon he wants and immediately puts them on ice. Everything else in the live box is released back into the sea. Reefnet fishing results in the highest-quality fish, since the netted salmon stay alive longer and are kept in much better condition than those caught using other fishing methods. In addition, there is no by-catch (taking of unwanted or prohibited species of fish).

You'll see reefnet boats anchored or in use at a couple of places around the San Juans. The little Shaw Island Historical Museum (360/468-4068) has one out front, and others are often visible in Fisherman Bay on Lopez Island, in Reid Harbor on Stuart Island, and along Lummi Island's Legoe Bay. Find out more online at www.lummiislandwild.com.

reefnet fishing boat

© DON PITCHER

## RECREATION

Bike rentals are not available on Lummi, so bring one over from Bellingham. Traffic is minimal, but roads are narrow and winding, with no shoulders—not the best for cyclists.

## ACCOMMODATIONS

On the west side of the island, **◖ The Willows Inn** (2579 W. Shore Dr., 360/758-2620 or 888/294-2620, www.willows-inn.com, closed Jan., $125–325 d) has nine rooms and cottages at the inn. The honeymoon cottage here provides additional privacy and a magnificent view of the San Juans, plus a jetted tub. A half mile away are a cabin, suite, and yurt at **Nettles Farm** ($165–245), along with two guesthouses ($285–295 d); add $30 for additional guests. Also available is a large beach house that sleeps six for $625. All guests at Willows Inn are served a full gourmet breakfast at the restaurant each morning and have access to an outdoor hot tub. There's a two-night minimum stay in summer. Whale-watching, kayaking, and sailing trips are available.

**Celtic Mariner B&B** (1611 Seacrest Dr., 360/758-2270, www.thecelticmarinerbandb.com, $120 d) has one guest room with a private bath, fridge, microwave, and separate entrance. Breakfast is served in the main house. No children or pets.

**Seaside Lodging Northwest** (360/758-7064 or 888/758-7064, www.seasidelodgingnorthwest.com) has a spacious home on the east side of Lummi Island that sleeps up to six guests for $425 nightly. The Cape Cod–style waterfront home has French doors opening to landscaped grounds, a modern kitchen, woodburning fireplace, and hot tub, plus luxurious bedding, granite countertops, and bath supplies you'd expect in a high-end hotel. A three-night minimum is required. Concierge services are available (extra fee, of course), including a personal chef, massage therapist, grocery shopping, and more.

Also check out **VRBO** (www.vrbo.com) for vacation rentals on Lummi Island; last time I looked there were more than 15 places available on a nightly or weekly basis.

## Camping

The **Washington Department of Natural Resources** (360/856-3500, www.dnr.wa.gov) maintains a free kayak-accessible campground near the south end of the island. This delightful spot is the only place to camp on Lummi Island.

## FOOD

The owners of The Willows Inn—Riley Starks and Judy Olsen—also run an organic farm (www.nettlesfarm.com) that grows vegetables and flowers and has 90 egg-laying hens. You can savor some of the garden bounty and other local fare at **◖ The Willows Inn** (2579 W. Shore Dr., 360/758-2620 or 888/294-2620, www.willows-inn.com, Wed.–Sun., closed Jan.). Under chef Blaine Wetzel, the restaurant has gained national acclaim, and in 2011 the *New York Times* labeled it one of 10 restaurants in the world worth a plane ride! A single seating at 7 P.M. (6:30 P.M. in winter) is available for the five-course prix fixe chef's tasting menu ($135 per person). The menu changes weekly but always includes vegetarian entrées. Reservations are highly recommended, especially with all those folks hopping the jet from New York. Breakfast is only available for lodging guests.

Downstairs at Willows Inn, the **Taproot Café** (360/758-2930, noon–7 P.M. Fri.–Wed.) generally has several specials on the menu board, along with sandwiches, burgers, quiche, salads, espresso, and a full bar. A limited dinner menu ($13–25 entrées) is available at the Taproot Monday and Tuesday evenings—when the main restaurant is closed.

Just south of the ferry dock, **The Islander** (2106 South Nugent Rd., 360/758-2190, www.islandergrocery.com, 6 A.M.–10:30 P.M. daily) has beer, soda pop, ice cream, and other necessities of life. A small **farmers market** takes place Saturday 10 A.M.–1 P.M. May–September.

North of the dock, **◖ Beach Store Café** (360/758-2233, www.beachstorecafe.com, 11 A.M.–9 P.M. Thurs.–Fri., 9 A.M.–9 P.M. Sat.–Sun., $10–22) is a casual bistro with award-winning clam chowder, plus wood-fired pizzas, fish tacos, sandwiches, and fettuccini alfredo. For breakfast (weekends only), get the corned beef hash or a chorizo omelet. Sit on the front deck to take in snowy Mount Baker when the skies cooperate. Free Wi-Fi.

## GETTING THERE

From I-5, take Exit 260 and travel four miles west on Slater Road to Haxton Way (location of Silver Reef Casino) on the Lummi Reservation, and follow it to the **ferry landing.** The county-owned *Whatcom Chief* ferry (360/676-6876) makes eight-minute trips between Gooseberry Point on the mainland to Lummi Island every hour from 6 A.M. to midnight (more frequently during the commute period). Round-trip cost is $13 for a car and driver, $7 for passengers and walk-ons, $7 for bikes, and free for kids.

# Marine State Parks

A number of the smaller islands in the San Juan archipelago are preserved as marine state parks. Locals often refer to these islands as the **outer islands,** and the parks are very popular with boaters and sea kayakers looking for a summertime escape. In addition to these, The Nature Conservancy's Yellow Island is also open to the public. The **San Juan Islands National Wildlife Refuge** is made up of 83 islands, almost all off-limits. Be sure to avoid these refuge islands, as they provide vital breeding and resting areas for birds and marine mammals. Boaters—including kayakers—must stay at least 200 yards away.

Several small island state marine parks are closed to the public to protect them from being damaged. Three of these undeveloped parks are offshore from Orcas Island: **Freeman Island State Park** near Point Doughty, **Skull Island Marine State Park** at the head

© DON PITCHER

Forested trails are found on many marine state park islands.

of Massacre Bay, and **Victim Island Marine State Park** in West Sound. Another closed area, **Iceberg Island State Marine Park,** sits near the southwest end of Lopez Island just off Iceberg Point.

## CAMPING AND MOORING

Most marine state parks have primitive campsites for $12 a night, available on a first-come, first-served basis. At the most popular parks—Clark, James, Jones, Matia, Patos, Stuart, Sucia, and Turn Islands—campsites often fill on weekends between mid-July and mid-August or over summer holiday weekends. There's generally space midweek.

Kayakers and canoeists will find **Cascadia Marine Trail** campsites for $12 on Blind, Burrow, Cypress, James, Jones, Lopez, Posey, Strawberry, and Stuart Islands. Park rangers try to prevent overcrowding but won't make folks move off-island if the sea conditions are unsafe. Campsite reservations are only available for group sites on Clark, Jones, Posey, and Sucia Islands; all the other sites are on a first-come,

first-served basis. The nonprofit **Washington Water Trails Association** (206/545-9161, www.wwta.org) has additional information on Cascadia Marine Trail campsites, but the areas are actually managed by Washington State Parks.

Most marine parks contain relatively protected coves with mooring buoys ($10/night). Other attractions include hiking trails and picnic tables, while some islands also have drinking water, docks, or floats. Most islands have outhouses, but you'll need to haul out any garbage. Pets are allowed in the marine parks but must be on a leash at all times.

## SEA KAYAKING

Quite a few companies lead sea-kayaking trips of varying lengths to the marine state parks. Companies based on San Juan Island are **Discovery Sea Kayaks** (360/378-2559 or 866/461-2559, www.discoveryseakayaks.com), **Outdoor Odysseys** (360/378-3533 or 800/647-4621, www.outdoorodysseys.com), **Sea Quest Expeditions** (360/378-5767

© DON PITCHER

**Adirondack shelters are available on Sucia and Jones Islands.**

© DON PITCHER

kayaks on a Jones Island beach

contains information on destinations, safety, difficulty ratings, and launching points.

## MOUNTAIN BIKING

Mountain bikes are allowed year-round on all marine state park trails, but cyclists need to avoid conflicts with other users. This means staying on trails, looking out for others, and riding slowly around camping areas. Bikes aren't allowed on piers, ramps, or floats. Local water taxis will transport bikes, and bike rentals are available from the three main islands: Orcas, Lopez, and San Juan, but the bike shop on San Juan Island will not allow bikes to be taken to the outer islands due to salt damage.

## INFORMATION

For additional information on the marine parks, call 360/376-2073 or visit the state park website (ww.parks.wa.gov) See Ken Wilcox's *Hiking the San Juan Islands* (Northwest Wild Books) or Dave Wortman's *San Juan Islands: A Guide to Exploring the Great Outdoors* (FalconGuides) for details on marine state park hiking trails.

Boaters heading out on their own to these smaller islands will want to pick up one of the cruising guides to the islands. *Gunkholing the San Juans* by Jo Bailey and Carl Nyberg (San Juan Enterprises) is packed with details on all the islands in the archipelago, and is interesting even if you don't have a boat or kayak.

## GETTING THERE

The state ferry does not stop on any of the marine state parks; access is limited to water taxi, airplane, private boat, or sea kayak.

### Water Taxis

A number of companies provide water-taxi service to the outer islands. Most operate seasonally, but **Paraclete Charters** (360/293-5920 or 800/808-2999, www.paracletecharters.com) provides year-round service. In business since 1992, the company runs three boats (the largest can carry 64 passengers) from Anacortes to anywhere in the San Juans. They serve homeowners on islands not on the ferry system,

or 888/589-4253, www.sea-quest-kayak.com), and **San Juan Kayak Expeditions** (360/378-4436, www.sanjuankayak.com). Orcas Island–based kayak companies are **Shearwater Adventures** (360/376-4699, www.shearwaterkayaks.com) and **Outer Island Expeditions** (360/376-3711, www.outerislandx.com). **Elakah Expeditions** (360/734-7270 or 800/434-7270, www.elakah.com) and **Moondance Sea Kayaking Adventures** (360/738-7664, www.moondancekayak.com) lead sea-kayak tours from Bellingham, while **Anacortes Kayak Tours** (360/588-1117 or 800/992-1801, www.anacorteskayaktours.com) has trips from Anacortes.

Sea kayaks are a popular island-hopping mode of transportation, but since some of the smaller islands are several miles out, be careful not to overestimate your ability. If you're planning a kayak trip to the islands, get a copy of Randel Washburne's *Kayaking Puget Sound, the San Juans, and Gulf Islands* (The Mountaineers, www.mountaineers.org). It

© DON PITCHER

**boats at Sucia Island**

along with other folks wanting to reach the islands. Prices depend on your destination and number of people, but you don't need to charter an entire boat, and they have room for kayaks, bikes, and pets. As an example, Anacortes to Clark Island costs $412 for one person round-trip, or $192 per person for five or more folks. Add $10 round-trip for bikes or $20 for kayaks.

Based at Skyline Marina in Anacortes, **Island Express Charters** (360/299-2875 or 877/473-9777, www.islandexpresscharters. com, open year-round) has two high-speed landing crafts with space for kayaks, bikes, and gear. Water-taxi rates vary depending upon your destination.

Based at Deer Harbor on Orcas Island, **North Shore Charters** (360/376-4855, www. orcasislandadventures.com) offers day trips and drop-offs to state marine parks on Stuart, Matia, Patos, Sucia, and other islands. The 26-foot biodiesel-powered boat costs $195 per hour for up to six people plus kayaks or bikes. Owner Marty Mead has years of experience

in local and Alaskan waters and was also the engineer on a 2007 crossing of the Pacific by *Earthrace,* a wave-piercing trimaran that set the record for the fastest time ever for a biodiesel-powered boat.

Also at Deer Harbor Marina, **Orcas Boat Rentals** (360/376-7616, www.orcasboats.com) has boat rentals if you want to head out on your own. The company can also provide water-taxi service to Jones Island, Yellow Island, and other nearby islands.

Based on the north side of Orcas Island, **Outer Island Expeditions** (360/376-3711, www.outerislandx.com) provides water-taxi service to Stuart, Sucia, Jones, Matia, and Patos Islands, with a four-person minimum.

**Humpback Hauling** (360/317-7433, www. humpbackhauling.com) provides passenger and freight service throughout the San Juans on a large landing craft. Owner Bob Miller—a highly experienced captain—also operates a smaller boat under the name Roche Harbor Water Taxi.

Based in Friday Harbor, **San Juan Islands**

**Water Taxi** (360/317-5475, www.sjiwatertaxi. net) can transport six passengers anywhere in the San Juan Islands. Captain Gunnar Wickman has sailed all over the world, and the boat spent many years fishing in Alaska. It's not fast, but the boat is comfortable, with space for bikes or kayaks.

## By Air

**San Juan Airlines** (360/293-4691 or 800/874-4434, www.sanjuanairlines.com) has scheduled daily wheeled-plane service from Anacortes and Bellingham to San Juan, Orcas, Lopez, Decatur, and Blakely Islands; it will stop at most other island runways, including Center, Crane, Eliza, Sinclair, Stuart, and Waldron Islands on a charter basis.

**Northwest Sky Ferry** (360/696-9999, www.nwskyferry.com) offers flightpooling from Bellingham to Stuart, Shaw, Waldron, Crane, Decatur, and Center Islands. Flightpooling is similar to carpooling, where they put people together to travel at a reduced rate.

Based at San Juan Island Airport, **Island Air** (360/378-2376 or 888/378-2376, www. sanjuan-islandair.com) provides charter flights to most islands.

**Kenmore Air** (425/486-1257 or 866/435-9524, www.kenmoreair.com) has charter float-plane flights from Lake Union in Seattle to many of the remote San Juan Islands, including Cypress, Blakely, Jones, Stuart, Henry, Sucia, and Decatur.

## BLIND ISLAND MARINE STATE PARK

Blind Island (360/378-2044, www.parks. wa.gov) is a three-acre grassy island within Blind Bay on the north side of Shaw Island. It's a great place to watch the ferries pass, with the Shaw ferry dock just 0.25 mile away, and Orcas Village less than a mile away. Facilities are limited to four mooring buoys, picnic tables, fire pits, and a composting toilet. Bring your own water. The island's four primitive campsites ($12) are part of the Cascadia Marine Trail and are available only for the use of sea kayakers.

In the early 1900s, Blind Island was occupied by a squatter family who built several buildings and rock cisterns and had a garden. The buildings are long gone, but you can see the cherry, apple, and hazelnut trees they planted.

## CLARK ISLAND MARINE STATE PARK

Two miles northeast of Orcas Island, Clark Island (360/376-2073, www.parks.wa.gov) is a narrow 55-acre island. It's relatively close to the western shore of Lummi Island, making it a destination for sea kayakers and boaters. The island has pretty sand and gravel beaches for walking, sunbathing, fishing, or scuba diving, plus a 100-foot-high hill in the middle. Droopy madrone trees line the water, framing dramatic views of the Cascades to the east, or Georgia Strait and the setting sun to the west. Short paths connect the two sides of the island, but the once-popular south-end trail has been closed to protect nesting seabirds.

Currents can be strong on the west side of the island, and storms often bring big waves and powerful currents that create hazardous conditions. The island is popular for day use, but it's not advisable if the wind is blowing. In addition, there's heavy tanker traffic in the channel east of Clark Island.

Nearby is privately owned **Barnes Island,** with a few homes, plus a cluster of rocky islets just southeast of Clark Island called **The Sisters Islands.** These are frequently crowded with nesting gulls, cormorants, and other seabirds. Two of them lie within the San Juan Islands National Wildlife Refuge, and boaters must stay 200 yards away.

### Camping and Mooring

On shore are nine primitive campsites ($12) with pit toilets but no water. Most of these are on-the-beach sites open April–September only, but two are in the trees and available year-round. Groups can reserve one of the campsites by calling the park.

Mooring buoys are available on both sides of Clark Island, but buoys on the west side are exposed.

## Getting There

**Paraclete Charters** (360/293-5920 or 800/808-2999, www.paracletecharters.com, $208 round-trip for two people to Clark, add $10 for bikes or $20 for kayaks) runs boats from Anacortes throughout the San Juan Islands. Prices depend upon the number of folks.

Also based in Anacortes, **Island Express Charters** (360/299-2875 or 877/473-9777, www.islandexpresscharters.com, $148/person round-trip to Clark, plus $12 for bikes or $30 for kayaks) has high-speed landing crafts with plenty of room for kayaks, bikes, and gear.

## CYPRESS ISLAND

The fourth largest island in the San Juans, Cypress is just three miles northeast of Anacortes. It is surprisingly wild, with excellent recreational opportunities and beautifully rugged scenery. Featured attractions include tall stands of old-growth trees and more than 25 miles of hiking trails, along with campsites, pretty beaches and coves, a couple of small lakes, abundant wildlife, and some stunning hilltop viewpoints.

There are no cypress trees on Cypress Island. Captain George Vancouver named the island in 1792 but misidentified the trees; they're actually Rocky Mountain junipers. Coast Salish people once occupied the island seasonally, and a number of archaeological sites have been identified. American settlers came to homestead, farm, log, fish, or mine, but most of them gave up almost a century ago. In the 1970s, local environmentalists prevented the island from being developed into a planned resort and residential area. Today, the 4.5-mile-long island is mostly in public hands and managed as a natural area by the Washington Department of Natural Resources (360/856-3500). Download Cypress Island trail maps from the DNR website (www.dnr.wa.gov).

## Hiking

For an incredible view, climb to the 800-foot summit of **Eagle Cliff** on the northern end of Cypress Island. The shortest trail begins from Pelican Beach and is a bit less than three miles round-trip. As might be surmised from the name, this is a bald eagle nesting area. To protect them, the trail is closed February–mid-July. Other trails and dirt roads lace the island, going all the way from Pelican Beach to the southern tip of Cypress Island. Mountain bikes and motorized vehicles are not allowed on any of these. See Ken Wilcox's *Hiking the San Juan Islands* (Northwest Wild Books) or Dave Wortman's **San Juan Islands: A Guide to Exploring the Great Outdoors** (FalconGuides) for complete details on Cypress Island hikes.

## Camping

Free campsites are located at **Cypress Head DNR Recreation Site** on the east side of the island, where you will also find five mooring buoys and outhouses, but no drinking water— so bring plenty with you. The bay at Cypress Head is peaceful and gorgeous. **Pelican Beach DNR Recreation Site** is another picturesque place, with six mooring buoys, free campsites, a shelter, picnic tables, and outhouses, but no water. It is located on the northeast side of Cypress. Camping is only allowed in designated campsites.

## Getting There

Kayakers and boaters typically head to Cypress from Anacortes, but small vessels need to take precautions due to difficult currents and tide rips in Bellingham Channel.

Based in Anacortes, **Island Express Charters** (360/299-2875 or 877/473-9777, www.islandexpresscharters.com, $74/person round-trip to Cypress, add $12 for bikes or $30 for kayaks) has high-speed landing crafts with plenty of room for kayaks, bikes, and gear.

**Paraclete Charters** (360/293-5920 or 800/808-2999, www.paracletecharters.com, $128 round-trip for two people to Cypress, add $10 round-trip for bikes or $20 for kayaks) runs boats from Anacortes throughout the San Juan Islands.

**Kenmore Air** (425/486-1257 or 800/543-9595, www.kenmoreair.com) has charter floatplane flights from Lake Union in Seattle to Cypress Island.

## DOE ISLAND
## MARINE STATE PARK

Doe Island (360/376-2073, www.parks. wa.gov) is a delightful six-acre escape. The secluded island is heavily forested and has both rocky shorelines and a gravel beach. It is located just southeast of Orcas Island, less than a 0.5-mile kayak paddle from the hot tubs at Doe Bay Resort & Retreat on Orcas. There are no mooring buoys, but a seasonal float extends from the north shore. Hiking trails circle and cross the island, and five simple campsites ($12) are available. No drinking water is available, but there are picnic tables and pit toilets. Be sure to check out the archaeological site in a little pocket cove on the north side; you can still see the place where the Lummi cleared rocks to beach their canoes.

Guided kayak trips to Doe Island depart Doe Bay Resort & Retreat on a regular basis in the summer; contact **Shearwater Adventures** (360/376-4699, www.shearwaterkayaks.com) for details. The closest access point for boaters and kayakers heading to Doe Island is the county's Obstruction Pass boat ramp on Orcas Island.

## JAMES ISLAND
## MARINE STATE PARK

Less than a half mile east of Decatur Island and just four miles from the Anacortes ferry terminal along Rosario Strait, James Island (360/376-2073, www.parks.wa.gov) is a cliff-faced and scenic little place. The island was named for an American sailor, Reuben James, who died during a naval battle in Tripoli while saving the life of Stephen Decatur. It was one of many places named during the 1841 Wilkes Expedition.

Covering 114 acres, James Island is shaped like an hourglass, with coves and mooring buoys ($10) on both sides of the "waist." The east cove offers a better anchorage for boats if the buoys are already taken, and the west cove has a floating dock. Beaches on both sides are steep. Kayakers need to be especially cautious in the waters north of the island, where deadly rip currents can form.

Two Anacortes-based companies provide transport to James Island: **Island Express Charters** (360/299-2875 or 877/473-9777, www.islandexpresscharters.com) and **Paraclete Charters** (360/293-5920 or 800/808-2999, www.paracletecharters.com). Bikes and kayaks can also be transported for an extra fee.

### Camping

Pitch a tent ($12) at one of 13 primitive campsites, or at the Cascadia Marine Trail campsite if you're in a kayak. The island has the usual complement of deer, birds, and raccoons, the last of which can be real pests when the sun goes down. You'll need to bring your own water. Picnic tables, a shelter, and pit toilets are present, however, and a network of short trails traverses the forests and twin 200-foot-high hills of James Island.

## ◖ JONES ISLAND
## MARINE STATE PARK

One of the most heavily visited of the San Juan marine parks, Jones Island (360/376-

Excellent trails cross Jones Island.

© DON PITCHER

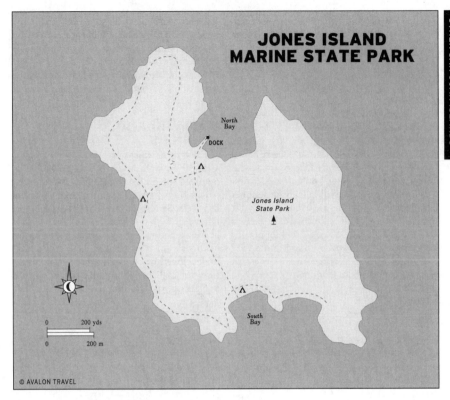

JONES ISLAND
MARINE STATE PARK

North
Bay

DOCK

Jones Island
State Park

South
Bay

0    200 yds
0    200 m

© AVALON TRAVEL

2073, www.parks.wa.gov) is a 188-acre island just a mile from the southwestern tip of Orcas Island, or a two-mile boat ride from Friday Harbor. The island is named for Jacob Jones, an American naval captain during the War of 1812, and is yet another place named during the 1841 Wilkes Expedition. It is a wonderful destination, either as a day trip or a multi-night family adventure. Two coves provide boat anchorage and access to the island's pleasures, and boaters can tie onto one of seven mooring buoys ($10). North Cove is a better anchorage and also has both a dock and seasonal moorage float. Local boaters recommend avoiding North Cove in high-pressure conditions, when winds blow from the north; avoid South Cove during low-pressure systems, when winds are reversed.

Jones Island has a mixture of old-growth forests (some of which were flattened in a fierce 1990 windstorm), stands of stately madrone, oak, and juniper trees, and grassy meadows. The shoreline is equally diverse, containing both rocky stretches and sandy beaches in pocket-size coves. Two unusual plants—prickly pear cactus and Garry oak—are present in protected areas on Jones Island.

A wide, nearly level 0.5-mile path leads through the forest from North Cove to South Cove, passing an old apple orchard along the way. South Cove is actually comprised of two adjacent small bays, each with a fine sandy beach—perfect for Frisbees, sunbathing, a picnic lunch, or just hanging out. A second trail follows the western shore of the island from South Cove, leading past interesting tidepools and up rocky slopes where you can watch sailboats and kayakers plying San Juan Channel. The trail continues to the north end of the island, where vistas extend to British Columbia's Gulf Islands.

## Camping

Jones Island Marine State Park has 24 primitive campsites ($12) with picnic tables, pit toilets, and potable water. Two Adirondack shelters ($23) at the South Cove have bunk beds; North Cove has a large kitchen shelter. Jones Island is often crowded. Camping is only allowed at designated sites, and these fill quickly on summer weekends. Reservations are available only for a group campsite and the Adirondack shelters on Jones Island; call 360/378-2044 for details. Kayakers will find two Cascadia Marine Trail campsites ($12) on a gorgeous southwestern beach facing San Juan Channel.

## Getting There

Jones Island is exceptionally popular with boaters, sailors, and sea kayakers. Several water-taxi companies are happy to get you to the island. Located at Deer Harbor Marina, **Orcas Boat Rentals** (360/376-7616, www.orcasboats.com) is just a 10-minute boat ride from Jones Island. Rent a skiff to head over on your own, or take a water-taxi service to the island for $100.

Operating from Friday Harbor on San Juan Island, **Captain Carli's Charters** (360/378-0302 or 888/221-1331, www.carlicharters.com, $125/person round-trip) offers transportation to Jones Island in a speedy six-passenger boat.

Other water taxis providing service to the island include **Island Express Charters** (360/299-2875 or 877/473-9777, www.island-expresscharters.com) and **Paraclete Charters** (360/293-5920 or 800/808-2999, www.paracletecharters.com) from Anacortes, along with **North Shore Charters** (360/376-4855, www.orcasislandadventures.com) and **Outer Island Expeditions** (360/376-3711, www.outerislandx.com) from Orcas Island.

Natalie Herner of **Gnat's Nature Hikes** (360/376-6629, www.orcasislandhikes.com)

leads boat-and-hike trips to Jones Island in the spring from Orcas Island. There's a three-person minimum and a six-person maximum.

**Kenmore Air** (425/486-1257 or 800/543-9595, www.kenmoreair.com) has charter floatplane flights from Lake Union in Seattle to Jones Island.

## MATIA ISLAND MARINE STATE PARK

Located three miles northeast of Orcas Island and a mile from Sucia Island, Matia (pronounced ma-TEE-uh; 360/376-2073, www.parks.wa.gov) Island is a mile long and covers 145 acres. Sandstone bluffs line the shore, and tall old-growth forests of Douglas fir, western hemlock, and western red cedar fill the center of the island. It's a beautiful and essentially undeveloped place. Matia received its name from the 1791 expedition of Francisco Eliza; in Spanish, the word means "no protection."

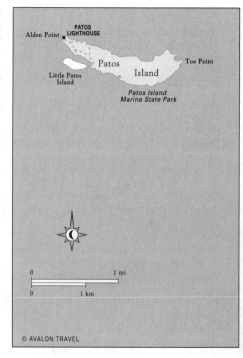

© AVALON TRAVEL

Matia was for decades the quiet home of a Civil War veteran, Elvin Smith, who got a regular workout rowing the three miles to Orcas and walking another two miles to Eastsound to buy his groceries. On his last trip in 1921, he and another elderly friend headed out from Eastsound in seas that suddenly turned rough. Pieces of the boat were later discovered near the Canadian border, but the two men were never found.

Most of Matia Island lies within the **San Juan Islands National Wildlife Refuge,** but the five-acre **Matia Island Marine State Park** centers on Rolfe Cove on the western end. Here you'll find a seasonal dock (generally Apr.– Sept.), two mooring buoys ($10), six primitive campsites ($12), and a composting toilet. No water is available, and wood fires aren't allowed on Matia, though you can use charcoal briquettes in the fire stands.

A scenic one-mile **hiking trail** starts at Rolfe

Cove and loops across the island, passing scattered remnants of Smith's old homesite and taking you through dense forests and along rocky shores. This is all part of the national wildlife refuge, so stay on the trails to protect the land and wildlife. Pets are not allowed on Matia Island trails. Boaters cannot approach Matia closer than 200 yards, except at the state park.

Immediately east of Matia is **Puffin Island,** with an active eagle nest, various nesting seabirds, seals, and sea lions. Puffins no longer nest there, though they apparently did in the past.

### Getting There

Matia Island is popular with kayakers and boaters but has potentially treacherous currents. The closest water-taxi service is through **Outer Island Expeditions** (360/376-3711, www.outerislandx.com), based on the north side of Orcas Island.

**North Shore Charters** (360/376-4855,

PATOS, SUCIA, AND MATIA ISLANDS

www.orcasislandadventures.com, $195/hour for up to six people plus kayaks or bikes) provides day trips and drop-offs to Matia Island from Deer Harbor on Orcas Island.

**Paraclete Charters** (360/293-5920 or 800/808-2999, www.paracletecharters.com, $312 round-trip for two, add $10 round-trip for bikes or $20 for kayaks) runs boats from Anacortes to Matia. Prices depend upon the number of folks.

Also based in Anacortes, **Island Express Charters** (360/299-2875 or 877/473-9777, www.islandexpresscharters.com) has a high-speed landing craft with plenty of room for kayaks, bikes, and gear.

## PATOS ISLAND MARINE STATE PARK

Northernmost of the San Juan archipelago, Patos (properly pronounced PAW-tohs, though you'll also hear PAY-tohs; 360/376-2073, www.parks.wa.gov) covers 208 acres and is six miles north of Orcas Island or two miles northwest of Sucia Island. The Southern Gulf Islands of British Columbia are only a few miles away. Wild, remote, and quiet Patos Island was named during a Spanish expedition in 1792. The name means "duck" and may have possibly come from a rock formation on the east side of the island that resembles the head of a duck.

The lack of a dock on Patos limits access, but you can anchor at two mooring buoys ($10) in **Active Cove.** Located on the southwestern side of Patos, it's sheltered behind **Little Patos Island.** During high-pressure systems, the moorage is exposed to winds blowing down the Strait of Georgia, creating a rough anchorage; otherwise, it's fairly protected.

Seven primitive campsites ($12) on Patos have picnic tables, fire pits, and outhouses, but no water. A 1.5-mile loop trail circles the western side of the island, passing through dense forests before opening onto the barren northwest tip at Alden Point. A 0.25-mile spur leads to picturesque **Patos Lighthouse.** Built in 1893 and now automated, the lighthouse sits atop a rocky bluff. **Keepers of the Patos**

**Light** (www.patoslightkeepers.org) works with the Bureau of Land Management (which owns the site) to preserve this historic structure.

For a lovingly written reminiscence of growing up on Patos in the early 1900s, see *Light on the Island* by Helene Glidden (San Juan Publishing). The author was a lighthouse-keeper's daughter and tells of her adventures with scoundrels, native people, and even Teddy Roosevelt.

### Getting There

Patos is not the place for novice kayakers or folks in small boats. There are few areas offering any protection, and the currents and riptides can be treacherous. Kayakers typically head to Patos from Sucia Island, rather than attempting the four-mile open-water crossing from Point Doughty on Orcas Island.

Based on the north side of Orcas Island, **Outer Island Expeditions** (360/376-3711, www.outerislandx.com) has three-hour trips ($89/person) to nearby Patos Island. The trip includes a guided 0.5-mile hike to the lighthouse and the chance to see porpoises and other wildlife.

**Orcas Island Eclipse Charters** (360/376-6566 or 800/376-6566, www.orcasisland-whales.com) leads informative four-hour lighthouse tours ($89 adults or $59 kids) once or twice a month April–August. Some of these include an onshore visit to Patos Lighthouse, while others take you by boat past this and three other lighthouses in the San Juans.

**North Shore Charters** (360/376-4855, www.orcasislandadventures.com, $195/hour for up to six people plus kayaks or bikes) provides water-taxi service to Patos Island from Deer Harbor on Orcas Island.

Based in Anacortes, **Island Express Charters** (360/299-2875 or 877/473-9777, www.islandexpresscharters.com) has a high-speed landing craft with plenty of room for kayaks, bikes, and gear.

**Paraclete Charters** (360/293-5920 or 800/808-2999, www.paracletecharters.com, $312 round-trip for two, add $10 round-trip for bikes or $20 for kayaks) also runs boats from Anacortes to Patos. Rates depend upon the number of folks.

## POSEY ISLAND MARINE STATE PARK

This pinprick of an island covers just one acre and is located a quarter mile north of San Juan Island's Roche Harbor. Posey Island (360/378-2044, www.parks.wa.gov) is named for the small and abundant wildflowers that carpet the ground in midsummer. Shallow waters and two Cascadia Marine Trail campsites ($12) make this a favorite spot for folks in kayaks and canoes in search of their own island. It's a great place to watch the parade of boats heading into or out of busy Roche Harbor. Campsite reservations ($10 extra; call 360/378-2044) are taken for mid-May to mid-September and must be made at least seven days in advance. Call early in the year (reservations open in Jan.) to be sure of a peak-season campsite on the island. In the off-season, campsites are on a first-come, first-served basis.

The island sees heavy daytime use by kayakers, and camp spaces fill quickly. A three-night maximum is allowed, but try to limit your stay to one night to give someone else a chance. Because of its location close to numerous summer homes and the harbor entrance, you shouldn't expect a quiet night during the summer. No water is available on the island, but picnic tables and a composting toilet are here. A maximum of 16 people are allowed to camp on Posey, which is really far too many for such a tiny spot.

## SADDLEBAG ISLAND MARINE STATE PARK

This 24-acre island in Padilla Bay is just two miles northeast of Anacortes and half a mile east of Guemes Island. It might be a stretch to call Saddlebag part of the San Juan archipelago, but the island is a marine state park (360/757-0227, www.parks.wa.gov). Facilities include five primitive campsites ($12) and an outhouse; no drinking water, buoys, or floats are available. A Cascadia Marine Trail campsite ($12) is available for sea kayakers. The

southeast corner of Saddlebag Island almost touches tiny **Dot Island,** part of the San Juan Islands National Wildlife Refuge. To protect nesting sites for seabirds, boaters aren't allowed within 200 yards of Dot Island. **Hat Island,** a larger island southeast of Saddlebag, is also closed to the public to protect wildlife.

## ◖ STUART ISLAND

Stuart Island, five miles northwest of San Juan Island's Roche Harbor, has two bucolic harbors just a stone's throw apart, along with a densely forested, hilly landscape and a classic old lighthouse. The island sits in the middle of Haro Strait, where killer whales are a common summertime sight. Canadian waters are less than a mile from the western end of Stuart Island. The three-mile-long island is predominately private, but **Stuart Island Marine State Park** (360/378-2044, www.parks.wa.gov) covers 88 prime acres, including 4,000 feet of shoreline. There are no stores of any kind on the island, so bring whatever you need when you come.

The island's two large and well-protected harbors—both within the state marine park—are favorites of boaters. Located on the southeast end of Stuart Island, **Reid Harbor** has 15 mooring buoys, linear moorage, and a dock, along with two floats at the head of the bay and a marine pump-out station. The 640-foot summit of Tiptop Hill (no public access) rises to the south, with a narrow dirt road providing access to other parts of the island. A trail connects Reid Harbor with **Prevost Harbor,** with seven mooring buoys, linear moorage, and a dock. It's an easy 200-yard walk, but boats enter Prevost Harbor from the north side of Stuart Island.

The 1841 Wilkes Expedition named Stuart Island for the captain's clerk, Fredrick D. Stuart. Loggers, fishermen, and a few farmers later settled the island. Today, Stuart is home to 20 or so year-round residents, augmented by another 150 folks with summer homes. Privacy is a priority here, and many areas are posted with No Trespassing signs. Fortunately, some of the most interesting sights are accessible by public trails or county roads, including Stuart

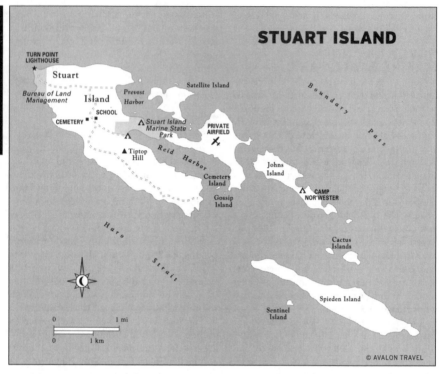

Island Marine State Park and a beautiful lighthouse on the westernmost end.

Several relatively short trails (three miles maximum) cut through the marine state park, offering ridge-crest views; open forests of madrone, cedar, and Douglas fir; and rocky shorelines along the way. Check the information kiosks at either harbor for details. For something a bit more ambitious, head up the county road that begins on public land at the head of Reid Harbor. This dirt road climbs uphill for 0.75 mile to a white one-room **schoolhouse.** Built in 1902, it now serves as a library. Adjacent is a newer school that closed in 2007 after the number of students dwindled. It was one of the last American public schools without electricity or flush toilets. Take a gander at the quaint **Treasure Chest,** a big wooden box filled with locally printed T-shirts available

on an honor system basis, including some fun pirate ones for kids.

Continue just past the school to a road junction and turn right. A short distance beyond is an unmarked road on the left leading to the **Stuart Island Cemetery,** with graves dating to 1904. Look for the distinctive headstone of Little Wolf, a local character who crafted copper bracelets that supposedly offered medical benefits. Back on the main road, you'll meet placidly grazing cows and horses at the next road junction. Turn right to Prevost Harbor, or left at the sign and pass an airstrip before continuing another 1.5 miles to **Turn Point Lighthouse.** The last portion of this hike is delightful, and the trail eventually emerges atop a tall cliff (stay away from the edge) where the panorama encompasses Haro Strait, the Southern Gulf Islands, and Vancouver Island. You'll see a parade of freighters, tankers, and

© DON PITCHER

Turn Point Lighthouse on Stuart Island

smaller boats, and you might even spot a pod of killer whales. It's a fantastic picnic spot.

Completed in 1893, the lighthouse has been automated since 1974. The lighthouse and surrounding 53 acres are owned by the Bureau of Land Management, which allows day use only. The nonprofit **Turn Point Lighthouse Preservation Society** (360/376-5246, www.tplps.org) assists in preserving this historic site. Working with the BLM, the group plans to create a small museum with a full-time keeper in the summer.

Just uphill from the lighthouse are large solar panels used to power the lighthouse. Visit www.siei.org for details on how one Stuart Island home has been transformed into a high-tech site where solar energy produces hydrogen, which is then used to make electricity for rainy days.

Turn Point marks the transition between Haro Strait to the south and Boundary Pass to the north. Large ships threading these channels must make a sharp turn here, and so do the often-turbulent tidal currents. The boundary waters are the deepest in the San Juan archipelago, reaching a maximum of 1,200 feet. It's a 6-mile round-trip hike from Reid Harbor to the lighthouse, or 3.5 miles round-trip from Prevost Harbor.

**Orcas Island Eclipse Charters** (360/376-6566 or 800/376-6566, www.orcasisland-whales.com) leads informative four-hour lighthouse tours ($89 adults, $59 kids) once or twice a month April–August. Some of these trips include an onshore visit to Turn Point Lighthouse, while others take you by boat past this and three other lighthouses in the San Juans.

## Boating and Kayaking

Powerful currents and tidal rips make the waters around Stuart Island challenging for small boats and kayaks; paddling here is not for beginners or the faint of heart. The closest access is Roche Harbor on San Juan Island, but you'll need to pass through the frequently swirling flows of Spieden Channel. For details on the best way to proceed, see Randel Washburne's

*Kayaking Puget Sound, the San Juans, and Gulf Islands* (The Mountaineers, www.mountaineers.org).

## Camping and Lodging

Stuart Island Marine State Park straddles the isthmus between Prevost and Reid Harbors, and includes 18 campsites ($12), picnic tables, seasonal drinking water, fireplaces, and pit toilets. Drinking water is limited and the system often runs dry by mid-July, so call ahead to make sure it's available. Four Cascadia Marine Trail campsites ($12) are available for sea kayakers on the east side of Reid Harbor.

A modern **waterfront cabin** (206/619-1965, www.vrbo.com/335147, $450/day with a 10-day minimum) is available on Stuart.

## Getting There and Around

**North Shore Charters** (360/376-4855, www.orcasislandadventures.com, $195/hour for up to six people plus kayaks or bikes) provides day trips and drop-offs to Stuart Island from Deer Harbor on Orcas Island.

Based in Anacortes, **Island Express Charters** (360/299-2875 or 877/473-9777, www.islandexpresscharters.com, $176/person round-trip to Stuart) has high-speed landing crafts with space for kayaks ($30 extra), bikes ($12 extra), and gear.

**Paraclete Charters** (360/293-5920 or 800/808-2999, www.paracletecharters.com, $312 round-trip for two, add $10 for bikes or $20 for kayaks) runs boats from Anacortes to Stuart. Prices depend upon the number of passengers.

Based on Orcas Island, **Outer Island Expeditions** (360/376-3711, www.outerislandx.com) has four-hour trips to Stuart Island ($139/person). The trip includes a guided 1.5-mile hike to the lighthouse and the chance to see orcas and other marine mammals. Water-taxi service to Stuart is also available.

Also try the Friday Harbor–based **Captain Carli's Charters** (360/378-0302 or 888/221-1331, www.carlicharters.com, $150/person round-trip) for transportation to Stuart Island in a speedy six-passenger boat.

**Outdoor Odysseys** (360/378-3533 or 800/647-4621, www.outdoorodysseys.com) has three-day sea-kayak tours ($605) that depart San Juan Island for Stuart Island, and more leisurely four-day paddles ($759) to Stuart, Jones, and other islands.

**San Juan Airlines** (360/293-4691 or 800/874-4434, www.sanjuanairlines.com) will fly to Stuart Island on a charter basis. **Kenmore Air** (425/486-1257 or 800/543-9595, www.kenmoreair.com) has charter floatplane flights from Lake Union in Seattle to Stuart Island.

**Northwest Sky Ferry** (360/696-9999, www.nwskyferry.com) offers flightpooling from Bellingham to Stuart Island. Flightpooling is similar to carpooling, where they put people together to travel at a reduced rate.

## Nearby Islands

Johns, Satellite, Sentinel, and Spieden Islands are nearby, and **Cactus Island** and several surrounding tiny islets are within the San Juan Islands National Wildlife Refuge. Boats aren't allowed within 200 yards of refuge islands to protect habitat for seals, sea lions, and seabirds. Cactus Island, along with a few other places in the San Juans, has Puget prairie vegetation, with native grasses and various rare plants, including the prickly pear cactus—the only species of cactus native to western Washington. You'll also find these unusual conditions at minuscule **Gossip Island** and **Cemetery Island,** near the mouth of Reid Harbor. These two islands are undeveloped state parks with day use only allowed and no picnics. There's a pretty white beach at Gossip Island.

## ◖ SUCIA ISLAND MARINE STATE PARK

Sucia Island (commonly pronounced SUE-sha, but you may occasionally hear the original Spanish pronunciation, sue-SEE-uh; 360/376-2073, www.parks.wa.gov) is the gold standard for Washington's marine state parks, with something for almost everyone. The shoreline has delightful sandy beaches for sunbathing, exploring, clamming, and crabbing, plus

© DON PITCHER

mushroom rock on Sucia Island

bizarre water-carved sandstone formations and lounging seals. Offshore, you can scuba dive on an artificial reef created by three sunken wrecks. Hikers and mountain bikers will find 10 miles of scenic trails, campers revel in the many primitive campsites, and boaters tie up at buoys, linear moorage, or docks in a half dozen small bays. Picnic tables and shelters dot the coves.

Shaped like a horseshoe, Sucia Island is 2.5 miles north of Orcas Island and almost to the Canadian border. In addition to the main island of Sucia, nine smaller islands (some privately owned) are adjacent, including the Finger Islands, Little Sucia Island (closed to public access when bald eagles are nesting here), Justice Island, and Ewing Island. All together, the islands cover almost 750 acres. Two other popular marine destinations are nearby: Patos and Matia Islands.

Sucia Island is the largest and one of the most popular marine state parks in Washington, with more than 100,000 boaters annually. Don't expect to be the only visitor on Sucia Island; on a summer weekend, the waters around the island are jam-packed with U.S. and Canadian vessels of all descriptions. You can avoid some of the mob scene in midweek or during the slower spring and fall months.

The first European to discover Sucia Island was explorer Francisco Eliza in 1791. He named it for the Spanish word that means "dirty" or "foul," a nautical reference to the shoal-filled waters surrounding Sucia.

The San Juans have long been a haven for smuggling, and its multitude of coves and sculpted sandstone rocks made Sucia Island a center for everything from illegal booze during Prohibition to Chinese laborers in the late 19th century. During the early 1900s, sandstone quarried from Sucia was used to pave Seattle's streets. In the 1950s, a wealthy Californian prepared to buy Sucia Island from its local owners, intending to subdivide it for vacation homes. Word quickly spread in the Puget Sound yachting and boating community, and a drive was mounted to raise $25,000 to purchase the island. In 1960, the Puget

Sound Interclub Association donated Sucia to the State of Washington, thus preserving this marvelous island for the public.

## Mooring

Sucia Island wraps its two long arms around **Echo Bay,** where you'll find 17 mooring buoys and two sets of linear moorage ($10). **Shallow Bay** is right across a narrow isthmus from the head of Echo Bay and has a pleasant beach, eight buoys, and colorful sunsets. An eroded sandstone cliff, filled with many small nooks and crannies, borders the northeast side of Shallow Bay. Known as **China Caves,** these niches were supposedly used by 19th-century smugglers to hide illegal Chinese laborers from immigration officials. It's a good tale, but probably apocryphal.

On the southern end of the island is **Fossil Bay**—named for marine fossils scattered along the beach—with 16 buoys, two docks, and a park ranger's station. Families have fun finding the fossils, but it's illegal to take them. A low, sandy isthmus (great for hanging out on a sunny day) separates it from **Fox Cove,** which has four buoys. **Snoring Bay,** with two buoys, is near the south end of the island, while **Ewing Cove,** with three buoys, occupies the northeast end of the island facing Ewing Island.

## Hiking and Biking

Despite the abundance of summertime boaters in Sucia, it is easy to escape the crowds by simply heading inland on one of the trails that lace the island. The land is surprisingly diverse, with a variety of forests—including Douglas fir, shore pine, Pacific madrone, and Rocky Mountain juniper—along with sea cliffs (use caution hiking with small children), sandy beaches, odd rock formations, and all-encompassing seascapes.

Trails start from all the popular bays and coves, offering options of varying lengths. If you were to hike from Johnson Point on the southern end of the island to Ewing Cove on the northern end, it would be a round-trip walk of nine miles. Of note is the one-mile hike from Fossil Bay to the end of **Ev Henry Finger,** a

narrow peninsula with steep cliffs and killer views of Orcas Island and points south. The hike to **Ewing Cove** is another delightful option, with a wooded trail that follows the shoreline to this beautiful and out-of-the-way cove. There are some steep drops along the way, so watch your step.

All of these trails are also open to mountain bikers, and biking the main roads is quite easy, but it's best to leave the narrower trails to hikers.

## Camping

A total of 55 primitive campsites ($12) are located at Echo Bay, Fossil Bay, Shallow Bay, Fox Cove, Ewing Cove, and Snoring Bay. Picnic shelters, fireplaces, firewood, and composting toilets are all available at the various campgrounds. Drinking water is here early; call ahead to check availability, or bring your own. Camping is only allowed at designated sites. The campsites at Ewing Cove and Snoring Bay are a bit more isolated and may be a better choice in the peak summer season when the island is a frenzy of activity. Reservations are available for three group campsites and an Adirondack shelter on Sucia Island; call 360/376-2073 for details. Groups can also reserve a picnic area along Fossil Bay.

## Getting There and Around

It's relatively easy to get to Sucia via sailboat or motorboat, and many others paddle kayaks from North Beach or Coho Lodge on Orcas Island. A number of regional kayak companies offer guided trips to Sucia for those who prefer a knowledgeable guide when crossing these sometimes-difficult waters filled with odd currents, sudden winds, and dangerous reefs. Don't take chances!

Two companies offer sea-kayak day trips from Orcas to Sucia: **Shearwater Adventures** (360/376-4699, www.shearwaterkayaks.com) and **Outer Island Expeditions** (360/376-3711, www.outerislandx.com). A five-hour trip includes a water taxi to Sucia and guided kayaking in the protected bays ($159 adults or $99 kids). Both companies use the water taxi from Outer Island Expeditions, based on the north side of Orcas and just a 15-minute ride to Sucia. If you just want to hike and play on Sucia, the water-taxi cost is only $45 per person round-trip. Highly recommended.

Friday Harbor–based **Captain Carli's Charters** (360/378-0302 or 888/221-1331, www.carlicharters.com, $175/person round-trip) runs transportation to Stuart Island in a speedy six-passenger boat.

**North Shore Charters** (360/376-4855, www.orcasislandadventures.com, $195/hour for up to six people plus kayaks or bikes) provides day trips and drop-offs to Sucia Island from Deer Harbor on Orcas Island.

Based in Anacortes, **Island Express Charters** (360/299-2875 or 877/473-9777, www.islandexpresscharters.com, $164/person round-trip to Sucia) has high-speed landing crafts with space for kayaks ($30 extra), bikes ($12 extra), and gear.

**Paraclete Charters** (360/293-5920 or 800/808-2999, www.paracletecharters.com, $312 round-trip for two, add $10 for bikes or $20 for kayaks) runs boats from Anacortes to Sucia.

**Kenmore Air** (425/486-1257 or 800/543-9595, www.kenmoreair.com) provides charter floatplane flights to Sucia Island.

## TURN ISLAND MARINE STATE PARK

Just a quarter mile from San Juan Island's east shore, Turn Island (360/378-2044, www.parks.wa.gov) is within easy kayaking distance of Friday Harbor. The 35-acre island is both a marine state park and a part of the San Juan Islands National Wildlife Refuge. The island was named by the British in 1858 to denote the abrupt change in course required when navigating the San Juan Channel here.

For such a little place, Turn Island has more than its share of attractions, including three mooring buoys ($10), two pebbly beaches, camping, nearby scuba diving, and three miles of hiking trails. One path completely circles Turn Island, with another cutting through its densely forested center.

Campers can pitch a tent at one of 12 primitive campsites ($12), which fill quickly. The island has picnic tables and compost toilets, but no water. **Campfires and charcoal grills are not allowed, so bring your cookstove and fuel.** The proximity to Friday Harbor makes this island both easy to reach and close to the noises caused by all that summertime activity, resulting in something less than a wilderness experience.

### Getting There

Turn Island is a very popular place for day-use picnickers and hikers who arrive by small boat or sea kayak. The closest access is from a little parking lot on Turn Point Road just 1.5 miles east of Friday Harbor; it is locally called Pinedrona Cove. From here, it's 0.2 mile to the island. Note, however, that the channel between Turn Island and San Juan Island can have strong currents and wakes from passing ferries. You can also put in at the Friday Harbor dock.

Based in Friday Harbor, **Captain Carli's Charters** (360/378-0302 or 888/221-1331, www.carlicharters.com, $100/person round-trip) has custom charters to Turn Island in a six-passenger boat.

# Private Islands

Scattered across the San Juans are islands that are predominately—or entirely—owned by private individuals or nonprofit organizations. Not all of these islands are restricted to landowners, however, and a number of these have at least some publicly accessible areas.

Some islands have only a single home; others host a few dozen residences and an unpaved airstrip. None have more than 80 or so people. Privacy is closely guarded on many of these islands, and visitors—particularly those who trespass on private land—are not appreciated.

Anyone interested in buying their own island should look over local real estate publications or a website such as www.privateislandsonline.com. When I last checked, Ram Island (near Lopez) was for sale at the bargain price of only $3.5 million.

Note that even those islands that are entirely in private hands may have beaches and tidelands that are accessible to the public if you arrive by boat. The Washington Department of Natural Resources (360/856-3500, www.dnr.wa.gov) produces detailed State Public Lands Quadrangle Maps showing public beaches in the San Juans and elsewhere.

## BLAKELY ISLAND

As the state ferry heads west from Anacortes to the San Juans, it threads its way between two large and privately owned islands, Blakely and Decatur. Blakely is the namesake of Johnston Blakely, a U.S. naval commander in the War of 1812, and was named during the 1841 Wilkes Expedition. Today, Blakely is sometimes called the "Flying Island." Many residents are pilots whose homes are adjacent to the airstrip; they taxi right up their driveways and park.

Blakely has a heavily wooded interior (all second-growth forests from logging in the 1950s), two lakes, a 100-foot-high waterfall, several large hills (one is 1,042 feet), and miles

© DON PITCHER

Many of the outer San Juan Islands are privately owned.

of private roads. A public marina is located on the northern tip of Blakely across from Obstruction Island. Visitors are welcome here, and guest moorage is available, along with a post office, picnic tables, a barbeque shelter, fuel, showers, washers, and dryers. A good little general store (360/375-6121) has food, basic supplies, ice, and even espresso. Beyond this, almost the entire island is private and completely off-limits. A handful of locals live on the island year-round, with more flying or boating in seasonally. In addition, Seattle Pacific University (360/375-6224, www.spu.edu) owns 967 acres on Blakely and operates the Blakely Island Field Station, which it uses for marine biology and ecological research; there is no public access.

### Getting There

You can't stay on Blakely without permission, but you can at least get there and check out the marina.

**Paraclete Charters** (360/293-5920 or 800/808-2999, www.paracletecharters.com, $128 round-trip for two, add $10 for bikes or $20 for kayaks) provides service to Blakely from Anacortes.

Also based in Anacortes, **Island Express Charters** (360/299-2875 or 877/473-9777, www.islandexpresscharters.com, $74/person round-trip to Blakely) has high-speed landing crafts with space for kayaks ($30 extra), bikes ($12 extra), and gear.

**San Juan Airlines** (360/293-4691 or 800/874-4434, www.sanjuanairlines.com) has daily scheduled flights to Blakely Island from Anacortes and Bellingham. **Kenmore Air** (425/486-1257 or 800/543-9595, www.kenmoreair.com) provides charter floatplane flights to Blakely.

## CANOE ISLAND

Halfway between Shaw and Lopez Islands is this privately owned 50-acre island, home to the **Canoe Island French Camp** (360/468-2329, www.canoeisland.org), a nonprofit language and culture summer camp that attracts children from around the nation. The coed

© DON PITCHER

Blakely Island

camp opened in 1969 and is staffed by French speakers who work with the 45 campers, ages 9–16. Kids don't need to know any French to attend, and there's a 1:3 staff-to-camper ratio. All counselors are fluent in French, and many come from France and other French-speaking countries.

Campers stay in tepees, and mornings are filled with French-language classes and activities, such as theater, fencing, music, and French cooking. Afternoons include games, kayaking, swimming, sailing, and boating. Four sessions are offered each summer, each lasting two or three weeks, and rates start around $2,000 for a two-week session. Three-day family camps ($250/person) take place over Memorial Day and Labor Day weekends, providing a great intro for younger kids. The program is semi-immersion, in which the campers are encouraged to use French as much as possible. The island is not open to the general public, though the tidelands are public below mean high tide.

## DEADMAN AND GOOSE ISLANDS

These two little islands are sandwiched between Lopez and San Juan Islands and are owned by The Nature Conservancy (206/343-4344, www.nature.org). Deadman Island is just west of Shark Reef along Lopez, while Goose Island is a grassy isle off Cattle Point on San Juan Island. They are not generally open to the public, but access may be allowed if you contact TNC in advance. Deadman is used by the University of Washington Friday Harbor Laboratory for marine research.

The Conservancy also owns the publicly accessible **Chuckanut Island** within Chuckanut Bay just south of Bellingham. This five-acre island is popular with kayakers and features graceful madrone trees and a short trail.

## DECATUR AND CENTER ISLANDS

Decatur Island is just east of Lopez Island and immediately south of Blakely Island. This large island is privately owned and home to 60

or so people year-round and hundreds more seasonally. The island has a post office, grade school (smallest one in Washington with 4–6 students), boat launch, and airport, plus miles of scenic county roads open to the public. The island is not on most travelers' agendas because you can't get off the roads to explore the private lands, and the beaches are not readily accessible. Experienced kayakers sometimes visit pretty **White Cliff Beach** on the southeastern side of Decatur, walking the public tidelands.

Decatur Island received its name during the 1841 Wilkes Expedition and is named for Stephen Decatur, a famous U.S. naval officer during the War of 1812 and various skirmishes in northern Africa. He is best known for his nationalist maxim that has become a right-wing standby, "Our country, right or wrong." Decatur was killed in a duel with a fellow captain at the age of 40.

**Center Island** is a 222-acre private island sandwiched between Decatur and Lopez Islands. It has quite a few summer homes and an airstrip.

### Lodging

The country store on Decatur—and the island's only business—closed a few years ago, but check **VRBO** for island rentals. A three-bedroom home (206/817-1557, www.vrbo.com/183309) is available for $2,100 per week, along with a three-bedroom cabin (www.vrbo.com/144298) for $1,790 per week.

### Getting There

**Paraclete Charters** (360/293-5920 or 800/808-2999, www.paracletecharters.com, $128 round-trip for two, add $10 for bikes or $20 for kayaks) provides service to Decatur and Center Islands from Anacortes.

Also based in Anacortes, **Island Express Charters** (360/299-2875 or 877/473-9777, www.islandexpresscharters.com, $74/person round-trip to Decatur or Center Islands) has high-speed landing crafts with space for kayaks ($30 extra), bikes ($12 extra), and gear.

**San Juan Airlines** (360/293-4691 or 800/874-4434, www.sanjuanairlines.com)

has daily scheduled flights to Decatur from Anacortes and Bellingham. **Kenmore Air** (425/486-1257 or 800/543-9595, www.kenmoreair.com) lands at Decatur Island on a charter basis.

**Northwest Sky Ferry** (360/696-9999, www.nwskyferry.com) offers flightpooling from Bellingham to Decatur and Center Islands. Flightpooling is similar to carpooling, where they put people together to travel at a reduced rate.

## JOHNS ISLAND

A little more than a mile long, this privately owned island has a mixture of rocky bluffs and quiet beaches, but no public facilities—unless you count the popular summer camp (Camp Nor'wester). The island lies immediately east of Stuart Island and north of Spieden Island.

Two Anacortes-based companies provide water-taxi service to the island: **Island Express Charters** (360/299-2875 or 877/473-9777, www.islandexpresscharters.com) and **Paraclete Charters** (360/293-5920 or 800/808-2999, www.paracletecharters.com).

### Camp Nor'wester

Johns Island is the home of Camp Nor'wester (360/468-2225 year-round or 360/472-1382 in summer, www.norwester.org), a coed summer camp for ages 9–16. The camp has been in existence since 1935, though it only recently moved to the beautiful 132-acre Johns Island site from Lopez Island; billionaire Paul Allen bought the old camp site.

Kids take part in such traditional summer-camp activities as camping, sailing, kayaking, canoeing (on a 35-foot Haida-style canoe), and natural history, along with a ropes course, biking, and arts and crafts. The emphasis is on working with peers to develop friendships and to learn together rather than independently. Sessions include a maximum of 170 campers with a staff of 75. Four-week sessions for ages 11–16 cost $3,775–4,075, and two-week camps for ages 9–10 are $1,975–2,275; prices include transportation to and from Seattle. In late August, a special four-day "preview session"

provides an introduction for parents and kids ages 7–12. The cost is just $300 per person, including transportation from Anacortes. This is a great way to introduce your child to summer camp.

## OBSTRUCTION ISLAND

This triangular island is wedged between Blakely and Orcas Islands. The state park campsites at Obstruction Pass on Orcas are less than 400 yards away. Entirely private, Obstruction Island has rocky shores, tiny beaches, and a dozen or so homes. Public access is not allowed. The island covers 217 acres and is heavily forested. Even though you can't go ashore, kayakers often put in at Obstruction Pass and paddle around the island.

## SATELLITE ISLAND

The Seattle YMCA's Camp Orkila (206/382-5009, www.seattleymca.org) owns 107-acre Satellite Island, located just off the north side of Stuart Island at Prevost Harbor. The island was named for the H.M.S. *Satellite,* a steamship used for surveys by the British during the Pig War. Satellite Island has no permanent structures and is not open to the general public, though Camp Orkila uses it for adventure trips. (The only exceptions are areas below mean high water, which are publicly accessible at low tides.)

## SENTINEL ISLAND

Owned by The Nature Conservancy (206/343-4344, www.nature.org), Sentinel Island is a 15-acre forested island immediately south of Spieden Island. The island is preserved as habitat for eagles, black oystercatchers, and glaucous-winged gulls today, but it was once the home of June and Farrar Burn, who homesteaded here in 1940. June went on to write about life here in the autobiographical *Living High* (Griffin Bay Bookstore) and described their adventures sailing around the San Juans in *100 Days in the San Juans* (Long House Printcrafters & Publishers). Both books make for interesting reading if you're looking for a taste of a quieter era. Sentinel Island is not

# GUMDROP ISLANDS

Boats for the San Juans leave the Quackenbush Dock in Bellingham at seven. On a Puget Sound morning in winter, seven is pitch-dark night. In summer, it has been full day for two hours or more. In the fall and spring, it is pale dawn. That is how it was on this September day, but fresh and clear, as though the world had got up on the right side of the bed.

Little fishing boats rolled sleepily against their moorings. Another passenger-and-freight boat was loading. It left just before us. I watched its keel rip open the bright silk of the bay.

Later, I learned the names of the dark green islands we passed, but that morning they were mysterious and dreamlike. Eliza slipped behind. Lummi Island, elephant-big, reared up on its haunches in front of the boat, but we side-stepped it and went on. Eagle Cliff on Cypress, Blakely Island, Lopez, Shaw, Orcas, Deer Harbor, Waldron, Stuart Island.

From the narrow channel between Johns and Stuart, we saw a tall, long, lovely island just ahead.

"That's Spieden," the captain said. "Ed Chevalier lives there. His wife's father homesteaded part of it, and Ed has gradually got it all. Just on the other side of Spieden is the little island you are looking for."

Across another channel, seagulls screaming. Around the immense hip of Spieden – and there was Sentinel Island, like a green gumdrop, fir trees lifting their beautiful crowns into the sky, sedum-covered bluffs shearing straight down into the rich, green-blue water. from June Burn's *Living High*, an autobiography published by Griffin Bay Bookstore on San Juan Island.

generally open to the public, but access may be allowed if you contact TNC in advance.

## SINCLAIR ISLAND

Sinclair Island was named during the Wilkes Expedition of 1841 for Arthur Sinclair Sr., a U.S. naval captain during the War of 1812. During his heyday as a smuggler, Larry Kelly owned a third of Sinclair Island.

This small and mostly private island is less than a mile northeast of Cypress Island. A county dock extends from the southwest end of the island, providing access to the little village called Urban and to the dirt roads that crisscross Sinclair. It's a 0.7-mile walk to **Sinclair Island Natural Wildlife Area,** a 35-acre beachfront parcel on the southeast end of the island. By combining beach walks with the island's quiet back roads, you can spend an enjoyable afternoon wandering the island while remaining on public lands.

### Getting There

**Paraclete Charters** (360/293-5920 or 800/808-2999, www.paracletecharters.com,

$128 round-trip for two) provides service to Sinclair Island from Anacortes.

Also based in Anacortes, **Island Express Charters** (360/299-2875 or 877/473-9777, www.islandexpresscharters.com, $76/person round-trip to Sinclair) has high-speed landing crafts with space for kayaks ($30 extra), bikes ($12 extra), and gear.

**San Juan Airlines** (360/293-4691 or 800/874-4434, www.sanjuanairlines.com) will fly to Sinclair Island on a charter basis.

## SPIEDEN ISLAND

Located between Stuart and San Juan Islands, Spieden (pronounced SPY-den) Island covers 480 acres and is privately owned with no public access. The island is informally known as John Wayne Island. In the early 1970s, Wayne and two taxidermists bought the entire island and began importing exotic animals for wealthy trophy hunters to bag. Environmentalists protested the sham, and locals feared stray bullets would be a hazard for people on nearby San Juan Island. After three years, the game farm closed. Most of the axis deer, Japanese

# KING OF THE SMUGGLERS

Smuggling along the U.S.-Canadian border has always been a fact of life, and the items transported back and forth have always been the same: liquor (particularly during the United States' foray into prohibition), illegal drugs, illegal Chinese immigrants, and even Canadian wool and silks.

An Irishman named Larry Kelly was the most infamous of all the smugglers, though perhaps not the most successful at staying away from the law. Kelly arrived in America simply by jumping ship in New Orleans. He fought in the Civil War on the Confederate side. Not long after the war, he arrived in Seattle. He had heard about the "hole in the fence," meaning the easy smuggling across the Canadian border – especially through Puget Sound – of liquor, opium, and Chinese laborers.

Kelly bought an old sailboat in 1872 and sailed north to Guemes Island, where he set up shop. He learned it was easy to hide from the revenue cutters because they ran on a set schedule. Kelly made a nice profit smuggling opium, which he bought at $15 a pound from factories in Victoria and sold for three times that in Seattle. The opium was packed in watertight tin cans, and to each can Kelly tied a chunk of salt as a sinker in case he was caught and had to dump the opium. After the salt dissolved, the can would float to the surface so Kelly could go back out and retrieve it.

Kelly charged about $50 for smuggling a Chinese laborer out of Canada into the United States. Although he denied ever killing one, other smugglers weren't averse to chaining a boatload of immigrants together and dumping them overboard to drown if a revenue cutter approached. It is likely he did some of the things common among his fellow smugglers, such as putting laborers down on a beach in British Columbia and telling them they were in America.

Kelly was caught in 1882 with 40 cases of Canadian whiskey and fined. He wasn't caught again for another four years, but that time he had 567 tins of opium. For this he was sent to McNeil Island Federal Penitentiary. In 1891 he was caught for the final time, on a train with opium in his traveling bag. He was put away again, and while in prison decided to change his life. He wrote to the Louisiana Chapter of the Daughters of the Confederacy to see if any of his old friends from the Civil War were still alive. He found some in a Confederate old soldiers' home in New Orleans, and it was there he went on his release from prison, never to smuggle again.

At least, he was never caught at it.

---

sika deer, Spanish goats, Corsican mouflon sheep, Barbary sheep, Indian blackbuck, and other animals gradually disappeared, though mouflon sheep and sika deer may be seen grazing in the distinctive open grasslands lining the south side of Spieden. Forests carpet the north side of the island, and Steller sea lions are sometimes seen on rocks off the eastern end of Spieden. The island is now owned by billionaire James Jannard (www.jannard.com), founder of Oakley Sunglasses and creator of the RED digital cinema camera; it's said he paid $20 million for the island. You'll hear all sorts of wild rumors from locals about the island, including ones of high-tech surveillance equipment to keep intruders away.

## WALDRON ISLAND

This large, mostly private island is 1.5 miles northwest of Orcas. The locals don't generally take kindly to outsiders, but the roads are open to the public, along with the dock at Cowlitz Bay. There are no stores, electricity, or phone service on the island, though it does have a small post office, cemetery, grade school, and landing strip. The year-round population is around 100, but it doubles when summer residents show up. Waldron Island was named for two members of the 1841 Wilkes Expedition: Thomas W. Waldron and R. R. Waldron.

Much of Waldron Island is flat and marshy, though the south end rises to 600 feet at Disney Mountain. **Waldron Island Preserve** encompasses 478 acres along Cowlitz Bay and Disney Mountain. These lands are jointly managed by The Nature Conservancy (206/343-4344, www.nature.org) and the San Juan Preservation Trust (www.sjpt.org), with only day use allowed. The Conservancy has a steward on the island; call for access information.

Waldron gained a measure of infamy in 1997 when drug enforcement officers swarmed across the island in search of marijuana growing operations. Several residents were arrested, and 886 plants were seized. The operation led to finger pointing in all directions, and still leaves a bad taste with islanders who cherish their leave-me-alone privacy.

### Getting There

**North Shore Charters** (360/376-4855, www. orcasislandadventures.com, $195/hour for up to six people plus kayaks or bikes) provides day trips and drop-offs to Waldron Island from Deer Harbor on Orcas Island.

**Paraclete Charters** (360/293-5920 or 800/808-2999, www.paracletecharters.com,

$312 round-trip for two, add $10 for bikes or $20 for kayaks) provides service to Waldron Island from Anacortes.

Also based in Anacortes, **Island Express Charters** (360/299-2875 or 877/473-9777, www.islandexpresscharters.com, $170/person round-trip to Waldron, add $12 for bikes or $30 for kayaks) has two high-speed landing crafts.

**San Juan Airlines** (360/293-4691 or 800/874-4434, www.sanjuanairlines.com) will land at the Waldron Island airstrip on a charter basis.

**Northwest Sky Ferry** (360/696-9999, www.nwskyferry.com) offers flightpooling from Bellingham to Waldron Island. Flightpooling is similar to carpooling, where they put people together to travel at a reduced rate.

### ◖ YELLOW ISLAND PRESERVE

This 11-acre slice of paradise is virtually equidistant from San Juan, Shaw, and Orcas

Yellow Island Preserve

© DON PITCHER

Islands. Yellow Island, owned by The Nature Conservancy (206/343-4344, www.nature. org) is famous for its lush wildflower displays that peak mid-April–early June, when more than 50 species are in bloom. The lack of deer and strong preservation efforts keep the island in a pristine state. Long and thin, Yellow Island has sand spits and grassy meadows on both ends, with a swath of evergreens across the middle.

Yellow Island was home for many years to Lewis and Tib Dodd, who lived a life that followed Henry David Thoreau's philosophy of self-sufficiency and harmony with nature. Lewis died in 1960, and Tib continued to spend summers on the island for many more years before donating the land to The Nature Conservancy in 1980. The simple driftwood and rock cabin built by the Dodds now serves as the caretaker's seasonal home.

## Visiting the Preserve

Yellow Island is managed as an ecological preserve with a very stringent set of regulations. Visitors can only visit between the hours of 10 A.M. and 4 P.M. daily and will generally need to land their kayak or small boat on the southeast beach. No camping or overnight mooring is allowed, and you can't bring pets, food, or beverages onto the island. Groups larger than six people will need written permission to visit. A 0.5-mile trail rings the small island; pick up an interpretive brochure before heading out.

## Getting There

Most visitors to Yellow Island arrive by sea kayak or motorboat from Orcas Island or San Juan Island. Located at Deer Harbor Marina on Orcas, **Orcas Boat Rentals** (360/376-7616, www.orcasboats.com) is a short boat ride from Yellow Island. Rent a skiff to head over on your own, or ask about water-taxi service for $100 per person round-trip.

Natalie Herner of **Gnat's Nature Hikes** (360/376-6629, www.orcasislandhikes.com) leads boat-and-hike trips to Yellow Island from Orcas Island each spring. There's a three-person minimum and a six-person maximum.

Also timed for the peak of the flowers, **Shearwater Adventures** (360/376-4699, www.shearwaterkayaks.com, $85 per person) guides springtime kayak day trips to Yellow Island from Deer Harbor Marina for.

**North Shore Charters** (360/376-4855, www.orcasislandadventures.com, $195/hour for up to six people plus kayaks or bikes) provides day trips and drop-offs to Yellow Island from Deer Harbor on Orcas Island.

Friday Harbor–based **Captain Carli's Charters** (360/378-0302 or 888/221-1331, www.carlicharters.com, $69 adults or $59 kids) runs custom charters to Yellow Island in a speedy six-passenger boat.

## Other Wasp Islands

Yellow Island is one of the Wasp Islands. Others in the group include Bird Rock, Cliff, Coon, Crane, Low, McConnell, Nob, and Shirt Tail Reef. Crane Island is the largest of these, covering 222 privately owned acres. McConnell Island is also private, but a tombolo (narrow sandy strip) links it to diminutive **Northwest McConnell Rock State Park,** a popular lunch spot for kayakers. Look along the shore of McConnell for remains of an old miniature railroad that was once used to entertain kids.

# BACKGROUND

## The Land

### ISLAND NAMES

A look at a map of northern Puget Sound will reveal a mélange of Spanish, British, and American names. None of the original Native American names remain in the San Juans, though surrounding areas kept a few indigenous terms, including Lummi Island, Samish Bay, and Skagit Island.

The Strait of Juan de Fuca is named for Apostolos Valerianos, a Greek who sailed for Spain under the alias of Juan de Fuca. The first European to sail the Northwest Coast of the United States and Canada, he entered Puget Sound in 1592, believing that he had found the fabled Northwest Passage. The Spaniard Francisco de Eliza and his assistant, Lopez Gonzales de Haro, explored these waters more thoroughly in 1791 and 1792, labeling the San Juan Islands, Haro Strait, Rosario Strait, and Orcas, Lopez, Eliza, Sucia, Patos, Matia, Guemes, and Fidalgo Islands.

Many regional landmarks—including Vancouver Island, Puget Sound, Georgia Strait, Cypress Island, Whidbey Island, Possession Sound, Mount Baker, and Mount Rainier—were named during English expeditions by Captain Cook in 1778 and Captain Vancouver in 1792.

Another major player in the naming game was Lieutenant Charles Wilkes of the U.S. Navy,

© DON PITCHER

who sailed through the San Juans on an 1841 scientific expedition. Wilkes applied the names of his naval heroes (along with several crewmembers) to everything in sight: Allan Island, Barnes Island, Blakely Island, Burrows Island, Clark Island, Decatur Island, Frost Island, Henry Island, James Island, Jones Island, Shaw Island, Sinclair Island, Spieden Island, Stuart Island, and Waldron Island. He also tried to rename the main islands of Orcas, San Juan, and Lopez, but his choices didn't stick.

## THE SALISH SEA

In recent years, biologists have begun using the name Salish Sea for the waters surrounding the San Juan Islands. This great inland sea—named for the Coast Salish people who first made this their home—encompasses Puget Sound, the Strait of Juan de Fuca, and the Strait of Georgia off the west side of Vancouver Island. Enormous glaciers carved out the basin that became the Salish Sea more than 14,000 years ago.

The Salish Sea is a fertile place, with twice-daily tides that sweep massive amounts of water upwards over submerged ridges, thus bringing nutrients to the top layers and surface oxygen to lower depths upon tidal retreat. Rivers and streams supply additional nutrients to the mix, and the temperate climate supports a diverse ecological web. The result is an incredibly productive environment for all forms of marine life. Steve Yates's *Orcas, Eagles, and Kings* provides an in-depth introduction to the Salish Sea.

## GEOLOGY

The San Juan Islands are composed of a complex and jumbled assemblage of rocks that were laid down in ancient oceanic trenches and then pushed up into mountains by tectonic forces. Over the last three million years, they were further shaped by a series of enormous glaciers that pushed southward from Canada and bulldozed everything in their path. The land that would later become the San Juans was buried several times beneath hundreds of feet of ice. When the last of the glaciers retreated around 12,000 years ago, they left behind evidence of their passing, including glacial erratics (large boulders that were carried atop the ice) and bedrock that shows the scratches and gouges of glaciers.

Other unusual rocks found on the islands include marine fossils on Sucia Island (in Fossil Bay, of course), impressive pillow basalts (created when lava flowed under the Pacific Ocean) along San Juan's west coast and Lopez's south side, and substantial limestone deposits on the north end of San Juan Island. This limestone was mined extensively in the early 1900s and used for the production of Portland cement. The old limekilns are still visible at Roche Harbor Resort and Lime Kiln Point State Park. For a more detailed look at San Juan Islands geology, pick up *Roadside Geology of Washington* by David Alt and Donald Hyndman.

## CLIMATE

Noting their location—in the middle of northern Puget Sound—one might assume that the San Juan Islands suffer from Washington's notoriously wet weather. Fortunately, such is not the case. Mountains on the Olympic Peninsula and Vancouver Island force clouds to drop much of their moisture before they reach the San Juans, creating a rain shadow effect. Summertime visitors are pleasantly surprised by the warm and sunny weather that predominates. Winters are typically overcast and rainy, though still drier than many other parts of Washington.

The San Juans do most of their tourist business between Memorial Day and Labor Day, when the weather is delightful. For locals, September and October are the best months of the year: The tourists are gone (and they left their cash behind), and the weather is still warm and relatively dry, with highs in the 60s and lows in the 40s or 50s.

### Rain, Fog, and Wind

Rainfall amounts to around 29 inches per year on the San Juans, compared with 37 inches in Seattle. Precipitation varies across the islands, with the driest areas closer to Anacortes or

© DON PITCHER

trail signs at Turtleback Mountain, Orcas Island

southern Lopez and the wettest on the northwestern end of San Juan Island.

The sun shines an average of 247 days a year, much of that during the summer months; July and August each average only an inch of rain per month. May, June, and September are also relatively dry. November, December, and January make up the rainiest season, with more than four inches of precipitation typically falling each month. Snow is uncommon in the San Juans—only around seven inches fall per year—and it rarely stays around for more than a few days. The one exception is the summit of Mount Constitution, half a mile up on Orcas Island, where snow occasionally gets two feet deep before a warm spell melts it again.

Fog can get thick around the islands at times, particularly in late summer. Fortunately, it is generally gone by early afternoon.

Winds are typically mild in the San Juans, but passes often funnel them, causing very different conditions depending on your location around an island. Sailors take advantage of

these winds, which often top 20 knots in open straits and channels. Small boaters—particularly sea kayakers—need to avoid such areas when the winds are blowing. Occasional winter storms can bring extreme events, such as the December 1990 nor'easter that flattened thousands of old-growth trees, particularly on Jones Island.

## Temperatures

Temperatures on the islands are generally quite comfortable. Midsummer days are typically in the upper 60s and low 70s, and only rarely top 85°F; the record high was 92°F on July 17, 1941. Nighttime lows in the summer average 50°F.

The record low for the San Juans was 8°F on January 13, 1950, but most winters the thermometer doesn't even come close to zero. In January (the coldest month), daytime highs are typically in the low to mid-40s, with nighttime minimums a few degrees above freezing. The thermometer dips below freezing approximately 34 days a year.

## Weather Updates

Get current weather and marine forecasts for the San Juan Islands—and anywhere else in America—from the National Weather Service's website (http://weather.noaa.gov). Another useful web source for weather is linked through the *Journal of the San Juans* (www.sanjuanjournal.com). Boaters can also get the latest forecast on their VHF radios (channels 1, 2, and 8); weather reports are broadcast continuously.

## Water

Water—or the lack thereof—is a serious problem on the San Juan Islands, particularly during the all-too-frequent drought years. Relatively low annual precipitation, limited underground aquifers, and only a handful of year-round creeks and lakes make water a scarce commodity. As the population increases and development grows, the demands for water escalate. Old wells are drying up, and new ones are often contaminated by saltwater intrusion as the underground aquifers are drained. Most bed-and-breakfasts and other lodgings use low-flow showerheads and other means to conserve water. Do your part by not wasting a drop. This means avoiding long showers, not leaving the water running while brushing your teeth or shaving, and not flushing the toilet as often.

## PUBLIC LANDS
### State Parks

A number of state parks (360/902-8844, www.parks.wa.gov) are scattered across the San Juans. **Moran State Park** on Orcas Island is the biggest and most famous of these, covering more than 5,200 acres of heavily forested terrain. It includes the islands' highest point, 2,409-foot Mount Constitution. A paved road leads to the summit, and the park offers camping, swimming, boating, fishing, and more than 30 miles of hiking trails. Smaller parks are **Spencer Spit State Park** on Lopez Island, a popular camping spot; **Lime Kiln Point State Park** on San Juan Island, a day-use-only park famous for views of killer whales from shore; and two small places on Orcas Island:

**Obstruction Pass State Park** and **Point Doughty Marine State Park.**

Several smaller islands contain **marine state parks** that are open to hiking and camping and are accessible only by boat or floatplane. These include Blind, Clark, Doe, Jones, James, Matia, Patos, Posey, Stuart, Sucia, and Turn Islands. Small marine state parks are also located on Orcas and San Juan Islands.

## National Wildlife Refuge

The San Juan Islands National Wildlife Refuge encompasses 83 islands and islets, most of which are off-limits to tourists, to protect birds and other animals. These islands provide vital nesting spots for bald eagles and seabirds, and the rocks are used as haul-out areas for harbor seals, California and Steller sea lions, and elephant seals.

Boaters (including sea kayakers) must stay at least 200 yards offshore from these islands. Landing is permitted only at two designated areas, on Turn and Matia Islands. The refuge is managed by the U.S. Fish & Wildlife Service (360/457-8451, www.pacific.fws.gov) and is based in Port Angeles; contact the agency for a small map of the islands. Marine navigation charts also show which islands are within the national wildlife refuge.

## San Juan Island
## National Historical Park

The so-called Pig War is memorialized in the 1,750-acre San Juan Island National Historical Park (headquarters: 640 Mullis St., Friday Harbor, 360/378-2240, www.nps.gov/sajh). Established in 1966, the park is divided into two sections. American Camp occupies a beautiful grassy peninsula on the southeast end of the island, while English Camp is in a wooded, peaceful cove on the opposite side of San Juan. Both of these areas are worth a visit, not only for the handful of historic buildings but also for excellent hiking trails and gorgeous beaches.

## Other Public Lands

Seven **San Juan County parks** (360/378-8420, www.co.san-juan.wa.us/parks) are

# PRESERVING THE SAN JUANS

To vacationers, the San Juans may seem like a recreational playground, but for island inhabitants, they provide sustenance. Puget Sound is becoming increasingly developed as the population spirals upward, leaving the islands as a place to rediscover the natural world. But the islands themselves are also under pressure as new homes encroach old farms or carve openings into remote shorelines, as public areas are closed off because the access trails cross private lands, and as increasing use impacts the natural areas. It's yet another case of wild places being loved to death. Several nonprofit organizations are working to protect the San Juans through land purchases and environmental action.

## SAN JUAN PRESERVATION TRUST

In existence since 1979, the San Juan Preservation Trust (360/468-3509, www.sjpt.org) works with local landowners to protect special features of their lands for future generations through conservation easements and donations. Over the years the trust has protected more than 9,300 acres of land, including working farms, forests, picturesque shorelines, and wildlife-rich wetlands. Most of the property preserved by the trust remains in private hands, with public access by permission only.

## SAN JUAN COUNTY LAND BANK

Established by a 1990 ballot measure, the San Juan County Land Bank (360/378-4402, www.sjclandbank.org) is a public program funded by a 1 percent real estate transfer tax. These taxes raise $1-2 million annually (depending upon the real estate market) to acquire land or conservation easements. More than 3,500 acres have been protected in natural areas, including such places as Hummel Lake and Upright Head Preserves on Lopez, Crescent Beach and Turtleback Mountain Preserves on Orcas, and Westside and Limekiln Preserves on San Juan.

## FRIENDS OF THE SAN JUANS

Based in Friday Harbor, Friends of the San Juans (650 Mullis St., 360/378-2319, www.sanjuans.org) is a local environmental group with nearly 2,000 members. The organization focuses on land use issues and beach research, and pushes for shoreline preservation throughout the San Juans.

## THE NATURE CONSERVANCY

An international organization, The Nature Conservancy (206/343-4344, www.nature.org) owns Deadman, Goose, Sentinel, and Yellow Islands and has 480 acres on Waldron Island. Only Yellow Island is readily accessible to the public.

---

on the ferry-served islands: Agate Beach, Blackie Brady Memorial Beach, Odlin, and Otis Perkins County Parks on Lopez Island, Ruben Tarte and San Juan County Parks on San Juan Island, and Shaw Island County Park on Shaw Island. Camping is available at Odlin, San Juan, and Shaw Island County Parks; the others are for day use only.

The **Washington Department of Natural Resources** (DNR: 360/856-3500, www.dnr.wa.gov) has considerable land on Cypress Island, with primitive campsites, hiking trails, and protected moorages. It also manages a campsite on Lummi Island.

The federal **Bureau of Land Management** (BLM: 360/468-3754, www.or.blm.gov) manages small natural areas on Lopez, Stuart, and Patos Islands. All have hiking trails and are for day use only. They also have a small office on Lopez with maps and additional information.

The **San Juan County Land Bank** (360/378-4402, www.sjclandbank.org) has acquired more than 3,100 acres in 13 natural areas scattered around the islands. These are open to the public for day use only.

**The Nature Conservancy** (206/343-4344, www.nature.org) owns several small San Juan islands, plus 480 acres on Waldron

Island, but only Yellow Island is readily accessible to the public.

The **University of Washington's** Friday Harbor Laboratories (360/378-2165, http://depts.washington.edu/fhl) manages several natural areas around the San Juans, but only Cedar Rock Biological Preserve on Shaw Island is open to the public.

# Flora and Fauna

Plant and animal communities on the San Juans reflect local topographic and weather conditions. Forests dominate in many areas, but the islands also contain broad expanses of grassland, open meadows and fields, rich marine areas, marshes and lagoons, and a long and diverse shoreline that includes rocky cliffs, sheltered bays, and sandy beaches. There are even islets so dry that cacti grow.

## HABITATS
### Forests
Dense coniferous forests (or ones regenerating after logging) cover large portions of the islands, and are typically dominated by Douglas fir, western hemlock, and western red cedar. Common understory plants include salal, Oregon grape, red elderberry, thimbleberry, salmonberry, blackberry, wild roses, and various ferns. Dry, rocky sites commonly have picturesque groves of Pacific madrone, particularly along island shores. At higher elevations and on exposed ridges, shore pine often grows.

Forests are home to Columbian black-tailed deer, raccoons, beavers, mink, river otters, bats, shrews, and various introduced species of squirrels, along with such birds as ravens, woodpeckers, winter wrens, and owls. Good places to explore island forests include Moran State Park and Madrona Point on Orcas Island, English Camp and Jackle's Lagoon on San Juan Island, Odlin County Park on Lopez Island, Cedar Rock Biological Preserve on Shaw Island, and the boat-accessible marine state parks on Jones, Matia, and Sucia Islands.

### Meadows
Meadows may be either natural grasslands, hilltops, and mountain slopes, or spaces created by the clearing of land for agriculture. Some of the best grasslands to explore include American Camp and the top of Mount Young on San Juan Island, Mount Constitution on Orcas Island, the wonderful floral displays on The Nature Conservancy's Yellow Island, and fallow agricultural land on all four of the main islands.

Animals commonly seen in island meadows include nonnative European rabbits, voles (meadow mice), shrews, alligator lizards, red foxes (a nonnative species on San Juan Island), and small birds, such as vesper sparrows, savannah sparrows, and American goldfinches. Overhead you might see birds of prey, such as bald and golden eagles or northern harriers. A few small islands (including Cactus, Gossip, and Cemetery Islands) contain areas called **Puget prairies,** with distinctive plants like the lance-leafed stone and even prickly pear cactus—the only species of cactus native to western Washington.

### Wetlands
Swamps, lagoons, marshes, ponds, and other wetlands are vital areas for wildlife on the islands and are home to river otters, muskrats, beavers, raccoons, garter snakes, red-legged frogs, Pacific tree frogs, rough-skinned newts, red-winged blackbirds, great blue herons, Canada geese, belted kingfishers, and many species of ducks. Good places to find wetlands include Jackle's Lagoon and Egg Lake on San Juan Island, the Frank Richardson Wildlife Preserve on Orcas Island, and Spencer Spit Lagoon on Lopez Island.

### Shorelines
San Juan County contains more than 375 miles of shoreline—the most of any county in

the lower 48 states. This coast varies widely, from rocks to sand to mud, and supports an equally varied population of animals. Intertidal areas are particularly productive.

Beautiful **sandy beaches** are found on all the larger islands, with some of the best at American Camp on San Juan Island, Obstruction Pass State Park on Orcas Island, Spencer Spit State Park and Agate Beach County Park on Lopez Island, Shaw Island County Park on Shaw Island, Pelican Beach on Cypress Island, and Shallow Bay on Sucia Island.

**Rocky shores** are ubiquitous in the San Juans and are welcoming areas for wildlife, including many species of birds. Good places to find them include San Juan County Park and Lime Kiln Point State Park on San Juan Island, Madrona Point and Point Doughty on Orcas Island, Shark Reef Park and Point Colville on Lopez Island, Cedar Rock Biological Preserve on Shaw Island, Eagle Cliff on Cypress Island, Doe Island Marine State Park, Turn Point on Stuart Island, and Ev Henry Finger on Sucia Island.

## Marine Areas

The rich waters around the San Juan Islands abound with marine plant and animal life. The area is justly famous for killer whales, and a surprisingly large business has grown up around whale-watching. Other marine mammals spotted here include minke whales, harbor porpoises, Dall's porpoises, California sea lions, Steller sea lions, harbor seals, and elephant seals. Of course, these waters also contain many species of fish and other creatures. Divers are attracted to the vibrant undersea world of the San Juans, commercial whale-watching trips are a summertime staple, and fish are caught commercially and for sport.

One of the best ways to see killer whales—without impacting them in any way—is from the shore at Lime Kiln Point State Park on San Juan Island. Folks riding the Washington State Ferries are certain to see gulls and various seabirds along the way and may also spot bald eagles and the occasional whale. San Juan Islands National Wildlife Refuge covers 83 islands and rocky points, providing protected breeding and resting areas for an incredible array of seabirds and mammals.

## TREES

The most distinctive and photogenic tree species on the San Juan Islands is the **Pacific madrone,** commonly called madrona or arbutus. These trees grow on rocky sites and are conspicuous as they angle out over the shoreline. Madrones are characterized by dark and leathery evergreen leaves and peeling reddish-orange bark that exposes a smooth underskin. Pacific madrone grows from California to British Columbia.

Washington's state tree, the **western hemlock,** is common in dense, shady forests throughout the archipelago. These trees can reach 500 years old, topping out at 200 feet. Look for the droopy crowns of western hemlock to distinguish them from other trees at a distance.

**Western red cedar** has distinctive flat sprays and a stringy bark. The Coast Salish

Pacific madrone on San Juan Island

© DON PITCHER

# SLUGS

If western Washington had an official creature, it could easily be the common slug; the region is famous for them. The damp climate is just what slugs need to thrive: not too wet, because slugs aren't waterproof (they will absorb water through their outer membranes until their bodily fluids are too diluted to support them), and not too dry, because insufficient humidity makes them dry up and die. Optimum humidity for slugs is near 100 percent, which is why you'll see them crossing the sidewalk very early in the morning, at dusk, or on misty days.

During the dry parts of the day, slugs will seek refuge under the pool cover you casually tossed onto the lawn, or under the scrap lumber piled in the back of your lot.

Slugs look like snails that have lost their shells, or like little green or brown squirts of slime about 3-5 inches long. Though more than 300 species of slugs exist worldwide,

the Northwest is home to little more than a dozen. The native **banana slug,** light green or yellowish with dark spots, has been rapidly outnumbered by the imported European **black slug,** which is now far more common in area gardens than the native variety. Slugs can curl up into a ball to protect themselves, or flatten and elongate themselves to squeeze into tight places. They move on one long foot by secreting mucus that gets firm where the foot must grab hold and stays slimy under the part that must slide. They see (probably just patterns of light and dark) with eyes at the ends of a pair of tentacles; they have a mouth and eat primarily plants and mushrooms.

Getting rid of slugs is no easy matter. Traditional home remedies include salt shakers and beer traps; both require a strong stomach. Most residents just try to avoid stepping on them.

© DON PITCHER

people prized this tree, using it for dugout canoes and splitting the wood for planks to build their houses. The sweet-smelling wood is resistant to decay. Western red cedar is a member of the cypress family and is not a true cedar.

One of the most important trees on the San Juans, **Douglas firs** can grow to six feet

in diameter. They are commonly found with western hemlock and western red cedar. Heavy ridges mark the bark of mature Douglas firs, and lower limbs fall off as the tree grows, making them a favorite of loggers who appreciate the knot-free wood.

**Pacific yew** has sharply pointed needles

and grows in moist areas, particularly along streams. Yews are slow growing and never get very tall. The Coast Salish used the dense wood to carve paddles and bows. Today, the tree is best known as the source for a potent anti-cancer chemical, taxol.

**Big-leaf maples** are distinguished by—you got it—their big leaves, which can reach a foot in width. The trees can grow quite large (to 100 feet high), with spreading trunks. One of the largest is on the grounds of English Camp on San Juan Island. The yellow leaves of maples are particularly beautiful in the fall. Two other related (but smaller) species are also present on the islands, the **vine maple** and **Douglas maple.**

**Shore pines** are a subspecies of lodgepole pine and are generally found on high, windswept bluffs, such as the summit of Mount Constitution on Orcas Island. Most are relatively stunted in height. The trees are well adapted to fire, with some cones that only release seeds when heat melts the sticky covering.

The **Rocky Mountain juniper** is commonly found in the Rockies, but also exists on the San Juans and nearby islands. The trees are stunted, rarely topping 20 feet in height. Cypress Island was misnamed by Captain George Vancouver when he sailed past it in 1792; the "cypress" he saw were actually Rocky Mountain junipers.

Other common trees on the San Juans include **grand firs**, recognizable by their long, flat needles with white undersides; **Sitka spruce,** which grows fast and tall and is common near the shore; and **red alder,** a common fast-growing plant in moist areas.

# WILDLIFE
## Wolf Hollow

Located on San Juan Island, north of Friday Harbor, Wolf Hollow Wildlife Rehabilitation Center (360/378-5000, www.wolfhollowwildlife.org) is a nonprofit organization that works with injured, sick, or orphaned wild animals. Most of these animals were injured by human activities. Since its founding in 1983, Wolf Hollow has treated more than 200 species—from hummingbirds to seals—and has a songbird aviary, raccoon pen, and eagle flight cage. It offers educational programs at local schools and parks, but the facilities are not open to the general public. If you find an injured or orphaned animal on the San Juan Islands, call Wolf Hollow; the staff is available 24 hours a day.

## Land Mammals

**European rabbits** were brought to the islands in the late 19th century as caged meat animals but were released when the breeders ran out of money. The rabbits are now common in grassy parts of San Juan and Lopez Islands and also occur on other islands in the San Juans. Most of them remain underground during the day, emerging at dusk. Bald and golden eagles, red-tailed hawks, northern harriers, and red foxes all feed on them.

**Columbian black-tailed deer** are found almost everywhere on the San Juans and may even be seen swimming between the islands. The deer are quite small, generally under three feet high and only rarely more than 200 pounds. Keep your eyes open for them in old fields and orchards or in brushy areas. During the summer, deer are commonly seen early in the morning or late in the day, when temperatures are cooler.

Other island mammals include raccoons, beavers, mink, river otters, vagrant shrews, white-footed (deer) mice, Townsend's voles, and several species of bats. Flying squirrels were recently discovered on San Juan Island and are presumably native. Introduced species include muskrats, Norway rats, and house mice, plus Townsend's chipmunk on Lopez Island and red foxes and European ferrets on San Juan Island. Three types of squirrels—eastern gray squirrels, eastern fox squirrels, and Douglas squirrels—have been introduced. Surprisingly, skunks, porcupines, and coyotes are not found on the San Juans. Elk were once found on the islands, but 19th-century market hunters killed off the last of them.

Red foxes are an introduced species on San Juan Island.

© DON PITCHER

## Reptiles and Amphibians

There are no poisonous snakes on the San Juans, but you might encounter three species of garter snakes (the double-striped common garter is most often seen). Other regional species include northern alligator lizards, Pacific tree frogs, red-legged frogs, northwestern toads, and rough-skinned newts, whereas bullfrogs and western painted turtles were introduced.

## Whales and Dolphins

The most famous local mammal—the **killer whale**—attracts more than half a million visitors to the San Juans each summer. An excellent source for information about these strikingly marked and social animals, as well as other marine mammals around the islands, is The Whale Museum's website (www.whalemuseum.org).

**Minke whales** are gray or brownish in color, with diagonal white bands on their pectoral fins. They are generally seen as solitary individuals, moving slowly and with a blow that is often inconspicuous. Minke are the most numerous of the world's baleen whales and are frequently seen around the San Juans in the summer, but not at other times of the year. Minke whales feed by driving schools of small fish to the surface and then opening wide to engulf them. They also take advantage of clusters of fish that have been schooled together by other fish or birds; minkes pop to the surface through this ball of fish, sometimes scattering gulls and other birds when they emerge. Minke whales can reach 30 feet long, and the larger females may weigh up to 10 tons.

**Gray whales** are bigger than minkes and lack a dorsal fin. They have a mottled gray body and are often covered with patches of barnacles, especially on the head. They are generally seen in shallow coastal areas and migrate some 9,000 miles, from Alaska to Baja. In recent years, a few gray whales have stayed in the waters of northern Puget Sound through the summer, but they are not commonly seen.

**Humpback whales** can reach up to 55 feet

© DON PITCHER

Male killer whales have a distinctive dorsal fin.

long and are slate gray or black, with irregular knobs on the head and jaw and a short dorsal fin. Their blows are strong and obvious. Humpbacks are rarely seen around the San Juans, but are fairly common in more northern waters.

Other species of cetaceans sometimes seen around the San Juans include **false killer whales,** a relatively small whale that is mostly black; and **Pacific white-sided dolphins,** with a gray-black upper body accented by a white belly and grayish sides.

## Porpoises

Visitors often think that the black-and-white sea creatures riding the bow waves of their tour boat are baby killer whales, but these playful characters are **Dall's porpoises.** They feed primarily on squid and small fish and can reach lengths of 6.5 feet and weights of up to 330 pounds.

The **harbor porpoise** is Puget Sound's smallest cetacean, growing to nearly six feet long and 150 pounds. Although similar in appearance to the Dall's porpoise, the much shyer harbor porpoise is rarely spotted in the wild. Accurate counts are impossible, but the population around the San Juan Islands has been estimated at fewer than 100.

## Seals and Sea Lions

**Harbor seals** are the most abundant marine mammals in the San Juans. They can be seen at low tide sunning themselves on rocks in isolated areas, but they will quickly return to the water if approached by humans, particularly kayakers. Though they appear clumsy on land, these 100- to 200-pound seals (some males can reach 800 pounds!) are poetry in motion underwater; they flip, turn, and glide with little apparent effort, staying underwater for as long as 20 minutes. Harbor seals have a bad reputation with area salmon anglers, although studies of the seals' stomach contents and fecal material indicate that they feed primarily on flounder, herring, pollock, cod, and rockfish, as well as some mollusks and crustaceans.

The **California sea lion** is a seasonal visitor

to northern Puget Sound. These dark-brown sea lions breed off the coast of California and Mexico in the early summer, and then some adventurous males migrate as far north as British Columbia for the winter.

The lighter-colored **Steller sea lions** are often seen in the spring around the San Juan Islands, particularly Spieden Island. Males of the species are much larger than the females, growing to almost 10 feet in length and weighing over a ton, while the females are a dainty six feet long and 600 pounds.

Recent years have seen an increased population of the **northern elephant seal** in waters around the San Juans. Adult males have a large elephantine snout, and the biggest may weigh upward of four tons. Females are much smaller. Both have a brownish-gray color and occasionally haul out on local beaches.

If you come upon a stranded seal, sea lion, whale, or other marine mammal, do not handle it, but instead immediately call the **Stranded Marine Mammal Hotline:** 800/562-8832.

## BIRDS

More than 200 species of birds live or travel through the San Juans, including large numbers of shorebirds in the spring and fall, nesting seabirds, great blue herons, trumpeter swans, Canada geese, wild turkeys (introduced in the 1970s), belted kingfishers, common ravens, rufous hummingbirds, and such predators as bald eagles, red-tailed hawks, sharp-shinned hawks, northern harriers, turkey vultures, and great horned owls. San Juan Island National Historical Park and local bookstores sell a nicely designed *Wildlife of the San Juan Islands* checklist that includes all these birds, along with local mammals, reptiles, and amphibians. You can get it directly from Archipelago Press (360/378-5571).

The **National Audubon Society's** Washington state office (http://wa.audubon.org) has detailed information on birds and birding in the state. Call its rare bird alert line (425/454-2662) for unusual sightings in the San Juans and elsewhere. Another useful source is the **Tweeters** website (www.scn.org/tweeters); click the "Latest Postings" link for recent sightings.

The **San Juan Islands Audubon Society** website (www.sjiaudubon.org) lists recent sightings, upcoming bird walks, and other birding info. They generally have birding walks on San Juan Island twice a month (except in July). Barbara Jensen of **Bird the San Juans** (360/378-3068, www.birdthesanjuans.com) leads birding, natural history, and cultural history tours of San Juan Island. A three-hour trip for up to four people is $135.

## Bald Eagles

The San Juan Islands are home to the largest year-round population of bald eagles outside Alaska. They are common sights soaring over the bays and channels or riding the thermals atop Mount Constitution on Orcas Island or Mount Findlayson and Mount Dallas on San Juan Island.

In the past, bald eagles were often blamed for the deaths of sheep and other domestic animals. Actually, eagles much prefer dead and dying fish to anything running around on hooves; their common fare, aside from dead

family of Canada geese

© DON PITCHER

salmon, is sick or injured waterfowl or rabbits that didn't make it across the road. An aggressive bird, the eagle will often purloin the catch of an osprey or other bird in favor of finding its own. The large nests of bald eagles, sometimes measuring more than 8 feet wide and 12 feet high, are often found in old-growth spruce and fir snags (standing dead trees).

The adult bald eagle's distinctive white head and tail make it easy to spot. But it takes four years for it to acquire these markings, making the immature eagle difficult to identify, as it may show whitish markings anywhere on its body. In contrast, the somewhat similar golden eagle has distinct white patches on its tail and underwings.

## Great Blue Herons

Another large bird seen throughout the San Juans is the great blue heron, a long-legged bird that wades in shallow bays and marshes. Their diet consists of frogs, small fish, snakes, crabs, and other creatures. Look for them in places such as the Frank Richardson Wildlife Preserve on Orcas Island, English Camp on San Juan Island, or Weeks Wetland on Lopez Island; the long legs, slate-blue coloration, yellow bill, and ornate black plumes are distinctive.

# History

North America has been inhabited for a very long time. Low ocean levels during the Pleistocene epoch (some 30,000–40,000 years ago) offered the nomadic peoples of northeastern Asia a walkable passage across to Alaska. One of the earliest records of humans in the Americas is a caribou bone with a serrated edge found in northern Yukon Territory. Almost certainly used as a tool, the bone has been placed at 27,000 years old by carbon dating. As the climate warmed and the great ice sheets receded toward the Rocky Mountains and Canadian Shield, a corridor opened down the middle of the Great Plains, allowing movement farther south. Recent scientific evidence suggests that ancient peoples also sailed or paddled along the coast from Asia to North America.

## THE COAST SALISH

Humans have occupied the San Juan Islands for thousands of years. Recent discoveries of bison bones in Orcas Island peat bogs revealed cut marks on the bones caused by human hunters, providing evidence that people have been on the islands for nearly 14,000 years. When the first European explorers sailed around the San Juan Islands, they found them populated primarily by the Lummi and Samish tribes, though the Songhees and Saanich were present on parts of the western and northern islands. These closely related tribes are all considered Strait Coast Salish people. Lummi legends tell of a man named Swetan who landed on San Juan Island where he built a home, probably at Garrison Bay. His descendants became the various family groups that settled the islands and surrounding shores. Nobody knows exactly when Swetan arrived, but he may represent the earliest influx of people to the area. The Salish culture underwent changes over the eons as people developed better ways to catch and preserve fish and shellfish.

Although the Coast Salish were a peaceable people, their Haida and Kwakiutl neighbors to the north were infamously aggressive, and the Salish found themselves under periodic threat from marauding parties that swept through the islands in 50-man war canoes. Salish men were often killed in these attacks, while the women and children were taken away as slaves. Once captured, a slave's only hope was to run away, since he or she could never marry a nonslave and was treated as property. To defend their territory against such raids, the Salish constructed rock stockades and armed themselves with whalebone clubs; these ancient fortifications are still visible on Lopez Island. Unfortunately, the northern tribes were some of the first to obtain firearms from Russian traders, making life even more difficult for the Salish. By the middle of the 19th century, the raiders were attacking not only the Salish but also white settlers in the region.

## The Cycle of Life

Strait Coast Salish life revolved around access to foods such as salmon, clams, and edible plants. The arrival of summer meant the return of salmon, and the Salish prepared by moving their families to temporary camps on the islands where they would be close to the migrating schools of fish. The salmon were caught in reefnets suspended from dugout canoes, and the fish were then preserved by air drying or smoking over a fire. Reefnets are still used today in the islands. Other important foods included clams, cockles, oysters, sea cucumbers, crabs, sea urchins, chitons, snails, barnacles, mussels, and various species of fish. Edible plants included wild strawberries, blackberries, gooseberries, huckleberries, purple great camas bulbs, horsetails, and tiger lilies. The Coast Salish used nets to catch black-tailed deer and ducks.

Men had the primary responsibility for fishing, hunting, house building, and carving canoes, while the women gathered, cooked, and preserved the food and made clothing, wove mats, and coiled baskets. Clothes were woven using processed cedar bark or roots, duck down, nettle fiber, wool, animal skins, and other materials. In the summer, Coast Salish people often went naked. After the busy summer season of hunting and gathering, the families returned to their winter village, which might be on the islands or the mainland. Fall was often a time for big potlatches. Guests were invited from throughout the region, and the festivities always included games, canoe races, mock battles, intertribal marriages, and an elaborate potlatch ceremony in which the host gained prestige by giving away gifts.

Winter quarters—cedar plank houses and enormous longhouses used for potlatches— were built along protected beaches. A number of families lived inside each plank house.

Sleeping platforms lined the outside walls, and mats hung from the rafters as partitions and to insulate from the cold. Families cooked over a central fire that also heated the house; smoke escaped through a hole in the roof. Western red cedar was important not just for the Salish homes but also in their carvings and dugout canoes, some of which reached 30 feet in length.

## Death of a Culture

The Pacific Northwest tribes were introduced to the byproducts of the white man's culture, such as knives, guns, and the deadly smallpox virus (to which they were not immune), before ever laying eyes on a white explorer. The first disease outbreak in this era of death swept through in 1782, followed by additional plagues in the 1830s and early 1850s. Over this 75-year period, some 80–90 percent of the Coast Salish died from disease. They were not the only ones; the population of Native Americans in the entire Pacific Northwest may have numbered one or even two million before the diseases struck, but their numbers plummeted to 180,000 by the time Europeans arrived. Smallpox Bay on San Juan Island is named for an incident in the 1860s when many Salish died after two sick sailors were forced ashore from an unknown ship to keep them from contaminating other sailors.

It wasn't just disease that killed the Coast Salish. Alcohol took a deadly toll, and San Juan Island became known far and wide for its saloons, where drunkenness and violence were the norm at any time of the day or night. And direct conflicts with whites pushed the Salish from areas they had inhabited for thousands of years. This combination of diseases, repeated raids by northern tribes, alcohol, and aggressive white settlers decimated the Coast Salish. By the 1840s, the San Juan Islands had no year-round residents; the survivors had moved to the Washington mainland or Victoria. The **Point Elliott Treaty** of 1855 established the Lummi Indian Reservation near Bellingham. The book *Lummi Elders Speak,* edited by Ann Nugent, has an insightful quote from one village elder,

Herman Olsen. Describing Mitchell Bay on San Juan Island, he said:

*A white fellow moved in there. They home-*
*steaded the whole thing. They just plain*
*homesteaded it wrong and everything.*
*Then on the other side of the bay, what*
*there was left, the Lummis moved across,*
*just a stone's throw across the bay; they*
*had two great big houses there. Then they*
*had some more small houses, cabin-like,*
*that they stayed in that got homesteaded*
*so the Lummis just lost out there too. White*
*people came and homesteaded the darn*
*place and never even left their ground for*
*the Lummis.*

For additional information on the original San Juan settlers, read Julie K. Stein's *Exploring Coast Salish Prehistory: The Archaeology of San Juan Island* (University of Washington Press, www.washington.edu/uwpress). The book details excavations at a seasonal camp near American Camp and Salish winter quarters at English Camp. Both of these camps were used for thousands of years, and English Camp may have been in use up until just before the English soldiers showed up in 1859. There are literally hundreds of other archaeological sites on the islands. Also worth a read is *San Juan Island Indians,* a self-published work by Gary J. Morris that's available in local libraries.

## THE EUROPEANS ARRIVE
### Spanish Explorers

In 1592, exactly a century after Columbus made his landfall in the Caribbean, a Greek explorer using the Spanish name **Juan de Fuca** sailed along Washington's coast and claimed to have discovered the fabled "Northwest Passage," an inland waterway crossing North America from the Pacific to the Atlantic. Later explorers did find a waterway close to where de Fuca indicated, but it led only into today's Puget Sound, not all the way to the Atlantic Ocean.

Spain, hoping to regain some of its diminishing power and wealth, sent out several expeditions in the late 1700s to explore the Northwest Coast. In 1774, Juan Perez explored as far north as the Queen Charlotte Islands off Vancouver Island and was the first European to describe the Pacific Northwest coastline and Olympic Mountains before being forced to turn back by sickness and storms.

In 1775, a larger Spanish expedition set out, led by Bruno de Heceta and Juan Francisco de la Bodega y Quadra. Heceta went ashore at Point Grenville, just north of Moclips on the Washington coast, and claimed the entire Northwest for Spain. Farther south, Bodega y Quadra sent seven men ashore in a small metal craft for wood and water; they were quickly killed and their boat torn apart in the whites' first encounter with coastal Native Americans. The two ships sailed away without further incident; Quadra named the island Isla de Dolores (Isle of Sorrows), today's Destruction Island off the Olympic Peninsula. Quadra continued his explorations as far north as present-day Sitka, Alaska, while Heceta sailed north to Nootka Sound. Heceta failed to note the Strait of Juan de Fuca, but he did come across "the mouth of some great river," presumably the Columbia, though the death or illness of much of his crew prevented further exploration and robbed Spain of an important claim.

It was not until 1791 that the first Europeans finally saw the San Juan Islands up close. In that year the Spanish explorer **Francisco Eliza** sent his schooner *Santa Saturnina* into what his pilot, Lopez Gonzales de Haro, described as "an indescribable archipelago of islands, keys, rocks, and big and little inlets." The Spaniards returned to the San Juans the next summer, this time better equipped to explore the islands in depth. But when they arrived, they found two other ships already present, the *Discovery* and *Chatham,* captained by their English competitors under George Vancouver. Despite the often-hostile relations between the Spanish and English, the two decided to work together as they explored the area. This cooperation may have been an augury of the later Pig War on San Juan Island in which two nations chose cooperation over conflict.

## English Explorations

England was *the* force to be reckoned with in the battle for the Northwest. In 1776, Captain **James Cook** took two ships and 170 men on an expedition that brought him to the Hawaiian Islands, the Oregon coast, and Vancouver Island's Nootka Sound. Though he charted the coastline from Oregon to the Bering Sea, he made no mention of the Strait of Juan de Fuca. Hostile Hawaiians killed Cook in a 1779 dispute over a boat, and his crew returned to England.

Other English sailors continued in Cook's footsteps, and in 1787, Charles Barkley and his wife, Frances, explored and named the Strait of Juan de Fuca. Best known today, however, is the expedition led by **George Vancouver** in 1792. His goal was to explore the inland waters and make one last attempt at finding the Northwest Passage. The names of Vancouver's lieutenants and crew members read like a list of Washington place-names: Baker, Rainier, Whidbey, and Puget. (Many of the place-names were attached to curry political favor back home; almost anyone in a position of power had his name stuck on something.) The expedition carefully charted and thoroughly described all navigable waterways and named every prominent feature. Vancouver's survey crew reached the Strait of Juan de Fuca in May 1792, and one of his boats landed at Blind Bay on Shaw Island, where they found a Coast Salish settlement. Some of the Coast Salish people paddled canoes out to trade with the Englishmen, providing them with three freshly killed deer and a live fawn for venison.

## American Explorations

An American, **Robert Gray,** sailed out of Boston to explore and trade along the Northwest Coast in 1792. Stopping first at Nootka Sound—the hot spot to trade on Vancouver Island—Gray worked his way south and spent three days anchored in today's Grays Harbor. Continuing south, Gray discovered the mouth of the Columbia River and traded there with the Chinook before heading home without finding Puget Sound and the San Juans.

His explorations helped establish American claims to the Pacific Northwest.

The first American survey of the San Juan archipelago took place in 1841 under the leadership of Lieutenant **Charles Wilkes.** The surveyors were only in the islands for three days in July but managed to see much of the country and to apply American names to virtually everything in sight. The predictable choices were American naval heroes from the War of 1812 or Tripoli, along with members of his expedition, including Stuart Island for his clerk, Fredrick D. Stuart, and Waldron Island for two of his crewmembers. Fortunately, some of his other name choices—Navy Archipelago instead of the San Juan Islands, Hulls Island instead of Orcas, Rodgers Island instead of San Juan Island, and Chauncys Island instead of Lopez—were later rejected by saner folks. Wilkes's charts of the islands did, however, later prove vital in the designation of the San Juans as American, rather than British, property.

## SETTLING THE ISLANDS

During the time between the early exploration and the permanent settlement of the Northwest, British and American trading posts emerged to take advantage of the area's abundant supply of beaver and sea otter pelts. Two English companies, the North West Company and Hudson's Bay Company, merged in 1821; American fur-trading outfits included many small, independent companies as well as John Astor's Pacific Fur Company and the Rocky Mountain Fur Company.

The most influential of them, the **Hudson's Bay Company,** built its temporary headquarters on the north side of the Columbia, 100 miles inland at Fort Vancouver. The settlers planted crops, raised livestock, and made the fort as self-sufficient as possible. At its peak, 500 people lived at or near the fort. When settlers began arriving in droves and the beaver population diminished in the late 1840s, the Hudson's Bay Company was crowded out and moved its headquarters north to Fort Victoria on Vancouver Island.

## Manifest Destiny

In the 1840s, the United States and England jointly occupied "Oregon Country," land north of the 42nd parallel. It included lands that today make up Washington, Oregon, Idaho, and parts of Montana, Wyoming, and British Columbia. The westward movement gained momentum when a New York editor coined the phrase "Manifest Destiny" to symbolize the idea that all the land west of the Rockies rightfully belonged to the United States. Ironically, if you exclude trappers, prior to 1843 there were barely 40 white settlers west of the Rocky Mountains.

Between 1840 and 1860, more than 50,000 American settlers moved west to Oregon Country to take advantage of the free land they could acquire through the Organic Act of 1843 and the Donation Land Law of 1850. Under the Organic Act, each adult white male could own a 640-acre section of land (one square mile) by simply marking its boundaries, filing a claim, and building a cabin on the land. The Donation Land Law put additional restrictions on land claims: 320 acres were awarded to each white or half-white male who was an American citizen and had arrived prior to 1851; another 320 acres could be claimed by his wife.

The promise of free land fueled the "Great Migration" of 1843, in which almost 900 settlers traveled to Oregon Country, six times the number of the previous year. More pioneers followed: 1,500 in 1844 and 3,000 in 1845. Most settlers came by way of the Oregon Trail from St. Joseph, Missouri; they followed the North Platte River, through southern Wyoming and southern Idaho into Oregon, then headed north to the Columbia River. Soon the route looked like a cleared road; traces of it can still be seen where the wagon tires dug ruts in stone and where wheels packed the ground so hard that grass still cannot grow.

## Divvying Up the Northwest

Britain regarded the westward expansion with dismay, watching as the lands it claimed were increasingly populated by Americans. The Oregon Treaty of 1846 settled the dispute, giving possession of all lands south of the 49th parallel to the United States. Although the problem appeared resolved, the treaty failed to adequately describe the boundary through upper Puget Sound, causing both the United States and Britain to claim the San Juan Islands. Over time this issue came back to haunt both nations. Thirteen years after the treaty signing, an incident involving a potato-loving pig and an angry settler on San Juan Island nearly precipitated a war. The issue would not be finally resolved until 1872, when an arbitrator awarded the islands to the United States.

## Smuggling Takes Hold

Smuggling was an important part of life on the San Juans for many years, and some of the earliest businesses were illegal booze joints for soldiers, settlers, and Native Americans. Around 1880, large numbers of Chinese laborers began arriving on San Juan Island, working both in local potato fields and at the limestone operation along Roche Harbor. Smuggling of Chinese workers from Vancouver Island through the San Juans to Seattle became a big business. An even more lucrative one was (and still is) illegal drugs. The drug of choice at the time—primarily for Chinese workers in the United States—was opium. Legal in British Columbia, it was refined in factories there. Opium smuggling became an important source of income for many island folks, including the best-known smuggler, Larry Kelly.

During Prohibition, the islands were a way station for booze destined for Seattle speakeasies, and a new generation of profiteers emerged. Today, there are still occasional busts of people attempting to transport drugs through the islands, and a few folks have even been caught with drug-packed sea kayaks.

## THE 20TH CENTURY

Once the Americans had successfully ejected the English from the San Juans, one of their first actions was a tax revolt. When Whatcom County imposed a tax, the locals managed to get the legislature to carve out a separate San Juan County for the 200 or so settlers on the islands. The initial seat of power was a rag-tag and boozy settlement called Old Town that was located near American Camp on the south end of San Juan Island. Eventually, the more civilized town of Friday Harbor became the island's primary settlement, and it remains so to this day.

In the late 1800s and early 1900s, Roche Harbor on San Juan Island developed into one of the world's largest limestone mining operations under the leadership of "boss" John S. McMillin. Another industrialist, Robert Moran, had a more lasting impact, however. A shipbuilder and former Seattle mayor, Moran retired early on Orcas Island, built a mansion (today's Rosario Resort), and donated thousands of acres of land for Moran State Park, one of the finest parks in Washington.

One surprising product of the islands from the 1890s through World War I was fruit, particularly apples, plums, and pears. Orcas Island was the primary fruit producer, but orchards spread across Lopez, Shaw, and San Juan as well. Insect infestations and competition from fruit growers in eastern Washington eventually doomed growers on the San Juan Islands, but many of these trees still produce today, more than a century after they were planted. In recent years, as the grow-local movement has caught on, fruit trees are again being planted on farms throughout the archipelago. Fresh apples are sold in weekend farmers markets, and one business on San Juan Island is even producing traditional hard cider, gin, and apple brandy.

## Cars and Ferries

Early in the 20th century, the San Juan Islands were home to a rough mix of farmers, fishers, miners, loggers, and smugglers. Tourism remained of minor importance on the San Juans until the middle of the century, when cars and ferries made the islands increasingly accessible to the masses.

Washington's ferry system had its origins in the early 1900s when a number of companies sailed Puget Sound waters in small steamers known as the "Mosquito Fleet." Competition and consolidation forced most of these companies under, and by 1935 only one remained, the Puget Sound Navigation Company, better known as the Black Ball Line.

That same year, the first auto ferry linked the islands with Anacortes and Sidney, British Columbia. As automobiles became an increasingly important part of the transportation mix in Puget Sound, Black Ball ferries acted as a link across the wide expanses of water. Prior to the ferries, steamers had sailed out of Seattle or Bellingham to deliver freight and passengers around the islands.

The State of Washington jumped into the ferry business in 1951 when it bought out Black Ball's ferries, terminals, and most other assets. The state ferry system was originally intended to be a temporary measure until bridges could be built across Puget Sound, but the legislature rejected that idea in 1959. Since then, Washington State Ferries has become the largest ferry system in the nation (Alaska's is vastly longer, however), with 20 ports of call served by 22 vessels, the largest of which can carry 2,500 passengers and more than 200 vehicles. Today, Washington ferries transport more than 11 million vehicles and 23 million people annually around Puget Sound. The run from Anacortes to Lopez, Shaw, Orcas, and San Juan Islands and then on to Sidney, British Columbia, is not only extremely popular but also the most scenic of all the cross-sound sailings.

## DESTINATION ISLES

For the last 50 years or so, the San Juans have increasingly been a place of recreation and relaxation rather than industry. Small farms and pastures are still important, particularly on Lopez Island, and a number of commercial fishers call the islands home, but the real engines driving the economy are tourism and retirement. In the last decade or so, the islands have attracted national attention as a place to retire, and as a spot for affluent young professionals who work out of their homes. During the 1990s, San Juan County had the second fastest–growing population in Washington.

As the population grew, development

pressure led to water shortages, the loss of public access to island shorelines, and overpriced housing. Despite these troubles—which are minor compared with the vast wasteland of development spreading along the shores of Puget Sound—the San Juan Islands are an eminently livable place where the natural world still dominates. After all, even with a 45 percent increase in the last 30 years, the total population on the islands is still just under 16,000 people. Starting in 2009, the San Juan Islands economy was hit by the same forces that affected the national economy. Housing prices actually declined for the first time in decades, and businesses struggled to make it through the winter months.

# Entertainment and Events

If you've come to the San Juans in search of nightlife, you are probably in for a disappointment. The islands are all about getting away from the hustle and noise of city life, with most travelers opting for an evening stroll along the shore over a steamy night on the dance floor. There are, however, a few bars and restaurants on San Juan, Orcas, and Lopez that offer live music, particularly on summer weekends. San Juan and Orcas also have movie theaters.

Many artists call the San Juans home, displaying their works at local galleries, particularly around Orcas Island and in the town of Friday Harbor. The Lambiel Museum on Orcas displays hundreds of pieces from the finest island artists. Orcas, Lopez, and San Juan Islands all have modern community theaters that host performing arts, musical programs, and other productions year-round.

## FESTIVALS

Some of the biggest island celebrations take place over the **Fourth of July** weekend, when parades, fireworks, barbecues, street dances, and other events draw locals and tourists to Friday Harbor, Roche Harbor, Lopez Village, and Eastsound. **Memorial Day** in late May is another time for play, with a parade, artist studio open houses, a Spring Celebration on San Juan Island, and the Bite of Orcas restaurant sampling at Eastsound. The **Celebrity Golf Classic** on San Juan in early June is the county's top fundraising event. San Juan Island National Historical Park puts on an impressive **Encampment** at English Camp in August, with British and American "soldiers" and others in 19th-century period costume.

The islands burst with musical performances all summer, including classical and rock music festivals on Orcas Island, weekly brown-bag concerts in Eastsound, musical weekends at the Lopez Center, and weekly concerts on the lawn in Friday Harbor.

Don't miss the premier playtime of the year, the **San Juan County Fair,** held on the third week of August in Friday Harbor. Other popular events include the **Splash of Summer Color** in July on San Juan, **Orcas Island Fly-In** in August, **Tour de Lopez** bike ride in April, and **Shakespeare Under the Stars** in July and August at Roche Harbor. San Juan, Orcas, and Lopez all have holiday arts-and-crafts fairs a couple of weeks before Christmas.

Boaters take part in **Whidbey Island Race Week** in mid-July, the **Round Shaw Row** in early August, and the **Shaw Island Classic** yacht race the first weekend of August.

# ESSENTIALS

## Getting There

There are no bridges to the San Juan Islands, but ferries ply these waters, scheduled air service is available, and the islands are popular with boaters and kayakers who head out on their own. The main regional airports are Seattle's Sea-Tac International Airport and Vancouver International Airport. From either of these, you can rent a car and drive to Anacortes, where the Washington State Ferries depart for the islands. Shuttle buses also run from Sea-Tac directly to the Anacortes ferry dock. Scheduled flights connect the islands with Seattle, Anacortes, Bellingham, and Victoria.

### WASHINGTON STATE FERRIES

If you can only take one ride aboard a Washington State Ferry (206/464-6400 or 888/808-7977, www.wsdot.wa.gov/ferries), the trip from Anacortes to the San Juans should be the one. The scenery is so beautiful that even point-and-shoot photographers can get spectacular sunset-over-the-islands shots. In the summer, ferries leave Anacortes at least a dozen times a day, 4:30 A.M.–12:15 A.M., stopping at the north end of Lopez Island, Shaw Island, Orcas Village on Orcas Island, and Friday Harbor on San Juan Island. It takes

roughly two hours to ferry from Anacortes to Friday Harbor. Not every ferry run stops on each island, but nearly all of them pull into Friday Harbor.

Ferries between Anacortes and Sidney, British Columbia, run twice a day in the summer and once daily in fall and spring; there's no service January–March. Vehicle reservations are *highly recommended* for service between the San Juans and Sidney. The ferries have food and drinks onboard, with a duty-free shop on ferries heading to British Columbia.

## Traveling Tips

The **Anacortes ferry terminal** is three miles west of town. A restaurant is nearby, and the bulletin board notes current campsite availability at San Juan Islands parks (meaning, often, that none are available). Ferries between Anacortes and the San Juans have onboard **Wi-Fi** service through Boingo (800/880-4117, www.boingo.com/ferrywifi) for a daily or monthly charge.

The ferry system operates on a first-come, first-served basis, with reservations available only for the routes from Anacortes to Sidney, British Columbia, and from Orcas Island or San Juan Island to Sidney. No reservations for travel to the San Juans; just get in line and wait like everyone else. In Anacortes, tune your radio to **AM 1340** for broadcasts of current ferry status, including any backups or other problems.

If you're taking your car across during the peak summer season, it's wise to arrive at least two hours early on Friday and Saturday, or an hour early on weekdays. Bring a book to read on holiday weekends since you may find yourself in line for up to five hours! Heading east from the San Juans in the peak season, try to arrive an hour and a half or two hours in advance of your sailing. Find current wait times on the ferry system website (www.wsdot.wa.gov/ferries).

Avoid the crowds by traveling midweek, early in the morning, late in the evening (except Friday evenings), or better yet, by foot, kayak, or bike. Leave your car in the lot at the

ferry docking at Friday Harbor

© DON PITCHER

terminal ($25 for three days) and stroll aboard; there's always space for walk-on passengers. Credit cards can be used to purchase tickets at any of the ferry terminals, or you can buy them online. (Note, however, that tickets are only good for seven days.)

If you are boarding a ferry and returning to the U.S. mainland from the islands, try to avoid sailings that started in Sidney, British Columbia; these all must clear customs in Anacortes, and the process can cause substantial delays.

Want a glimpse of travel aboard the ferries? Point your computer to www.ferrycam.net for current ferry conditions and to see photos of the trip from Anacortes to Friday Harbor.

## Anacortes to the Islands

For travel to the San Juan Islands from Anacortes, the state ferry system charges higher rates in the summer. Fares from Anacortes to Friday Harbor (the last American stop) are $11.50 for passengers and walk-ons, or $53.80 for a car and driver. Bikes are $4 extra, and kayaks cost $17.50 more. Summertime fares to the other islands from Anacortes are $11.50 for passenger or $37.75 for car and driver to Lopez Island, and $11.50 for passenger or $45.30 for car and driver to Orcas or Shaw Islands.

Ferry travelers are **only charged in the westbound direction.** Eastbound travel within the San Juans—such as from Orcas to Lopez, or from the islands to Anacortes—is free, with no tickets required. The only exception is for travelers eastbound from Sidney, British Columbia. If you're planning to visit all the islands, save money by heading straight to Friday Harbor and then working your way back through the others at no additional charge.

## Interisland Ferries

Once you're on the San Juans, there is never a charge for passengers, walk-ons, or bikes to travel to another island in either direction. Also, there's no charge for cars heading east within the islands, but the westbound charge is $23.80, whether it is just across the waterway from Shaw to Orcas, or all the way from Lopez to Friday Harbor. Rates are lower in the off-season.

Here's a tip that isn't widely publicized: If you're planning a short stop on one of the islands and then continuing westward to another island within 24 hours, request a **free vehicle transfer.** This is useful if you're on Lopez and heading to Friday Harbor (free stops at Shaw and Orcas), or going from Lopez to Orcas (free stop at Shaw). It saves you $23.50 for each stop, but you must ask for it on your departure island. Note that you cannot stop for more than 24 hours when using a vehicle transfer.

## Anacortes to Sidney, British Columbia

Washington State Ferry (206/464-6400 or 888/808-7977, www.wsdot.wa.gov/ferries) service connects Anacortes with Sidney, British Columbia. Sidney is just 20 miles from the beautiful city of Victoria, and BC Ferries head east from Sidney to the Gulf Islands and Tsawwassen (near Vancouver). Service between Anacortes and Sidney is twice daily in the summer (mid-June–Sept.), and once daily in the fall (Oct.–Dec.) and spring (Mar.–mid-June), with no ferries at all in the winter (Jan.–Mar.). One-way tickets cost $16.85 for passengers and walk-ons, or $56.45 for a car and driver. The charge is the same in the opposite direction (Sidney to Anacortes) or from Sidney to Friday Harbor, but if you stop in Friday Harbor, there are no additional charges to continue east all the way to Anacortes. Reservations are highly advised for ferry runs between Anacortes and Sidney.

Once a day, the Anacortes-Sidney ferry stops at Friday Harbor in both directions. If you get on in Friday Harbor, the passage westward to Sidney costs $6.30 for passengers or $29 for a car and driver. Vehicle reservations are recommended to travel westward from Friday Harbor to Sidney and should be made at least 24 hours in advance. Contact the ferry system for reservations.

When crossing between the United States and Canada, adults of either country will need a passport. All baggage is subject to inspection.

## PRIVATE FERRIES AND DAY CRUISES
### From Seattle

The passenger-only *Victoria Clipper* (206/448-5000 or 800/888-2535, www.clippervacations.com) runs high-speed catamaran day trips between Seattle and San Juan Island. The round-trip cost is $80 adults or $40 kids if you wait till the last minute, but you can save substantially by booking at least a day ahead: $70 round-trip for adults and free for kids under 12. Combine transportation from Seattle with a 2.5-hour whale-watching trip for $30–40 extra. Cruises operate daily mid-May–early September, and on weekends only the rest of September. The company has a multitude of other travel options in the Northwest, including packages that add a night's lodging on San Juan Island, or a three-day/two-night visit to San Juan Island and Victoria. You can also use this as transportation to the islands from Seattle, going up on one day and returning at a later date. In addition, *Victoria Clipper*

has year-round service between Seattle and Victoria for $107–147 round-trip.

### From Port Townsend

**Puget Sound Express** (360/385-5288, www.pugetsoundexpress.com) provides passenger-only service between Port Townsend and Friday Harbor. The boat leaves Port Townsend daily May–October, staying in Friday Harbor long enough for a quick three-hour visit, or you can overnight and return to Port Townsend later. The charge is $89 round-trip ($49 kids ages 2–10), and bikes and kayaks are $15 extra. This isn't a whale-watching trip, but it isn't uncommon to sight orcas en route.

### From Bellingham

**San Juan Cruises** (360/738-8099 or 800/443-4552, www.whales.com, Fri.–Sat. May–Sept.) departs Bellingham for all-day cruises to the San Juan Islands on the 149-passenger *Victoria Star 2*. These trips combine a two-hour stop in Friday Harbor with a three-hour whale-watching voyage and lunch. The cost is $99 adults, $50 ages 6–17, free for younger kids.

## WATER TAXIS

Water taxis provide a quick and easy way to reach a specific place in the islands without dealing with ferry lines or vehicles.

Operating out of Anacortes, **Paraclete Charters** (360/293-5920 or 800/808-2999, www.paracletecharters.com) has been in business since 1992 and has a very experienced crew. They run three passenger boats—the largest is 58 feet long and can carry 64 passengers—to anyplace in the San Juans. This is the place to go for transportation to destinations off the route of the state ferry system, including the private islands. Rates depend upon the destination and number of passengers. As an example, Anacortes to Cypress Island costs $72 for one person round-trip, or $52 per person for five or more folks. In addition to passengers, Paraclete will haul anything from motorcycles and appliances to furniture and construction material. There's no charge for pets, and kids get discounted rates. Add $10 round-trip for

Charter sailboats provide a distinctive way to explore the islands.

© DON PITCHER

bikes, or $20 for kayaks. The boats are designed for all weather conditions and even provide 24-hour emergency transportation when planes aren't able to fly.

Based in Anacortes, **Island Express Charters** (360/299-2875 or 877/473-9777, www.islandexpresscharters.com) has two high-speed landing crafts (one can carry 42 passengers) with plenty of deck space for kayaks, bikes, and gear. Rates depend upon the number of passengers. Skipper Rey Rubalcava provides transportation almost anywhere in the San Juans.

Based on Orcas Island, Marty Mead of **North Shore Charters** (360/376-4855, www.orcasislandadventures.com) provides water-taxi service to Stuart, Sucia, Matia, Patos, and other islands. The boat can hold up to six passengers, plus kayaks and bikes; the cost is $195 per hour.

Operating from Orcas Island, **Outer Island Expeditions** (360/376-3711, www.outerislandx.com) leads daily summertime tours to remote islands in the San Juans and provides water taxi service to Stuart, Sucia, Jones, Matia, and Patos Islands.

## MULTI-DAY CRUISES

Based on San Juan Island, **Fantasy Cruises** (360/378-1874 or 800/234-3861, www.sanjuanislandcruises.com) operates summertime cruises that begin in Seattle and take in the San Juan Islands, Victoria, Whidbey Island, Port Townsend, and other waypoints. The 130-foot *Island Spirit* has 16 staterooms, and eight-day cruises cost around $6,000 for two people.

Operating from Bellingham, the **Northwest Navigation Co.** (360/201-8184 or 877/670-7863, www.northwestnavigation.com) takes six passengers onboard the *David B,* a distinctive and lovingly maintained 1929 vessel. Two-night San Juan trips are $695; kayak mothership trips are also available.

Based on Orcas Island, **Emerald Isle Sailing Charters** (360/376-3472, www.emeraldislesailing.com) has multi-day San Juan Islands charter trips onboard a gorgeous 54-foot pilothouse ketch. Trips start at $997 per person for a three-day voyage.

**Sail the San Juans** (360/671-5852 or 800/729-3207, www.stsj.com) offers six-day fully crewed charters around the islands, departing from Bellingham for $2,095 per person. The 50-foot *Northwind* comfortably accommodates six guests.

## FLYING INTO WASHINGTON

Anyone flying into Washington will almost certainly be landing at **Sea-Tac Airport** (206/787-5388 or 800/544-1965, www.portseattle.org/seatac), 12 miles south of Seattle. The airport has undergone a significant upgrade in the last few years and is a pleasant place to spend a couple of hours in transit. The central terminal has enormous windows facing the runways and a good selection of reasonably priced dining choices. All major domestic, and many international, airlines operate out of Sea-Tac, and foreign travelers can change money in the main terminal. A **Visitor Information Booth** (open daily May–Sept., brochures available anytime) is close to the baggage claim area.

The least expensive way to reach downtown Seattle from the airport—just $3—is aboard a **Sound Transit** (206/398-5000 or 800/201-4900, www.soundtransit.com) light rail train. Trains run every 15 minutes (or less) daily 6 A.M.–11 P.M. and take you directly to Pioneer Square or University Street. City buses provide connections to other parts of Seattle.

### Car Rentals

All the major national car rental companies have desks near the baggage claim at Sea-Tac Airport. I've found the best rates with a web search at www.travelocity.com, www.expedia.com, or www.orbitz.com. AAA or Costco members should be sure to ask about any additional discounts. **Thrifty Car Rental** (www.thrifty.com) and **Payless** (www.paylesscarrental.com) often have some of the lowest rates and provide a starting point for price comparisons. For wheelchair-friendly van rentals, contact **Wheelchair Getaways** (425/353-6563 or 800/854-4176, www.wheelchairgetaways.com).

# GETTING TO THE ISLANDS FROM SEATTLE

The San Juan Islands are 65 air miles northeast of Seattle, with access by air, boat, shuttle van and ferry, or car and ferry.

## By Ferry

You will see a constant parade of Washington State Ferries departing from downtown Seattle, but none of these go to the San Juans. Instead, you'll need to get to Anacortes, where ferries head to the islands. There is, however, a private passenger-only ferry, the *Victoria Clipper* (206/448-5000 or 800/888-2535, www.clippervacations.com), with daily service to the islands from Seattle.

## Shuttle Vans

Getting to the islands from Sea-Tac is easy. **Airporter Shuttle** (360/380-8800 or 866/235-5247, www.airporter.com) makes connections between Sea-Tac and the ferry terminal at Anacortes, along with Bellingham and points north all the way to Vancouver. The one-way cost is $33 ($20 kids) to the ferry terminal. Vans run ten times or so a day and generally take three hours.

**Island Airporter** (360/378-7438, www.islandairporter.com) provides direct van service daily from Sea-Tac to San Juan Island. The bus departs the airport and heads straight to the Anacortes ferry, where it drives on for San Juan Island, and then continues to Friday Harbor ($50) and Roche Harbor ($60). You'll need to add the ferry fare, but it's approximately half the standard rate since you're on a bus. Vans operate once a day in each direction Monday–Saturday in summer and Monday–Friday in winter.

## Trains and Buses

**Amtrak** trains serve Seattle from the King Street Station (3rd Ave. South and S. King St., 206/464-1930 or 800/872-7245, www.amtrak-cascades.com). The Amtrak *Cascades* train connects Seattle with Vancouver, British Columbia, stopping at Mount Vernon and Bellingham twice a day in each direction. Trains do not stop in Anacortes (where Washington State Ferries depart for the San Juan Islands), and the closest station is 18 miles away in Mount Vernon.

**Greyhound Lines** (206/628-5526 or 800/231-2222, www.greyhound.com) has daily bus service throughout the lower 48 and to Vancouver, British Columbia, from its bus terminal at 9th and Stewart. It's the same story here as for Amtrak; Greyhound's closest stop is the town of Mount Vernon.

## By Car

If you're driving from Seattle, it's 80 miles (92 miles from Sea-Tac) to Anacortes, where you catch the Washington State Ferries to the San Juans. The ride is very straightforward: Follow I-5 north to Mount Vernon at Exit 230 and turn west onto Highway 20, which goes straight into Anacortes. The ferry terminal is three miles west of downtown Anacortes via 12th Street.

Be sure to fill your tank in Anacortes before driving on the ferry. Because of the extra cost of shipping fuel (and because they can get away with it), gas stations on the islands charge at least 30 percent more than on the mainland.

# FLYING TO THE ISLANDS

The quickest way to reach the islands is by air, but there are no direct flights from Sea-Tac Airport. You'll need to take a free shuttle to Seattle's Lake Union or Boeing Field to connect with Kenmore Air flights.

## Kenmore Air

The San Juans are served by a legendary floatplane company, Kenmore Air (425/486-1257 or 800/543-9595, www.kenmoreair.com). In business since 1946, it is the world's largest full-service seaplane operation, with two-dozen planes and a summertime staff of more than 200. Kenmore is best known for its De Havilland Beavers (a workhorse of Alaskan bush pilots), but also flies larger turbine Otters and Cessna Caravans. Its yellow-and-white floatplanes are a familiar sight on Lake Union in Seattle and nearby Lake Washington in Kenmore. Kenmore Air is a partner with

© DON PITCHER

**Kenmore Air has daily floatplane flights from Seattle to the San Juans.**

Alaska Airlines, providing 250 air miles for each flight.

Kenmore Air has daily scheduled flights from Lake Union and Lake Washington to Friday Harbor and Roche Harbor on San Juan Island; Fisherman Bay on Lopez Island; and Rosario Resort, Deer Harbor, and West Sound on Orcas Island. They also fly daily to various places along British Columbia's Inside Passage, including Victoria and the Gulf Islands. A free shuttle provides transport to Lake Union from Sea-Tac. Pack light for your trip since a 24-pound baggage weight limit is in effect, and excess baggage costs $1 per pound.

Kenmore also offers flightseeing trips and charter service to other destinations in the San Juans—including Cypress, Sucia, Stuart, and Jones Islands. Wheeled-plane flights take place between Boeing Field in Seattle and airports on San Juan, Orcas, and Whidbey Islands. The baggage weight limit for these is 70 pounds.

## San Juan Airlines

San Juan Airlines (360/293-4691 or 800/874-4434, www.sanjuanairlines.com) has scheduled daily wheeled-plane service to the San Juans from Anacortes and Bellingham, stopping at San Juan, Orcas, Lopez, and Blakely Islands on a scheduled basis. Additional daily flights connect Victoria, British Columbia, with Orcas and San Juan Islands, Anacortes, and Bellingham. Flightseeing and air charters are available to other airports on the San Juans, including on Center, Crane, Decatur, Eliza, Sinclair, Stuart, and Waldron Islands.

## Northwest Sky Ferry

Northwest Sky Ferry (360/696-9999, www.nwskyferry.com) has twice-daily scheduled flights from Bellingham to San Juan, Orcas, and Lopez Islands, with flightpooling charters to other destinations throughout the San Juan Islands. Flightpooling is similar to carpooling, where they put people together to travel at a reduced rate. The airline will fly almost anywhere in the San Juans.

## Charter Flights

Charter flights to the San Juans can be cheaper than scheduled flights if you have four or more passengers. San Juan Airlines and **Island Air** (360-378-2376 or 888/378-2376, www.sanjuan-islandair.com) on San Juan Island provide charter flights throughout the region, including to Boeing Field in Seattle.

## FLYING INTO BRITISH COLUMBIA

The primary hub for flights into western Canada is through the city of Vancouver, though there are also quite a few flights into nearby Victoria on Vancouver Island. There are no airport shuttles between **Vancouver International Airport** (www.yvr.ca) and Anacortes, but car rentals at the Vancouver airport are an option if you want to drive south across the border to Anacortes and then catch the Washington State Ferries to the islands.

If you are flying into **Victoria International Airport** (www.victoriaairport.com), take a taxi to the town of Sidney, where the Washington State Ferries disembark for the San Juans.

# Getting Around

Information on local water taxis, charter flights, and flightseeing for each island can be found in the *San Juan Island, Orcas Island,* and *Lopez Island* chapters. Interisland ferry travel is detailed under *Getting There* in this chapter.

## CAR AND MOPED RENTALS

Avoid the lengthy summertime waits by parking at the Anacortes ferry terminal, walking onboard the ferry, and renting a car once you reach the San Juans. On Orcas Island, rentals are available through **Orcas Mopeds** (360/376-5266, www.orcasmopeds.com). Orcas Mopeds also rents mopeds and scootcars.

On San Juan Island, contact **M&W Auto Rentals** (360/378-2886 or 800/323-6037, www.sanjuanauto.com). Rates start around $50 per day for a compact or $70 per day for an SUV. Rental vehicles are allowed off the islands to the Washington mainland and Canada (with restrictions). **Susie's Mopeds** (360/378-5244 or 800/532-0087, www.susies-mopeds.com) rents mopeds and three-wheeled scootcars in Friday Harbor.

If you're flying to Sea-Tac and then heading to the islands for a week or more, you're probably better off renting a car at the airport, where rates are lower than on the islands.

## BUSES AND TAXIS

**San Juan Transit** (360/378-8887 or 800/887-8387, www.sanjuantransit.com) operates hourly shuttle buses around San Juan Island in the summer, providing a reasonable way to reach the most-visited points. The buses can also carry bikes and luggage.

Taxis are available on San Juan and Orcas Islands, but not on Lopez.

Moped rentals are available on San Juan and Orcas Islands.

© DON PITCHER

# Recreation

The San Juans abound with outdoor pleasures: cycling, sea kayaking, camping, hiking, bird-watching, scuba diving, boating, sailing, whale-watching, skateboarding, and fishing, to name a few.

## BICYCLING

The San Juans are very popular cycling destinations, offering up mild weather, a wide diversity of terrain, gorgeous scenery, excellent facilities, and little traffic. If you have a family in tow or aren't in great shape, head to slow-paced Lopez with its pastoral countryside, good camping, comfortable inns, and friendly locals. Shaw is small but fun to explore, with quiet roads that are fine for families; no lodging, but there is a campground. Orcas has the most rugged rides—including a tough haul to the top of 2,409-foot Mount Constitution—and the most challenging roads, but the diversity and beauty make it unique. San Juan offers varied terrain, the most services (especially at Friday Harbor), and wide shoulders, but also the heaviest traffic.

You won't find any separate bike paths on the islands, and some roads can be narrow and winding with minimal shoulders. Use some common sense even if you are on vacation. Local bike shops carry maps that denote routes with problems (such as heavy traffic or narrow and winding roads), and they offer travel tips. The **San Juan Island Trails Committee** website (www.sanjuanislandtrails.org) also has details on San Juan Island bike routes.

### Bikes on Ferries and Buses

You can bring your own bike on the ferry for an extra $4 round-trip (far cheaper than hauling your car, and you won't have to wait). Ferry loading procedures vary, so be sure to follow the instructions of terminal personnel. Always walk your bike on and off the ferry. Space is always available for bikes.

**San Juan Transit** (360/378-8887 or 800/887-8387, www.sanjuantransit.com) on San Juan Island can transport bikes onboard their vans, providing an easy way to get around if your legs begin to tire.

### Bike Rentals

Bike rentals are available on the three major islands by the hour, day, or week. Most shops rent touring and mountain bikes for around $40 per day or $90 for three days, including bike helmets. Specialized equipment, such as tandems, racing bikes, kids bikes, panniers, child carriers, and bike trailers are also generally available, but reserve ahead to be sure.

### Bike Tours

Several companies guide multi-day cycling tours of the San Juans, with food, lodging, and a support vehicle included in the rate. Bike rentals are also available, and you can choose your own pace on these relatively leisurely tours. All of these differ in routing, amenities, and the number of participants, so call for their catalogs or surf the web to see which one works for you. Note that cycling trip prices are often substantially higher if you are a single traveler looking for a private room.

Based in Issaquah, Washington, **Bicycle Adventures** (425/250-5540 or 800/443-6060, www.bicycleadventures.com) leads a variety of cycling tours around the San Juans, starting at $1,995 for a four-day tour that includes biking, hiking, and kayaking, with lodging at island inns. They also lead seven-day loop tours starting in Seattle and going to Anacortes, Lopez Island, San Juan Island, Victoria, Port Angeles, and Port Townsend. These include cycling, kayaking, and other activities, plus luxury lodging and fine dining for $3,420.

Berkeley-based **Backroads** (510/527-1555 or 800/462-2848, www.backroads.com) has cycling, multisport, and hiking tours of the San Juans approximately 40 times a year. All sorts of options are available, including five- or six-day trips with lodging in casual or luxurious accommodations, multisport adventures with

© DON PITCHER

taking bikes on board the ferry on Orcas Island

lodging or camping, family multisport camping trips, and hiking trips. Multisport trips are especially popular, mixing cycling with kayaking, hiking, and other activities. These six-day trips are available with camping—guides set up and take down the tents—and meals included for around $2,000. At the luxury end, you'll pay $3,000 for a six-day multisport trip that includes upscale lodging and meals.

Based in Wisconsin, **Trek Travel** (608/441-8735 or 866/464-8735, www.trektravel.com) is another company with six-day San Juan bike treks for $2,695, lodging included. In addition, the YMCA's **Camp Orkila** (360/376-2678 or 206/382-5009, www.camporkila.org) leads a seven-day cycling program for teens that covers the San Juan Islands.

## Safety on the Road

A number of common-sense precautions are wise for anyone heading out on a bike in the San Juans:

• Always wear a helmet, even for short trips.

• Be especially cautious in the vicinity of ferry docks, particularly when a ferry has just disgorged its load of vehicles. Get off the road to let the traffic pass safely.

• Watch out for long lines of traffic heading up the road when a ferry has just docked.

• Always keep to the right and ride in single file.

• Ride straight ahead and avoid weaving into traffic.

• Keep your groups small, with three or four riders together spaced widely apart. Larger groups should divide up to make it easier and safer for cars to pass.

• Pull well off the road whenever you stop, particularly when visibility is poor, such as at hilltops or on corners.

• Stay off roads posted as private property.

• Avoid riding at night, and be cautious when roads are slick from recent rain.

• Wear reflectors and use strobes to show your presence when light conditions are poor.

## HIKING

Hiking trails in the San Juans are somewhat limited, and there are no overnight backpacking trips anywhere on the islands. The longest and best trails are on Orcas Island within Moran State Park and at Turtleback Mountain Preserve. Other pleasant day hikes can be explored within San Juan Island National Historical Park and at smaller state and county parks and other public lands on San Juan, Orcas, Lopez, Shaw, and Cypress Islands. Many of the marine state parks have trails, including delightful paths to old lighthouses or remote beaches; especially notable are those on Stuart and Sucia Islands.

Ken Wilcox's *Hiking the San Juan Islands* (Northwest Wild Books) and Dave Wortman's *San Juan Islands: A Guide to Exploring the Great Outdoors* (FalconGuides) are authoritative sources for anyone planning a hike on the islands. They cover not just the main islands in the archipelago, but also marine state parks, private islands, and trails on Whidbey, Camano, and Fidalgo Islands.

Natalie (Nat) Herner of **Gnat's Nature Hikes** (360/376-6629, www.orcasislandhikes.com) guides hiking trips in Moran State Park on Orcas Island and leads boat-and-hike treks to the marine state park on Jones Island and The Nature Conservancy preserve on Yellow Island. She has a background in environmental studies along with more than a decade of experience as a naturalist and guide on whale-watching boats.

Although best known for its cycling trips on the San Juans, **Backroads** (510/527-1555 or 800/462-2848, www.backroads.com) also guides six-day hiking-focused adventures for $2,500 including transportation, meals, and lodging. These begin in Anacortes and include time exploring sights on Orcas and San Juan Islands before ferrying on to Victoria, Olympic National Park, and back to Seattle.

## HORSEBACK RIDING

The rolling farm country in rural parts of the San Juans are perfect for horses and riding. Several outfits provide trail rides on the islands,

including Horseshu Ranch on San Juan Island and Orcas Island Trail Rides and Turtlehead Trails on Orcas Island. In addition to rides, some ranches also provide riding lessons and horse boarding.

## SEA KAYAKING

The relatively protected waters, diverse landscapes, rich wildlife (including killer whales), and myriad bays and coves make the San Juans a marvelous place to explore by sea kayak. This is one of the finest ways to see the islands, as more and more folks are discovering each year. A number of companies offer guided trips, and several will also rent kayaks to experienced paddlers. No kayaking experience is necessary on any of the guided tours, but it certainly helps to be in good physical condition. All necessary instructions and paddling gear are provided, and you'll typically use a stable two-person kayak.

### Guided Trips

Kayaking companies on San Juan, Orcas, Lopez, and Whidbey Islands, as well as in

© DON PITCHER

**kayaks on Whidbey Island**

Anacortes and Bellingham, all offer guided trips of varying lengths. Any of the listed outfitters will do a good job on a day trip, but for longer paddles, you may want to look around to find a company that best meets your needs. One of the most professional is **Shearwater Adventures** (360/376-4699, www.shearwaterkayaks.com), based on Orcas Island. In addition to day trips, guides teach kayaking classes, set up custom tours, and have a shop that sells paddling gear and kayaks. Other Orcas kayak companies are **Orcas Outdoors** (360/376-4611, www.orcasoutdoors.com) and **Outer Island Expeditions** (360/376-3711, www.outerislandx.com).

On Lopez Island, both **Cascadia Kayak Tours** (360/468-3008, www.cascadiakayaktours.com) and **Outdoor Adventures Center** (425/883-9039 or 800/282-4043, www.outdooradventurecenter.com) lead multi-night sea kayak trips.

Several San Juan Island–based kayak companies offer multi-day trips, including **Discovery Sea Kayaks** (360/378-2559 or 866/461-2559, www.discoveryseakayaks.com), which has a kayak shop in Friday Harbor. Other operators include **Outdoor Odysseys** (360/378-3533 or 800/647-4621, www.outdoorodysseys.com), **San Juan Kayak Expeditions** (360/378-4436, www.sanjuankayak.com), **Adventure Quest Expeditions** (360/378-5767 or 888/589-4253, www.sea-quest-kayak.com), and **Crystal Seas Kayaking** (360/378-4223 or 877/732-7877, www.crystalseas.com).

**The Sea Kayak Shop** (360/299-2300, www.seakayakshop.com) in Anacortes sells boats and gear and offers kayak classes. Rentals are available for experienced paddlers. Bellingham-based kayak companies include **Moondance Sea Kayaking Adventures** (360/738-7664, www.moondancekayak.com) and **Elakah Expeditions** (360/734-7270 or 800/434-7270, www.elakah.com).

Seattle-based **Northwest Outdoor Center** (206/281-9694 or 800/683-0637, www.nwoc.com) and **REI Adventures** (800/622-2236, www.rei.com/adventures) also lead sea kayak trips to the San Juans.

## On Your Own

From a ferry, the waters around the San Juan Islands often appear tranquil, and sea kayaking seems to simply involve getting in and paddling. Beginners may be fine on a calm day in a protected cove, but conditions can quickly turn treacherous in the more exposed channels; a simple rollover can quickly become a life-and-death situation. Particularly deadly are situations where strong tidal currents are pulling one way while winds are pushing in the opposite direction, creating large waves. Even experienced paddlers are best off starting out by taking a trip through a San Juan Islands–based sea kayak company where they can learn details of the local conditions before heading out on their own.

**SeaTrails** (www.seatrails.com) produces a number of excellent waterproof maps covering the San Juans. These cost $18 and are available in local kayak shops. The Canadian Hydrographic Service's (www.charts.gc.ca) *Tide and Current Tables* book is very useful for kayakers; find it in local marinas or bookstores. Randel Washburne's detailed *Kayaking Puget Sound, the San Juans, and Gulf Islands* is packed with information on destinations, tide rips, current and wind problems, difficulty ratings, and launching points and includes coverage for quite a few San Juan Islands paddling trips. Kayakers heading out on their own should probably read this book first.

## Minimizing Impact

Sea kayakers sometimes develop an unwarranted degree of self-righteousness. After all, they're the ones paddling, while other boaters are tooling around wasting fossil fuels and polluting the air. The reality is that kayakers can be particularly damaging to the environment even while attempting to have a low impact. Many sailors and some motorboaters "camp" in their boats, while San Juan Islands kayakers always depend on the fragile islands for a campsite. This can mean lots of trampled plants, and can impact the animals that live there as well. A park ranger told me of once seeing 72 kayak campers on Posey Island

Marine State Park (near Roche Harbor). The island covers a total of one acre, so the campers' "wilderness experience" was more like a crowded tenement with just one outhouse for everyone.

Kayakers also can have surprising effects on wildlife, particularly seals and sea lions hauled out on the rocks. To a snoozing seal, a paddler and kayak may look like a cruising killer whale scoping them out for a meal. Don't get too close to marine mammals, particularly at San Juan Islands National Wildlife Refuge islands, where all boats are legally required to stay 200 yards offshore. The Whale Museum's Soundwatch program (360/378-4710 or 800/946-7227, www.whalemuseum.org) recommends a number of other precautions for kayakers heading out to watch killer whales; pick up the *Be Whale Wise* viewing guidelines from the museum in Friday Harbor or download a copy from its website. Also on the website and at the museum is a pamphlet detailing **responsible kayaker code** guidelines to help protect marine wildlife. Important ones include having a trip plan, not positioning yourself in the path of whales or paddling into a group of whales, and staying 100 yards or more away from seal haul-outs and nesting bird sites.

If you come upon a stranded seal, sea lion, or other marine mammal, do not handle it, but instead immediately call the **Stranded Marine Mammal Hotline** at 800/562-8832.

## Cascadia Marine Trail

The Cascadia Marine Trail covers water-accessible campsites throughout Puget Sound, including more than a dozen in the San Juan Islands. These campsites ($12) are only open to those in sea kayaks and other small and beachable human- or wind-powered crafts. No sailboats with motors or motorboats where you row ashore in a dingy! All permit money goes to marine trail maintenance and expansion. Designated Cascadia Marine Trail campsites are not just for one tent, and you may have quite a few neighbors during the peak season. Limits, however, are placed on the number of

campers at the most popular marine state parks in the San Juans.

The nonprofit **Washington Water Trails Association** (WWTA: 206/545-9161, www.wwta.org) works to protect waterfront areas for public use, and its website provides detailed information on Cascadia Marine Trail campsites. The parks are actually managed by Washington State Parks, not the WWTA.

The following marine state parks, county parks, and Washington Department of Natural Resources lands in the San Juans contain designated Cascadia Marine Trail campsites: Blind Island, Burrows Island, Cypress Head (Cypress Island), Griffin Bay (San Juan Island), James Island, Jones Island, Lummi Island, Obstruction Pass (Orcas Island), Odlin County Park (Lopez Island), Pelican Beach (Cypress Island), Point Doughty (Orcas Island), Posey Island, Saddlebag Island, San Juan County Park (San Juan Island), Shaw County Park (Shaw Island), Spencer Spit (Lopez Island), Strawberry Island, and Stuart Island. On Whidbey Island, Cascadia campsites are located at Deception Pass State Park, Joseph Whidbey State Park, Fort Ebey State Park, and Windjammer Park (Oak Harbor).

## Water Taxis

Several companies provide transportation to the more remote islands in the San Juans. All of them will transport your kayak (generally $20–30 extra round-trip), and prices vary depending upon the destination and number of people. Anacortes-based **Paraclete Charters** (360/293-5920 or 800/808-2999, www.paracletecharters.com) has been in business since 1992 and operates three boats. Also operating out of Anacortes is **Island Express Charters** (360/299-2875 or 877/473-9777, www.islandexpresscharters.com), with two high-speed landing craft. From Orcas Island, hop aboard **North Shore Charters** (360/376-4855, www.orcasislandadventures.com), with a shallow-draft landing craft for service to Sucia, Patos, Matia, and other state marine parks popular with kayakers.

## SKATEBOARDING

Skateboard enthusiasts flock to the impressive **Orcas Island Skateboard Park** (www.skate-orcas.org), recognized as one of the best skate parks in the Northwest. No bikes are allowed, and helmets are required. On San Juan Island, the skateboard park (very popular with stunt bikers) is at the San Juan County Fairgrounds, and on Lopez it's in Lopez Village.

## WHALE-WATCHING

The waters around the San Juans are famous for whales, particularly the exciting killer whales, or orcas, that pursue migrating salmon. Other marine mammals commonly seen around the islands include minke whales, harbor porpoises, Dall's porpoises, harbor seals, California and Steller sea lions, and even elephant seals.

The best time to see orcas is mid-June to mid-July, but they are periodically visible anytime from mid-May to mid-September. Three resident pods, or families, of orcas are frequently spotted. They have been extensively studied for more than 30 years, and individuals are identifiable from distinctive body markings.

Watching whales is a favorite activity around the San Juans, and dozens of commercial whale-watching boats operate in the summer months; it's become a $10 million per year industry. Daily tours depart from San Juan and Orcas Islands, but whale-watching trips are also available out of Anacortes, Bellingham, Port Townsend, Seattle, and Victoria (see individual chapters for details on local operators). In the peak season, be sure to make advance reservations for these popular trips. During the winter, when the whales are elsewhere, some of these companies switch to wildlife-viewing cruises.

The excellent **Whale Museum** in Friday Harbor maintains a **Whale Hotline** for sightings and stranding information (800/562-8832, www.whalemuseum.org). If you're heading out in your own kayak or other vessel, be sure to stay at least 100 yards from whales (it's the law) and 200 yards from seal and sea lion haul-out areas since the animals are easily

spooked. Boaters and kayakers heading out on their own should pick up the **Be Whale Wise** viewing guideline pamphlet from The Whale Museum or download a copy from its website. Do your part to protect whales from harassment by following these guidelines:

- **Slow down,** reducing speed to less than seven knots when within 400 yards of the nearest whale.

- **Keep clear of the whale's path** and avoid abrupt course changes.

- **Do not approach** or position your vessel closer than 100 yards to any whale.

- **Always approach and depart whales from the side,** moving in a direction parallel to the direction of the whales. Do not approach whales from the front or from behind.

- **Stay on the offshore side of the whales** when they are traveling close to shore.

To lessen the likelihood of impacting the whales while watching them, the museum encourages visitors to watch from the shore; a great spot is **Lime Kiln Point State Park** on the west side of San Juan Island.

## BOATING

The San Juan Islands are one of the top three sailing destinations in the nation and are equally popular with power yachts. Boat charters are available at San Juan, Orcas, and Lopez Islands and from marinas throughout the area, particularly in Anacortes and Bellingham. Two types of charters are offered. For **bareboat charters,** the company provides the boat and you do everything else, from captaining to swabbing the decks. You'll be required to show navigational and on-the-water skills in advance or the charter company won't let you take the boat. (Some companies also offer learn-to-cruise classes for landlubbers.) **Skippered charters** are for those who either lack the knowledge to head out on their own or want someone else doing the work. These cost considerably more, of course, and typically include an experienced local skipper and three meals a day. Much to the relief of those who

© DON PITCHER

Watching whales from shore is the best way to lessen your environmental impact.

appreciate peace and quiet, **Jet Skis** and similar personal watercraft are prohibited anywhere in San Juan County waters. Take precautions not to disturb killer whales when boating in their vicinity.

## Charter Companies

Anacortes is home to one of the largest concentrations of bareboat charters in North America, with more than 350 power yachts and sailboats available. If you don't have boating skills, these companies can also provide a qualified skipper and a cook for absolute luxury. The largest Anacortes charter companies are **ABC Yacht Charters** (360/293-9533 or 800/426-2313, www.abcyachtcharters.com), **Anacortes Yacht Charters** (360/293-4555 or 800/233-3004, www.ayc.com), and **Ship Harbor Yacht Charters** (360/299-9193 or 877/772-6582, www.shipharboryachts.com).

Bellingham is another major center for boaters heading to the islands, with the following companies offering powerboat or sailing charters: **Bellhaven Charters** (360/733-6636 or 877/310-9471, www.bellhaven.net), **Bellingham Yachts Sales and Charters** (360/671-0990 or 877/310-9446, www.bellinghamyachts.com), **Northwest Explorations** (360/676-1248 or 800/826-1430, www.nwexplorations.com), **Par Yacht Charters** (360/200-6800, www.parcharters.com), **San Juan Sailing** (360/671-4300 or 800/677-7245, www.sanjuansailing.com), and **San Juan Yachting** (360/671-4300 or 800/670-8089, www.sanjuanyachting.com).

Nearly all bareboat sailing charters in the San Juans start from Anacortes, Bellingham, or other ports, but a few island companies have a limited number of sailboats for experienced yachtsmen. On Orcas, contact **Orcas Island Sailing** (360/376-2113, www.orcassailing.com); sailboat charters are available at **Deer Harbor Marina** (360/376-3037, www.deerharbormarina.com) and **Rosario Resort Marina** (360/376-2222 or 800/562-8820, www.rosarioresort.com). Companies on San Juan, Orcas, and Lopez Islands offer skippered sailing trips for an afternoon or a week.

## On Your Own

Boaters heading out on their own will want to pick up one of the cruising guides to the islands. Recommended is the oddly named **Gunkholing the San Juans** by Jo Bailey and Carl Nyberg. It's out of print but still readily available. By the way, "gunkhole" is slang for a protected anchorage. Also look over the **Waggoner Cruising Guide** (www.waggonerguide.com) for coverage from Puget Sound all the way to Prince Rupert, British Columbia. Regional visitors centers have copies of **SunCruiser Magazine** (www.suncruiser.ca), a free boating publication covering northern Puget Sound and the Strait of Georgia.

Boaters need to avoid most of the 83 islands within the **San Juan Islands National Wildlife Refuge** (360/457-8451, www.pacific.fws.gov). To preserve vital wildlife habitats, you are not allowed closer than 200 yards from these; the only exceptions are portions of Turn and Matia Islands. The refuges are marked on nautical charts.

The **San Juan Island Yacht Club** (360/378-3434, www.sjiyc.com) sponsors a dozen or so local cruises annually, along with the biggest sailing event of the year—the Shaw Island Classic—held the second Saturday of August.

Boaters heading out on their own should pick up the **Be Whale Wise** viewing guidelines from The Whale Museum or download a copy from its website (www.whalemuseum.org).

## Lighthouses

**Orcas Island Eclipse Charters** (360/376-6566 or 800/376-6566, www.orcasisland-whales.com) leads informative summertime tours ($89) to the four lighthouses within the San Juans: Turn Point Lighthouse on Stuart Island, Patos Lighthouse on Patos Island, and Lime Kiln Lighthouse and Cattle Point Lighthouse on San Juan Island.

## FISHING

Fishing for salmon (mainly king, silver, and sockeye) is best in August and September, with other fish—including blackmouth bass, bottom fish, halibut, and lingcod—available at other times of the year. Charter-fishing operators generally provide fishing gear and bait, but you'll need a current saltwater fishing license. Fishing trips on Haro Strait can often provide the opportunity to see killer whales.

Fishing is a popular activity in the San Juans.

© DON PITCHER

The **Washington Department of Fish and Wildlife** (360/902-2464, http://wdw.wa.gov) is in charge of fishing, hunting, and clamming on the islands. Pick up the fat *Fishing in Washington* pamphlet at sporting goods or other stores that sell fishing licenses. Annual freshwater fishing licenses cost $28 for Washington residents or $83 for nonresidents. Combination licenses for both freshwater and saltwater fishing, plus shellfish (including clams), are $53 for Washington residents or $122 for nonresidents. A two-day combination license for nonresidents is $27. Be sure to get (and fill out) a catch record card for salmon, sturgeon, steelhead, halibut, and Dungeness crab from the vendor who sells your license.

## Clamming

Clams and other mollusks were a major part of the diet of the Coast Salish people who first lived on the San Juans, and they are still dug today along many island beaches. For information on clamming, including regulations and safety issues, contact the Washington Department of Fish and Wildlife (360/902-2464, http://fishhunt.dfw.wa.gov).

Some years, an overabundant growth of microorganisms causes clams to build up dangerous levels of toxins, including domoic acid, a chemical that can cause seizures, cardiac arrhythmia, coma, and even death. Before digging, it's always a good idea to check the Department of Health's **Shellfish Safety Hotline** (360/796-3215 or 800/562-5632, www.doh.wa.gov/ehp/sf) for the latest on the edibility of area clams.

## SWIMMING

The three main islands all have popular lakes where swimming is allowed. On Orcas, Cascade Lake within Moran State Park is the main destination. On Lopez, it's Hummel Lake. On San Juan, you can swim at privately owned lakes at Lakedale Resort for a fee. Orcas, San Juan, and Lopez Islands all have swimming pools at health clubs, resorts, or summer camps that are open to the public.

## DIVING

Locals say the San Juans offer the finest cold-water diving anywhere, with something for all levels of ability. Beneath the surface, the waters are chilly (48–52°F year-round), with currents that feed an abundance of marine plants and animals, from plankton to killer whales. Jacques Cousteau considered the San Juans one of his favorite places to dive in the world.

The ocean floor around the archipelago is a garden of colors, with sponges, hydroids, corals, jellyfish, crabs, sea stars, sea cucumbers, kelp, and many species of fish, including sculpin, rockfish, scorpion fish, greenling, surfperch, prickleback, eel, ronquil, goby, clingfish, midshipman, and flounder. Many of the world's largest marine species are here, including the giant Pacific octopus, the two largest scallops, the world's tallest anemone (reaching three feet), and the largest sea slug, chiton, barnacle, and sea urchin. These waters are also home to dolphins, whales, seals, and other marine mammals.

All told, you'll find more than 500 dive sites here, covering a diversity that will please all levels, from those who learned at a Mexican resort to tech divers using rebreathers. In addition to wall dives, reefs, and pinnacles, there are dozens of wrecks to explore—including a 366-foot destroyer that was intentionally sunk off the southern Gulf Islands. Local currents are important in your dive planning, since they can reach seven knots when the tides are in full flux. There are, however, a number of beginning shore dives and some very good dives close to the islands. The best diving is often in the winter, when visibility increases due to less phytoplankton in the water.

For additional information, see Betty Pratt-Johnson's *99 Dives from the San Juan Islands in Washington to the Gulf Islands* or Edward Weber's *Diving and Snorkeling Guide to the Pacific Northwest*. *Northwest Dive News* (www.divenewsnetwork.com) is a free monthly publication available from ferry brochure racks and regional visitors centers.

## Heading Out

**Anacortes Diving & Supply** (2502 Commercial Ave., 360/293-2070, www.anacortesdiving.com) is a full-service shop that runs a variety of dive trips to the San Juans and surrounding areas. Bellingham shops include **Gone Diving** (1740 Iowa St., 360/738-2042, www.gonediving.org) and **Adventures Down Under** (2821 Meridian St., 360/676-4177, www.adventuresdownunder.com). There are no full-service dive shops in the San Juans, but **Friday Harbor Dive** (360/378-6702, www.fridayharbordiveservices.com) provides air, nitrox, and rental gear.

## Safety

The diving around the San Juans is superb, but it can also be treacherous, with cold water,

powerful currents, and a host of other hazards. Stay within your limits, and never take chances. If you lack experience in cold water and currents, get local training and go with a knowledgeable operator who can safely get you into these spectacular waters.

At least five divers have died in the San Juans over the last decade or so. In 1998, a physician and highly experienced diver drowned while shooting underwater videos in a strong current near San Juan Island. At the time, he was utilizing a rebreather apparatus. In 2001, an experienced young diver drowned at a popular spot off Orcas Island while diving with her mother. Her body was found in 90 feet of water with a full tank of air and working equipment, but the regulator was not in her mouth. The cause of her death remains a mystery.

# Accommodations

## LODGING CHOICES

The lodging scene on the San Juan Islands comprises a mix of small hotels and inns, luxurious bed-and-breakfasts, resorts, and vacation rentals. Budget accommodations are scarce, and they are even more difficult to find when

families start planning their summer vacations and school lets out. Most places on the islands have just a few rooms, so space is at a premium. It also costs a premium; only a handful of places have rooms for less than $110 d in the peak summer season. Hostel-type accommodations

coastal homes on San Juan Island

© DON PITCHER

# BUYING PARADISE

Many San Juan visitors dream of moving to the islands and living out their fantasies of a simpler life, where they would sit on the deck along their private cove, sip champagne, and watch the sailboats, eagles, and killer whales play. OK, that works for Bill Gates and other Microsoft billionaires but is a bit of a stretch for mere mortals. As with other resort areas, housing prices on the San Juans are high, and property values remain some of the highest in Washington. The severe recession of the last few years had a major impact on island home sales. At the market peak in 2008 the median home price was around $800,000, but by 2011 it had plummeted to under $300,000. Several real estate businesses closed over that time span, and as of 2011, you could even find a few places – primarily older condos and fixer-uppers – for under $100,000! Feeling flush with cash? At the high end, you'll still see many waterfront mansions going for over $2 million, but even magnificent places have dropped in price. When I last looked, a spectacular home with 161 acres near Deer Harbor was available for $11 million – reduced from the original asking price of $15 million. Many homes stay on the market for a long time; some for as long as three years.

Many of the homes are occupied only seasonally or belong to retirees. (Because of all these retired folks, the median age of islanders is 12 years over the statewide average.) Don't come to the islands with the expectation of getting rich, since half of the local jobs are in the services sector. The islands are, however, a great place if your money flows in from outside sources or a trust fund from your late Aunt Judy; dividends and investments make up more than half the income for the average islander.

Anyone considering a move to the islands should take into account not just the economics of the venture, but also the environmental problems associated with increased growth and development on the islands. Water is in short supply and will only become a greater problem as more people move to the San Juans. If you are planning a move to the islands, try to make it one that doesn't involve building a new place on undeveloped land.

If you're in the market, or just want to indulge your island dreams, a number of local real estate companies will be happy to assist you. State ferry brochure racks are packed with glossy publications from island brokers, and you can cruise through property descriptions on their websites.

### SAN JUAN ISLAND
### (AND ALL ISLANDS)

Coldwell Banker San Juan Islands (360/378-2101 or 800/451-9054, www.sanjuanislands. com)

Island Group Sotheby's International Realty (360/378-2151 or 800/258-3112, www.islangroupsir.com)

Pat O'Day Real Estate (360/378-4111 or 800/552-8594, www.patodayrealestate. com)

Windermere Real Estate San Juan Islands (360/378-3600 or 800/262-3596, www.windermeresji.com)

### LOPEZ ISLAND

Lopez Island Realty (360/468-2291 or 866/632-1100, www.lopezislandrealty.com)

Lopez Village Properties (360/468-5055, www.lopezisproperties.com)

Windermere Real Estate Lopez Island (360/468-3344 or 866/468-3344, www.wrelopez.com)

### ORCAS ISLAND

Cherie L. Lindholm Real Estate (360/376-2202, www.orcashomes.com)

Offshore Properties (360/376-5166, www.offshoreproperties.net)

Orcas Island Realty (360/376-2145, www.orcasislandrealty.com)

Windermere Real Estate Orcas Island (360/376-8000 or 800/842-5770, www.orcas-island.com)

are available at Bracken Fern Lodge or Doe Bay Resort & Retreat on Orcas Island and Wayfarers Rest on San Juan Island.

If you're in doubt about where to stay, visit **TripAdvisor** (www.tripadvisor.com) or **Yahoo Travel** (www.travel.yahoo.com) to see what other travelers say, or see the annual **AAA TourBook** for Washington; it's free to AAA members (www.aaa.com), who often get discounted rates.

You may want to also consider bidding sites such as **Priceline** (www.priceline.com) and **Hotwire** (www.hotwire.com). Most San Juan Island places aren't on these bidding sites, but they can be quite useful for booking lodging in Seattle. Try starting your bidding around 40 percent lower than the lowest official rates, and make sure you have everything correct before you submit a bit since refunds are virtually impossible. See **Better Bidding** (www.betterbidding.com) or **Bidding for Travel** (www.biddingfortravel.yuku.com) for helpful tips and to see the deals others have found on the bidding sites.

Throughout this book I list prices for lodgings as one person (single or s) or two people (double or d). Add a total of 9.7 percent (7.7 percent state sales tax plus 2 percent lodging tax) to all lodging rates quoted in this book, including bed-and-breakfasts.

## The High Season Shuffle

The San Juans are immensely popular in the summer, particularly during the peak season of July and August. If you plan a visit during these times, there may well be no room at the inn, and not a lot of mangers available either. Save yourself a headache by making reservations far in advance. At the older and more established bed-and-breakfasts and resorts, this means calling at least four months ahead for a midsummer weekend reservation! This is particularly true if you want a place for less than $140 a night in August. Do *not* arrive in Friday Harbor on a Saturday afternoon in July and expect to find a place—you won't. Anyone looking for space on Memorial Day, the Fourth of July, or Labor Day should make reservations up to a year in advance.

Many resorts, inns, and cottages also offer weekly rates and require a minimum summertime stay of at least two nights (sometimes up to a week). Also note that most island bed-and-breakfasts cater almost exclusively to couples and do not allow kids. Families are often better off with a vacation rental by the week or a campsite at one of the island parks.

In the winter you'll find fewer fellow travelers, lower lodging rates (sometimes less than half the summer prices), and less of a problem getting a room, but the weather won't be quite as inviting, the scenery won't be as green, and some businesses will be closed. The lowest rates are typically Sunday–Thursday October–April. Winter holidays (especially Christmas to New Year's) are likely to be booked well in advance.

## Vacation Rentals

Several real estate companies on the islands offer weekly and monthly home rentals starting around $800 per week. Another option is through one of the international online vacation rental brokers, such as **VRBO** (www.vrbo.com), **Homeaway** (www.homeaway.com), **CyberRentals** (www.cyberrentals.com), and **Vacation Homes** (www.vacationhomes.com).

## Home Swaps and Freeloading

Visitors to the San Juans may also want to investigate a house exchange. A number of online companies list homeowners on the islands who are interested in a trade if you have an upscale home. If you live in Hawaii, Costa Rica, or Aspen, your home might be a hot property. If you live in North Dakota, good luck. Companies worth investigating include **Home Exchange** (www.homeexchange.com), **Home Link** (www.homelink.org), and **Intervac** (www.intervac-homeexchange.com). Also check out such websites as **Airbnb** (www.airbnb.com), **CouchSurfing** (www.couchsurfing.org), or **GlobalFreeloaders** (www.globalfreeloaders.com).

© DON PITCHER

camping at San Juan County Park on San Juan Island

## CAMPING

Public campsites are most abundant at beautiful **Moran State Park** on Orcas Island, but even these fill up almost every day in July and August. San Juan Island has a handful of spots at **San Juan County Park,** and additional public camping can be found at **Odlin County Park** and **Spencer Spit State Park** on Lopez Island, along with **Shaw Island County Park.** County and state park campsites can be reserved ahead of time (strongly advised in the summer). Walk-in campsites (no reservations) are at **Obstruction Pass State Park** on Orcas Island, while **Griffin Bay Marine State Park** on San Juan Island and **Point Doughty Marine State Park** on Orcas Island are accessible only by kayak. In addition to these, many of the more remote marine state parks have primitive campsites accessible by boat or kayak.

San Juan, Orcas, and Lopez Islands all have private campgrounds, offering a mix of standard tent sites and RV spaces with water and electrical hookups.

# Food and Drink

Food prices on the islands are somewhat higher than in Anacortes or Victoria, so you may want to stock up on groceries before climbing onboard the ferry. There are no 24-hour stores in the San Juans, and some dinner restaurants close as early as 9 P.M., so call ahead.

## RESTAURANTS

Given the location, it should come as no surprise that seafood gets center-stage treatment at many local restaurants. Fresh salmon and halibut are always favorites, along with fresh oysters from Westcott Bay on San Juan Island or Judd Cove on Orcas Island. Competition is stiff among island restaurants, and there are some real Northwest cuisine standouts. Reservations are wise at the nicer restaurants, especially in peak season. All three main islands also have excellent unpretentious eateries with nicely prepared meals. Fish and chips are a delicious fast-food option. And speaking of fast food, you won't find McDonald's, Burger King, Taco Bell, or any of the other grease factories on the islands, though you can always slake your urgings in Anacortes or Victoria.

Anyone who has spent any time on the web knows Yelp (www.yelp.com), Urbanspoon (www.urbanspoon.com), and TripAdvisor (www.tripadvisor.com), three sources for up-to-date restaurant reviews. Don't take everything you read at face value—some contributers clearly have their own agendas—but when all the reviews are consistently positive (or negative), you should take note.

## FARM FRESH

Farming was once a substantial business on the islands, and peas, fruit, hay, and dairy products were all important at one time or another. Many of the old apple, pear, and plum orchards dotted around the islands still produce fruits more than a century after they were planted.

Small-scale agriculture is increasingly popular, particularly on Lopez and San Juan Islands, where dozens of farms produce such specialty products as kiwifruit, goat milk and cheeses, organic wines, apple cider, and even oysters and clams. For a complete list, get *Farm Products Guides* for San Juan and Lopez Islands from local visitors centers or the Cooperative Extension (360/378-4414, http://sanjuan.wsu.edu).

Saturday **farmers markets** are a fun summertime event where you can buy local produce, flowers, crafts, clothing, and art. These take place not just on San Juan, Orcas, and Lopez Islands, but also in Bellingham, Anacortes, and Whidbey Island.

## ALCOHOL

Local grocery stores all sell beer and wine, and you can buy the hard stuff from state liquor stores at Eastsound and Orcas Village on Orcas Island, Lopez Village on Lopez Island, and Friday Harbor on San Juan Island. Small wineries are located on Lopez, San Juan, and Whidbey Islands. Note that all Washington State bars and restaurants and most other public places are entirely **smoke-free,** which might be one more reason for smokers to quit.

# Tips for Travelers

## CROSSING THE BORDER

Ferry and commercial aircraft passengers crossing between British Columbia and the San Juans will be checked by either the U.S. Customs Service or Canada Customs. The **U.S. Customs and Border Protection** (800/562-5943, www.cbp.gov) has stations at Roche Harbor (360/378-2703, mid-May–Sept.) and Friday Harbor (360/378-2080, year-round) on San Juan Island. Travelers heading from the San Juans to Vancouver Island will need to clear customs in Sidney operated by the **Canada Border Services Agency** (204/983-3500, www.cbsa-asfc.gc.ca).

Crossing between the United States and Canada is not nearly as simple as it was in the days before bomb-sniffing dogs, surveillance cameras, and legitimate terrorism fears. Adult citizens of either country need a **valid passport** to cross the border in either direction. Your driver's license, birth certificate, social security card, a note from your high school principal, or MasterCard—even a platinum one—doesn't count. **Children under age 16** traveling with their parents will need either a passport or a certified copy of their birth certificate, and if only one parent is with the child, the parent will need to provide a signed and notarized permission note from the absent parent, including a phone number where they can be reached. Anyone 16 and older needs a passport, and it's wise to get a passport for all children to avoid any future hassles or travel delays at the border. All other foreign visitors must have a valid passport and may need a visa or visitor permit depending upon their country of residence.

Canadian law prohibits individuals from bringing guns, mace, pepper spray, and similar items into Canada, and a felony or DUI conviction will probably prevent you from crossing the border. Anyone **entering Canada by private plane or boat** must call the **Canada Border Services Agency** (888/226-7277) in advance for a list of official ports of entry and their hours of operation.

## Driving in Canada

U.S. and international driver's licenses are valid in Canada. All highway signs give distances in kilometers and speeds in kilometers per hour. Unless otherwise posted, the maximum speed limit on the highways is 100 kph (62 mph).

Use of safety belts is mandatory, and motorcyclists must wear helmets. Infants and toddlers must be strapped into an appropriate child's car seat. Before venturing north of the 49th parallel, U.S. residents should ask their vehicle insurance company for a Canadian nonresident interprovincial motor vehicle liability insurance card. You may also be asked to prove vehicle ownership, so carry your vehicle registration form.

If you're a member in good standing of an automobile association such as AAA, take your membership card—the Canadian Automobile Association provides members of related associations full services, including free maps, itineraries, excellent tour books, road and weather condition information, accommodations reservations, travel agency services, and emergency road services. For more information, contact the **British Columbia Automobile Association** (604/268-5600 or 877/325-8888, www.bcaa.com).

## Returning to the United States

On reentering the United States, if you've been in Canada more than 48 hours, you can bring back up to $800 worth of household and personal items, excluding alcohol and tobacco, duty-free. If you've been in Canada fewer than 48 hours, you may bring in only up to $200 worth of such items duty-free.

If you're planning to make any large purchases in British Columbia, pick up a brochure describing what you can bring back without being charged extra duties.

## TRAVELING WITH CHILDREN

The San Juans seem custom-made for families. They're a quick ferry ride from the mainland and provide all sorts of fun activities, from whale-watching and cycling to hiking and horseback rides. Children under age six travel free on **Washington State Ferries,** and older kids get reduced fares. Most attractions and activities have lower rates for children, and some also offer one-size-fits-all family rates.

**Sea kayaking** is a fun activity for older kids, and some companies provide special kayaks with middle seating for children as young as five. An impressive lavender farm on San Juan Island offers the chance to pick fragrant bouquets. Orcas is home to two great activity options: **The Funhouse,** where science and play meet, and **Orcas Island Skateboard Park**—one of the finest swaths of curving concrete in the Pacific Northwest. Check out www.orcas-familyfun.com for more options.

Lopez Island is the most family-friendly island for **cycling,** with relatively level terrain, a diversity of scenery, good camping opportunities, and a paucity of traffic. Bikes, kid trailers, and strollers are available for rent on San Juan, Orcas, and Lopez Islands.

Several **summer camps** are scattered across the islands, including Camp Orkila, Four Winds-Westward Ho Camp, and Camp Indralaya on Orcas; Camp Nor'wester on Johns Island; and Canoe Island French Camp. In addition to traditional summer camps, the YMCA's Camp Orkila (360/376-2678 or 206/382-5009, www.camporkila.org) also offers reasonably priced day camps that are perfect if you're on Orcas for a week and need some time away from the kids. Drop-in **child-care centers** are available on San Juan, Orcas, and Lopez Islands.

Anyone traveling with youngsters today should bring a laptop or tablet computer stocked with movies and games for those times when parents want the kids to quiet down. And don't forget the headphones so you don't need to hear *Rio* for the 348th time.

## SENIOR TRAVEL

The San Juans are an easy and popular summer destination for seniors traveling by car or RV.

© DON PITCHER

Kids of all ages can find something to enjoy on the islands.

Island museums and some tour companies have discounted rates for those over 65, and visitors to national parks can get an Interagency Senior Pass that allows entry to all parks for a one-time charge of $10. The ferry system knocks half off the price for senior drivers and passengers over 65, but this only applies to the passenger portion of your ticket, not your vehicle.

## TRAVELERS WITH DISABILITIES

Quite a few hotels, resorts, and bed-and-breakfasts in the San Juans provide ADA rooms with wheelchair-accessible facilities. A partial list includes Lakedale Resort, Roche Harbor Resort, Friday Harbor Inn, and Friday Harbor Suites on San Juan Island; Outlook Inn, Rosario Resort, and Turtleback Farm Inn on Orcas Island; and Lopez Farm Cottages and Edenwild Inn B&B on Lopez Island.

Get wheelchair-friendly van rentals through **Wheelchair Getaways** (425/353-6563 or 800/854-4176, www.wheelchairgetaways.com) in Edmonds. Washington State Ferries have half-price fares for disabled passengers, but this is only for the passenger portion of your ticket, not your vehicle.

## GAY AND LESBIAN TRAVEL

The San Juans are a fairly tolerant place, and most islanders don't care about one's sexual orientation. This is, however, a place to relax, so visitors shouldn't expect a San Francisco or Miami party scene.

Several island B&Bs and restaurants have gay or lesbian owners and may promote themselves on such places as www.purpleroofs.com or www.gaytravel.about.com, while many other San Juan places are listed on these sites as gay-friendly. Some conservative B&B owners may not be especially accepting of same-sex couples, but most lodgings welcome lesbians and gays.

## PETS

The three main islands—San Juan, Orcas, and Lopez—all have veterinarians and kennels for dogs and cats. Anacortes has a veterinarian and pet boarding, along with a popular downtown dog park. Keep animals on a leash when traveling on ferries or around the islands, especially in natural areas. Some parks and preserves are closed to dogs.

## HEALTH AND SAFETY

The closest full hospitals are in Anacortes or Victoria, but San Juan Island has a 10-bed hospital with limited services. Both Orcas Island and Lopez Island have medical clinics with at least one physician available 24 hours a day. All three islands also have dentists, massage therapists, and a range of alternative medical practitioners.

For medical emergencies and fires, call 911 from a land line or cell phone; EMTs and paramedics are available, and a helicopter or fixed-wing plane can transport patients to larger hospitals in Seattle or elsewhere.

In 2005, Washington State passed a comprehensive ban on smoking in all indoor public places and workplaces, making it one of a handful of states to go almost entirely smoke-free. **Smoking is prohibited in all restaurants and bars,** though it remains legal in some tribal casinos.

### Safety in the Outdoors

There are no bears, mountain lions, or poisonous snakes on the San Juan Islands, and the greatest threat to campers is probably the drive up I-5 from Seattle or that double cheeseburger, fries, and 24-ounce soda you inhaled in Anacortes. Mosquitoes are not particularly bad, but yellow jackets can be a problem in the summer, particularly for those with allergies. They can also be a major nuisance for anyone dining outside, and you may end up fighting a losing battle keeping them off your burger. West Nile virus cases have occurred in Washington, so it's wise to use mosquito repellents. Head to www.doh.wa.gov for more on this potentially fatal disease.

Another potential threat is **hantavirus,** which is spread by deer mice. The disease it causes can be fatal, and at least one infection has been reported from the San Juans.

Prevention is the best strategy, and it simply means minimizing your contact with rodents. Never handle deer mice, stay away from their nests, and sleep inside a tent when camping—not on the open ground. For additional hantavirus information and safety precautions, see the Centers for Disease Control and Prevention website (www.cdc.gov).

# Information and Services

## TRAVEL INFORMATION

For maps and other information before you arrive, contact the **San Juan Islands Visitors Bureau** (360/378-6822 or 888/468-3701, www.visitsanjuans.com) to request its official *San Juan Islands Official Visitors Guide.*

### Chambers of Commerce

Each of the three main islands has its own local chamber of commerce visitors centers stocked with local brochures. Island chambers of commerce are **San Juan Island Chamber of Commerce** (360/378-5240, www.sanjuanisland.org), **Orcas Island Chamber of Commerce** (360/376-2273, www.orcasislandchamber.com), and **Lopez Island Chamber of Commerce** (360/468-4664, www.lopezisland.com).

For gateway cities, contact **Anacortes Visitor Information Center** (360/293-3832, www.anacortes.org, **Whidbey-Camano Tourism** (888/747-7777, www.whidbeycamanoislands.com), **Bellingham Whatcom Tourism** (360/671-3990 or 800/487-2032, www.bellingham.org), **Seattle Convention and Visitors Bureau** (206/461-5840 or 866/732-2695, www.visitseattle.org), and **Tourism Victoria** (250/953-2033 or 800/663-3883, www.tourismvictoria.com).

### Island Publications

Two free publications are found onboard the ferries and in racks around Friday Harbor and Anacortes: *San Juan Islands Springtide,* published by Sound Publishing (www.islandssounder.com), and *San Juanderer,* published by the *Anacortes American* (www.skagitvisitor.com). Both offer helpful details on the islands and are full of ads from local businesses. They generally come out in May for the busy summer season. Also check out another free publication, *The Book of the San Juan Islands,* with relocation info and tons of factoids about the San Juans. It's published by *The Journal of the San Juans* (www.sanjuanjournal.com).

### More Websites

Virtually all San Juan lodgings and many other local businesses maintain websites. A number of general sites are also worth investigating in addition to the visitors bureau site. The **San Juan Islander** (www.sanjuanislander.com) is a web-only newspaper with community news, events, weather, classified ads, the local police blotter, links to regional newspapers, and useful visitor information. It's updated daily and is a fine way to keep abreast of local events before (or after) your visit to the islands. A number of other private websites provide island information and links. Check out www.sanjuandirectory.com, www.sanjuanupdate.com, www.orcasisle.com, and www.orcasisland.org.

At **Island Cam** (www.islandcam.com), you'll find live webcam images from 14 places around the San Juans, including Roche Harbor and the Friday Harbor ferry landing on San Juan Island, Rosario Resort and the ferry landing on Orcas Island, Fisherman Bay and Lopez Village on Lopez Island, and the Anacortes ferry landing. It's a good way to check the ferry lines and weather, or to see what special deals are offered by local bed-and-breakfasts and air taxis.

## MONEY

Canadian and other non-U.S. currency can be changed at banks on San Juan, Orcas, and Lopez Islands. **Travelers checks** are probably the safest way to carry money, but buy them from a well-known U.S. company, such as American Express, Bank of America, or Visa. They are accepted without charge in most stores and businesses, though you see them less and less. It's not wise to travel with travelers checks in non-U.S. currency.

Most travelers do fine using just credit cards and ATM cards. The major **credit cards**—especially Visa and MasterCard—are accepted virtually everywhere. **Automated teller machines** (ATMs) are located at Friday Harbor on San Juan Island, Eastsound on Orcas Island, and Lopez Village on Lopez Island, but not on Shaw Island. These ATMs tack on a charge (typically $2) in addition to your own bank's fees, making this an expensive way to get cash, especially for small amounts.

## COMMUNICATIONS AND MEDIA
### Newspapers
Two surprisingly good weekly newspapers provide useful print and online info for the San Juans. In business since 1906, *The Journal of the San Juans* (360/378-5696, www.sanjuanjournal.com) has its editorial staff in Friday Harbor on San Juan Island. *The Islands Sounder* (360/376-4500, www.islandssounder.com) is headquartered at Eastsound on Orcas Island. Both papers come out on Wednesday.

Based on Lopez Island, *The Islands' Weekly* (360/468-4242, www.islandsweekly.net) is an advertisement-filled paper distributed to all local residents for free. It is also sold in a few places around the islands, primarily on Lopez. You won't find much in the way of hard news coverage, but it does have community events and other features. Sound Publishing Company (www.soundpublishing.com)—the state's largest newspaper publisher—owns all three of these papers.

### Phone Calls
The area code for northern Puget Sound, including the San Juans, is 360. All phone calls among the various San Juan Islands are local calls. Cellular service is reasonably good on the main islands, but may be nonexistent in hilly areas or where other islands block the signal. Dial 911 for emergencies, even from your cell phone.

### Internet Access and Wi-Fi
A number of places provide online access if you want to check email or surf the web while traveling in the islands. **Libraries** on San Juan, Orcas, and Lopez Islands all have computers you can use for free, as do those in Anacortes, Bellingham, and most other American cities. Computer rentals (with web access) are available in Friday Harbor on San Juan Island and Eastsound on Orcas Island.

Many hotels and B&Bs in the San Juans, along with quite a few cafés, coffeeshops, and other businesses, provide free **Wi-Fi** access. These Wi-Fi hotspots can be found by just popping open your laptop or tablet computer to see what's available, or by visiting www.wifiareas.com or a similar website for an up-to-date listing.

### Post Offices
Post offices are on Orcas Island at Eastsound, Deer Harbor, Olga, and Orcas. On San Juan, they are located at Friday Harbor and Roche Harbor. Lopez Island has its post office in Lopez Village, and the Shaw Island post office is right next to the ferry dock. Most of these are open 8 a.m.–5 p.m. Monday–Friday, though some may also open for a few hours on Saturday. When closed, their outer doors usually remain open, so you can always go in to buy stamps from the machines. Many grocery store checkout counters also sell books of stamps with no markup.

## WEDDINGS
Grand scenery, sunny weather, picturesque settings, luxurious bed-and-breakfasts, and excellent caterers combine to make the San Juans an idyllic place for weddings and honeymoons. The best source for details on island weddings—from caterers and florists to wedding planners and DJs—is the **San Juan Islands Visitors Bureau** (360/378-6822 or 888/468-3701). Request its printed wedding directory

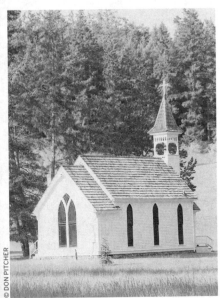

© DON PITCHER

Victorian Valley Chapel is a quaint spot for Orcas weddings.

or find the same info on its website (www.visitsanjuans.com). Visit **Orcas Island Weddings** (www.orcasislandweddings.info) for links to wedding service providers on Orcas.

Marriage licenses are issued by the **San Juan County Auditor** (360/378-2161, www.co.san-juan.wa.us/auditor), and a three-day waiting period is required.

For wedding planning on Orcas, contact **Orcas Events** (360/376-8376, www.orcasevents.com), **Weddings on Orcas/Sandy Playa** (360/376-5531, www.weddingsonorcas.com), or **Patina Floral & Planning** (360/376-3737, www.patinafloral.com).

Good regional wedding photographers include **Steve Horn Photography** (360/468-2100, www.stevehorn.net), **Wed in Washington** (360/378-3686, www.wedinwashington.com), **Fleischer Art Photography** (360/376-4050, www.rockisland.com/~flash), **KP Studios** (360/299-2566, www.kp-studios.com), and **Kathleen Ballard Photography** (360/317-7012, www.kathleenballardphotography.com).

## Resort Weddings

Anyone planning a wedding should start as early as possible since some of the most popular island sites are booked a year in advance.

**Roche Harbor Resort** (360/378-2155 or 800/451-8910, www.rocheharborweddings.com) on San Juan Island is exceptionally popular with wedding parties, and the staff can help with all the arrangements. The location is particularly beautiful, with a gorgeous flower garden and a chapel that doubles as the only privately owned Catholic church in America. Wedding site fees range from free for a Thursday afternoon wedding to $8,000 for a pull-out-all-the-stops midsummer Saturday afternoon affair. Most cost $1,500–3,500. Only one wedding is allowed per day, so book far ahead for the peak season.

At **Rosario Resort** (360/376-2222 or 800/562-8820, www.rosarioresort.com) on Orcas Island, the wedding ceremony site fee is $2,000 for a one-hour service on a point of land affording a 360-degree bay view.

At both of these resorts, you'll need to add in the other associated costs (food and drinks, entertainment, decorations, makeup artists, musicians, ad infinitum) for the reception. Not to mention lodging, transportation, photography, flowers, cake, and the myriad other expenditures that appear when those wedding bells chime, along with credit (or marriage) counseling afterwards.

## San Juan Wedding Spots

In addition to Roche Harbor, several San Juan Island sites are popular for weddings, including the historic schoolhouse at **San Juan Vineyards** (360/378-9463 or 888/983-9463, www.sanjuanvineyards.com), the lakeside lodge at **Lakedale Resort** (360/378-2350 or 800/617-2267, www.lakedale.com), and eco-friendly **Juniper Lane Guest House** (360/378-7761, www.juniperlaneguesthouse.com). Groups looking for lodging together may want to consider the **Tucker House B&B** (360/378-2783 or 800/965-0123, www.tuckerhouse.com) and Harrison House Suites in

Friday Harbor. These adjacent properties have the same owners and together provide space for 60 people.

Public places popular for weddings include **San Juan Island National Historical Park** (English Camp, American Camp, and South Beach), and **San Juan County Park** on San Juan Island.

## Orcas Wedding Spots

Rosario Resort is especially popular for weddings, but equally picturesque is **Victorian Valley Chapel** (360/376-3289, www.victorianvalleychapel.com), a miniature New England–style church for storybook weddings in a hidden valley. Also popular are **Outlook Inn** (360/376-2200 or 888/688-5665, www.outlookinn.com), **Deer Harbor Inn** (360/376-4110 or 877/377-4110, www.deerharborinn.com), and **Camp Orkila** (360/376-2678 or 206/382-5009, www.camporkila.org).

**Orcas Hotel** (360/376-4300 or 888/672-2792; www.orcashotel.com) is an extremely popular wedding destination. The latter is a lovely building, with a big lawn and a restaurant for receptions, though noisy ferry traffic makes for a less than peaceful (or private) setting. One major advantage of Orcas Hotel is the ease of access for visitors. Guests won't need to take a car on the ferry since the hotel is right at Orcas Landing. Wedding packages are $1,200 plus the rental of all 12 hotel rooms (space for 32 guests overnight).

Also well worth a look are **The Inn at Ship Bay** (360/376-3933 or 877/276-7296, www.innatshipbay.com), near Eastsound, and **Doe Bay Resort & Retreat** (107 Doe Bay Rd., 360/376-2291, www.doebay.com), with spacious grounds along a pretty bay. **Madrona Point** at Eastsound is a pretty waterside park for weddings, with the historic Odd Fellows Hall nearby for receptions.

# RESOURCES

## Suggested Reading

### TRAVEL

Bower, Holly, and Sarah Eppenbach. *With Love and Butter: An Island Cookbook and Memoir.* Lopez, WA: Hummel Lake Press, 2002. This is a beautiful blend of great recipes and Lopez Island history, with arty block prints. Author Holly Bower owns the respected Holly B's Bakery.

Crockford, Ross. *Victoria: The Unknown City.* Vancouver: Arsenal Pulp Press, www.arsenalpulp.com, 2006. Filled with little-known facts and interesting tales, this book describes how to get the best seats on BC Ferries, where to shop for the funkiest used clothing, the history of local churches, and more.

Harrison, Lorrie. *Kindred Spirits: Stories, Passions, and Portraits from the Heart of Community.* Anacortes, WA: Island Time Press, 2001. This book's sharp design and attractive black-and-white photos immediately grab your attention, and the stories of the eccentrics who populate the island keep your interest. Nowhere in the book is this mysterious place identified, but here's a hint: the island starts with "L" and ends with "Z."

Hempstead, Andrew. *Moon Victoria and Vancouver Island.* Berkeley, CA: Avalon Travel, www.moon.com, 2009. A great source for up-to-date coverage of Vancouver, Victoria, and the Gulf Islands.

Meyer, Barbara. *Sketching in the San Juans... and a Bit Beyond.* Eastsound, WA: Paper Jam Publishing, www.rockisland.com/~paperjam, 1996. This attractive book is filled with hundreds of colorful and expressive watercolor sketches, created during Barbara Meyer's quarter century on the islands.

Mueller, Marge, and Ted Mueller. *The Essential San Juan Islands Guide.* Medina, WA: JASI Publishers, 2007. Focuses on lodging, restaurants, shopping, and tours. Unfortunately, the book reads at times like a P.R. handout from the various businesses.

Mueller, Marge, and Ted Mueller. *The San Juan Islands: Afoot & Afloat.* Seattle: The Mountaineers, www.mountaineersbooks.org, 2008. A relatively complete guide to natural areas within the San Juan archipelago, including the smaller islands.

Veal, Janice, and Dawn Ashbach. *San Juan Classics Cookbook.* Anacortes: Northwest Island Associates, 1987. A delightful introduction to cooking, San Juan Islands style. Recipes are from local chefs and the authors' own collections.

Veal, Janice, and Dawn Ashbach. *San Juan Classics Cookbook II.* Anacortes: Northwest Island Associates, 1998. The second in a set of nicely illustrated books by local authors. The emphasis is on natural ingredients from the Northwest.

Wilcox, Ken. *Hiking the San Juan Islands.* Bellingham, WA: Northwest Wild Books, 2001.

A fine pocket-sized guide with dozens of hiking trails on the San Juans and surrounding areas, including Whidbey Island.

Wortman, Dave. *San Juan Islands: A Guide to Exploring the Great Outdoors.* Guilford, CT: FalconGuides, www.falcon.com, 2005. A helpful guide to hiking trails throughout the San Juans.

## ON (AND IN) THE WATER

Bailey, Jo, and Carl Nyberg. *Gunkholing the San Juans.* Seattle: San Juan Enterprises, www.paracay.com, 2000. A chatty boater's bible with 300 fact-filled pages about cruising the islands. Worthwhile for sailors, motorboaters, and kayakers, and also of interest if you're just looking for details on hidden parts of the islands. Not only does it cover all the San Juans, but also surrounding areas, including Guemes, Cypress, and Lummi Islands, along with Deception Pass, Bellingham, Anacortes, and La Conner. Now out of print.

Canadian Hydrographic Service. *Canadian Tide and Current Tables Volume 5: Juan de Fuca Strait and the Strait of Georgia.* Canadian Hydrographic Service, www.charts.gc.ca. This detailed Canadian government publication is available at local marinas and bookstores. It provides vital information that is especially useful for those traveling in small boats and sea kayaks around the San Juans.

Douglass, Don, and Reanne Hemingway-Douglass. *Exploring the San Juan and Gulf Islands: Cruising Paradise of the Pacific Northwest.* Anacortes, WA: Fine Edge Productions, www.fineedge.com, 2003. Part of a series of respected cruising guides by the authors, this one details anchorages and attractions in the islands, with suggested itineraries, GPS way stations, and distance tables.

Hale, Bob. *Waggoner Cruising Guide.* Bellevue, WA: Weatherly Press, www.waggonerguide.com. An authoritative annual guide

for boaters, this book covers the waters from Puget Sound to Prince Rupert, British Columbia, including the San Juans. It contains text on anchorages, piloting, and what to expect at each port, along with a bit of history.

Pratt-Johnson, Betty. *99 Dives from the San Juan Islands in Washington to the Gulf Islands.* Surrey, British Columbia: Heritage House Publishing Co., www.heritagehouse.ca, 1997. The most up-to-date guide to island diving.

Scherer, Migael. *A Cruising Guide to Puget Sound and the San Juan Islands: Olympia to Port Angeles.* Camden, ME: International Marine/McGraw-Hill, www.mhprofessional.com, 2004. A comprehensive spiral-bound guide for boaters.

Vassilopoulos, Peter. *Anchorages and Marine Parks.* Vancouver: Seagraphic Publications, www.marineguides.com, 2008. A useful guide for boaters along the British Columbia coast, this book also includes limited coverage of the San Juans.

Washburne, Randel. *Kayaking Puget Sound, the San Juans, and the Gulf Islands.* Seattle: The Mountaineers, www.mountaineersbooks.org, 2002. Filled with details on destinations, routes, ratings, and launching information, this guide explores the nooks and crannies of this fascinating waterway, including nine paddling trips in the San Juans.

Weber, Edward. *Diving and Snorkeling Guide to the Pacific Northwest: Includes Puget Sound, San Juan Islands, and Vancouver Island.* Houston: Gulf Publishing Co., 1993. A useful (but dated) guide for scuba divers heading to the San Juans.

## LITERATURE

Blanchet, M. Wylie. *The Curve of Time.* Sidney, British Columbia: Gray's Publishing, 1968. This lovingly written book is the classic memoir of a newly widowed woman and her five children who explored the waters off

Vancouver Island in the 1920s and 1930s. It's a wonderful book to read while boating in the San Juans and points northward.

Burn, June. *Living High.* Friday Harbor, WA: Griffin Bay Bookstore, 1969. A delightful autobiographical story about June and Farrar Burn, who homesteaded on tiny Sentinel Island in 1919. The island is now managed as a natural area by The Nature Conservancy.

Burn, June; edited by Theresa Morrow and Nancy Prindle. *100 Days in the San Juans.* Friday Harbor, WA: Long House Printcrafters & Publishers, 1983. In 1946, June and Farrar Burn purchased an old sail-rigged rowboat from the Coast Guard and spent 100 days sailing through the San Juans. Their stories appeared that year in the *Seattle Post-Intelligencer* and were later collected to form this book. Out of print, but available in used bookstores in the area.

Glidden, Helene. *Light on the Island.* Woodinville, WA: San Juan Publishing, 2001. Originally published in 1951, when it was a regional best seller, this volume tells the adventures of a Patos Island lighthouse-keeper and his family. A good read, but not necessarily the gospel truth.

Guterson, David. *Snow Falling on Cedars.* Vintage Books, www.randomhouse.com, 1995. This slow-paced but evocative novel is set in the San Juan Islands, and portions of the movie of the same name were filmed on the islands. The love story/murder trial tale is a fine read, bringing to the fore the nation's mixed emotions about Japanese-Americans living in a white town after World War II. The movie is even sleepier than the book.

## HISTORY

Morris, Gary J. *San Juan Island Indians.* A Xeroxed publication from 1980 available in island libraries, this work is filled with details about the lives of the islands' original settlers.

Orcas Island Historical Society and Museum. *Orcas Island.* San Francisco: Arcadia Publishing, www.arcadiapublishing.com, 2006. Part of the Images of America series, this interesting history book is filled with historical photos from Orcas.

Peacock, Christopher M. *Rosario Yesterdays: A Pictorial History.* Eastsound, WA: Rosario Productions, 1985. Available from Rosario Resort and local bookstores, this book provides a fascinating history of Robert Moran and the mansion he built on Orcas Island.

Richardson, David. *Pig War Islands.* Eastsound, WA: Orcas Publishing Co., 1990. Written in a way that vividly brings the past to life, this book provides a detailed overview of island history with an emphasis on the Pig War and various scandalous events. His treatment of Native Americans is dated (the book was first published in 1971) and bordering on racist at times, but the book remains a fascinating read.

Stein, Julie K. *Exploring Coast Salish Prehistory: The Archaeology of San Juan Island.* Seattle: University of Washington Press, www.washington.edu/uwpress, 2003. Written by a curator of archaeology at UW's Burke Museum, this small book provides an introduction to Native Americans based on evidence from two important sites within San Juan Island National Historical Park.

Vouri, Michael. *The Pig War.* Friday Harbor, WA: Griffin Bay Bookstore, 1999. The definitive book on the Pig War by a longtime ranger from San Juan Island National Historical Park.

Vouri, Michael. *San Juan Island (Images of America).* Friday Harbor, WA: Journal of the San Juans, 2010. A fine collection of historical photos and commentary on San Juan Island.

Walker, Richard. *Roche Harbor (Images of America)*. Friday Harbor, WA: Journal of the San Juans, 2010. A fine collection of historical photos and commentary on Roche Harbor.

## NATURAL HISTORY

Adams, Evelyn. *San Juan Islands Wildlife: A Handbook for Exploring Nature*. Seattle: The Mountaineers, www.mountaineersbooks. org, 1995. This isn't what you might expect. Although it does contain details about wild animals on the islands, it is primarily a series of Adams's nature essays. The writing is strong but a bit pompous.

Alt, David D., and Donald W. Hyndman. *Roadside Geology of Washington*. Missoula, MT: Mountain Press Publishing Co., www. mountain-press.com, 1984. A fine book for anyone with an interest in geology, with easy-to-understand descriptions of how volcanoes, glaciers, floods, and other processes shaped the state's topography over the eons.

Atkinson, Scott, Fred A. Sharpe, and David Macaree. *Wild Plants of the San Juan Islands*. Seattle: The Mountaineers, www.mountain-eersbooks.org, 1993. The definitive guide to island plants, with descriptions of more than 190 species, arranged by the habitat in which they are found.

Baron, Nancy, and John Acorn. *Birds of the Pacific Northwest Coast*. Renton, WA: Lone Pine Publishing, www.lonepinepublishing. com, 1997. Nicely illustrated, this is the best all-around guide to identifying birds found on the San Juans.

Folkens, Peter. *Marine Mammals of British Columbia and the Pacific Northwest*. Vancouver: Harbour Publishing, 2001. In a waterproof, foldaway format, this booklet provides vital identification tips and habitat maps for 50 marine mammals, including all species of whales present in local waters.

Ford, John K. B., Graeme M. Ellis, and Kenneth C. Balcomb. *Killer Whales*. Vancouver: University of British Columbia Press, www. ubcpress.ca, 2000. Written by scientific experts, this is the finest book on the natural history and genealogy of orcas in Washington and British Columbia. It includes a photographic genealogy for field identification of individual whales and is nicely illustrated, too.

Lewis, Mark G., and Fred A. Sharpe. *Birding in the San Juan Islands*. Seattle: The Mountaineers, www.mountaineersbooks.org, 1987. Detailed information on the islands' birds and where to find them. This is not, however, a field identification guide.

Yates, Steve. *Orcas, Eagles, and Kings*. Seattle: Sasquatch Books, www.sasquatchbooks. com, 1994. This beautifully written and photographed book takes readers on a tour through the Salish Sea, the inland waterway that includes Washington's Puget Sound and British Columbia's Georgia Strait.

# Internet Resources

### San Juan Islands Visitors Bureau
www.visitsanjuans.com

This website has many links to local businesses and is a good starting point for Web surfers. The Visitor Information Service also produces an excellent printed booklet, *San Juan Islands Official Visitors Guide.*

### San Juan Island Chamber of Commerce
www.sanjuanisland.org

Start here for specific San Juan Island information.

### Orcas Island Chamber of Commerce
www.orcasislandchamber.com

The official Orcas Island business website.

### Lopez Chamber of Commerce
www.lopezisland.com

A useful starting point for Lopez Island information.

### Anacortes Chamber of Commerce
www.anacortes.org

A good source for info on the primary entry point to the San Juans.

### Whidbey-Camano Tourism
www.whidbeycamanoislands.com

Whidbey Island details and links to most local businesses.

### Bellingham Whatcom Tourism
www.bellingham.org

The official spot for visiting Bellingham.

### Seattle Convention and Visitors Bureau
www.visitseattle.org

Everything you'll need for a visit to Latteland.

### Tourism Victoria
www.tourismvictoria.com

Tourism Victoria's website has all the details on British Columbia's beautiful capital city.

### Travel to Canada
www.westerncanadatravel.com

Website of Andrew Hempstead, author of a comprehensive guide to Vancouver Island and the Gulf Islands.

### Washington State Parks
www.parks.wa.gov

This site has details on San Juan state parks, along with many others across the state.

### Washington Department of Fish and Wildlife
http://fishhunt.dfw.wa.gov

Head to this official website for details on fishing licenses and seasons. You can even buy your license online.

### Washington State Ferries
www.wsdot.wa.gov/ferries

The state ferry system's very helpful website, with details on schedules, fares, system delays, and much more.

### San Juan Island National Historical Park
www.nps.gov/sajh

This small national park offers a fine blend of history and scenery; check here for more information.

### San Juan County Parks
www.co.san-juan.wa.us/parks

Check here to get details on county parks and to make campsite reservations.

### San Juan Islands National Wildlife Refuge
**http://pacific.fws.gov**
The refuge is scattered across 83 islands, islets, and rocky reefs in the San Juans. Learn more at this website.

### U.S. Customs & Border Protection
**www.cbp.gov**
Customs stations are located on San Juan Island at both Roche Harbor and Friday Harbor.

### Canada Border Services Agency
**www.cbsa-asfc.gc.ca**
Travelers heading into Canada from the San Juans will need to clear customs at Sidney, British Columbia.

### Tourism Vancouver Island
**www.vancouverisland.travel**
An excellent base for Vancouver Island details.

### Don Pitcher
**www.donpitcher.com and www.facebook.com/ donpitcherphotography**
Author Don Pitcher's website and Facebook page provide details on his guidebooks and photographic projects.

# Index

# List of Maps

# www.moon.com

DESTINATIONS | ACTIVITIES | BLOGS | MAPS | BOOKS

**MOON.COM** is ready to help plan your next trip! Filled with fresh trip ideas and strategies, author interviews, informative travel blogs, a detailed map library, and descriptions of all the Moon guidebooks, Moon.com is all you need to get out and explore the world—or even places in your own backyard. While at Moon.com, sign up for our monthly e-newsletter for updates on new releases, travel tips, and expert advice from our on-the-go Moon authors. As always, when you travel with Moon, expect an experience that is uncommon and truly unique.

**KEEP UP WITH MOON ON FACEBOOK AND TWITTER**
**JOIN THE MOON PHOTO GROUP ON FLICKR**